OUR LIGHT

A Kundalini Awakening Testimonial

By Mary E. (Betsy) Rabyor

This book can be purchased at http://ourlightbody.com

Cover Painting by Kazuya Akimoto, "Blue Human Chrysalis", © 2009, Used by Permission

http://www.kazuya-akimoto.com

Our Light Body: A Kundalini Awakening Testimonial

ISBN-10: 0985466308
ISBN-13: 978-0-9854663-0-5

Rabyor, Mary E., 1958-
Includes index.
1. Light Body. 2. Kundalini Awakening. 3. Human Metamorphosis. 4. Merkaba.
5. Ascension. 6. Enlightenment.

Credits
Cover Painting entitled "Blue Human Chrysalis" by Kazuya Akimoto, © 2009
Cover design by Corey A. Larson
Interior design by Mary E. Rabyor

Medical Disclaimer
This book is not intended as a substitute for the services of health care professionals. Neither the author nor publisher is responsible for any consequences incurred by those employing the remedies or treatments reported herein. Any application of the material set forth in the following pages is at the reader's discretion and is his or her sole responsibility.

Printing information
First paperback printing, April 2012
Originally published in United States of America, by Mary E. Rabyor, 2012

Dedicated to

BeiYin

Benjamin

Corey

Zachary

Tanka: Allowing Deep Sleep

~

Allowing deep sleep

a liquid pool engulfs me

dissolving my parts.

In dark unknown of pupae

a butterfly grows its wings.

~

Betsy

December 27, 2007

CONTENTS

INTRODUCTION

Human beings are currently evolving into a new species, popularized as the light body. Each day more people are experiencing kundalini awakening symptoms, which are signs of our human metamorphosis. Our light body starts to grow when our vibration is high enough to activate DNA instructions that exist in our genetic code. The growing force that permeates everything is increasing the vibration of all objects over time. Eventually we reach a point where the old body design can no longer thrive in the increased vibratory field and a species wide metamorphosis is triggered. That is where we are at today. We have no knowledge about our evolution to a new species because our recorded history is not long enough. When it happens to people today they have no idea about what is happening to them, and there is little information about it. For this reason, I share my story of transformation to my light body as well my theories about how and why this is happening.

I had the typical American life, growing up in small towns in a military family and we moved often. After getting a college degree, I married, had children, and enjoyed the suburban life in a city with all the material comforts. Life seemed great but unbeknownst to me, an inner darkness was growing and eventually nothing I gained satisfied me. Around this time in 1990, I investigated spiritual topics and started to meditate. From then on, I did meditation twice per day and worked with alterative therapies over the years. In 1999, I had a spiritual awakening with a barrage of kundalini symptoms. I quit my job and my focus after that was on self-realization. In late 2005, when working with Reiki, I started having kundalini awakening symptoms. In January 2006, at forty-seven years, the full-blown kundalini transformation triggered. When it happened, I had no idea what it was so I searched the Internet for answers. I found the name for this phenomenon was kundalini awakening. Back then, there was little support and information about it. I had many questions and wanted to talk to someone who had been through it. There were a few groups in the Internet, but I could not find answers for my immediate concerns. It was a difficult time because my family and friends thought I was crazy, which made me feel more alone.

Fortunate for me, my intuition worked well and I got the answers I needed to continue in the transformation. Many of those insights I share in this book. I would have loved to find a book like this. It would have helped me understand this is a long process, much sooner than I was willing to admit and it would have given me ideas how to handle the different situations that arose.

It is common that kundalini awakening symptoms appear suddenly, and people tend to think there is something physically wrong. Many people go to a doctor, who cannot find the cause and will tell them there is nothing wrong. I publish my book primarily for those going through kundalini awakening, to let you know you are not alone, the transformation is real and you are not going crazy! The opposite is the case; you are becoming wide-awake.

When my kundalini awakening started, I did not think there was something physically wrong. I knew what the cause was, because I had been working for years to increase my self-realization level. I was elated to have this happen, but also surprised at how intense and amazing the symptoms were. I strongly felt it had evolutionary importance, so I went to physicians and wrote to people in professional fields, offering them the opportunity to observe and record this amazing phenomenon. I think most did not believe me and thought I was crazy as nobody accepted my offer. I feel physicians soon will report these phenomena, and then this book will interest physicians, consciousness researchers and researchers of human evolution and morphological processes.

Part I, of this book discusses the current evolution of the human species and the acceleration of human metamorphosis occurring today, owing to the increased energetic vibration we are living in. Human evolution is synonymous with self-realization, a gradual and biological process, moving us toward a new species with a light body. Learning about kundalini transformation is important, because it is a question of our continued survival.

When the kundalini transformation was well under way, I had no doubt that I was changing into a new kind of human being. When we look at the human fossil record, there is ample evidence that human beings have been various species. I know it is difficult to accept that human metamorphosis is occurring now. In 2006, I made a new website for kundalini awakening where I blog and write articles about my journey.[1] Since that time, more people contact me each year, reporting they are going through it. My experience is evidence that kundalini transformation is occurring and the experiences of many people that write me as well.

---

[1] http://phoenixtools.org

Part II, discusses the two aspects of the human being. One aspect is formed and physical and the other is unformed and spiritual. The first is the current physical structure of our evolutionary form as is reflected in most human beings today by the structure of personality. The second is the source energy behind that created structure, which I call the higher-self. Part II, discusses the current human being and what drives human evolution. I explain what the higher-self is and how the higher-self is the driving force behind this metamorphosis.

Part III of the book discusses the mechanics of human metamorphosis and the main stages of kundalini transformation. It has a chapter to define kundalini terms and has my conclusions about the kundalini transformation and common questions and answers about kundalini awakening. Part III, answers questions such as:

Are humans evolving to a new species right now?

What condition triggers evolution to a new species?

Is self-realization a biological process?

How does metamorphosis happen in a living form?

What triggers activation of DNA strands?

What are the stages of self-realization and kundalini transformation?

Part IV, is my kundalini testimonial, which is the core of the book and consists of a journal of daily notes, insights and dreams. When the kundalini awakening started, I took notes each day about what was occurring and what I did. This journal covers the period of November 1, 2005 to December 31, 2006, which is approximately the first year. After the full-blown kundalini awakening, I did a self-guided fulltime retreat for three years. I went into isolation, removed distractions and only did bare necessities such as cleaning and eating. During this time, I did around twelve-thousand hours of meditation, Reiki acupressure and stretching sessions. The intensity of the workouts grew so strong that I could let go of body control and my body moved spontaneously. Often there was extreme tension in the body, which became unbearable and I would have to do a session to get relief. In a few hours, the tension would return. Each day I prayed it would finish and wondered how much longer. I often thought this day was the hardest and then would face more difficulty the next day. If I would not have recorded this information, I would have little memory today of it. Each time I read these notes, it takes me back to how it was when I went through it. As of April 2012, I am in my seventh year of the kundalini transformation; I make great progress and feel it will finish soon.

Kundalini transformation is a private matter and I feel vulnerable sharing such detail with the world at large. However, I felt it was worth the risk to publish because increasing numbers of people are going through the transformation and little information is available. My heartfelt mission is to help people awaken and publishing this may help others.

The contents of this book are from my experience and are not copied from other sources, besides a few quotes. If I have written something similar to published material, then it is here because I came to the same conclusion. Having experienced kundalini transformation is my qualification for writing this book. I do not claim this information is factual or that I have all the answers about it. Kundalini transformation occurs to me, and I try my best to make sense of it. The conclusions I reach in this book are my 'current theory'. I say theory because I cannot be sure it is valid. I do not seek validation for my theories. Validation is only interesting for the personality. I am beyond the validation game of personality and can easily drop my theories, when facts indicate they are no longer valid. Finally, my testimonial comes from observations colored by my history and interpretation, and therefore should not be considered factual.

I have not edited the journal material to incorporate my current understanding of the kundalini transformation or to cover my naiveté while I went through it. I felt it was more important to relay how it was when I went through it, thinking others going through the transformation might therefore relate more closely to the experience. Hindsight is great; I see many mistakes and false assumptions I made and I am sure that I am making similar mistakes today. The reality is we do not know something until we have experienced it. That is how it is living on the edge of the unfolding present moment. Rising awareness is about letting go and adapting to changing circumstances, which includes letting go of things we believe may be true. I believe when this process finishes I will have more certain answers. I still have many questions about kundalini transformation, seek answers and welcome new insights.

What is it like to be fully enlightened?

What benefits will the new light body have?

Can enlightened humans pass their genes to their children?

How many people is this happening to today?

Is there anyone currently alive that has completed this transformation?

How long does kundalini transformation take?

What happens at the end of the transformation?

What is the average age of full-blown kundalini transformation?

Is a species-wide human metamorphosis affecting all age groups?

Why is this happening to many women when they reach the age of menopause?

Are there striking differences in kundalini symptoms between men and women?

 My experience is not going to be like someone else's experience, it is colored by my personality, by my constitution, by my spiritual work, by my history and finally by my physical reality. I had a difficult time with the transformation because I have a congenital defect with malformed hip, shoulder, neck and skull bones. When I felt intense pain, it was from opening and moving bones that had been fused and crooked since birth. With that said, not everybody is going to have a difficult time with this physically. However, I do believe that no matter the personal background, each person going through the kundalini transformation will be challenged. It is difficult to let go of all our resistance and allow the fire of transformation energy to consume us. Physical difficulty is proportional to nature and number of physical defects. Mental and emotional difficulty is proportional to remaining cognitive and emotional issues that have not been addressed. Always, the more we resist transformation, the more difficult and drawn out it is.

Lastly, there is a glossary, which I recommend reading in full before diving into the journal. Reading it will help you understand the language I use for the transformation and symptoms. I invented terminology when I knew no other term for it. I have edited the journal to standardize my descriptions to fit the terminology so it is more consistent. I have created an index, with references to symptoms, insights and dreams, so be sure to reference it when needed to find items of interest.

The greatest transformation of human history is happening right now and I humbly offer my personal testimony as evidence it is unfolding.

Betsy

PART I: THE NEW LIGHT BODY

Chapter 1: Overview

To Survive We Must Learn To Spontaneously Adapt

We have not reached our full potential as human beings, unless we can respond with full presence and spontaneity to our world as it unfolds. It is paramount that we learn how to do this, because if we do not our survival as a species is threatened. It is our habit of not being willing to change that contributes greatly to pain, disease, suffering and increased destruction in the world today. The ability to adapt to changing conditions is the evolutionary process that has been going on slowly in human beings over eons. These changes are evident in our archeological history, as changes in our brain and in the size and shape of all bones of the skull. It is theorized that the majority of human beings use a small percent of their brain potential. What is different today is that we are gaining extraordinary knowledge about how to increase our brain capacity, from the scientific side through studies of brain plasticity and biofeedback, and on the spiritual side, from people who have practiced meditation and worked with alternative therapies. Scientists and spiritualists are making amazing discoveries today about how we can increase our potential.

Human Beings Are Created In The Image Of The Creator

A long-standing spiritual wisdom expressed by visionaries throughout the ages is that human beings are created in the image of The Creator. Over the ages, enlightened people have promised that if we lead a spiritual life and follow certain guidelines, then we will receive amazing powers and be full of love and joy. Many people today claim to be enlightened but do they have Godly powers? It seems we get mostly what we expect and because the majority widely agrees about our limited potential, then what we get for living a contemplative life seems mediocre at best.

There is truth to what the visionaries have said that human beings were created in the image of The Creator. The first thing human beings have, is the unique ability to process thought and make decisions, and to put our energy into the decision we made via action. We can focus our intention and manifest what we want to create. Human beings are creators. The second thing is we have a huge energy potential on reserve inside. We have sufficient energy to heal ourselves of any physical defect, disease or problem. We have sufficient energy to change our existing structure of personality in the mind to a different one. We can release this power to transform and heal ourselves by learning how to do it. It is sad to know we have this huge abundance of energy inside that could heal and transform us, and then to see many sick and dying people that do not know how to access our abundant energy reserve.

When we cut our finger, the wound closes, the skin grows back, and the finger heals. In a little time there is no evidence we cut our finger. An obese person can undergo a strenuous exercise regimen and remain on a healthy diet, and change their appearance from obese back to a slim and muscular person. During this healing process, all the tissues of the body are changed. Intuitively we know our living body is a dynamic and changing system and our body will try to maintain a homeostasis because this is beneficial for our survival. Given we know this, the next question might be, if the body tries to maintain a homeostasis and there is sufficient energy available, then why are many people sick, have diseases, are unhappy or are dying? The answer is that it has to do with how we use and direct our energy, what we focus on grows stronger.

The Game Of Personality

Many people are unknowingly using their life-force energy to animate their personality primarily to get validation for their self-image. That concisely is the game of personality and this old habit uses most of our time and energy. Human beings are creating things all over the world, but mostly we create things with the motivation to gain something for ourselves. Because our eyes are focused on the visible aspects, our time and energy is used for materialistic creation and concerns of survival. Rarely is energy given with no idea to gain something for ourselves. It is mostly a dog-eat-dog world where most people are secretly trying to survive and outlast the other, to win and feel security from what they can gain. This prevailing materialistic attitude is the main reason there are wars, hatred, violence and much despair and sickness in the world.

By playing this game, we are combative with others and the world's resources are something to be owned, used or destroyed. When we are trapped in this survival game, we rarely feel compassion for other beings, because we cannot see beyond our own blinders. What we are essentially doing is striving to maintain a self-image that is a made up fiction.

The self-image is not a real entity, but while we keep focused on our materialistic attributes of thinking and feeling, it seems real and we will remain in the mode to defend our self-image with all our means. We are living in a dream world we are weaving and are using all our energy to build and maintain our ghostly self-image. If we were not using our energy this way we would have abundant resources for self-healing, transformation of self and others and the world would be a much more loving, healthier and happier place. We would have peace on Earth.

Healing Happens When We Sleep

Most of us get a mini-healing each night when we fall asleep. Sleep starts at exactly the moment when thinking subsides. When we lay down to rest, this automatically raises our energetic vibration. When the energetic vibration gets strong enough, our internal healer stops the thinking and simultaneously, we fall asleep. During sleep, our internal healer goes to work to clean the damages sustained during the day and works on things in the brain that needs attention to maintain our health.

After reaching maturity, if we are not aware of the game of personality then we will continue to divert all our energy to our personality and it will get more complicated and developed. As the personality gets larger, there are negative side effects, there is less energy to repair the body and our awareness level reduces. Over time, the growing personality becomes a heavy weight. As the personality gets bigger, it causes more damage each day to the system, and consequently more time is needed each night in the quiet mind state to repair the day's damages. All of us will eventually reach the point when we age or get sick because the nighttime sleep cannot restore us to a healthy balance.

Now here is the secret. To stop the building of the personality to larger proportions, we need to learn how to divert from using our energy that way. What we focus on, increases. If we learn to divert energy from animation of our personality, the side effect is energy stored in the personality releases. The personality dissolves and there is reduced influence of this structure on our life. The released energy is in the free and unformed energy pool of our body and can be used for healing and transformation to our light body.

To heal and transform, each day we need to practice letting go of our old habit to chatter with our mind, which is the cause of animation of the personality. By doing this we will effectively get more time in the sleeping state, where healing automatically happens. This is difficult because we do not want to give up our precious time for something where it feels as if we are not doing anything and are losing control. When we divert energy from the old habit of animating the personality, we immediately feel a loss. It is difficult to allow the mind to settle and the first time we try it, it feels as if we are dying. Nothing could be further from the truth. Living our life as the personality is like living as a zombie, and when we are successful to let it go, we feel vibrantly alive with intense presence and feel full of joy.

Evolutionary Advantage Of Being Human

What distinguishes us from our ape ancestors and other animals is our advanced brain. With the complexity and current structure of our brain, it allows us to process stimuli picked up with our sensory apparatus by using reflected consciousness. As we live our life, events trigger memories of experiences and provoke thoughts and feelings, similar to what has gone before. This was an evolutionary advantage because it allowed us to compare past experiences to current ones and allowed more choices to respond to situations. We have an advanced capability to self-reflect, partly owing to mirror neurons in our brain, of which complexity is missing in other species.

As things go, the existing model can always be improved and human beings are now facing that reality. When something has been in a specific shape for a long period, then it happens that the structure eventually becomes a burden. Static rigid forms are something that never last in nature. We know that a bridge has a solid shape and will not last forever. Wind, rain and the elements of nature slowly cause erosion and eventually the bridge will collapse. The world we can observe is flowing, changing and dynamic in nature. It can be argued that human beings die, because they have not yet learned how to be dynamic. It can be argued that the destruction we see around us with global warming, deforestation, pollution, loss of animal, insect and plant populations, is partly the result of human activity and decisions.

Cataclysmic Change

The reality is the old world is breaking down and simultaneously a new world is arising. This has to do with the law of energy conservation, that when one thing is destroyed it is changing shape to another form. Nothing is ever lost, the reality is transformation and that includes us. Even when we die, we do not lose ourselves, we only change shape. When our bodies can no longer support life, we leave it with the convulsions of the body in the death process.

Huge forces of energy are released with a cataclysmic change of shape, such as when a bridge collapses, a person dies or when a volcano blows its top. The Earth will eventually experience a cataclysmic change because the growing force of the sun is increasing over time. Being bathed in the energy of the cosmos and owing to the principle of entrainment, when one object we are in contact with vibrates faster, we also vibrate faster. As the vibration of objects increases, it creates stress to static structures and causes them to develop fissures and cracks subsequently causing them to break down.

There is a limit to how long a structure can thrive in the same energetic vibration range. Eventually the living form can no longer thrive in the increased vibration, which puts stress on the old form to evolve to the next level. This has been the Earth's history over millions of years, as we see evolution through our archeological record. As the sun is getting hotter over time, the vibration of all objects it shines upon always increases. There will always be a level reached which forces a transformation of the entire biomass of the planet. This has happened many times in the past, and explains the growing life cycles on Earth. We are not aware of this, because the cycle is longer than our recorded history.

Another way to see this is to look at one Earth cycle. Suppose there is a cataclysmic change with volcanic eruptions, earthquakes and floods, and most life is destroyed on the planet. What are left afterward are organisms that can survive the onslaught, and from that DNA gene pool, the next round of species is grown. The planet is full of raw materials, as most was destroyed and pulverized in the last eruption. All life upon the Earth starts growing again and new species arise.

Now zoom into our current cycle on Earth. We can look back and see when the last cataclysmic change happened, when the dinosaurs mysteriously disappeared, and know this is how long this cycle has been going on. From that moment to now, has been the history of humanity. We can imagine that the entire Earth's abundance of raw materials released in the last cataclysmic cycle has been slowly transferred to the growing human population. To grow our population we need energy, and the Earth and Sun have been our sources. As the population increases, it puts more stress on the environment and all other living systems, as we need more energy to sustain the existing population. An infinitely growing population is unsustainable, and eventually we will reach a threshold where a cataclysmic change will happen to move our evolution forward and find a new balance. The same scenario occurred with the dinosaurs and we will face that precipice again.

As population increases and resources deplete, it increases stress as well the stress induced by humanities increasing large egos themselves. Many people want more but there are limits to everything. As the biomass of the planet is transferred to the growing mass of humanity, eventually a breaking point will be reached and transformation will be eminent. As disease, violence and stress increase and as resources decrease, it causes even more stress on people. The increased stress is a sign of fracturing of the old structure. As stress increases, it becomes increasingly painful to remain the same, and this motivates people to drop identification with the old form of human being and push them to the next species.

Our growing population creates stress in many places at once as we change and affect the landscape. By burning fossil fuels, over fishing, driving out native plants and animals, over developing, pollution and waste of resources, we contribute to planetary imbalance and increase the stress as a whole. Planetary stress moves us closer to cataclysmic change. Today, it is known that global warming is happening. Humans contribute to global warming by burning fossil fuels, but I believe the main reason the planet heats up is due to the current Earth cycle and increased energy from the sun. As the earth heats, the core gets hotter and this creates pressure. The pressure can only be contained for so long before it will find a way to release. From our past, we know that pressure releases in the form of volcanoes, earthquakes and tidal changes. After pressure is released, the Earth will cool again. What time this cataclysmic change will happen is unknown, but it does seem to be on the horizon of the next few hundred years. I suspect that surviving this violent upheaval will be humanities next global challenge. By accepting we are currently within a human metamorphosis period, we can survive this cataclysmic change by transforming our old structure to the new one. After we have metamorphosed into the new human form, we will be able to adapt quickly to the changed conditions and have increased ability to survive.

Our Love Affair With Personality Prevents Adaptation

The main thing that prevents us from adapting to changing conditions is our habit of responding to life in conditioned ways. We do this by responding to life with our mental ability, which we cannot help do because it is how our brains are structured. This results in our behaving as repetitious beings even if this behavior is not beneficial to our survival and well-being. It usually takes extreme pain or discomfort before we are willing to change our behavior. The disruptive forces occurring now on Earth can be seen as positive, because they motivate us to change.

What prevents us from adapting to changing conditions is due to our identification with our personality. The personality is a collection of memories of experiences, including our beliefs about the world and our knowledge. Our personality is the 'main asset' we do not want to lose because it gives us a false sense of being alive. To keep this illusion going, we focus our attention inwardly and react with thinking and emotion, recalling memories and processing what has already gone by and is past. Then it is normal we make our decision about how to respond to life, from our reactive thinking. We often repeat, responding as we did before to something we feel is similar. This 'old habit' is why we respond in predictable ways and cannot respond in new ways to life, which is continually unfolding as new expressions.

Personality exists owing to the current structure of our brain and is a stepping-stone to reach further steps in evolution. The personality allows us to self-reflect, and once we become aware of our true nature by using that ability then it has served its purpose. After spiritual awakening, the next step is to dissolve this structure thereby changing our brain to a new structure, which allows spontaneous response. Dissolving this structure happens gradually, each time we divert energy from the activity of mind-chatter.

Arising Of A New Species

Many of us have worked with self-realization for years. We are taking steps to change our conditioned behavior, by meditating and doing transpersonal work. As more of us do this, the collective worldwide self-realization level rises. When we stop responding like programmed robots and respond creatively to life, it causes changes to appear in the world. The more our self-realization level grows the less harmful and more loving these expressions are which reduces the stress of the world. This creative self-expression will then affect people all over the Earth through chain reactions. When one person changes in a new way, the world changes with them because we are connected. The more people that make a positive change, the more the world changes in a positive direction.

Each day more of us respond in loving ways to situations that need help, versus the old way of us only acting for the purpose to gain something for ourselves. Each day more of us are awakening to the reality of living in the present moment. We are looking often to the outside, seeing what is really around, and responding to what is needed for the good of the whole. The good news is that the more of us who do this, it will put pressure on people who are not changing and by our example give them motivation to change. Therefore, we see that as the old structure is breaking down, a new one is arising simultaneously. This follows the laws of energy conservation, nothing is ever lost and nothing is ever gained, rather it is all transformation. Our current evolutionary challenge is to learn how to live as one with the cosmic transformational energy and learn how to 'go with the flow'. When successful we will live in a new Earth as free, peaceful, loving, alive, energetic and flowing spiritual beings.

I know it is difficult to believe that we are developing into a new species right now. We see in our archeological record that animals and human beings are evolving into different species over time. This metamorphosis of the human species is evident by rising awareness occurring in many people. Many of us that are awakened still do not know that self-realization manifests and is reflected as a change in the physical form, thus it is partly a metamorphosis or biological process. Einstein's famous equation of $E = MC^2$ (Energy = Mass times the speed of light squared), tells us that every solid form is a vibrating mass of energy and all solid forms are composed of energy. Energy and mass are interchangeable. We are forms as well and a change in our consciousness is reflected on both sides of the equation.

Evolution And Kundalini Transformation

I feel we have been evolving into a new species over many eons and the instructions for this new human species have always been present in our DNA. I see that all life forms on Earth have the same instructions in their DNA, and thus all lower life forms are evolving to become like human beings.

To survive and thrive, human beings need to learn to adapt to a world that is more quickly changing. As the sun ages its output of energy and vibration increases, which affects all living systems within its range, causing them to vibrate faster as well. The more our internal vibration accelerates the more stress this puts on our existing form, and provokes the necessity for us to change our form to adapt to the new external vibration.

The sense of this evolution of human beings is we are developing into a new species that can respond and react to the events around us, away from duality or reflected response to one of unity or direct response in body. This is an evolutionary advantage because we can quickly adapt to the changing conditions around us as the vibratory field we exist in continues to accelerate. The alternative is for our form to be destroyed in the cataclysmic change, and start over which can take many eons to reach the level of our current physical form.

There is an acceleration of human metamorphosis today evidenced by numerous things such as planetary stress, increased neurological symptoms, disease and larger numbers of people spiritually awakening. People who have done spiritual work over the years (past lives count) can detect the difference between quiet and noisy mind, and work with this metamorphosis. The changes occurring in the body are preparing for the ability to move the body and react to stimuli without needing thought. What many people are encountering is uncharted territory, and history supports the notion that this has never happened.

Spontaneous body movement is not like the voluntary movement of the body that we are used to doing. To have awareness with all our attention in the 'present moment', it needs a quiet mind, and to do that we must have the same capability in the body. As the nervous system changes gradually in quiet mind states, the body changes with it. The kundalini transformation is creating a new light body that can respond without the need for 'reflected thought'. To move voluntarily, we think and make a decision, and then the muscles get the signal and the body moves. All of this takes precious time. To move spontaneously we move without thinking about it.

Another reason for the metamorphosis is understood sometime after we recognize our true nature as intelligent energy. We see we have a God-like nature and understand that we have created ourselves and our ultimate destiny is to be a creator. You learn how to become a creator by going through physical transformation of recreating yourself. Once you have learned how to do that, then you can change your form again when you feel it is necessary to do so. This ability itself is the prime one that allows us to adapt to increased vibration and live in a 'different world'. We are not currently aware about this world, as it is not physical like the one we know today and exists in another dimension. The ability to transform ourselves is ultimately about moving to another plane of existence that protects us from being destroyed from these physical cycles.

The Second Awakening

There have been several enlightened people in the last thousand years and major religions have been established around these rare people today. I see this as the first mass awakening of humanity and there were only a handful of people. It seems every culture has one person resulting in the major religions of today. Many religions have a common belief these enlightened souls will come back to Earth at an 'end time' to save the rest of us or bring us to enlightenment. How I understand it, is these people were like forerunners leaving us with information on how we could achieve what they did. Their teachings are the doctrine of the major religions. Humanity has had the essential information needed to awaken for thousands of years. Many people over all these years have listened and led contemplative lives, and thus we get the result today that many people are awakening.

I think we are now in a second mass awakening of humanity, where many people will become enlightened like those few from our past. I think the second awakening is about becoming enlightened ourselves; it is not about people returning to save us! This time, there will not be a few sages scattered in far reaches that alone possess the information we need for enlightenment. The information from previous enlightened masters has been around for a long time and anyone seeking information to become enlightened can easily obtain it.

To be clear, the old paradigm of being believers or following religions, gurus, sages, masters or enlightened ones that worked in the past, is not what it is about today. We have all the information we need to become enlightened, our task now is to become it. The time to start is now, because we do not know when the full-blown cataclysmic change will trigger. What we each need to do is have the desire to change and then start asking the questions. Then we can change our programming and renew ourselves. When we ask essential questions about our true nature, we will receive the answers we seek. Please do not be led astray and miss the awakening that is happening now. The message today could not be clearer: DO NOT FOLLOW ANYONE! Rather find the light you already possess that is inside each of us and can be found simply by starting to look for it. The truth is we all have the information and we all have direct access to it. We only have to turn our focus from the outer world to our inner world, and we will find our answers there. Each answer we receive enlightens us and moves us closer to full enlightenment with our light body.

PART II: TWO ASPECTS OF THE SELF

Chapter 2: The Personality

This topic is difficult to explain because of our tendency to identify with our personality. My mentor BeiYin has spent his lifetime writing about this topic, and I feel his words are a great way to open this topic. Below I have included his colorful description defining the personality and his answer that tells you how to go beyond it.

*"'Personality' is an illusion, created as part of the human condition and nature in its momentary state of evolution. Personality is like moving pictures projected to a screen. What you see seems real; people are talking, fighting, suffering, enjoying, etc. However, these are only lights and shadows on a flat and empty surface, although you see it in three dimensions and feel it is real. It is only an illusion of reality. You can go into it, engage yourself and try to change something about the pictures you see. On the other hand, your personality is changed through dramatic and traumatic influences, turning you upside down. Whatever you do and whatever happens to you, you are still caught in your illusion picture world, so keeping and holding your 'personality' intact. Of course, this is your most precious possession, because you do not know anything else and as you are bound and limited to it, you will defend it with all means. 'Personality' gives you the feeling of existence." - **BeiYin**

Q270: "How am I escaping from reality?"[2]

BeiYin: In plain words: I have the key and I offer it to everybody who asks for it. You are asking, so you will find it within yourself. I am giving hints for this in my writings, at my website and here in this book. The *key* is free, but you will need to work on yourself to use the secret key.

There is no way to escape your reality, because that is what you are, even though it is a *fake reality*. You are identified with it and that is what makes your personality. You may feel this to be a straitjacket, but you cannot let go of it because it has become your skin, bones

---

[2] This is question number 270 from BeiYin's book: <u>The Secret Key</u>

and blood. You then may ask what is needed to go beyond it or how can I jump over my shadow?" Indeed, that is the dilemma. Nevertheless, it is possible!

First, you need to understand yourself, gain knowledge about human nature and understand why you are in this 'straitjacket'. Then you will discover that this has to do with the evolution of humankind that is still primitive with a limited development of awareness. There is much to investigate and by doing so it will cause personal reactions, because your established worldview filled with concepts and your self-image will be shattered. Your *fake reality* will fall apart. Do not get sucked into the craziness of this world. Calm down and be aware of your *existence* that is not colored by the manipulation of this society. You are confused because you are identified with your personality, resulting from the programs and concepts given to all human beings, putting them into a straitjacket. You see your present confusion in a positive and creative way, because you are ready to get out of the game of the personality. You cannot force anything and running away does not work, as you still carry your 'luggage of personality' with you.

InkyPinkie: 'Freedom' is a concept. The idea of it is held in the mind and there is identification with it, which results in a state of mind that has little or nothing to do with reality. However, it seems very real to us. The identification can be so strong in the mind that our entire existence becomes limited to this created fake reality. We can even be willing to die to defend our identity or convince others of our concepts. Indeed this is absurd. 'Freedom' becomes the cage we escape to, so we can keep our little fake reality intact. We do this so we do not have to confront *freedom*. *Freedom* does not need identification games and the fake realities of our personalities are left behind. "Freedom is when there is nothing left to loose."

BeiYin: *Freedom* is not only a state of mind. The mind only represents one part of the whole. As a word and concept, it is limited to the mind and is part of the identification game of the personality. Real *freedom* is a state of *being* and is not limited to parts, that is what freedom means or not? Yes, of course, the image 'freedom' is used by politicians and others who manipulate people, by feeding them the picture that they will gain everything they desire when they buy or follow certain things. Real *freedom* is a rare experience because it is the result of a growing process and this is not the common state of evolution of humankind, only in rare exceptions. Talking about it is senseless, because it only creates another concept that is integrated into the database of the mindset of personalities. Because that is the truth, I will shut up now.

What Is The Personality?

The personality is a combination of emotional, attitudinal, and behavioral response patterns of an individual. These response patterns are mostly habitual, and create an energetic expression where we identify with this energetic expression as ourselves. Personality exists owing to two parts, as is true for all things that exist. Part of personality is physical and part of personality is energetic. The physical aspect is the visible animation of our body when we express ourselves and the energetic aspect is our source energy that fueled our self-expression. Personality is an intermediate structure in our evolution as human beings. This structure is primarily formed in the brain and results from the current combination of DNA instructions that are activated.

Human beings have developed personalities because that is what their soul energy and DNA currently can create. Our physical aspect reflects our actuality, but our spirit contains our potential, not yet manifest. All forms are composed of two parts, the unformed source energy and the reflected aspect, the visible created and manifest form. The created form reflects the current capability of The Creator within. Most of us are identified with our created visible aspect, but 'visible aspect' means it is merely a reflection in the mind.

Ability To Self-Reflect Gives Our Sense Of Self

A significant part of what we know as the personality is our ability to process thought. Our inner energetic source is not visible, but when we think, the thought is a physical form that can be observed. Thinking makes consciousness visible. Mirror neurons (more on that below) in our brain give us the capability to internally think things over when we encounter various stimuli. The main difference between human beings and other life forms, in that we are capable to self-reflect, to see our thoughts and to be aware of ourselves in the world and what effect we have on it. Animals cannot recognize themselves in a mirror, but people can by the age of two years. The ability to recognize ourselves and be self-conscious is an intermediate evolutionary step toward enlightenment.

Most people understand their personality is themselves, it is the 'me' we are all familiar with. Yet, what many people do not see is that this 'me' is primarily made by internal reflection made possible by the complexity of the organization of the brain.

Mirror Neurons

Recent brain research has identified specialized neurons in the brain called mirror neurons, which development in the human infant is encouraged from the activity of imitation. Mirror neurons allow us to process information from the outside that we have picked up with our senses and reflect it within to give it a value. Science has shown that when we want to recall the sound of a peanut snapping, what we do is replay a scenario in our brain of holding a peanut and snapping it. When we watch a person picking up an item the same neurons fire in our brain and activate motor sensors in the same fingers, we saw the person using to pick up the item. The mirroring capability of the human brain is advanced, and animals with high intelligence all have some mirroring capability. The mirroring capability gives the illusion we are seeing, hearing, touching, smelling and tasting things. The sensing is occurring in our mind and nervous system but the illusion generated seems so real that it traps us in our mind.

Halves Of Brain Correspond To Motor And Sensory Nervous System

Our brain is organized into halves, which correspond to our motor and sensory nervous system. One-half of our brain processes information and makes decisions and the other half receives information. Our sensory system picks up signals from the outside as vibrations and characterizes them according to the sensitivity of the sense, so we get sight, sound, touch, taste and smell. This information is then sent to the brain along the sensory tract to the right hemisphere for feeling interpretation and is processed in the left-brain with the mirroring functionality. After receiving information we can decide to act on what we have encountered, which then sends charges down the motor neuron tract into the body, allowing us to move various muscles and our body according to what we have decided to do.

We are all familiar with conscious control of our body with voluntary muscle movement. We want to read that book, we decide to pick it up, our arm muscles charge with energy and we can pick up the book and read it. This seems a great thing; we choose and can move our body according to how we decided. Well, it is more than most animals can do, because they can only react in mostly instinctive ways to what presents. In human beings, there is the capability in the middle to think it over and choose how to react to modify our behavior.

Personality & Split-Brain Organization

The phenomena of personality partly exists in human beings, because of the way that the brain is organized into left and right hemispheres and the mirroring capability, which creates a distortion in how we see the world and ourselves and interact with it. This split organization of the brain is reflected throughout the body. The main distortion occurring is information is mirrored in the mind, and with our ability to mirror we process images. We tend to interact with the world all in the space of our mind. We are not seeing, hearing or experiencing what is occurring in the outside world in 'real time'. Because we are occupied with processing information after an event has happened, it is similar to living our life always in the past. The continual processing of information blinds us to what is occurring now.

This results in the distinctly human capability to reflect on our thoughts and feelings. We can manipulate complex images, daydream, recall memories and project into the future. While this describes the basic process, many of us are not aware enough to observe our thoughts and feelings that occur constantly as reactions to stimuli. If we look closely, we will see we are rarely present to observe what is occurring in real time. We are rarely present to see what is unfolding now. We cannot see that our reactions are responses to things that no longer exist. Not knowing about our internal processing, we do not know how our experiences, biases and judgments are internally coloring what we see.

What Is Me?

When we do not understand how our mind, nervous system and reactions work, we react in an autopilot fashion in habitual and instinctive ways to stimuli. The main autopilot response that happens is we use most of our attention for the task of thinking. From the thinking process, emotions are generated according to the undertone of our thoughts. Emotions are reflected in the muscles in the face and body, where an actual energetic charge goes into the muscles that animate, showing what we are feeling. For most of us, thinking occurs during all waking hours and manifests as continual chatter (mind-chatter) or talking to ourselves (mind-voice). We rarely 'shut up', and take pause to reflect on events and review our reaction we had to it.

When we are not aware of our constant chatter, we cannot listen to another person nor have a meaningful conversation. We cannot see and experience what is going on in the world around us. Chattering creates blindness because while we are occupied with processing stimuli with our thinking, our attention is turned inward. With our mind organization, we can only put our attention on one thing at a time. When our attention is turned inward with thinking, we simply are not 'present' to see what is happening in the outside world. Reality unfolds real-time and we miss it often because we are busy thinking. When we think, we are always processing information from events that have already past. In the non-awakened human, thinking is an automatic and reflexive reaction that happens every time we encounter events. If we are not knowledgeable about this reaction of mind-chatter, then we are blind.

Immediately after we meet someone, our mind kicks in to make the person understandable to us, by giving them identifiers. Thinking is done with our ability to process images and recall memories. What we think is thus heavily influenced by our experiences. If we meet a new person, they may remind us of someone we knew from our past. Now we see that person like the person we knew from the past. Alternatively, we may meet an old acquaintance and remember how they were. We do not take the time to see how they are today; instead, we see them how they were through our memory. They can be a different person than our recollection but we cannot see it. If it's someone we don't know then we categorize them as pretty, ugly, gay, straight, religious, white collar, smart, stupid, tall, short, thin, colored, rich, poor, famous, or any of numerous labels. When we categorize the pure data, we no longer see the person as they are without our labels. In all these cases, we have not looked into the eyes of the other person and simply felt who they were, all of our interacting with them occurred in the mind. Many people rarely meet or see each other and have the true capability to listen and hear each other. These kinds of fake interactions go on all over the planet, it is like both people are immersed in their internal world and neither can see or connect truly with the other. I wrote a poem, which summarizes the problem more succinctly.

Lost in inside world
making sense of images
connecting the dots.
Isolated bubble views
a planet full of dreamers.

If we understood this happens owing to how our brain is organized and from our old habit of focusing our attention in the mind, then we would clearly see what is making us blind and be motivated to drop the habit. A big reason why we are hooked on this habit is because the mind-chatter produces the feeling of 'me' and of having a personality. The internal sound of the reflected thoughts and mind-voice gives us our feeling of self. Before this topic is understood, the 'me self' is precious to us, and we are very afraid to discover that this self is not real. To acknowledge this truth, means that who we thought we were was a lie, and we have no idea what we would be without this illusion. To acknowledge this truth is like dying, because we have nothing known to attach to when the illusion is shattered. The 'me self' is a phantom of vibration energy, projected from our imagination and ability to emote, which we have created and maintain owing to our unique ability to focus energy inward with the capabilities of our mind. This phantom is so precious to us, that we will fight to the death to protect our illusion, rather than admit that how we are is a lie.

Brain Plasticity

If the section above, explaining why we are blinded by our mind, was not enough to convince us to start the journey of self-realization this one may be a stepping-stone. Brain plasticity research is showing that a contributing cause of old-age forgetfulness and dementia is owing to people responding to life by repeating the same program. When we continue to respond to life from what we learned long ago, it is similar to creating a track in our brain from using the same response. Overtime by using the same responses, it reduces the capability of the brain to learn new things, it drains overall energy and eventually memory problems surface. The brain becomes static and rigid and loses elasticity to learn new things over time. Research is showing that this situation is not something that we have to accept as part of our future. They have seen that new neurons are made and regenerate when we challenge ourselves to learn new things, thus more energy flows in the brain resulting in a more robust, healthy and elastic brain. Prior to this, it was not known that neurons could grow and regenerate. Besides doing meditation, which is more effective, learning new things is a good measure to ward off problems such as old-age forgetfulness, dementia and decreasing health.

Caricature Of Personality

Besides using our minds robotically, we also move our bodies in habitual ways responding to stimuli. Over time this programmed body movement (strongly related to programmed mind and facial expression), results in decreased elasticity all over the body. As we age, a caricature shape is reflected in our body and is especially notable in our face. We have a common saying for it, that as people age they develop character. For most our life, we walk the same way, we move our arms the same way, we present our smile and face the same way, we keep the same posture and we move our muscles the same way doing many things. These repeated voluntary movements of the body reduce elasticity of the mind and body and create energy blocks all over the body. A pocket of reduced energy in the body is known as an 'energy block'. An area of muscular tension from overuse or strain, or an area of under use characterizes an 'energy block' with little energy getting to it. In both scenarios, that area of the body suffers from attrition. In a typical adult human, there are thousands of energy blocks in the mind and body, which are due to habitual use of the mind's programming.

Phi – Golden Ratio – Divine Proportion

In math and art, Phi, also know as divine proportion and golden ratio, is a mathematical constant approximately equal to 1.6180339887. Two quantities are in the golden ratio, if the ratio between the sum of those quantities and the larger one is the same ratio between the larger one and the smaller. The golden ratio is seen everywhere in nature, plants, fractals, skeletons and crystals. It seems a universal truth that life forms are more beautiful the closer they are to The Creator, or having a higher energetic vibration.

Phi finds its fullest realization in the human form. The human body and face is based on the divine proportion. Human bodies have the possibility to reflect the divine proportion, because they were 'created in the image of God'. The more measurements of divine proportions present in the human body and face, the more beautiful all people think a person is. This has been proven with experiments, whereby many people ranked a set of different faces from prettiest to ugliest with different ratios in the same way.

When we grow spiritually, then the change we have made to ourselves by reducing the influence of behaving as conditioned personality eventually is reflected as a change to our physical appearance. The physical changes are moving toward this golden ratio and are gradual and barely perceptible on a daily basis. By doing daily meditation, we can change how we look as the body cells will change according to our energetic vibration. As it is below, so it is above. Very spiritual people often appear more attractive and younger than their physical age. I think we are instinctually attracted to the physical quality of the golden ratio in all life forms, because it reflects a God like quality that is the source of pure love, which we are all seeking.

Facial Asymmetry

When a baby is born, it has many measurements containing the divine proportion present in its face and body. That is a main reason why we are attracted to a babies face and want to love them. However, as people age our body and face tends to get lopsided, and we move away from the divine proportion. People gain character as they age.

You can see the influence of the right-brain and left-brain mind, reflected in the body as the caricature of personality in most people. To see this, take any photograph with the person looking squarely to the front, bring it into a photograph editor, and split the photograph down the middle and dissect the face. Then make two photographs from the one photograph with a left-face and right-face image. When completed, you will notice that the two faces look entirely different. I have done this with a photograph of myself below.

From left to right: right-face mirrored, original photo, left-face mirrored.

Each face has different physical appearance reflecting the left-brain and right-brain and body responses of the person to life. One face will reflect dominance, defensive, protective or masculine side of the personality, whereas the other face will reflect receptivity, integration or feminine side of the personality. One face side characteristics reflect adaptation, integration and our ability to respond to new stimuli; it is our energy gaining or growth aspect. This can be seen as the survival adaptation or flight response. Our other face side characteristics reflect our ability to fight or protect what we currently have when encountering new stimuli; it is our energy protecting or self-preservation and survival aspect. This can be seen as the fight response.

These effects in the body are due to our repetitive self-expression and get more pronounced with age. My theory is that an enlightened person will have a balanced face and body and will not move their body in repetitive ways. If you could realize the state of not having any conditioned habits and repetitive behaviors, you may stop aging and even reverse age, becoming like a baby or with the face of an angel.

The Cord Of Personality

If someone had perfect divine proportion, their energy flow would be equally balanced between the left and right sides of the body. This person would have no preference to use either the left or right brain or the left or right body; all parts would be in balanced alignment and have equal and spontaneous capability to react to stimuli.

The reality is that as we age, the balance between left and right sides of the body become more lopsided. This imbalance, seen in the growing character of the face as we age, is reflected underneath in the energetic flows in the spine and nervous system all over the body. Basic energy flows in the body connect all the parts together continuing in a circular path to the brain. For example, with a repeated body movement, such as hand expressions while talking, an energy path runs along all the muscles in the body from tip of finger to the brain that allows us to make that movement. We do not think about this movement, it happens automatically which tells us it is programmed in the mind and the body. This path is owing to the brain organization of two halves, which correspond to our motor and sensory nervous system.

Now take all the individual programmed ways we express ourselves and collectively it creates a right body and left body energetic flow, which when lopsided takes this energy away from a strong vertical pattern centered along the spine and into all body parts. When we experience events that harm or injure us, we create energy blocks in the body by mentally protecting those areas from being hurt again. These energy blocks affect the main paths of energy flow that connect one joint to another, and subsequently connect an appendage to the spine. This creates a lopsided flow of main energy running through the body, which I call the energetic cord of personality. The majority of our energy, which flows along the paths of skeletal movements, is contained in this cord. This cord flows between the sacrum, hip girdle, spine, shoulder girdle joints and jaw joints. One long cord of energy like this exists in the body, which creates a complete circuit traveling through the brain as well. The shape and location of this cord varies among people according to the location of their stronger energy blocks. The cord carries the main flow of energy through the body, which reflects the person's physical use of energy in movement. Observing how a person walks or stands can easily show the cord and its effects. This cord is not a straight up-and-down cord; rather it zigzags as it connects between the joints into the spine. I theorize that most bodies will have a cord on each side of the body, which represents right and left-brain influences. The cord of personality contains more energy on the defensive side of the body, and it is interesting that this side of the body is the one prone to injuries and disease. We use that side to protect ourselves, so present it first when we fall. That side has more injuries and thus has more energy blocks. If our left-brain is dominant, our left eye is stronger, and our right body dominates. If our right-brain is dominant, our right eye is stronger and our left body dominates. The right-brain controls the left body and vice-a-versa.

I feel the cord of personality contains the majority of energy held in tension and this energy animates the personality. This cord contains much energy and much transformational pain is felt along it, as kundalini transformation proceeds. A synonym for this cord is the 'pain cord'. As parts of the body are healed through release of energetically held tension (energy blocks are removed), the cords weaken and are gradually removed from the body. When energy releases from this cord it is sent to the spine and the 'free energy store'. The freed energy is used to change the mind and later the body changes as neurons and cells are grown to reflect the new mind organization. Essentially, that pocket of resistance is removed from the body. Over time in transformation, the cord slowly dissolves and vibration in the body grows proportionally stronger as the mind and nervous system expand. Energy is released from the personality and is used to create the light body. The vibration increase is obvious to all people going through kundalini transformation. In kundalini transformation, you will notice over time that your body becomes more elastic and the skeletal structure is moving toward balance on both sides of the spine and the splits in the mind also dissolve.

Building Of The Structure Of Personality

For the majority of humankind, the structure of personality exists from the moment we are conceived, and at its basic level is inherited from our genes and is influenced by our soul energy. This structure is in place because of the genetic instructions we inherited responsible for organization of the brain. During conception and from birth onward, additional layers are added to the structure of personality, which happen through imprinting and include mental, emotional and physical aspects of the personality. These develop as we grow into our full stature. Each layer is built on top of the previous layer.

Imprinting – How Layers Are Added To The Personality

We exist in a changing world. As such, we are changing and evolving life forms. Imprinting allows us to build on our history and pass this along through our genes. Imprinting goes on collecting our energy in the existing life form, building it over each generation. As far as human history is considered, the imprinting going on is primarily building more energy in the structure of the mind that we are familiar with as personality. Imprinting is occurring each day from encounters we have with other forms of energy around us. All forms are made of mass and energy and it is well known from Einstein's equation of $E=MC^2$, that energy is equal to the mass times the speed of light squared. From this equation, we know that energy and mass are interchangeable, and that we are vibrating objects of energy. From Newton's law of motion we know that when objects encounter each other they affect each other, according to the object's force, velocity and mass.

Imprinting can happen on different energetic levels in us, which include mental, emotional and physical aspects. In short, we are affected each day by that which we encounter, and we keep accumulating experiences and over time modify our response pattern to encountered events. This process is expanding our memory banks and building more complicated response patterns stored in the brain and body. It takes energy to store and maintain this information.

Anytime we encounter a certain event there is an energetic character and we detect all kinds of information about it, which comes from our experience. In the blink of an eye we search our vast memory banks, and we know if this event is unknown or familiar, agreeable or disagreeable, weaker than our energy or stronger than our energy, to name a few. We will respond to it according to how we have read the situation with the underlying motive to survive or gain an advantage.

If we are not afraid, then we are open to the energy that we encounter, are getting harmonious with that energetic vibration, and can be said to be in communication with it.

This is the ideal state, which can lead to adaptation and change to existing response systems, where we can learn something new and modify our old way of responding. If we fear the energy can overpower or destroy us, we will run away from it to protect our existing structure. In running away, we preserve the existing system and rarely learn something new. Protecting ourselves is an important option and way to conserve our energy for a time when we are ready to face something stronger. Lastly, if we feel the other energy is dangerous and we feel strong enough to take it on, then we will confront or destroy it, to protect others or ourselves. This is another case where we act to preserve the existing system and rarely learn anything new. The existing thing we are protecting can be a physical form, our point of view or a habit. We will continue to add new strategies in each situation we encounter, to survive and keep ourselves intact. If we flee, we find a new way to flee, or if we fight, we find a new way to fight, or we could be adapting to the energy as a means to make ourselves invisible. Adaptation is another survival strategy, not the true stance of wanting to change our conditioned response pattern. To change something in an essential way requires a new creative response. Creativity comes from our source, not from our programmed responses.

All our encounters affect us in numerous ways and on many levels. Over time, our personality keeps getting more complicated and energetically 'heavier'. The unformed pool of energy that was our source energy was first used to grow us into our full stature and later is used to build and store complex survival mechanisms in the brain and body.

Layers Of Personality According To Age

The gestation period is nine months, and it is interesting that if you double that nine months successive times, you arrive at a template, which shows the layers of personality and stages of growth of the human being as seven stages.

Conception to Birth, 9 months, Core Inherited Layer

1. 0 - 18 months, 1.5 Years, Baby, Emotional Layer

2. 18 – 36 months, 1.5 - 3 Years, Toddler, Cognitive Layer

3. 36 – 72 months, 3- 6 Years, Child, Survival Strategy Layer

4. 72 – 144 months, 6-12 Years, Preteen, Validation of Personality

5. 144 – 288 months, 12-24 Years, Teenager, Differentiation of Personality

6. 288 – 576 months, 24-48 Years, Reproduction years, Expansion of Personality

7. 576 – 1152 months, 48-96 Years, Awakening, Transformation, Death

This insight came when I asked 'the cosmos' how long the kundalini transformation would take. I was amazed to see the growth stages so clearly. I do not think everyone follows this roadmap exactly; they are average ages for the various stages. I feel the awakening timeframe would depend on what you have achieved in past lives, and your current soul vibration level. These days increasing numbers of youth are spiritually awakening in the fifth stage in the early twenties. I presume they are aware enough to understand they can skip the personality expansion stage and immediately start meditation to dissolve the layers that have built-up. The baby boomers on average seem to have spiritual awakened around age thirty-five and the kundalini awakening on average occurs in the later part of the sixth stage, when hormones are changing and when men and women enter the menopause years. This makes sense because when reproduction slows down in the body it creates an energy surge. Reproduction is no longer the focus. The new focus becomes self-realization and the body boosts the energy by shutting down unneeded function to make that event more likely. The majority of kundalini awakening cases I have heard about all have onset in the sixth stage. The table shows the possibility to regenerate ourselves by dissolving our personality, rather than only having the option to succumb to gravity, conditioning and degeneration and ending with death.

Finally, I think this table is interesting because there are seven physical stages from birth to death, which has many parallels. It is a cosmic number representing the seven notes of the scale, the seven colors, the seven chakras of the body and the seven days that God created the world in the Christian story of creation, to name a few. From intuition, this table tells me that it will take one year of dedicated work to heal each layer of the personality in the kundalini transformation. At the time of this writing, I am in my sixth year, and feel I am on target to complete the transformation this year, which would be in December of 2012. I am not attached to any specific date but I am excited about completing the transformation.

Core Inherited Layer (Soul Energy To Birth)

The core aspects of personality are part of us the moment we are conceived. The genes we inherit determine the basic shape and operation of our brain, as well our body organization. However, even the genes inherited from our parents are not the final determination of what we become. The recently discovered epigenome is an energetic layer that affects the genome and can turn certain DNA switches off and on. The DNA is like the hardware and the epigenome is the software, where the programming and instructions happen and determine what is expressed through the DNA. I suspect this energetic layer is heavily influenced by our soul energy, which is intrinsically part of the growing human. I think our soul energy can influence our inherited genes, affecting what switches are turned off and on. Many spiritual people believe we choose our parents, selecting them for the correct environment and background that will help us learn our next life lesson.

Energetic influences can be inherited from our ancestors. For example, there was a study of a family over many years, whose ancestors had experienced strong drought. Scientists could determine that this emotional disturbance and 'fear of drought' was passed on to children through the gene pool. Finally, there is the subject of past life influences and our soul energy that occupies our body. These subjects are beyond the scope of this book but I feel it is good to mention them for completion.

Emotional Survival Strategy: Love & Self-Survival (0-1.5 Years)

During the conception period, in the birth process, and to about age one and a half years, the emotional layer is built in the personality. I call it an emotional layer, because before the cognitive facilities of the brain are developed, we primarily interact with the world through feelings. For the baby, it is all about getting love and not getting hurt. The baby is vulnerable to outside influences, needs protection, and a primary concern is survival. The most important learning experiences during this period are about surviving, and thus the first survival strategy of the personality is learned at the level of feelings. This layer is primarily built because there is a lack of unconditional love. If we had an abundance of unconditional love, we would be nurtured and protected and would have no reason to protect ourselves. The world is not like that, so we build a strategy to get love and to protect ourselves.

Psychological research has determined there are nine basic types of survival strategies according to how we respond to events through our emotional response system. These strategies have been well documented and are in the body of knowledge known as the enneagram. Energetically, we can react to any event in three basic ways. We can try to overpower the energy by fighting against it, or we can escape the energy by fleeing from it, and last we can integrate with the energy by adapting to it. When you take all permutations of the three possibilities of flee, fight, adapt, you get the nine basic enneagram types. Each personality has a dominant passion (use of emotional energy) that corresponds to the nine basic types. These passions determine the enneagram core type. Anger, pride, deceit, envy, avarice, fear, gluttony, lust and sloth are the passions. Besides the core enneagram type, each person uses two other enneagram types. One type is used when we feel stressed and the other type is used when we feel secure. These are the positive and negative sides of the personality, known as masculine (protective) and feminine (nurturing) attributes, or the left and right face. All our responses are done to ensure our survival and validate the personality. Determining our enneagram type is helpful to see our passion in action when it arises, so we can heal this layer.

When we grew as a baby, many experiences had a huge emotional impact on us when they happened. We may have a vague memory or heard stories about certain experiences we had, but today they seem insignificant. During these early years, a survival strategy is developed with patterns of emotional response to life events. This survival strategy is the deepest core layer of our personality, besides inherited aspects. Because it is the deepest layer, it affects all our responses to life and is invisible to most of us. This childish emotional response pattern, because it was not learned cognitively is difficult to detect in operation. This layer is also called the 'inner child'. After this layer is healed, we stop walking in circles by repeating the same overall response pattern, and we stop behaving like a child when we do not get our way. This layer cannot be healed until the outer layers are healed, because healing happens in reverse order of the construction of the personality. Healing of the personality is like taking a backward walk through time.

The walking around in circles that affects every decision we make in life, is essentially about finding love and security in the outside world. What we do not know is that this love will never be found in the outside world. When we turn our eyes inward and look for the love within, then we will be near to healing the first layer we built around our core, which contains the kernel of love we seek.

Cognitive Survival Strategy: Validation, Social Layer (1.5 - 12 Years)

As the brain develops, there is a preference to process information by thinking about it versus feeling about it. Now, the building of the cognitive survival strategy starts. This layer is built on top of the emotional survival strategy. We construct complex scenarios on how to respond according to the emotional charge we get as reactions to our encounters. We have already decided on our preferred way to respond emotionally to events (one of the nine enneagram types), which does not change over the lifetime of building the remaining layers of our personality.

This phase is about refining how to get validation from the outside world, for that which we want our personality to be. We are developing a complex upside and downside response pattern that involves thinking about the event, then choosing how to respond to it. Our underlying motive with this behavior is to survive, but it is not physical survival, it is about the survival of the entity of personality that we are building in our mind. Here we will discover, develop and refine our best way to respond to events when we like them and when we do not like them, using our choice and ability to react back to the world with our growing physical, emotional and mental capacities.

Adult Individualization, End Of Growing, Relationships (12 – 24 Years)

In these years, we are focused on differentiating ourselves from others and are busy accumulating attributes for our personality. Sexual maturation occurs in this period and creates another layer of identity depending on our sexual attributes and experiences we have. These attributes include many things depending on what we value for ourselves or how we get our validation from the outside world for 'who we are' or 'how we want others to think we are'. Attributes that we decide to acquire are heavily influenced by our environment, societal values, by family position, by our parents or lack of parents, teachers, direct experiences, peers and from media sources. What we value and want to acquire as attributes, will largely depend on our emotional and cognitive survival strategy we determined in the prior years and our unique way of viewing the world, and from all our experiences to date. We are all individuals and no person is the same, because everyone has a unique gene pool and set of experiences that shape them. People value many things for attributes, even if they do not seem valuable. Valuable for us, means it helps to get validation from the outside world and from people for that which we believe ourselves to be. We might value being ugly, beautiful, fat, thin, stupid, smart, wise, foolish, rich, poor, helpless, powerful, weak, to name a few. Parents often unknowingly encourage the attaining of these properties to their children, by repeating things to them such as 'you are so smart or stupid, or 'you are so pretty or ugly', or 'you are good at this or that'. The child then thinks that this is how they are special, accepts it as truth, and builds survival strategies to reinforce and prove it. The most important thing is to receive the validation, not the attribute.

This stage is mainly about proving that our viewpoint is the right one and that we know. The upside defense strategy is about getting validation for what we know, and the downside defense is to fix it when we do not know. After a failure, we think about it and devise a new concept to know more or to be right more often. We will use the new concept until it fails. When we do not get the validation we seek, we are at a loss on what to do. This process continues for most of our life, until we awaken to the futility of this endless concept swapping game and stop doing it. After this long process, our basic belief is, "I think therefore I am." This belief is a property we value highly and is rarely questioned. This phase is about developing the layer of knowing, we have the need to feel we know and actively seek confirmation that we do know something. This layer is built on top of the layers of seeking self-validation and of seeking for love; all these strategies are constantly in play in the outside world.

The main thing we have been doing all these years is building a structure with a defense system for the structure of personality; it is not about physical survival at all. For this purpose, these properties are very valuable, as the most important thing is to get validation and proof that "I am alive." We highly value these properties because they are the building blocks to erect our self-image; the quality of the property is not as valuable. This entity does not exist in the real world; rather it exists as a figment of our imagination. The end of growing of the personality stops when the body stops growing. This is approximately when the medial prefrontal cortex has reached final maturity, when we have reached our full height and after eruption of the last wisdom teeth. On average, this is twenty-four to twenty-six years.

Expansion Of Personality & Reproduction (24 – 48 Years)

After our brain has reached full maturation, the basic structure of our personality is fully formed. Now, it is a matter of going out in the world and testing our full power and ability to influence people, places and things. This phase is mostly about expanding on what we have already learned and it's predominately about accumulating further properties and making ourselves 'bigger' in our mind's eye. The growth occurring here is primarily an accumulation of energy to expand the existing structure of personality, we want to get bigger so we can have more influence and feel ourselves even stronger as the phantom self. We want to influence the world with our knowledge and power, by reproducing ourselves either physically or by getting others to adopt our beliefs or become leaders. We believe we are more likely to survive, and feel stronger the more we can influence the world and other people.

We are mainly occupied with self-expression, reproduction of ourselves both physically and mentally and creating physical things in the outside world and of acquiring even more properties that at this point are mostly power related and external. Properties in this sense includes, career, schooling, degrees, religion, apprenticeship, learning skills, knowledge, marriage, children, starting businesses, getting a house and as many more things as possible. Of course, our driving motivation in all this is looking for love and satisfaction in all physical outside forms and activities as possible. As properties are accumulated and held in place and valued, more energy is needed to keep those structures 'erected'. Therefore, the more we own and accumulate the less life-force energy we have in a non-fixed form. As this expansion continues, our energetic vibration declines, we become more rigid and eventually health problems will surface.

Male & Female Menopause, Aging & Decline (48 – 96 Years)

Aging accelerates around forty-eight years, and continues unless a transformation of personality occurs. Once the main structural elements of the personality have formed, it is as if the energy in the body gets used to traveling repeatedly on the same fixed pathways. These pathways exist in the brain and have a corresponding flow of energy through the body, which I call the cord of personality.

This creates an imbalance of energy flows in the body. Over time, parts of the body that are not stretched have reduced energy flow and health problems appear in those areas. Other important ways that energy flows are reduced in the body occur when we adopt a new defense strategy to protect ourselves, or by mentally protecting an area of our body from further pain due to a recent trauma, or by projecting a larger than life self-image. It takes much energy to keep this illusion going 'while in the public eye'.

As time goes on, if the structure of personality is not dismantled, the areas of the body with low levels of energy affect systems related to it, and free energy in the body continues a gradual decline over time. As health problems build, it is like there is never enough energy at night in the sleep period to repair the day's damage and restore us to full vibrant health. The energy keeps depleting over time and degeneration continues to go on each day, then we see that we are aging.

It is also common near the age of forty-eight, that male and female menopause starts as hormones change and divert energy from reproduction, and thereby returns much energy back to the free pool of energy. This energy gives a boost in awareness and it is common that spiritual awakenings happen then. This can be an important turning point in our life, where we springboard off this energy surge and change our focus away from material pursuits and toward nonmaterial pursuits. Traditionally these are known as the wise years. Remember, what we focus on increases. We can change our focus toward our nonmaterial aspect of higher-self by doing new things such as self-inquiry and meditation. When we do, we will discover the declining path we were on reverses or stalls. As the dissolving of the personality progresses, our energy increases, diseases are healed, and we notice an increase in agility. The kundalini transformation is now under way.

Human Tendency Is To Stay The Same

The structure of personality tends to stay in place and heavily influence our lives for several reasons. We mostly respond to life events habitually. This is known as conditioned response, and we do it because it is easy and the outcome is predictable. We are pain avoidant, and whenever we have to undergo a transformational change of body, mind, emotions or habits, it hurts to do so, and this we do not want. Lastly, getting validation for our self-image (how we perceive ourselves) is a large factor in our staying identified with our personality and not moving beyond this evolutionary form.

1. Conditioning

The main way we move our energy through our physical aspect is in a conditioned way, which we previously learned through thought, feeling and action. Rarely do we question that there might be another possibility, and thus we are mostly acting like programmed robots. Conditioned behavior partly results from our duality organization of our body and brain and our tendency to avoid change, which is painful. The other reason is a lack of information about our personality and higher-self, which we do not have because we have not asked about it. There is much information available, but first we must ask the question to receive the answer. The longer we stay the same, the harder it becomes to change ourselves because of our increased rigidity, reduced vibration and low awareness level and the quicker we age and decline.

2. Pain Avoidance

We are pain avoidant and understandably so. The survival strategies of the personality developed in our earliest years were done to help ourselves survive and protect us from pain. These were useful strategies then, but eventually this protection mechanism will cause more harm than good. We have difficulty to break our habit of pain avoidance, because the habit is so deeply ingrained and such a familiar part of ourselves.

A child will hurt their leg and limp to protect the leg so they will not feel more pain. The limping behavior can go on long after the leg has healed. The limping can become a habit, and delay and prevent healing of the leg. As the leg heals, pain will be felt due to the tissues repairing, which can reinforce the limping behavior. When we mentally and physically try to protect an injured area with the intent to avoid pain, what we are doing is not allowing energy to enter that area. Energy needs to get into this area to heal it. When tissues heal, transformational pain will be felt.[3] Eventually the leg is healed, but it may not have been restored to the prior vitality and balance if the child limped. Energy will find a path to get to the leg to heal and maintain it, but it will not be the ideal path. When young, the leg is in a growing process and can become deformed, shortened or out of alignment with the hip socket, which in turn will affect the feet, ankles, knees, spine, shoulders and skull alignment.

The child can still fear hurting the leg and the limping can continue subtly long after the leg has healed. A simple protection strategy like this can stay in place after an injury well into the adult years, and can remain for a lifetime. This proactive stance is then an unconscious habit and is blocking energy flow to that area. Later on, problems will happen in that area or in related areas, because energy was not allowed to penetrate and heal the area. Much later in life, problems will develop along a line in the body related to the old injury site.

Another experience many of us have is a traumatic experience of being harmed by another human, usually related to the first sexual encounters. This often causes us to create an invisible armor protecting the chest, buttocks or genital areas, depending on where the damage was experienced as most painful. These experiences are harmful because large areas

---

[3] For more information about transformational pain, see Chapter 4.

of the body can be walled off, and are typically close to the spine, resulting in reduced flows of energy along the spine. This type of energy block often has a huge emotional component as well, so the defense system in the body often has trapped emotional energy related to the site of injury.

With traumatic events such as rape, beatings, or severe injury, there is a large energetic impact of being hit or hurt by the other object as well a strong emotional component. That area of the body is mentally walled off to suppress the memory so the person does not have to recall the horror of that experience. This kind of protection serves well in the initial stages after an event like this, to keep our sanity, heal and return to normal. However, rarely do we ever drop this defense because the memory is suppressed and eventually it becomes very problematic, resulting in mental or emotional dysfunction. We can understand that defense systems are in place to protect us from pain. Transformational pain is a symptom of the healing process and to heal we need to accept the pain, which is counterintuitive.

When an old emotion is recalled, we can bawl like a baby for days on end. This hurts like hell, but it is healing as old pent-up emotion is released through crying. When we cut our finger, our nervous system detects it has happened, and we quickly withdraw our finger away from the knife. We see the blood and know we are cut, and then we feel the pain. This pain is not from the cut, that we did not feel, the nervous system reaction was automatic. The pain we feel is from an intense energy localizing by the cut, to repair the tissues, the pain we feel is the heat and fire of the transformation. This experience does not have to be experienced as painful, once we understand what is going on. We can detach and observe the feeling occurring in our finger, and we will not have the experience of pain. Instead, we will observe the sensation of tissues repairing and of an energetic vibration working strongly in the area.

If we have severely injured a limb, and it has been in a cast and has taken a long time to heal, then it will take even more energy and pain to restore it to the flexibility it once had. As the limb is healing, adhesions and scar tissue develop and the muscle fibers become weak from nonuse. The first time we stretch the limb it hurts like hell. This is transformational pain, it results from intense energy going into the tissues and starting to remove the energy blocks and open and heal the limb. It takes much energy to open a broken ankle or hipbone, the pain is proportional to what is needed to heal it.

If our desire is strong enough, we will rehabilitate the leg and be willing to go through the transformational pain required to get what we want. After we begin this healing process, we may see the truth that we can get through this kind of pain and not experience it as painful. We look deeper and understand this pain comes from our mental resistance to accept the healing energy and to become one with it. When we resist the healing process, it is more painful and prolonged. Resistance takes energy. The less we resist the faster we heal. The more transformational pain we are willing to endure, the more we heal.

These words can be misunderstood. I am NOT saying that pain should be sought, nor self-inflicted, or that pain has to be our experience. With advanced stages of self-realization, you can go beyond having the experience of pain as tissues are mending and transforming.

3. Validation Of Personality

Validation is probably the most important reason that the structure of personality is so persistent and difficult to go beyond. We have two main ways to get validation for our self-image. Self-image refers to how we perceive ourselves, how we perceive people and how the outside world perceives us. We have an image we hold in our mind about who we are and how we behave; it is the essence of what is meant by 'me'.

This topic is difficult to discuss because I know many will not understand what I am saying. If what is written is misunderstood, it is because we are still under the influence of perceiving the world through the validation structure of the personality, which primarily happens in the mind. This message is difficult to get through, because the mind filters out what the self does not want to know. To understand it clearly, would be the beginning of the end of the illusion currently operating.

The illusion in operation is that we believe who we are is the mind-voice and the emotional energetic charge generated from the internal story we are constantly weaving with our mind-chatter. Mind-chatter is a constant dialogue we make with our thoughts, about everything that is occurring to us. We chatter and give opinions about everything that occurs all day. We know no other world than this. We have no idea what is meant by clear sight or seeing reality, because we are essentially living internally in our mind and think we see. This state has been described by mystics as blind, asleep, clouded by a veil, in the dark, or not awake. Unfortunately, reading about it does not open the eyes, but I will try again to make it clear.

This illusion and the belief that we are the mind-voice gets constantly reinforced in the outside world by us deliberating provoking the outside world, to give us the reason to react back with strong emotional energy. We are constantly looking for reasons to react so we can build a strong energetic emotional charge, so we can feel ourselves as strong energy. The stronger the energy we can build up, the more alive we feel. Our main motivation for doing this is it serves as a kind of entertainment and it makes us feel alive, even if the energy we generate is not pleasant. That is the game played by the personality, and as personalities are getting bigger today, there is more energy to put behind our response and thus the game is increasingly harmful to everyone and everything. If we take an honest look, we cannot deny that there is an escalation of violence, chaos, destruction, destitution and harm increasing all over the world today. The longer we stay immersed in this illusion and game, and if enough people do not go beyond it, it is sure to get worse as time goes by.

The stronger we react to something that happens, the more alive we feel, and the more it reinforces the belief that the entity we are operating through is in fact real. Personalities love drama and seek it. Drama is the fuel that keeps the reactive cycle going. We need to get validation for our self-image, which we do by creating drama. That is the way that that this illusion continues. The illusion will stop, when we see through the illusion, and realize that we are 'pretending'. Then we can learn to divert energy from the old way of responding, whenever we observe we are starting to stir up trouble. We stir up trouble, by pushing the button of another or by creating a drama situation.

We each have a positive and negative reaction pattern that we use to respond to events in our life to get validation for our self-image and keep the illusion going. Both of these responses happen constantly and automatically in varying degrees of intensity. Before we know about our programmed aspects, we have no idea we are responding in an autopilot way to many of life's events.

The positive response is about getting validation for our self-image and the negative response happens when we do not get validation for our self-image. When we are operating entirely under the influence of the personality, then our actions are mostly driven by the need to reinforce an existing attribute or to get a new attribute as a property that helps reinforce our idea of self. Personalities are never satisfied with what they own, they always need more of whatever substance is valuable to them, this fact keeps us always focused on the better days ahead. It is a rare person who gives something without wanting something in return. As most people do not even know they are in the illusion, then they are not aware of their hidden agenda. We think we are generous, but we are not aware that we are greedy. We are blind to our motives, while operating under the blinder of the personality.

We are happy if we get what we want, and stay happy and always are asking for validation of what we believe we are. The more you give people validation the happier you keep them and the more stuck you keep them in their illusion. If you want to help people, tell them how they are, but that is dangerous to do. When we do not get what we want from the outside world, either in material or from other's approval, then our pain response comes. Each individual has their own type of pain response, and some of them are violent. If there is a strong response, either positive or negative, it is normal that we will act to reinforce our concepts and belief system by getting more attributes. For instance, if we no longer can get confirmation, we can fall into a depression and think about what else we might need to do. We dream up another concept to try in the outside world, thinking we are changing ourselves by doing something different. However, what we are doing is adding on another layer of programming and making the illusion that much stronger. This is how it goes and sadly, some people continue like this their entire life and never see beyond the veil blinding them. Okay, this is probably more than you want to know, so I will move on to the next topic. I hope that I have not lost your attention here. This topic can be difficult to read, because it does not give validation like 'the personality' is seeking, and we can get a strong reaction when reading it. If this is the first time, you have encountered this topic, it can feel unknown and scary, and you might even get the feeling to close or burn this book, to get away from it as fast as possible. If you are feeling this, take a deep breath, relax and go on to the next topic.

Structure Of Personality Is An Intermediate Form

Many people think our spiritual energy is dormant; lying coiled somewhere waiting in the wings for the right opportunity to jump out. However, it not dormant, rather it is used for an important intermediate evolutionary step of development of the personality. Before a new step in evolution can happen, the prior step must be completed. Many people are still building the personality. Building the structure of the personality is the activity of accumulating energy from experiences into our self-image, which later will be the fuel for the metamorphosis that will follow, as this structure breaks down.

People Today Have Big Egos

Most people are in the state of having evolved structures of personality and big egos, as we are all growing along the same evolutionary timeline together. A big ego means the structure is getting heavier, the mind is becoming more complicated and more energy is needed to project our illusion. Big egos are not a bad thing, what they represent is that enough energy has been accumulated in experience. Another way to see it is that over time the aspect of self that exists, as personality gets heavier with more energy as the structure expands. As egos enlarge, the static heavy weight creates an inherent weakness, and the structure of personality is near the breaking point, where transformation to a new species is eminent.

Large egos exerting their influence in an increasing population is a contributing factor to poverty, super-rich, war, pollution, stress, violence and destruction of natural resources. This should not be seen as negative because large egos mean we are ready to transform, it is simply our current reality. Increased cosmic vibration creates pressure when we refuse to change and adapt to the growing force. This pressure and pain is what motivates us to let go and be open to change and evolve. An evolutionary step happens in this way with the old form eventually reaching its practical usefulness for survival and continued growth, it wears out, and energy from that old form is used to build the new form.

When the old breaks down, there will be tears as transformation is always difficult! However, as the old is breaking down, the new is built simultaneously and there is great joy. The truth is, all is transformation, nothing is lost and nothing is gained, when one thing goes away, another takes its place, we are eternal and will have many shapes into the eternal future.

An Evolutionary Step Happens When Higher-Self Is Recognized

The more problematic our ego becomes, the more driven we are to discover the root of our problems. When we finally turn our attention towards our true self, it is the important first step to begin our journey of self-realization. Through the practice of daily meditation, we will eventually become aware of the mind-chatter and later can observe the phenomena, of 'activated personality' arising when it happens in our life.

We take an evolutionary step when we recognize the invisible source energy behind our visible reflection as our true self. We see through the pretender and realize we are the intelligent source behind the mind and not the thinker. Ultimately, this recognition is possible because of our brain organization with the capability to self-reflect. We use our mind to query ourselves. At this time, confusion naturally arises and the question, "Who Am I?" arises.

This self-recognition happens in the space when we suddenly forget 'the me'. A quiet mind, absent of thinking is the requirement for this event to happen. This can happen in various ways, in meditation, by praying intensely, by getting very quiet to hear an answer, from a sudden shock or trauma, by looking at a spiritually creative art work or something beautiful in nature, to name a few. Through self-questioning and asking, "Who Am I", each of us will eventually discover that we are not the reflection; instead, we are the source energy behind the reflection.

Dissolving The Structure Of Personality

When this fact is seen first hand by the questioner, then it is the beginning of the end of the old structure of personality, it has served its evolutionary purpose. After this truth is realized, there is no longer a need for the existing brain organization and transmuting the structure of personality to free-form awareness in the body has begun. This event is known as spiritual awakening, and is an important turning point in our life, where we seek connection with source rather than be attached to external forms. We are on the path of spiritual growth.

Once we know this fact, we often turn attention to ourselves and practice meditation. Meditation is gratifying because when we unite with higher-self we feel loved and complete and we learn about our other layers of conditioning. We see that when we act in conditioned ways out of personality that it causes harm to self and others and keeps us from love. We continue to meditate and query ourselves and let go of our conditioned responses one-by-one. Our awareness increases and each day we feel more loving and compassionate. We respond to life events in creative ways and help others. The meditative state becomes easier and starts to happen in daily life. Meditation is creating a space for our higher-self to emerge. The more we are quiet in mind, the more energy is released back to the pool of free energy in our living system, which then is used by our higher-self to make a change to our system. Briefly, this is the process of dissolving the personality. When we consistently work this way, the influence of the personality is gradually reduced and the influence of the higher-self is increased.

Chapter 3: The Higher-Self

Seeker: *"I've been looking for my true self but I can't find it, can you tell me where it is?"*

Master: *"That which you are seeking is the part of you looking for it."*

The Basic Question: Who Am I?

Spiritual masters over the ages have stated that the most important question we can ask is, "Who Am I?" I agree this is the most important question because our unseen aspect of self is revealed by using our ability to reflect about ourselves. Most people do not use their mind to query themselves, rather they mainly use it to query objects in the outer world.

This is understandable, as when we were first born, that is how we learned about the world, through our capability to self-reflect with mirror neurons in the brain. Since we were born, we identified with the reflection that comes back to us from the outside. We learned to get our identification from the reaction of the other in the outside world to what we did. From that, we inherently assume that we are the formed and visible part of ourselves, as this is what we can see. However, this visible aspect of ourselves, that we see is a reflection in the mind, it is not physical. It seems physical due to how the mirror neurons work, and how we process external images internally with our mind. In short, we are identified with our reflection.

Because of this identification, we get our satisfaction from things we can obtain from the outside world for our reflection, which includes properties and validation for our self-image. It is a normal human activity to attain many properties for the self-image. While we are identified with the physical world, we always have a goal to get something believing it will make us feel complete and happy when we get it. However, we are never happy with what we attain, and set the next goal to get the next thing we desire. The quest for material assets for our self-image will go on until the material assets no long make us happy.

Near the same time the material acquisition game is worn out, we will feel a large hole inside, a dullness of living is prevalent, and signs something is seriously wrong may manifest. There can be disease, mental illness, addiction to substances, divorce, loss of job, thoughts of suicide, intense desire to find our soul mate and many things like this.

At first the difficulties that plague us, are blamed on the world and we feel like a victim. The world, the cancer, the drugs, or people cause our problems. We can put up a valiant fight against the outside, to try to prove our problem has an external cause. Eventually, we will lose this fight because the cause is not external. The cause of our problems is due to focusing our attention in our ability to reflect and thereby animate the personality. When we focus our energy in the mind to animate the personality, we lose energy, which could be used to attain higher levels of self-realization and to heal. The longer we play this game and avoid taking responsibly for our problem, the sicker and more depleted we become. When we stop blaming others for our problems, then we are ready to take responsibility for and ask, "What part am I playing in this?" We are empty inside and we have no idea how to fill this void. Now we are open to try something different. When there is enough pain and difficulty in life, it is exactly the moment we ask, "Who Am I" or "What is God". When we ask these questions, it is an important turning point in our life. We no longer solely use our mind to validate our self-image through the outside world; we now use our ability of mind to query the source.

Self-Observation

At the point we turn our focus away from the world of created objects and turn it toward our source, we gain self-knowledge. Self-knowledge can easily be misunderstood. Self-knowledge is not about textbook learning, and memorization of rote terms, and regurgitating information that has been read off pages. Self-knowledge is learning firsthand about how we physically work and when we gain that knowledge, we can sort the fake from the real and locate the higher-self that is hidden within. The true nature of higher-self is rarely revealed right away; it takes time for our 'light' to be revealed. This is because there are many layers of materialistic forms laid on top of the higher-self that hide our core. To reveal the higher-self, we must unpeel the layers covering it up. These layers exist as conditioned patterns of behaving, and are difficult to uncover because they feel part of ourselves so that we cannot easily see them.

At this point, we no longer desire material things, we declare a new goal to become spiritual and connect with The Creator. We are interested in healing and becoming a better person. The spiritual path has begun and we will read books, join groups, go to therapy, and do daily spiritual practice and healing regimes. At this point, we still desire to attain properties for our self-image; we have merely substituted a materialistic goal with a spiritual goal. We are doing this because we have not changed enough to act different, we still favor processing of information through our mind's eye. Going after a spiritual goal is a materialistic pursuit. However, there is no other place to start from except this point, as this is our current capability.

Now that our focus is turned inward for self-discovery, we will observe and learn about ourselves, gaining self-knowledge from those observations. By meditating regularly, we get skillful at observing our thoughts and response to events and learn more. Once we are skilled at querying the reaction people have to our expression, then we can determine the cause of our reaction. A good question is, "Why did that person respond that way to me"? It can be insightful to ask friends and family to tell us about our good and bad characteristics. Continuing with questions like this and observing our reactions to life events, we get insights about how our personality operates. We notice that we respond in autopilot ways, we see how we rarely reflect before responding, we see the world differently. With each new insight, we have directly received self-knowledge that we never would have understood from reading in a book.

Each insight changes our perspective and we review all information we hold true. It is normal that we drop limiting beliefs we had about the world, societies, governments, religions and many other things. Dropping beliefs itself, can open an entirely new worldview. After a large insight, our spirit soars. After we experience our spirit soaring, we feel lighter and joyous and have a reason to go on living and it motivates us to continue self-realization.

After this event, some people will believe they are enlightened. Then they will attach to that accomplishment as a materialistic gain, which stalls their enlightenment process. It does not matter if this happens; eventually the growing weight of the personality will become unbearable and will motivate us to return to our source. If we understand this, we can take a shortcut and not quit before the transformation has finished. It is very easy to fool ourselves into believing we are enlightened while we are still identified with our self-image. Do not be fooled, by the great pretender!

To gain self-knowledge we are going to have to ask some difficult questions where we will not want to hear the answer. It is not easy to get to the truth about our personality and to give up old habits. It is difficult when we see how we have been hurting others and causing pain with our unconscious responses. It is difficult to see how we have been hurting ourselves. It hurts to heal on all levels, mental, emotional and physical. It hurts to discover that everything we thought we were turns out to be a big empty lie. It takes strong desire to get to the truth of the matter, but persistence pays off in the end. Once we start asking questions such as these, the answer will always come. We can trust in that, that we are supported in this effort, because the most important thing for us to attain in our life is enlightenment.

Transforming The Personality & Free Will

One of the most important tools we have is our ability to decide and move ourselves in the world, with our attention set on the focus of the decision. In this way, we manifest what we focus on. Activated personality happens due to our habit of focusing in thinking and responding to life events from the story, we are weaving there. When we are as the personality, then our motivation is purely materialistic and everything we do has the motive to build our self-image. When we focus in reactive mind, all our conscious capability and energy is used to keep the pretending game going.

Once we realize there is another aspect of our being, then we have the choice to divert energy from the old habit of animating the personality and set our focus to another point. This point is away from use of mind to simple gazing, which is the meditative state. The more we do that, the more we grow spiritually. We manifest what we focus on. There is a counter-part to this truth, and that is what we do not focus on will decrease. Each time we divert energy from animating the personality, personality will diminish in influence and higher-self will increase in influence. This happens slowly over time, but if we keep at it, we will continue to change. In our growing process of diminishing personality and increasing higher-self, insights will continue to be received and each will give us more self-knowledge and move us to the next level.

Surrendering To Higher-Self

Surrender as used in this context means to practice diverting our energy from the old habit of activation of our personality, which primarily is driven by the phenomena of mind-chatter. Surrender practice is normally done using meditation techniques to quiet the mind-voice, by setting our focus on an object of attention that does not require use of our mind. Meditation at first feels strange and is hard, because there is nothing to do or think about. We are so used to constantly chattering, that it is difficult to stop it. It is difficult to do nothing except sit for an hour; we want to rise and do something material. To meditate we put our focus on an object that does not need the help of our thinking, such as observing your breathing that happens automatically. This is all the information you need to do meditation. The mind-doer of course wants to make it into something, so even simple meditation instructions will be embellished by the mediator still identified with the personality. Anyway, all mediators and those new on the spiritual path, can know they are not alone. We all start here. With diligence and continued patience, we will achieve seconds of quiet mind, and over time, these spaces will get longer. It only needs a few seconds for a profound change to be made in your mind, every second counts here! Each change to our mind makes us stronger.

I had the question for over a year, "What does it mean to surrender?", and finally I found out, you do it every night right in the moment when you fall to sleep. When you divert energy from mind-chatter then 'lower-self' falls asleep. When your lower-self falls asleep, your higher-self arises and goes to work changing and healing your body.

Higher-self is the same as our internal healer. The body is a reflection of the brain organization. To change something in the body or to heal it, a change must first be done on the energetic level, which happens in the brain. If we are using our brain to think and emote, then higher-self cannot arise, because we are busy using our attention in another way. A change can only be made to the mind when we are not using it! In truth, there is only one real self, it is the higher-self and the other one is fake.

The statements such as "you can observe your thinking", or "I can multitask", is not true if you are using your mind. It has recently been shown by scientists that the mind cannot multitask. We only have the ability to set focus on one thing at a time. Many teachings that discuss meditation say, "You observe your thinking." or "You see your thoughts like clouds in the sky". It is not possible to observe our thinking real time. If we are thinking then we are not aware. It is one state or the other. When we are immersed in thinking, we are essentially blinded. What is true is we can REMEMBER that we were thinking, or realize we were lost in thought, and this happens by reflected thought. The higher our self-realization, the easier we can detect when thinking starts and have more control to stop it. When we recognize we were lost, we shake out of it and reset our focus to gazing on the object of our meditation. In meditation, we do no more than this simple gazing. Any use of mind, takes us out of the meditative state. Meditation techniques, which use visualization techniques or constant mantra repetition the entire session, do not allow the practitioner to reach deeper states of meditation because the mind never settles.

Kundalini transformation and all healing happen when there is a rise in energetic vibration. A rise in energy often creates a better opportunity for higher-self to take over; because it shakes us out of the conditioned energetic loop, we are stuck in with the activity of engaging with our reflection. The rise in energy shakes us out of our mesmerized state of daydreaming. Surrender practice, inherently has the side effect to raise our energetic vibration, so is another good reason to do it.

What Is The Higher-Self

This is a question where the answer cannot be understood by the mind and by a person identified with their mind. The answer to this question is hinted at all over this book and if you are ready to hear this answer, you will receive it. However, the true answer to this question WILL NOT come from the words, as the answer is never found in a formed object. However, it is possible that reading these words can trigger the realization within you. This answer is only received experientially. In the moment recognition comes, higher-self will arise and we will KNOW the answer.

The higher-self is the real self, it is our soul, and it is our non-formed energetic aspect. The higher-self is not visible, has no shape, and is the source of everything that is us. The higher-self does not experience pain or fear and does not think, our higher-self is pure love. Our higher-self is vastly intelligent, can connect with other conscious intelligence, and thus is a vast reservoir of information. Our higher-self, contains memories of everything that has happened for all our lifetimes. Our higher-self is composed of material from the stars, and we come from the stars. Our higher-self is eternal and non-destructible and lives forever. There is no end to this journey.

Prior to enlightenment, we always are and always have been here. There are no long periods in Earth history where we have not been present to experience it. Our higher-self is constant, it is always with us, and it is our essence. Higher-self never dies we only change form from one shape to another. Look back as far as you can in your memory to a time before your birth and you will discover you can remember before your birth! Then you may realize you are here 'right now' and searching a vast memory bank. You realize you have no memory of being dead because you are here to review whatever has happened. Recalling a death from a previous lifetime drives this point home.

The higher-self is the driver of energy, the questioner and the receiver of information and the ultimate decision maker. Higher-self has created the lower-self, that I call the structure of personality. Higher-self had the reason to do that, so we can recognize the creator who made that structure. Higher-self is evolving through successive lifetimes on Earth, because through experience of living in the material world we eventually discover that we are not material, but are the energy behind the material. We understand that we are a creator, and it is as if we are in kindergarten, where Earth is our playground, and our most important task is learning to transform and recreate ourselves. After we have learned how to transform ourselves, then we are no longer dependent on physical earthly forms and enter another dimension of existence. We have learned all the lessons of the physical realm, and have no need to come back here again.

PART III: HUMAN METAMORPHOSIS

Chapter 4: What Is Human Metamorphosis?

"Human metamorphosis is the transmutation of the physical body into a body of light, done by our higher-self. By transforming ourselves we become a creator." - Betsy

Our Minds Are Expanding With The Universe

Over the long evolution of human beings, what is evident from our archeological record of our human ancestors is that the size of the skull is getter larger and more complex over time. The primary difference between species of human beings has been a growing capability of the brain. We can look through our history and see these brain changes as, the start of religions, the Renaissance, the age of enlightenment, the age of the agricultural revolution, and today with the information age. This shows that our brains are expanding in ability and our collective knowledge is increasing over time for human beings.

Part of this is positive and part of it is negative. Positively, as we evolve our energetic vibration is getting stronger, so we can accumulate more information and have greater storage capacity. Negatively, there is a limit to how long this can go on and how much information we can store because of the organization of the brain and the current human DNA pattern expressed.

Current scientific information about the cosmos shows that energetic vibration and speed is increasing in all objects since the Big Bang and continues to increase over time, not slowing as previously thought. This means that all objects under the influence of cosmic vibration are vibrating faster, and will continued to do so, which I feel is the primary reason for evolution. Increasing vibration means the same as 'we are in a growing process!' With any form of life, there is always a beginning and an end to the life cycle, no life form goes on forever.

Everyone knows that the sun is what causes things to grow on Earth. Without the energy source of the sun, nothing would exist and thrive on the Earth. The sun is our nearest cosmic influence, and it is burning hotter and vibrating faster as it ages, which of course makes us vibrate faster too. It is not illusion that we are moving faster and things are speeding up around us.

My Big Bang Theory

I believe there will be many Big Bang events in the cosmos. I think every Big Bang has a beginning and an end, yet the process is eternal. The Big Bang is one huge growing cycle, the beginning is the massive explosion of all matter from a black hole, and the end is all matter gradually being sucked back into another black hole. You can liken the beginning as accumulation of much material in a black hole, and all that material to be like an acorn seed. The acorn seed has all the instructions needed to make the mature form of the oak tree. Then the acorn seed explodes into tiny pieces and each piece holds a kernel of the same instructions to form the tree. As the pieces explode outward and coalesce, they all gain mass over time because they are in the growing stage. As the pieces coalesce, they eventually form the tree. The tree does not vibrate so fast, as energy is locked into form. When the tree is near the end of its life, it starts to break down. As the structure slowly dissolves, energy is released from the solid structure and collects as a vortex along its core. When all the energy is collected into the vortex, the tree dies and the shell that remains is returned to the earth. Yet, the seeds produced by that tree over its lifetime go on. Owing to the experience of years of living as the oak tree and the growing force affecting all living objects, the DNA in the new acorns is not the same. The acorn contains new instructions for the next round of life. When the seed is planted, the new lifecycle begins.

From the Big Bang, the growing force is in place everywhere while the material is moving as increasing speed. As material increases speed, vibration accelerates. This is evidence of the growing process that we experience and witness daily. Eventually a point will be reached when the structure developing across the universe from the material of the Big Bang, will run out of steam. This will happen when all the life forms have reached maturity and the structure gets too weak to support the weight and is ready to transform. At this point all material will decelerate which is the dying process, will collapse and be pulled and collected into a new black hole. Yet, the reality is that while the forms will die, the energy behind the form is eternal and do not die. In the collective energetic form of the entire universe is a new seed and cycle of life, which can recreate once the next Big Bang happens. This will be a different cycle and we will be part of it eternally or not? I had a vision about this years ago, that what intelligent life was trying to do 'on the grand scale', was to prevent our destruction in the physical Big Bang cycle. The Big Bang cycle of creating intelligent life forms such as human beings on Earth, has been going on for a long time and collectively we do not see how to get out of the big repeating loop that always destroys the forms. If this is true, it is quite the problem! Perhaps if we enlighten ourselves and live in another etheric dimension, then we can escape from the cycle of material destruction.

What Triggers DNA Activation?

My current theory is that species evolve by building energy across generations in the brain and DNA. Energetic vibration increases for all species in each generation. When the energy gets high enough then it triggers latent DNA growing instructions and a new species emerges. I find the missing links in the human species fossil record to be an interesting problem. Perhaps if in-situ metamorphosis occurs in human being or other species when they evolve, then we will never find an intermediate form.

A life form exists as that life form because of its structure. While the structure is strong, that form exists. However, we know as things age, structures get weak and develop cracks. Increasing vibration of a form will eventually change the structure. As the energetic vibration in human beings grows stronger in each successive generation, the existing structure of the species becomes weaker and moves closer to a metamorphosis. This is the basic reason for evolution.

The more pressure (*energy*) that builds inside an existing structure, the closer the structure comes to breaking apart to release the energy needed to make a new life form. Much energy is needed as fuel to have this happen. This can be seen in nature as pressure building in a volcano; the more pressure there is in the structure the more instable the form is. When the pressure reaches its maximum capacity for the container then the pressure breaks apart the old container.

As the growing force of the cosmos continues to accelerate, all life forms will experience increased vibration. Eventually the point is reached where the structure can no longer maintain its current form given the increased vibration. At this point survival of the species is threatened and for life to continue, it must metamorphosis into a new species that can survive in the changed conditions. The fuel for this feat has been accumulating energetically in the forms, as increased awareness through experiences and learning. All life forms become more conscious over time.

Once the consciousness level is high enough in the form, it has enough energy to flip the latent DNA switches on to trigger the old form to morph into the new form. All instructions for this new form have always been present in our DNA; they are only not activated. It is known that the DNA of most species has the same genetic instructions, what differentiates species is which parts of the DNA are activated. As I see it, all life on Earth is growing toward expression as a human being. When the trigger point is reached in a human being, the old brain reorganizes. This reorganization releases energy, which is used to metamorphosis into a new species, with a new brain organization in the same body.

All Structures Eventually Weaken And Transform

When the vibration grows too strong for the containing structure, the structure that held the previous form in place will break down. This is true for many forms, even the ego mind. As the old form breaks down, the released energy collects as a vortex of energy, gaining energy from the dissolving mass. When enough of the old has dissolved, the energy vortex is strong enough to break apart the solid structure that was the frame holding the energy in that shape. The energy is released through the violent breakup of the old to make the new structure. This is what happens in the physical death and in mini-deaths that happen with metamorphosis. As each part fails or quits using energy in that part, the energy is extracted and moves to the spine. The spine is the center of the central nervous system, and the right and left sides of brain control the opposite sides of the body. As energy moves to the spine, the right and left sides of the body activate and create a pumping force, which creates the double helix around the spine. This double helix then forms into a vortex, similar to a mini-tornado. Exactly then, the last energy leaves the body and moves into the vortex around the spine, the vortex sucks the energy up through the brain and out of the body and it can be said that the person has died. When a part of the living structure breaks down, then the released energy is used to make something new in the living structure. In the case of physical death, the energetic core leaves the body, and is the seed to make the next life form. In truth, there is no such thing as death; there is only transformation from one form to the next.

Law Of Conservation Of Energy

"The Law of Conservation of Energy states that the total amount of energy in an isolated system remains constant and the total energy is conserved over time. For an isolated system, this law means that energy can change its location and form within the system. For instance, chemical energy can become kinetic energy, but that energy is neither created nor destroyed." -- Wikipedia

Energy is neither created nor destroyed; it only changes from one form to another. In the same moment that energy was released during the eruption destroying the previous form of a volcano, a new form was created from the old. The volcano is now a crater of empty space with new life-forming material spewed onto the earth. The same happens in a living form in various ways.

This describes metamorphosis. In a living system, energy is constant and is distributed differently over time as the life form takes on new characteristics and subsequent vibrations. We may see that the evolutionary path human beings are on is resulting in bodies with higher vibrations over time growing toward the source that created us, which some call God.

What Is Human Metamorphosis?

Metamorphosis is a biological process, by which an animal physically develops into a new form or structure, after its birth through cell growth and differentiation. It is not widely known that human metamorphosis is possible, because it is only beginning to happen to some people today. I can tell metamorphosis is accelerating in the human population because more people contact me each year telling me it is happening to them. I know it is possible, because it is happening to me! As I see it, human metamorphosis is a biological process that reorganizes the structure of the brain and nervous system, subsequently causing a new cell growth in the body to reflect the new organization of the brain. The process is triggered by certain DNA switches activating owing to increased vibration in the body. This increased vibration is synonymous with a high level of self-realization.

In-Situ Metamorphosis

Story of the butterfly: a caterpillar is born and eats until it has enough energy to fuel its metamorphosis. Hormones are released and it finds a place to attach itself to a branch, then a chrysalis comes out of its head and slowly covers it. Of course, the caterpillar has gone into a deep sleep state. While the chrysalis formation goes on, its old skin is shed and the entire body is covered by the chrysalis. Then its entire body is dissolved into a pool of nutrient rich liquid, and instructions for existing cells not previously expressed in the caterpillar are activated and the new form of butterfly grows from the liquid pool that was the caterpillar. When the butterfly cannot grow any further because the cocoon is restrictive, the butterfly will break out of the cocoon and spread its wings. Some amazing facts about this are 1. During the development of the adult, the chrysalis loses almost half its weight. This shows that metamorphosis consumes a tremendous amount of energy. 2. The DNA of the caterpillar and the butterfly life forms are identical. 3. The caterpillar and butterfly are the same entity and has been present through all stages. Now, I wonder if the butterfly can remember its previous life of having been a caterpillar.

Metamorphosis is happening with some people today, but it happens when we choose to quiet our mind, so we do not have to make a cocoon. This process occurs in a living life form but instead of the old body destroying such as happens in physical death, the life form does smaller in-situ transformations.

A new brain and nervous system is built in the existing body, breaking down the old structure and using this released energy as fuel to make the new body based on the new genetic instructions activated when the process triggered. After this completes the person is a new species and from reproduction can produce offspring of the new species. I believe this phenomenon happens widely to many individuals in the same species simultaneously, as all are affected by outside changing conditions in similar ways and have been evolving a similar amount of time. When the vibration level is high enough, latent DNA switches activate and a jump is made to the next species in the evolutionary track. Thus, a species wide metamorphosis is initiated. I think it is likely that other life forms will undergo a metamorphosis simultaneously as human beings. Another theory similar to this has been proposed for a species wide metamorphosis in the topic of morphogenetic fields.

I believe we do not know about human metamorphosis because it leaves nothing for us to discover in the archeological record and we have not been recording history long enough to have seen it happen. Perhaps it has been observed, but we did not understand then what it was. I think it will not be long before human metamorphosis is widely accepted as truth.

In-Situ Metamorphosis Happens When We Are Quiet

In-situ metamorphosis accelerates when we do not use our energy to animate the personality. When we are not using our mind, we can use our energy to reorganize our mind. The mind cannot be changed if we are busy using it. When we are quiet and non-reactive, our higher-self is present and can reorganize our brain. This transformation happens to a lesser degree in the night while we sleep. When we fall asleep, our higher-self goes to work to change the organization of the brain in the same way. It is not coincidental that dreams occur in various sleep states. Dreams are a symptom of brain reorganization. When we willing quiet our mind, transformation happens and our energetic vibration increases. Increased energetic vibration is evidence of brain reorganization and of self-realization. It is like slowly creating a new organization in our brain and later when new cells are replaced in the body, the body and mind reflect this new and more efficient organization. It is almost like making a change to the epigenome.

Rising Awareness Is A Biological Process

I believe that higher levels of self-realization manifest in the body due to a biological change and reorganization made to the mind and the nervous system. In the archeological record of human beings, we observe that the brain keeps getting larger. Over the years, I have been through many spiritual steps where each dissolved some aspect of my personality. It was obvious to me that my self-realization level was gradually increasing and increased each time a new insight was received. When the kundalini transformation was triggered, it was obviously physical, and then I was sure that self-realization had a biological aspect. Since I have been in the transformation, my vibration increases each day and I have an increased ability to stay calm and non-reactive. The structure of personality continues to dissolve and awareness keeps rising over time. It feels like light is expanding and is filling every niche in my body, and why I call the new human species the light body.

Healing Vibration & Tingling: Neuromuscular Junction Link

When I give myself an acupressure treatment I feel the energetic vibration moving and increasing to higher levels in my body as the session goes on. I believe I feel this vibration because there is an electric charge building in the muscle fibers. I think that healing work in the body always happens through the foundation of the muscles. Muscle fiber is stretchy and can be charged to do work.

I often notice a vibration working in a part of my body, it stays in one place and a small area of tissue is pummeled repeatedly. I call this an 'energetic hold'. I know this symptom happens when blocked energy in my body is being opened energetically. I know a block is removed but it does not tell me what is occurring physiologically.

I suspect at a micro scale that an energetic block is an area of tissue where the neuromuscular junctions are weak owing to nonuse or overuse. Neurons and muscle fibers are the only excitable cells in the body and both carry electricity through the body. This is the way a decision to move a body part, is sent down the motor neuron pathway to the skeletal muscles. The neuromuscular junction is where the nervous signal is passed to the muscles. I think an 'energetic hold' happens in tissue where the neuromuscular junctions need to be strengthened. An 'energetic hold' often continues for some time, with tension localized in the body that I call transformational pain. Clearing a block happens when the neurons in the neuromuscular junctions are strengthened, thus allowing more energy to flow between the neuron and muscle fibers. Tingling, shivers, energy rushes and tones are often felt after clearance of a block, because the nerves excite due to increased electric flow across the neuromuscular junctions. This feels great when it happens. The tingling will often spread to other areas in the body after a block is opened. I guess it is like dominoes, when one neuromuscular junction opens wider it affects the next in order. I strongly suspect the tingling symptom is related to making new nerve connections.

My current theory is that energetic changes and healing in the metamorphosis of the body is mostly due to strengthening the neuromuscular junctions. The instruction to produce that change comes from the brain and travels through the nervous system to the neuromuscular junction. If this is true, then it explains why exercise is so important for healing. Stretching the fibers of muscles strengthens the neuromuscular junctions and increases the energy flow between brain and body. This increases the health and efficiency of the entire system.

The energetic holds and clearance of energy blocks happens almost constantly in the kundalini transformation. The main thing in kundalini transformation is feeling cramping tension building in various muscles groups, then feeling the release as the muscles open, which can be mild or strong, and feeling the tingling sensation as new energy flows into the opened area. Another phenomena of the kundalini transformation, is feeling vibration constantly working in the body and each day it gets noticeably stronger.

Transformation Pain

Pain is a sensation often produced after intense or damaging stimuli such as cutting a finger, breaking a bone, being burned, or putting iodine on a cut. Pain is part of the body's defense system, producing a reflexive retraction from the painful stimulus, and tendencies to protect the affected body part while it heals, and avoid that harmful situation in the future.

In this book when I mention pain, I am predominately talking about the transformational pain that is a symptom of kundalini transformation. Transformational pain is felt frequently and resolves promptly. I rarely talk about acute or chronic pain, which is due to unresolved disease or another problem. Transformational pain is experienced when something in our body is healing, if we understand this deeply we know that the area in question is changing shape from one form to another. One shape is going away and another is arising, this is the essence of metamorphosis. The pain we experience has to do with the form being healed, whether it is emotional, mental, or the physical body. It is painful to discover we may be wrong in our thinking, it is painful to remember old memories and cry, and it is painful to heal torn tissues or broken bones.

For a real change or healing to happen there must be a transformation of energy, from the old form to the new form. This process of the old dying and of the new forming is often perceived as a painful sensation. The transformation is biological and the intense heat given off as the old tissue releases the held energy and changes to the new tissue causes pain. Healing does cause pain and is a symptom of the transformation, of the old giving rise to the new.

Transformation Pain Is A Symptom Of Healing

In the moment, we experience a sudden damage to our body, as with an external injury, we do not feel transformation pain then. When we cut our finger, we immediately pull our finger away from the object that cut us. That is a reflex as no pain is felt then. A microsecond later, we feel pain in the finger as the tissues mend and stop the blood flow. What occurs is a sudden rush of energy travels along the nerve paths going to the site of injury, and as it localizes on that spot, heat rises and the strong vibration of a growing reaction is what makes it feel painful. There are many accounts of people who have had extreme injuries and have not felt pain. They do not even know what is damaged until they look with their eyes. It is when the healing process starts that the sensation of transformational energy is felt. The greater the injury, the more energy is diverted to heal in one location and the stronger the sensation is. Transformation pain is a symptomatic reaction owing to the intense heat and energy moving and working at the locus of the transformation site.

We Are Pain & Change Avoidant

We have pain sensors all over our body to protect us in case our life is physically threatened, so our innate tendency is to avoid the experience of pain and harmful situations in the future. To protect us physically this works well. The problem comes with our identification with our personality. We tend to believe that the personality is a physical entity and thus we avoid anything, which might cause pain and threaten the demise of this structure. Thus, we evaluate all experiences in the same way and avoid painful experiences, because pain for us is a signal that our life may be threatened. Another thing that causes us extreme discomfort is the unknown. We tend to get resistant and animate our personality in the face of the unknown because we fear the unknown. Change is always about entering the unknown. This can be problematic in the kundalini transformation, because the entire process requires a leap of faith and trust and readiness to enter unknown fields and dimensions.

What we need to know is that the energy held in the structure of the personality and in all forms is mutable, it is not our permanent self and it is not a permanent structure. If we allow this transformation of this energy, we will not die and we will not disappear. Allowing transformation to happen means we are allowing ourselves to adapt to changes occurring around us. With this attitude, we are physically mutable and thus much more likely to survive, then if we resist change. If we resist changing ourselves when events indicate, then what we are doing is becoming more solid or holding our energy as the personality in tension. This holding of energy to try to maintain static familiar shapes is that which restricts the flow of energy and causes pain and subsequently acquired disease, conflict, aging and illness to build in our physical body. All structures become weaker the more they resist change. In the moment, we drop our attitude of resistance, holding and trying to protect something or an area, pent-up energy used for this protection is automatically released from the structure of personality and returned to our free reserve of unformed energy. This released energy will be used for healing and transformation. Soon we will feel the transformational energy, as an old part of us goes away and a new part rises in its place. Know that nothing is ever lost, a new form always supersedes the old, and the new can better adapt to changing conditions around us. Updating ourselves and allowing change and transformation makes us much more likely to survive, than trying to protect worn out stagnant forms of energy.

Transformational Pain Need Not Be Experienced As Pain

Because kundalini transformation is a long growing process, transformational pain is experienced frequently. The transformation is much more effective and less painful; the sooner we accept it and learn how to relax our body and mind. When we are relaxed and our mind is quiet, we do not have the experience of pain from the transformation. Pain is usually transitory, lasting only until the stimulus is removed or the underlying damage or pathology has healed.

The transformation process does not need to be experienced as painful. The reality of this sensation is what we experience depends on our focus. When pain is experienced from transformation, it is a sign we are identifying with the symptom, meaning the personality has activated. When personality is activated, it is the same as resisting transformation on all levels. When we are directing, focusing and using our energy to animate our personality, we are not allowing our energy to change ourselves. When having the painful experience we may notice we are chattering with our mind-voice and generating strong feelings. We may be saying things such as, this hurts, I want my Mommy, I don't want more pain, this is not fair, I can't take any more, I want this to go away or I don't want to do this! When personality is activated, we can prolong the pain feeling long after the sensation is gone.

Alternatively, when we feel the sensation of transformational pain, it is best to learn not to focus on the symptom as unwanted or painful. In a state of acceptance and quiet mind, we can observe the phenomena and with practice, we will not experience it as painful. Later it can be experienced as pleasurable and even later as neither pleasurable nor painful, it only is. If we internally observe the energetic movement in the area, where we feel the pain sensation, we will see the transitory nature of this symptom. When we feel it, it is already past. Even if there are moments of intensity, we know they will be gone in an instant. Those instants can link and soon it is behind us. The more we learn how to do this the easier and more effective the transformation will be. Then we will see that to continue we must learn how to let go, and the symptom of transformation pain and learning how to not experience it as painful is what will be our guide to teach us how to fully detach from 'past forms'. This is the same as the awakened state. That is the ultimate result of the transformation, so it makes sense we learn how to do this, otherwise we will not achieve our goal. As systems around us continue to speed up, it will increase pressure on us to evolve. To refuse to do so causes unnecessary pain. Eventually the pain will motivate us to change and we will let go.

Metamorphosis Happens Spontaneously

The most critical thing that threatens our survival and ability to adapt to changing conditions will be the first priority of our internal healer to heal. Our internal healer will select energy blocks to clear where it can get the most energy in return. Our internal healer wants to heal us and is hungry for energy. The more free energy our system has to work with, the more power there is to transform us.

It is best to leave the task of healing in the hands of our higher-self, as this is not something we can figure out with our mind. We might not like a certain irritating symptom and focus our energy into trying to heal or alleviate that symptom, but this might not be the most effective use of our energy. We can relax a muscle knot in our trapezious with massage. Usually what will happen is because the cause was not treated then the knot will return. If we allow our internal healer to decide how to use the energy boost, an emotional trauma from our childhood may get resolved which caused repressed anger and created those knots. By healing the cause of the tension, we will stop generating the knots; they will dissolve and never return. We need to trust that our higher-self knows what needs to be healed first and will do the healing in the most efficient manner. The reality is we do not know how to heal ourselves as in how to mend a finger. The best thing we can do is to increase our overall energy, which then aids in the healing process that is taken care of by our higher-self.

Another way to look at this is to examine the subject of brain plasticity. In this field of study, it is shown that if we do not learn new things over time our brain becomes lazy and thinking is eventually affected and memory problems such as old-age forgetfulness, dementia and Alzheimer's manifest. The inelastic brain is similar to a map containing many tracks of all the things we learned long ago. When we do not learn new things, we traverse over the same track repeatedly and this creates a rut that reduces the health of the brain. Over time, this causes the brain to lose elasticity and results in disease like dementia. The offered cure to increase plasticity of the brain is for us to learn new skills and new ways to respond to life and problem solving to increase the number of tracks. This does work, but I think there is a better way to encourage plasticity or increased elasticity of the brain.

I think the most efficient way to increase brain plasticity is by erasing what we already know, not by learning something new. I think the most flexible, intelligent, intuitive and healthy brain is one with little or no programming. When energy is diverted from activating the personality by stopping thinking, then the neuron mapping of the old tracks that keep the thinking personality in place are broken down. The more we do this non-doing activity, the more the neurons branch out, like infinitely expanding fractals, and the more flexible our mind and body becomes. As our brain and body become more elastic, our insight increases and we can respond spontaneously and creatively rather than only in conditioned ways.

Only 'You' Can Release Your Personality

We are not enlightened because we are identified with our personality, where when animated fools us into thinking we are alive. Because this is the problem, it means there is only one way to remedy it. To transform ourselves, we only need to practice letting go of the old habit of chattering, which is the cause of animation of the personality. Each time we are quiet, our brain is rewired to be more efficient, a program is removed, we are partly healed, our energetic vibration raises and we are more aware. Each time we raise our vibration level, we have more energy at our disposal to heal things in our body, which needs more energy to accomplish. When programmed tracts are removed, neuron growth expands and branches out in that space with numerous connections which is what increases our vibration. As we continue in the transformation, deeper and older problems are corrected, even to the point of correcting the structural alignment of the skull and skeletal frame. The truth is only we can transform ourselves. Only we can stop 'pretending as the personality', nobody can stop us from doing that.

Enlightenment Has Always Been Going On

Enlightenment is a gradual growing process, where the organization in the brain is changing into a more efficient one-mind structure in the interval we do not use our mind. Spiritual enlightenment has been going on since the first life emerged on Earth, where all of us are in various stages of accomplishment. Successive generations of life forms, over all these eons have been increasing awareness, up to the present people of today. Our current structure of the brain and body gives us the capability to recognize our source as spirit and creator of ourselves. Then the next step for human beings is to become that spirit in the body. There is one more physical species of life form for human beings to become on Earth and it is happening now, we are growing bodies of light.

Growing numbers of people have had spiritual awakenings and it is difficult to find commonalities in the reports. The variety in reports is partly because spiritual awakening is not widely accepted as a real phenomenon and has not been studied by scientists. Another reason is that many of the symptoms are internally experienced due to changes in the nervous system. Because these symptoms are not experienced externally, there exists no language for it. Variation in testimonials is normal because each of us is an individual with unique experiences and what we observe and report will be heavily influenced from our past. Thus, reports across testimonials seem different even when we are describing the same phenomena. Finally, kundalini awakening is a continuous process with key stages. There is currently no clear definition about those stages, so all stories are lumped together in one basket, under the common name of kundalini awakening, even if they are miles apart. As more people share their accounts of kundalini awakening, we will increase our knowledge about the transformation and help each other get through it.

What is common to all who have spiritually awakened is they understand the truth that they are NOT the thinker. They encounter the higher-self as spirit; they meet their true self that is the life-force behind the body, behind the mind, behind everything. Many people that spiritually awaken believe they are enlightened, which then stalls their evolution to reach higher steps. This can happen because this phenomenon is not widely known and understood by society and there is a prevalent societal belief that enlightenment can happen instantaneously. Today this is changing, as more people are experiencing kundalini awakening symptoms. I hope my testimonial can motivate people to keep going so they can reach further stages.

The reality is that awareness rises gradually and it happens each time that we drop a part of our conditioning. After we spiritually awaken, we are no longer fully identified with our personality, so we have better ability to observe ourselves and be acutely present at times. Our personality is complex, was built over many years and is held together by our programmed responses to life events. We cannot let go of all our programming instantaneously, nor can we change the energy in our system in one fell swoop. It would be too much to take.

We can only relate and respond to that which we have knowledge of and changes in consciousness happen in steps. We cannot be aware of what is hidden, and what is hidden is our conditioning. Conditioning is hidden because it feels to be integral to ourselves. We cannot change something we cannot see. We change a part of ourselves when we have the desire to change and ask the proper questions to discover our hidden programmed influences. If we are happy how we are, then we will not change. It is normal we want to be comfortable with how we are for a while and we cannot instantly jump into the stream of constant change. When we are comfortable with the known, we feel secure and are building energy to be used later. However, we should not stay comfortable for too long.

Chapter 5: Four Stages Of Human Metamorphosis

What Is The Dark Night Of The Soul?

Dark night of the soul is a metaphor for a common phase that happens in spiritual awakening, marked by despair, intense fear, crying and wanting to die. I think a better name would be dark night of the personality, because the strong reactions do not come from the soul. The strong feelings result from identifying with our personality.

The personality is upheld in our mind's eye by identifying with our thinking. This happens when we tell a story and believe our story is truth. Our story's undertone causes an emotional charge in the muscles that produces the 'me' illusion. Chiefly, we identify with feeling energetically alive because of the story we are creating. When the thinking is dark, it will create a dark vibration in the body and we will feel dark. Once established, the dark vibration will continue to trigger similar thoughts. At this point, we are immersed in storytelling and the dark vibration. Our personality is strongly activated, and our soul is trapped in a circular reaction.

The Four Stages Of Physical Transformation

There are four main stages of physical transformation, each with a dark night and awakening. The number of stages we experience depends on our current state of evolution. We can spend a lifetime in any cycle. The first dark night is before spiritual awakening and the fourth awakening happens when the process is complete with enlightenment. By going through a long transformation, I realized there were multiple dark nights. With my third dark night, almost identical issues arose as the second dark night. I felt I was repeating and was a failure. The same issues arose with my fourth dark night, but this time I knew I was progressing. I had the same issues in each dark night, but saw healing was occurring in a different energetic layer of each issue.

Our personality stays intact due to identification with our mind, emotions and body. Enlightenment is the process of dissolving the personality, in reverse order, of how it was built. The outermost layer is cognitive, which we built from about three years to adulthood. The middle layer is precognitive or emotional, which we built from about conception to age three. The innermost layer is the physical body reflecting our DNA, which represents many lifetimes and inherited aspects from our ancestors, mother and father. The reason there are four stages of personal transformation is based on the fundamentals of how something is created. The personality is an object and goes through the same steps of creation and destruction. Physical transformation is about transmuting our personality into awareness as higher-self in the light body. The transformation is about learning to become a creator and our body is our field of learning.

How We Create Something

1. We observe an object in the physical world using our sensory apparatus. We think about what we have seen and ask questions about it. The answer comes from inspiration or thinking, and then we decide what to do and form our 'mental' goal. This is the thinking level.

2. When we have our goal, we need desire to do it. With our goal and desire, then the direction to use our energy is set. This is our intention. Energy charges move from the brain to the proper body muscles preparing us to move our energy from thought to feeling to carry out our goal. This is the feeling or emotional level.

3. Once our intention is determined and we are ready to act, our body muscles are charged and prepared for movement. This is the vibration level.

4. We move and do the action in the world. We created the thing we desired, by moving our energy from the external world to the inner world and back. This is the manifest object or body level.

Pattern Of Transformation: Awakening And Dark Night Cycles

Each layer of transformation goes through distinct phases. Our starting point is attachment with a layer. Because of our attachment, misery and dissatisfaction eventually result and then we are ready to let that layer go. In the instant, we drop attachment to a layer, higher-self arises and a spiritual awakening happens. Tremendous energy is released, which fuels the transformation. Transformation is a biological aspect of awakening accompanied by profound healing and spiritual reactions. It is normal to experience many charismatic symptoms such as, tones, flashing lights, rushes of internal wind, numbness, tingling, going out of body, insights, crystal clarity, visions, repressed memories, telepathy, amplified hearing, heightened vision, weight loss, elation, kriyas, laughing, and many more. Most of these symptoms are due to biological changes to the mind, body and nervous system. It is normal to feel elated for many days following a spiritual awakening. When higher-self arises, we make direct contact with our higher-self and feel spiritual and awake. The awakening has changed us permanently. We have received revelations, insights and wisdom that we will never forget. Our values have changed and we see everything differently. It is normal that we drop attachments to people, places and things associated with the layer we dropped.

The Dark Night Begins

Eventually the elation settles, yet healing is still going on. We may feel tired, have pain in the body or have strong emotions. The thoughts get dark and crying can be nonstop for days on end. We may have dreams and memories of past lives flood in to our consciousness. We no longer feel well, it seems we sacrificed much and what we gained was little. We may feel we have no reason to live. This scenario triggers the dark night of the soul. It is easy to identify with the heavy healing reactions and the personality dominates. Because we are energetically stronger, we can activate our personality stronger when we identify with our thoughts and feelings. When we feel we have lost something, we cling stronger to what is familiar. By identifying with thoughts and feelings, we are lost in the illusion and entrenched in the dark night of the soul. Even though this stage feels dark, it is still part of the transformation. Our vibration is higher and deeper blocks of the personality are healing. Every main awakening stage releases tremendous energy from fixed form. Crying is a vehicle to release stored energy from the mind and heart. After we cry hard, we will feel much better afterward. When it is the darkest, the light is near, hang in there.

How To Get Through The Dark Night Of The Soul

In the awakening event our body, mind, and nervous system are changing due to the released energy. The brain is reorganizing, and thinking and feelings are erratic. Many of the thoughts and feelings in the dark night are a reaction of the reorganization occurring in the brain. Eventually we will process information and react to events differently, owing to those changes.

We have more energy, but do not know how to direct this energy yet. It is likely we still have the habit to attach to the energetic layer of personality that is healing. The way to get through the dark night most efficiently and with the least pain, is to quiet the mind as much as possible whatever stage we are in. Do not identify with the strong symptoms occurring which include your thoughts and emotions. As much as we can, we should practice quieting the mind and seeking our center. When we are united with our source, we are still and free of resistance. When we are still, the transformation goes faster and is more efficient because we have no resistance, allowing the energy to change us. The image of a hurricane is helpful. Our physical self is in the twisting vortex of wind and our higher-self is in the eye, still and calm in the center. Seek center, to ride out the storm in the safety of the eye.

Many meditation tools can help us achieve quiet mind. The tools that work are partly preference, part experimentation and part what has worked for us in the past. The awakening event happened because we achieved quiet mind, so use what worked before. While there is a strong transformation occurring in the mind, we cannot rely on our thinking. It is best to do everything we can to divert ourselves from thinking. The more we practice meditation, the more skilled we get and it is easier to pass through stages that rewire the brain. Meditation is a skill we need to master, as each dark night requires a deeper stillness.

First Dark Night – I Think Therefore I Am – Identified With Objects

The first dark night can last a long time and is the reality for most people today. In this stage, we are primarily identified with objects and thought is the main object. Everything we do and receive in life is filtered through our thinking. We live our life completely in our mind. A constant inner dialogue is occurring all day. This dialogue often carries on into the night. Difficulty to sleep, or to fall asleep, is a sign we have little ability to stop the dialogue. We are in the stage of expanding our personality and are identified with our thinking. Before awakening, the mind chatter is mostly invisible and "I think therefore I am", is the main philosophy. All actions have the motive to gain attributes and get confirmation for our self-image. How we see ourselves, and how we believe others see us, is of primary importance.

Most of our actions are harmful to self and others, because our main motivation is to gain something. A materialistic gain is only made when somebody else loses. Because most of humanity is not awakened, it explains the dog-eat-dog world, full of violence, destruction, lying, stealing, killing, fighting and poverty. We can be happy for some time in this stage, if we are gaining enough attributes and getting satisfaction from them. As the personality expands, pain grows proportionately and pain will eventually divert our focus from material acquisitions to the search for our spirit. The first awakening is near when the material acquisition game no longer satisfies.

First Awakening –Higher-Self Arises As Vibration In The Mind

Eventually the material acquisition game wears out when we no longer feel any joy from whatever we receive. In this moment, we admit we are miserable and material things no longer make us happy. This is a huge turning point, where we divert our attention from the material world and toward our spirit or The Creator. We actively search for something to fill the empty hole inside. The material game did not make us happy, so we are open to explore alternatives. This is the seeking and healing stage. We explore spirituality, read self-help books, do therapy, join support groups and seek a connection with our Creator. This stage can last long, with many intermediate steps within it. It is about unraveling the layers of programming that make up the personality.

When we divert energy from material acquisition and focus on our source, we gain self-knowledge about ourselves. Self-knowledge reveals insights that slowly reduce attachment to our self-image. As attachment to our self-image reduces, moments of clarity happen and our thinking and emotions become visible. Increased clarity allows us to distance from our firm attachment we had with our self-image, and we see ourselves better. By using our energy to look at ourselves, we see how we are! Then we may ask, "Who is looking?" Each self-revelation is a mini-awakening that slowly raises our vibration. As we continue with self-discovery, an awakening event will happen when our vibration level is high enough in a moment when we stop the mind-chatter. Silence can happen after an accident or trauma, a sudden insight, seeing something beautiful, or while doing our meditation. What is significant is our mind was quiet long enough to release energy imprisoned by our nonstop mind-chatter. During that space of total quiet, our higher-self arises into our mind, we see our true nature, and now we know we are not the thinker. We experience ourselves as the source behind the thinking, we have seen beyond the veil, beyond that which blinded us. It is the first glimpse of our higher-self and we realize we are godlike creatures; we have awakened to our true nature.

Second Dark Night – I Am Spiritual - Identified With Mind

The first time we see our true nature, higher-self arises into the mind, a flood of information comes into our consciousness and we receive knowledge about our life purpose. Information is downloaded into our mind and thinking is fast like a computer. This information helps us continue our spiritual awakening and we understand why we are here and what our special gifts are.

Because we are still the storyteller, we tend to embellish the pure information we receive so that it makes sense. The embellishment creates strange stories of why we are here and what is our life mission. After the first awakening, some may think they are God's chosen one or that they are the reincarnation of a famous mystic. It is a natural inclination to want to save the world and while our intention is good, it is misguided, as we do not know any better. We tend to go into a head-trip after the first awakening and some people never get out of it and end in psych wards. We can be carried away with our newfound meaning and purpose in life and it becomes our new identification.

As we drop attachments with material possessions, it is still our nature to attach and so we latch on to the new one. This can be another long dark night, but not as long as the previous one. Each dark night gets shorter as we progress. After awakening, we identify with our spiritual aspect and tend to ignore our thoughts and feelings, which create a split identity. This is similar to what happens when people go crazy from identifying with their thoughts and feelings, but now we identify with our spirit. The split creates a fake identify of being spiritual. We feel awake and we know something real has happened. This is difficult to get out of, because we do not trust other viewpoints. We are awakened and think we see clear. If someone tells us we are acting crazy or irrational, we tend to dismiss it.

Hopefully, luckily, the message gets through and we see the new split we have created. We let it go and crash down from the pink fluffy cloud back to the hard earth and the second dark night of the soul. Now we cry harder than we ever have before. This crying jag releases a ton of held emotional energy; it is cleaning out old beliefs and values and is healing. As in the first dark night, we tend to attach to the strong healing reactions and have similar thoughts and feelings. As discussed prior, to get through do not cling to the edges, rather seek the center. After the big release of energy, we will feel more spiritual. It is like coasting downhill because our awareness is higher. If we remain diligent to uncover the hiding games of the personality, insights will continue and our awareness will keep rising.

Second Awakening – Higher-Self Arises As Muscle Vibration - Emotions

The second step can last a lifetime, and is the hardest to complete. It is difficult to go beyond all the myriad tricks we create to keep the pretending game going. It needs intensive inquiry to unravel the cognitive layers and to identify new games we create to keep the identification game going. Concepts of 'being' is a new game we learn and it can be so satisfying that we rarely question it. A concept of 'being' refers to performing in a certain way, which is done to get validation for our new spiritual identity. The common denominator is still attachment to our self-image, but now the self-image is spiritual. We get confirmation of our spiritual self-image by joining 'spiritual' groups, where we give each other validation for being spiritual. Concepts of 'being' are adopted or invented, and then performed to prove we can 'behave as spirit'. These concepts run the gauntlet of acting as an authority, giving advice, becoming a spiritual teacher or guru, developing a technique for self and others to follow and many more. We discover a new way to make a living and the activities are so satisfying that we lose motivation to find deeper hidden attachments. We tend to believe we are enlightened and therefore there is no longer a need to do this work.

If we do our meditation and continue to question ourselves with the desire for truth, we will discover the games and drop them. Going beyond the concept of 'being' is the hardest. We test out a concept of 'being' until it fails. Rather than giving up, we adopt or invent a new way 'to be'. It is like having mini awakenings and mini dark nights, one after the other. We receive a new insight and later crash when we understand we still are not enlightened. Even while this happens, our awareness is rising and our personality is reducing in influence.

Eventually our awareness will be high enough to discover the cause of this endless game of adopting new ideas and trying to make them into our self-image or way of being. We will discover that this behavior is driven by our belief that what we tell ourselves is truth. We believe 'our story' is truth, because it gives us the feeling we know. When we clearly see how we fool ourselves by believing 'our story' is truth, then we will drop 'our story' every chance we get.

Working diligently to stop the storytelling increases our awareness level, because storytelling consumes much energy. Our vibration level rises and we will encounter our higher-self again. This time it is not from realizing we are not our mind, but from realizing we are pure vibration. When this happens, we see that by being the storyteller we provoke our environment so we can react with strong emotion. The strong energy we create this way is what is fooling us. We thought this strong energy was aliveness. We see through the ruse by meeting our true vibration. Then we no longer want to do it anymore. The part of us that was pretending is gone. We are elated and many insights continue to come. The kundalini growing that is in progress becomes evident at the second awakening. At the first awakening, our vibration filled our mind, now it is stronger and has expanded to fill our body's muscles.

We clearly see the game of personality and know storytelling fuels it; we are done with that old habit. The only thing left to do is quiet our mind as much as possible. We know if we do that, we will grow. There is nothing more to learn about how to be spiritual, we need no more concepts or techniques, and do not adopt a new self-image and have nothing to enlarge. We are finished with seeking and games. Our life becomes a meditation, and we work on dropping the remaining attachments.

Third Dark Night – I Am Vibration – Identified With Emoting

After the second awakening, our awareness rises with consistent meditation. Insights continue and we are strong enough to drop our attachment to emoting. This is a transitory period where we feel between the two worlds of physicality and spirituality, belonging in neither. We know we are not aware and are not sure how to know without the use of our storytelling. We are confused and disoriented. We do not yet have reliable access to intuition and we do not trust our story and less the story of others. This is a phase of becoming independent of authorities where we learn to rely on getting answers direct from our source. It happens during this phase that strong emotions are provoked from most outside events. This is part of the healing after the second awakening event. Our emotions rage and we may feel crazy. We seriously question our sanity and wonder if we have made any progress when we see how crazy and emotional we are. We may think we are repeating and have not learned anything. That is a hard pill to swallow when we have been working so hard. Again, we feel like we have lost everything and enter the dark night of the soul. Another big cleansing is occurring with much crying, stronger than the prior episode. In this phase, the emotional energy of the inner child releases and a ton of energy is stored in this layer. The dark gets very dark, but simultaneously, the light expands rapidly. Eventually we will see the deep emotional layer, and understand why we have been acting this way all our life. After releasing this emotional layer, there is extraordinary freedom and independence from any person, place or thing. We stop walking in circles, which we have been doing all our life. The real world is now open before us.

Third Awakening – Higher-Self Arises As Body Vibration

After emotional cleansing, our vibration is high and meditation gets deep with increased ability to sustain the quiet mind state. Pre-kundalini awakening symptoms sporadically happen in the body. With our free time, we meditate to accelerate the transformation. Higher-self is driving more than lower-self. During this phase, our energetic vibration is growing rapidly and we become sensitive to energy inside and outside ourselves. Soon we will feel springy and light inside our body and higher-self will arise the third time. This time we feel it all over our body and in our mind as strong vibration and this time it does not fade, rather it gets notably stronger each day. Eventually the full-blown kundalini transformation is triggered and we enter the fourth dark night of the soul.

Fourth Dark Night – Death Of Body – Kundalini Transformation

The fourth stage is long and lasts many years. The rest of the personality is transmuted, that is stored in the bones, muscles and DNA and simultaneously the new light body is built. When enough energy has been withdrawn from the structure of personality, and our vibration is high enough then latent DNA instructions are activated to start the growth of the light body. This activation point is what I call full-blown kundalini transformation. After a few months of preparatory nervous system changes to the body, eventually changes move through the chest and neck to make changes to the physical structure of the skull and brain. The fourth dark night at its most intense is experienced as a form of physical death. To be reborn in the flesh, we truly have to die in the flesh. When dying we gasp as we take our last breath of air and make gurgling and choking sounds as the air is compressed out of our body, moves through our chest and into our brain. We shortly stop breathing when this happens. The challenge is to allow this feeling and go to deep center knowing we are in a transformational death.

We can only get through the fourth dark night with a total physical surrender of our body. However, do not worry, when we reach this step we are strong enough to do it, all we have done before has prepared us for this step. In this step, we are acutely present and of course, we live through it. After we have passed through the physical death, we will never go back to having a personality again, not now or in a future lifetime. We are now erecting a new structure that will serve us for the next part of our journey. There is no going back and there is no desire to do so.

Fourth Awakening – Higher-Self Arises In The New Light Body

It takes some time for the new light body to grow, but when it is done, the transformation will be complete. The end of the fourth dark night and the fourth awakening will happen in the same moment in the blink of an eye, as they are occurring simultaneously each day as the old is dissolved to create the new. When complete we will be enlightened, physically alive and present in our new light body. Hallelujah!

Chapter 6: All About Kundalini

What Is Kundalini Energy?

Kundalini, from Indian yoga, is a source of energy in the body, envisaged as a sleeping serpent coiled at the base of the spine. Kundalini is the intelligent conscious life-force energy of YOU distributed in your body's cells that keeps you alive and functioning. Kundalini energy is responsible for evolutionary development and for heightened states of consciousness and awareness, and is present in all living life forms. All life forms are evolving toward heightened awareness. Kundalini energy does not have any specific character, as pure energy it has no form or condition. When kundalini energy releases from fixed form, the base of the spine activates, felt as a fluttering sensation in the tailbone. After this, kundalini energy coils up the spine, like a serpent rising.

Before awakening, kundalini energy is in a fixed shape in the body and is at a low vibration level. Kundalini energy is dormant while used to animate the personality. Kundalini energy releases from fixed form, when elements of the personality dissolve which happen when we let go of our attachment to that element. A large quantity of kundalini energy releases in major awakening events. With each release of kundalini energy from fixed form, the body vibration rises.

After birth, the growing force is strong in our body; our body vibration is high, which is obvious from our rapid growing. Our growth rate and body vibration gradually decline as we grow into adulthood. This decline is due to energy converting into a structure, which is the personality of the developing individual. When growing stops, our kundalini energy is contained in the structure. The personality is partially created from growth and organization of the brain. This brain organization is reflected in the body as animated personality. Our unique vibration is held in shape by our physical structure, reinforced by our skeletal alignment, brain organization and epigenome.

After growing stops, the personality expands as we gain attributes for our self-image. Personality expansion happens due to our current brain organization and evolutionary state and is beneficial. As kundalini energy amasses in the expanding personality, it is collecting as an easily tapped supply of fuel. The energy building in the personality is kept in place through our conditioned use of the mind. In the moment we stop using our mind, some of this energy is released and is the fuel to transition to a higher state of consciousness. Kundalini energy is constant in the body. The law of conservation of energy, states that any object in nature is energetically a closed system and no mass or energy is ever gained or lost in a transformation. Kundalini energy is always conserved and nothing disappears. Atoms merely separate and reform into new shapes.

What Is Kundalini Awakening & Transformation?

A kundalini awakening happens when energy is released from the personality, when quiet mind is sustained and our vibration is strong enough to release it. After the energy release, the brain and nervous system reorganize and kundalini symptoms occur. All along our spiritual journey kundalini energy releases, over time the releases are closer together until they are continuous. Kundalini releases become detectable in the pre-awakening stage when we are near our first spiritual awakening.

Large amounts of kundalini energy release three times in our spiritual enlightenment as described in the previous chapter. These awakening events change us. When a large release happens, there is a barrage of symptoms such as, energy rushes, tingling, light explosions, tones, altered sensory perception, not needing to sleep, weight loss, and insights.

The first time energy releases, it rises into the mind and we awaken and understand we are not our mind. I call this spiritual awakening and the crown opening, where we discover our higher-self. The second time energy releases, it is stronger and fills the muscles and we realize we are not our vibration. The third time energy releases, it fills the entire body and then we realize we are not our body. The third event is the onset of the full-blown kundalini transformation. After this, kundalini energy releases continuously in smaller amounts with frequent kundalini symptoms.

Kundalini transformation is a gradual, biological growing process moving human beings toward enlightenment that also heals our body. Our higher-self orchestrates the transformation by releasing energy from our personality and using it to reorganize our mind and body. The changes result in a refined nervous system, higher vibration, increased awareness and less influence of personality, called the light body. Kundalini transformation is a metamorphosis into a new species of human, using the energy of the old body to create a new body. Kundalini transformation is synonymous with human evolution and metamorphosis.

It is only recently known that human beings can metamorphosis into a new life form, as more people report about kundalini awakening experiences. I believe instructions for a new species of human being exist in our DNA, and when conditions are right they are activated. Kundalini transformation is continuous over our long human history and everyone is at some stage of it. As human beings evolve, kundalini transformation accelerates and self-realization levels increase in the human population. Rising self-realization is due to kundalini transformation. Kundalini transformation is a biological process and therefore self-realization is too. I see no distinction between healing and kundalini transformation.

How Does Kundalini Transformation Happen?

Each time we divert energy from using our mind and are in the meditative state, energy is released from the personality. Kundalini transformation converts this energy into a new structure in the mind and body, giving rise to a spontaneous and aware life form. As we continue to do meditation, the structure of personality slowly dissolves and has less influence on our life over time. To convert the entire structure of personality into the new structure is gradual and takes many years to complete.

We can only reorganize our mind if we are not using our mind. The distribution of kundalini energy in our body depends on what we focus on. If we focus on animation of the personality, then personality expands and accumulates energy. If we focus on not animating our personality by meditating, then personality reduces by releasing energy from programmed forms. To change our structure, the brain must change. Brain organization is similar to the epigenome, which is similar to software instructions that influence our DNA. The epigenome determines which genes are activated in our DNA, and later dictates our body and mind characteristics. To effect our DNA and activate the latent growing, we need to change our software instructions. Released energy is the fuel necessary to change the brain. Energy cannot be released from the brain, nor can released energy be used to change the brain, if we are using the brain. If you read that carefully, you will notice there are two reasons quiet mind states are important. Releasing energy from the brain is one and allowing the change in the brain is the other.

Our higher-self is intelligent and knows exactly how to make these changes to the mind and nervous system and complete the metamorphosis. The transformation happens spontaneously, every time we are quiet. In the space when we are quiet, the brain organization changes, the epigenome changes and the DNA are affected. After the new programming is done, as cells are replaced in the body they physically reflect the new structure in the body.

The biological aspect of kundalini transformation is primarily changes to the central nervous system. I believe the central nervous system is reorganizing into a single brain structure, away from the dual brain and right and left body structure. The nervous system slowly branches out in the mind and body like an infinitely expanding fractal pattern and our body fills with light. A side effect expansion of the nervous system is increasing body vibration, due to the increased number of neurons in the neural network. It is like a reverse growing, using the old structure to make the new structure. The physical appearance changes little during the transformation, because it is mostly making changes to the central nervous system. As the central nervous system and brain reorganizes, it is increasing the body vibration. When this is complete, the body vibration will be high enough to trigger the final change to create the light body. The physical appearance will change after the rewiring is complete, resulting in a new species of human that is enlightened.

What Is Full-Blown Kundalini Transformation?

The full-blown kundalini transformation happens when the self-realization level or vibration level is high enough to activate latent growing instructions in the DNA. It typically happens after the third awakening that releases the emotional energy layer of the personality that surrounds the core of the self. After releasing this layer, the personality does not activate strongly, which further conserves energy and the meditative state deepens. When we have crystal clarity between quiet mind and non-quiet mind states, our ability to sustain quiet mind increases and meditation goes deep. Triggering the full-blown kundalini transformation is near when it is easy to sustain forty-five minutes of quiet mind each time we meditate. These long periods of sustained quiet mind, profoundly change the brain and increase our vibration. This event is part of human evolution and is triggered by our growing consciousness.

Full-blown kundalini transformation starts with connections between energy circuits all over the body in a cascade of reactions and energy rushes in the spine. Nervous system reorganization follows that lasts about a week. This is characterized by sections of the body going numb with stinging prickles in the skin for several hours. After each section completes, the body part expands in size. This starts at the feet and slowly moves up to include each area of the lower body. The brain is rewiring also, but numbness is not felt in the skull. The reaction is continuous and while the nervous system is reorganizing, it is difficult to perform normally.

What differs compared with prior awakening events is the reactions are stronger and continuous day and night, for the entire interval. When the brain reorganizes, it causes confusion and is like being in a strange dream that lasts a long time. It is hard to do anything else, so we succumb. We are in 'good hands', as the higher-self has taken over and is orchestrating the changes. It is common to receive insights and instructions from the higher-self that will help with the transformation going forward. It is wise to take notes so we can remember the information.

Full-blown kundalini transformation will not trigger until we can sustain the quiet mind state and our vibration is high enough to activate the DNA. Premature full-blown kundalini transformation makes no evolutionary sense, as we could never handle it. The higher-self would never start a process that would threaten our survival.

The Reason For Kundalini Transformation

Kundalini transformation is about reorganizing the brain and nervous system into a body of light. The structure of personality is removed in favor of a new structure. I think I am experiencing increased vibration in the body, due to an expanding and improved nervous system. I think the split-brain body and mind that uses self-reflection to process data is changing to a body and mind with a single brain that does not need the self-reflection apparatus. It is a strange thought to understand the human brain in its current organization is primitive. Still, the old organization is beautiful, because the self-reflection apparatus allows us to recognize the higher-self that is behind the body and mind.

As my body transforms, new circuits are made in the nervous system each day and is like a fractal expanding infinitely into finer branches. It is like a maze of nervous system paths expanding in billions of directions. When the outer layer of my skin changes, I feel numbness, tingling, itches and insect crawling sensations. When deeper layers of fascia change, I feel body elongations and the body feels elastic. When the organs change they cleanse, when the heart changes it jumps and when the brain changes I have an altered state of consciousness and hear tones and see flashing lights. When an energy circuit is strengthened or created along a main nerve pathway, all kinds of nerve symptoms are felt. As kundalini transformation continued, my senses became more acute and my intuitive ability rose. I often received images in my 3rd eye, heard messages, had visions and vivid dreams. This information helped guide me in the transformation.

Rebuilding The Spine And Elasticizing The Body

As I see it, the structure of personality, reflected as the two-brained programmed mind in the body blocks energy flow all over. The cord of personality is similar to a huge amount of energy, contained in a program that is fixed and nonflexible. The cord of personality reflects our programmed use of energy as a whole, and the body itself becomes nonflexible and fixed from using that program. I think much of the energy contained in the cord of personality is held in place due to the skeletal alignment, which formed during our growing into adulthood. Bone is the deepest and densest tissue and holds the most energetic vibration in the body. The skeletal alignment reflects our animated use of our body due to identification with our personality. Unbalanced cranial, sacral and spinal alignments are common; no person has perfect skeletal alignment.

To release energy that is locked in joints, spine and between sutures, the area must be stretched open. When stretched, the neuromuscular junctions are enhanced and nervous energy can more easily flow between the brain and bodies muscles. Stretching of muscles is the way the body does work. In kundalini transformation, stretching has the purpose to release energy held by skeletal alignment. Certain joints, vertebrae, skull sutures and sacrum sutures can be difficult to open. As I understand kundalini transformation, all bones and tissues will be stretched open, because all the energy of the personality must be recovered.

When kundalini transformation starts, these blocked areas slowly open and energy releases from them. The released energy is used to reorganize the brain and remove the program that created that energy block. Energy blocks in the body held from skeletal alignment, are released with spontaneous stretches. Kriyas gradually get stronger to move bones more firmly positioned. As transformation continues, the spine is rebuilding and loosening from the body. The body feels increasingly elastic, due to the enhanced nervous system.

Becoming Sovereign In The Transformation

Kundalini transformation has taught me how to be independent from authorities as I learned to trust in my higher-self. I think this was a necessary step, to learn to take the reins in my hands. I am learning how to be a creator, by recreating myself. I am guided by my higher-self to learn these things.

The main work I had to do with the kundalini transformation was learning how to surrender to the strong kundalini forces working in my body, on command. I found the more I surrendered the faster the transformation went and my vibration and intuition would rise exponentially. I was never given more than I could handle. My progress toward the light body was directly proportional to how much I surrendered. I let go of body control, because I trusted my higher-self took over when I did that.

I feel everyone must take this journey alone because only we can release the energy we are holding in tension as the structure of personality. However, we are not alone, only the personality feels alone. When we surrender, higher-self takes over and knows exactly what to do. Our higher-self is intimately connected with universal consciousness, so the wisdom of the universe is at our disposal. No matter where we are in our spiritual journey, the most important thing we can do is surrender and trust we are guided. We can trust that exactly what we need to grow will be given to us and we only need to respond to what is in front of our face. It is like this, that everything in life unfolds.

Main Patterns Of Kundalini Transformation

It is beyond the scope of this book to detail all the stages of the kundalini transformation. It is also beyond my ability to describe, because I have not finished the transformation. In this section, I describe some obvious patterns.

Body Activation Pattern

When the full-blown kundalini transformation triggers, new nervous connections are made connecting all main parts of the body together. This happens in a pattern, which I call the body activation pattern, and repeats throughout the entire transformation. The left leg activates first, then the left hip and then the left shoulder. After this, the right leg activates, the right hip activates and then the hips activate together and generate rotational energy in the pelvic bowl. This rotation activates the front of the spine, and then energy is sent up the front of the body to activate the right shoulder. Then energy traverses across the torso from left to right side repeatedly and creates a rotational energy in the shoulder girdle. After this, the arms activate. As the shoulder girdle rotation builds, it generates a rotational in the torso. This energy then goes down the front of the spine to the pelvic bowl.

After this, rotational energy in the pelvic bowl forms a large vortex, often with sexual sensations and then the tailbone will activate, which is the root of the spine. When the accumulated energy goes down to tip of spine, the tailbone activates and curls toward the perineum. In the early stages of kundalini transformation, this is felt as tingling in the genitals or as a fluttering sensation by the tailbone. As the transformation progresses, curling of the tailbone is physically felt, which I call a 'tailbone tuck'. Simultaneous spontaneous orgasms are common when the tailbone curls.

With or without orgasm, after the tailbone activates, energy goes up the back of the spine to the skull and activates the right side of the skull and then the left side. Last, energy in the two sides of the skull combines into an energy vortex strong enough to change the brain. After energy finishes working in the brain, energy goes back down the spine in a vortex shape. This energy sent down the spine is that which will change the nervous system and body according to brain reorganization. As this energy descends, it first works in the spine on both sides of the body. Next, you feel energy branching out to various places in the body from the spine, with the sensation the energy is making changes to the body as it moves around. I call this descent of energy 'freefall', and the changes made to the body as the 'growing phase'. I call this phase freefall, because it is relaxing and pleasurable and there is no tension in the muscles. You sink into it. In a little while, changes made from neuron growth, will result in higher vibration and more energy to clear the next block, and energy charges will again build in the muscle fibers causing tension. Enjoy the freefall while you can.

This pattern repeats for the entire kundalini transformation. The time between complete passes gets progressively shorter over time. Before spiritual awakening, it can take years. At onset of kundalini awakening, it can take three weeks or more to complete one cycle. Towards the later stages, it is nearly continuous and cycles in less than a minute. When the transformation is complete, there are no more passes. As new nervous system connections are made, there is more energy to change the body each time. The body vibration increases with each pass, due to the central nervous system changes, but the physical appearance does not change markedly. The chapter and section headers of the journal depict the various stages that repeat as the body changes.

Expanding Nervous System Changes, Vibrations And Tones

The vibration and inner sound changes over time. At first, you will feel vibration localized in certain body parts and hear a low tone. As the transformation continues, body parts connect with new energy circuits and later with energy vortices, which are felt when they form. An energy circuit or vortex forms due to a main change occurring in the spine, and tones are heard and strong rushes of energy of various forms are felt. When energy vortices form, the vibration encompasses much of the body, and it will shake even while resting. As the body vibration increases, the inner sound becomes melodic. Even later, vibration and the growing reaction are felt continuously all over the body. Over time, the constant background tone becomes finer and higher-pitched, showing energy is still working in the mind at increasing rate of speed. New energy circuits sporadically produce a high-pitched clear tone, similar to a clarinet. After a year or two, the vibration that rocked the body settles, but is still felt continuously, it is finer. Later the vortex patterns will establish in larger areas of the body, such as left body and right body and work together in a marching pattern, and later will merge as one larger vortex. Still there is more. It is like the light in your body is infinitely expanding as a fractal pattern. As you move closer to the completion point, you no longer feel meridians, chakras, marching patterns or strong swirling energy patterns in the body and the constant background tone grows faint. Nevertheless, you can still feel it and hear it. At the end, I believe you will no longer feel the vibration nor hear any tone. Seeing this progression tells me vibrations and tones are signs of the transformation working and when finished, everything will be calm and super quiet, yet very alive, blissful and wonderful!

Kundalini & Stretching Pattern

The muscles are the main 'work horse' of kundalini transformation, because they can respond to nervous system stimuli, exert force and move you. In kundalini transformation a vibration is constantly felt, which changes character over time. I think the vibration is due to the changes made to the nervous system, and this change occurs at the neuromuscular junction[4] between muscle and nerve cells. The first vibrations in the body occur at a fine

---

[4]For more on neuromuscular junctions, see the metamorphosis chapter.

level, in smaller part of the muscle fibers. As changes to the central nervous system continue, larger portions of muscles in the body are affected, and vibration continuously increases. With active kundalini transformation, the body vibration can be verified and measured by an EMG (electromyography), which is a machine that can test the electric activity of muscles.

Eventually larger muscles are changed enough, where spontaneous movements (kriyas) become frequent when in the surrendered state. Kriyas have the purpose to open larger areas of the skeletal frame and tissues, to release stored energy from the personality. Kundalini transformation is all about recovering the energy that supported the structure of personality and using that energy to build the new body. No pocket of energy that represents personality in the body will be left untouched.

Muscles stretch by vibrating at a micro level or on a larger scale with kriyas, and held energy releases from them and returns to the central nervous system in the spine. The body parts relevant for this cycle of change are stretched and release energy, in the body activation pattern explained prior. After energy moves to the spine, it collects in the pelvic bowl. When the cycle completes, energy in the pelvic bowl forms a vortex and goes to the brain for reprogramming, as discussed in detail above. After the nervous system changes are made in the body, tension will build in the muscles preparing for another cycle to remove more energy blocks and convert the energy to a new body. This pattern continues until the reorganization of mind and body are complete.

What Are Kundalini Kriyas?

Kriya refers to the outward physical expression of awakened kundalini and look like spontaneous yoga postures. A long time ago, kriyas occurred to people who meditated often, and these yoga-like poses are credited as the origin of modern yoga. Kriyas are spontaneous movements, because you do not voluntarily decide to move that way. A kriya happens unexpectedly. Kriyas happen due to higher-self, orchestrating the movement. Because higher-self does not use thought, it seems it happens spontaneously.

Like other kundalini symptoms, kriyas can happen at any stage in our life. Everyone has experienced tossing and turning in the sleep, and seeing a mangled mess of covers in the morning. That mess of covers is our only hint we were moving spontaneously in the night. Most are familiar with the spontaneous stretch in the morning, when our body stretches to the maximum, our toes point and out arms go over our head and the entire body quivers. We did not decide to stretch like that, it happened. That is how a kriya feels.

I feel kriyas have the purpose to remove energetic blocks out of the body, using the muscles and skeletal positions to help achieve that, by using leverage. The spontaneous movement of the kriya opens larger areas of the body. After having experienced many kriyas, I infer kriyas are working to separate the spine, cranial bones and all joints connected to the spine. Simultaneously they release the foundation of the personality, which is energy held at the deepest layer in the skeleton. The spine is the cornerstone of the body and must be fully released and remade. Over the course of kundalini transformation, kriyas become more frequent and involve larger portions of the body. They get so strong they are capable to move us into yoga-like positions while we are awake. Eventually the kriyas become continuous, fluid and non-jerky as higher-self becomes dominant in the new light body.

The Kriya Stretch

Kriyas happen due to charges building in paired groups of muscles in areas of the body holding energy blocks. After the muscles of a certain body area charge, they contract which causes a stretch reflex. The force of the stretch opens and energizes that area of the body. The kriya stretch itself is healing, strengthening neuromuscular junctions and is transforming energy. This kriya stretch can be active or passive. An active stretch involves movement of the body. In a passive stretch, the body does not move, stretching is occurring in the muscle fibers at a micro level, which I call an energetic hold. You feel the passive stretch as localized in the body with strong tension in the area, like a Charlie horse cramp in the leg.

The kriya stretch is accompanied by pain similar to working out with a new exercise routine or moving in a way you are not used to moving. This pain is a symptom of energy transformation that is opening the area of the body, releasing held energy and healing the tissue. The active or passive kriya stretch will persist until that area in the body releases the tension. When the tension releases, it feels wonderful and nervous system healing reactions follow such as tingling, shivers, energy fills, elongations or puff outs.

Kriyas Are Like A Baby's First Steps

As split-brained human beings, we move our body voluntarily, by deciding how to move. To move voluntarily needs heavy use of our mind, taking our attention from what is occurring in the world. This processing results in delayed response to outside events, which are unfolding in real time. We are rarely spontaneous. This is how the central nervous system is currently organized with its sensory and motor tracts. The new species of human that is evolving is retiring the split-brain organization of the brain and replacing it with a unified brain organization that allows immediate response to stimuli in real time. Of course, the new design is better, but we cannot create it until our self-realization is high enough.

When we surrender control of our mind and body to higher-self, we are as one with our higher-self. When we are like this, mind reflection is bypassed and kriyas happen directly without conscious decision. In the beginning of kundalini transformation, we think the kriya is occurring spontaneously because we are not well acquainted with our higher-self. As the transformation continues, we identify less with our personality and more with our higher-self. When the kriyas first started, I felt I was moved against my will and had a victim attitude. Eventually my personality dissolved enough and I directly saw the truth, "I am doing the healing" and have been since it started. As we continue into advanced stages of the kundalini transformation, the kriyas fully take over and it is clear we are stretching to become alive in the flesh. The truth is kriyas are like a baby's first steps; they are the sign of YOU coming alive and stretching to become alive in the flesh. Kriyas are awakening signs.

It is only by surrendering use of our mind and body to the higher-self that the energy of the personality can be removed. We cannot remove something we are busy using. When we quiet our mind, higher-self arises and transformation and healing happens. It is a beautiful design, that transformation happens this way and makes perfect sense.

Kriya Progression

As kundalini transformation progresses, the central nervous system has increased capability to strongly charge and move the larger muscles of the body. When our mind is quiet, our body moves spontaneously and we are certain we did not decide to make the movement. Kriyas increase over time. The first kriyas are like small jerks or spasms and typically involve a small section of the body or a few yoga-like poses. After the reprogramming of the nervous system that happens with the full-blown kundalini transformation, there is increased ability to surrender control of the body to the higher-self. The first full-body kriyas feel like we are suddenly coming alive and filling with light energy, but still we do not move. From consecutive surrenders of body control, the higher-self and kriyas gradually get stronger. As we get stronger kriyas affect larger portions of the body. Sometimes we are positioned into yoga-like poses, and feel energy releasing from areas of the body related to the pose.

As the transformation continues and the nervous system expands, the kriya movement becomes more flowing and yoga-like. This happens because the central nervous system has changed enough to move the body from a control center in the brain. The control center is wielded by the higher-self. Still the kriyas are not graceful like dancing and not enjoyable because they are done to open tissues in the body, and it feels more like an intense physical therapy. Eventually the kriyas will take over the body while in a meditative state. Sometimes the body moves fast and may roll around, similar to an epileptic fit. During these kriyas, it is common to hear bones and ligaments snapping and popping. When I was a few years into this, the kriyas were so smooth that you could not tell my body was moving with non-voluntary control. The kriya stretch became my focus, because allowing higher-self to take over body control was the most effective way to do the transformation. It is me after all.

What Is Genuine Kriya?

There are certain characteristics of kriyas and self-realization that cannot be faked. If a person is still identified with their self-image and is pretending it is easy to detect if you know what to look for. Not many people know what to look for and therefore cannot make a valid assessment for genuine kriya or self-realization.

If you are awake, you can see if another human is awake and can be meditative. If you have experienced kundalini kriyas, then you know what genuine kriya look like. To explain what they look like is an invitation to those still in the pretending game of personality to mimic the pattern so they can get confirmation for being kundalini awakened. Nonetheless, it does not matter because when people pretend they rob themselves of real transformation. With kriya movements, there is the pattern of body movement in a counterclockwise direction. The energy inside the body moves clockwise as one vortex and the movement outside the body moves counterclockwise in another vortex. The physical body moves against that energy in the muscles in a counterclockwise stretch. These are the two energetic poles of the body. The rotation pattern is related to the gravitational pull of the Earth, moon and sun and is the same in all human bodies.

Do All People In Kundalini Transformation Have Kriyas?

Some people claim kriyas are not experienced by all people in kundalini transformation; they say they are only experienced by those who have blocks that need to be removed. I partly agree, because I think kriyas have the purpose to remove energetic blocks. If a person has the structure of personality in their body, the programmed energy can be seen from their body's posture, animation and from caricature of their face. If programming remains, there must be energetic blocks that have not yet been removed. Before I would recant on thinking all people in kundalini transformation will have kriyas, I would have to meet somebody who is enlightened that shows no programming in the body reactions and mind. As far as I understand it, I believe all people in kundalini transformation will eventually experience kriyas, as that is the most efficient way to open the tissues to release the held energy.

As my transformation progresses, the kriya movements are stronger, more intelligent and fluid, and I have no doubt my higher-self is coming to life by making a place in my body, filling it with light. As I see it, the entire body is filled with a large block of energy comprised of thousands of smaller blocks, so everyone has blocks to remove. I suspect more frequent and stronger kriyas are experienced if you have more defects. I do not feel that anyone will escape kriyas, as the bones of the skull have little range of movement between the sutures, and there is a ton of energy locked into the facial bones. To release this energy the bones must open, and kriyas do this efficiently.

Kundalini Awakening Symptoms

Many kundalini awakening symptoms result from changes to the nervous system. It is easy to confuse symptoms from a neurological or biological condition as being due to kundalini awakening. In either case, symptoms are a sign of healing and of your body trying to maintain homeostasis or to increase your energy.

Kundalini symptoms happen all along the awakening process, before pre-awakening, at spiritual awakening and afterward leading to full-blown kundalini transformation. Symptoms are produced as signs of physical changes manifesting in the body after each event of quiet mind happens, no matter how long that interval was. Because self-realization is gradual and biological, our ability to sustain quiet mind grows over time. The longer you can sustain quiet mind, the stronger the kundalini transformation symptoms become. Kundalini awakening symptoms noticeably, get closer together over time if you are progressing in your spiritual transformation. After the full-blown kundalini transformation, symptoms are continuous 24/7, get stronger each day in different ways and do not stop until the transformation is complete.

Pre-Awakening Symptoms

The kinds of symptoms faced when near pre-awakening often are due to changes occurring in the mind. Visions, vivid dreams, insights, synchronistic events, seeing the world differently and many changes in perspectives and beliefs occur. There is often a questioning of ideas and beliefs about God and religion that you have held your entire lifetime. Energy is working in your mind to clear aspects about how you see yourself and how you see the world. In short, your eyes are opening as your mind quiets down and when you look outside you discover that everything is conscious. Sporadic nervous system reactions also occur.

Spiritual Awakening Symptoms

In a crown opening, you will feel a sudden rise of energy. You experience a change in perception and see nature differently with vivid colors. You have the sensation of time standing still and see the interconnectedness between objects in the world. It is like seeing the world moving in a connected way, instead of seeing still objects. You experience healing symptoms and feel rushes of energy, flashes of light and many other kundalini symptoms. You have visions, vivid dreams and know about things you never had before. It seems information is downloaded to you. In a crown opening, you receive information about your purpose and lesson for this lifetime. As your soul energy opens, you may remember some past lives. You may feel you are related to religious icons or may feel like you are God. There are many descriptions of the crown opening and they differ widely. Because people are still heavily influenced by their personality when it happens, colorful, mysterious and 'out of this world' stories are reported. Common to them all is they have seen beyond the illusion the personality creates, and have met their higher-self. Much energy has released from the personality and a profound rewiring of the central nervous system is underway. This is cause for the expanded perception and sensory abilities. Another common factor is the heightened abilities eventually fade. Then you will hear people state they still have the abilities, only they are now used to them. This is wishful thinking. In the end this does not matter, we have changed. Our eyes are now open. A barrage of nervous system kundalini reactions also occur, but fade after a while.

Healing Phase Symptoms

Later symptoms will be a combination of healing reactions, which can be illness in the body, signs of mental health problems, emotional problems and the like. All are signs of continued healing. Anxiety, depression, chronic fatigue syndrome, fibromyalgia, gallbladder and liver problems, tingling legs syndrome and others like this are common healing events after crown awakening. Healing of the body will increase as your vibration rises and healing of the body from diseases is a priority to gain more energy. As healing symptoms increase, we feel sick and notice reduced awareness level. We remember how we felt before and want that back, which motivates us to enter into a self-healing process and increase our meditation and spiritual work. It is hard to tell which came first, the sickness or the awareness and which caused the other, because both are part of the same.

Kundalini Symptoms

Prior to full-blown kundalini transformation, while meditative, you have kundalini symptoms such as feeling tingles or muscle twitches in various areas of the body. You may feel fleeting pain or cramps, quivering of the lips, flashes in the brain and sporadic jerks of body parts. You may feel sudden rushes of energy in the body, explosions of light in the brain and feel tingling or numbness in various body parts. When you feel these things, you have the ability to sustain quiet mind in meditation for increasingly longer times. This cannot be missed. You will be falling into a deep trance-like state and will fear you will lose yourself as the quiet increases. It is like falling asleep in your meditation, and you want to awaken and shake it off. Going beyond this initial fear, to allow yourself to fall asleep, will be part of deepening your meditation. If your meditative state is not deepening like this, you are probably at an earlier stage of spiritual awakening and it is unlikely the full-blown kundalini transformation is near to triggering. While in early awakening stages, it is easy to convince ourselves we are more advanced than we are, because of our identification with our mind-voice and from believing truth comes from our storyteller.

Because of widespread lack of information about kundalini awakening, symptoms tend to be colorfully described, which makes this experience seem stranger than it is. Many of the symptoms are due to changes in the central nervous system, are observed internally, and thus are unworldly. We do not have a common language to describe internal symptoms. To complicate matters further, the brain is rewiring, old memories are stirring up, hormones are rushing and strange sensations all felt all over the body. As more people come forward reporting their kundalini awakening and as scientists get involved and record cases, then our knowledge about this natural process will expand and it will be less mystical.

It is beyond the scope of this book to talk in detail about each symptom. Several common symptoms are defined in the glossary and the index contains reference to many symptoms I experienced. All or any of these symptoms happen at various stages along the path of spiritual awakening and healing, but are more like a barrage of symptoms which then fade. With kundalini transformation well under way, you will experience all these symptoms and some continuously on a daily basis. When kundalini transformation is in full force, the symptoms do not fade, they are felt every day, and get stronger over time. Eventually you reach a plateau when you are near the end phase and then all symptoms settle down. However, there is something consistent after full-blown kundalini awakening that cannot be missed: your vibration will increase each day as well your awareness level.

Common symptoms include: tingling, muscle twitches, kriyas, stinging prickles, freezing, hot flashes, sweating, hot bones, body vibration, pain in muscles, muscle cramps, flashes of light in the mind, rushes of energy moving on the spine, internal rain, drops of liquid, external rain, pulse in root and crown chakras, increased sexual energy, spontaneous orgasms, insights, frequent changes in sensory perception, amplified senses, altered states of consciousness, loss of all sensation, going out of body, organ cleansing, electric shocks, buzzing in body, itching, insect crawling sensation, shaking, shivers, hearing tones, change in sleep and eating patterns, hyperactivity, headaches, pressure in skull, visions, visits from extraterrestrials or guides, snapping, clicking and popping of bones and ligaments, numbness, spontaneous crying or laughing, mystical experiences and more.

Chapter 7: Common Questions About Kundalini

1. Is This Kundalini Awakening?

Increasing numbers of people are experiencing kundalini awakening symptoms, as humanity evolves. Kundalini awakening symptoms are produced all along our awakening journey. In early awakening, the symptoms are sporadic or last a few weeks and fade. As we progress in our self-realization, the kundalini symptoms become stronger, more closely spaced together and last longer. Three times, there are major awakening events with a huge release of energy and a barrage of symptoms. After the third event, full-blown kundalini transformation is underway and the symptoms are continuous and do not fade.

Most kundalini symptoms are common healing reactions. There is no difference between human metamorphosis and healing; they are the same. When we compare our symptoms to the list of kundalini symptoms, it is easy to infer we are experiencing kundalini awakening when we are not. The cause of the symptoms may be due to a neurological or medical problem. These issues are still a healing process, but they happen before spiritual awakening. Kundalini awakening is more likely if you have been working spiritually by doing meditation, praying, energy healing, yoga or Tai chi regularly. Kundalini awakening is a growing process, where many symptoms are experienced in a short time and the symptoms do not stay the same for more than a few days. If your symptoms have remained unchanged for a long period, it is not likely to be kundalini awakening. With kundalini awakening, the mind is reorganizing, so there are frequent altered states of consciousness and symptoms of the nervous system changing. You should feel like you are awakening, and should be receiving insights about your true nature and things you never knew before.

To know our stage of spiritual awakening is difficult because of the root problem of identifying with our personality. When identified with our personality, we seek information and confirmation for how we believe ourselves to be. If we value the attribute of being spiritually awakened, then we want to prove that is true. In our current evolution path, kundalini awakening is the current trend, and people want confirmation they are like that. When we receive information of this nature, we interpret it the way we want to see it, to give ourselves this confirmation.

Many spiritually awakened people are still trapped by the personality games, which is the hardest to overcome. When we think we are awakened, self-questioning stops as well spiritual growth. To continue to grow, we need to answer the questions, "Am I fooling myself?" and "Am I awake?" Reading the chapter on the four stages of human metamorphosis and my testimonial, can help determine your step. What is more important than knowing which step we are on, is to accept where we are now and to do daily meditation, then we will continue to grow. I feel my testimonial shows we are not enlightened until the physical step has completed. If we have not done this step, we have more to do. That is simple.

2. Is There Some Exercise I Can Do To Activate Kundalini?

I am asked this question often. I guess the increased interest is partially due to the growing force that is urging people to awaken and is partially due to spiritual people wanting to gain the trendy attribute of being 'kundalini awakened'.

Our kundalini can always be activated. Activated means, we raise our vibration higher than our current vibration level. Vibration increases when we quiet our mind. In the interval where we experience quiet mind, the brain reorganizes and changes us and our vibration increases. Every second we succeed in quieting the mind counts; change happens in that space spontaneously without us doing anything. The change lessens the influence of our personality, and increases the influence of our higher-self, by a little bit. The next time we meditate, our vibration is a little higher. When our vibration reaches certain levels, it will trigger release of larger amounts of held energy, which result in major awakening events. Each time we meditate, our free kundalini increases. With spiritual awakening, we cannot skip steps, because it is partially a biological process. I feel the best approach to activate kundalini is to establish a consistent and daily meditation routine.

There are various meditation techniques to help quiet the mind. We should try various ones until we find one that works for us. However, do not go into the game of learning many techniques and being the master at none. Try one technique for three months, and if it is not working then try another. We can use more than one technique per day, but keep it consistent. It takes consistent practice and time to get good at meditation. With meditation, because we start out heavily identified with our thinking, we can easily get lost in a thinking loop or technique and not be getting a result. Therefore, it is good to have our meditation checked by someone who is more advanced, so we can be sure our meditation is getting a result.

3. Can Kundalini Awakening Trigger Prematurely?

Kundalini is always working and shaktipat, an energy healing or something else can trigger an awakening event, which increases our energetic vibration through the principle of entrainment. When our vibration increases above normal, our mind suddenly goes quiet and in that space of time energy releases from our personality. When energy releases it produces healing reactions as kundalini symptoms. The awakening event we experience depends on our self-realization level. The awakening events are usually minor, but on rare occasions can be major.

Steps cannot be skipped in spiritual awakening, it is a biological process and steps are completed in sequence, in reverse order of building the personality. If we are starting self-realization work, we will experience a beginning awakening. If our self-realization level is high, due to transforming much of our personality, then full-blown kundalini awakening can trigger. Much energy is needed to trigger the full-blown kundalini transformation. It cannot trigger until we are ready for it and strong enough to do it. Whatever awakening result we get is what we were ready to face, because the truth is WE are healing ourselves. Our higher-self would never prematurely trigger a force that we are not strong enough to handle, as our well-being is the most important.

A single energy healing rarely raises our energy to the level needed to trigger any major awakening event. This has several reasons. The main reason is we are still holding energy in form as our personality. Energy held as personality is like a large shield of protection, which does not allow our vibration to rise very high. The second reason is an awakening event is only triggered when our vibration level reaches a particular threshold, which happens rarely in our life. People concerned with this question, are likely still closely identified with their personality, as fear of awakening kundalini comes from the personality, not from the higher-self. The higher-self is fearless.

4. Does Kundalini Awakening Stop After Activation?

Kundalini awakening is a growing process that continues our entire lifetime and has been going on for all of human evolution. The growing process continues until we reach enlightenment. When a baby's teeth come in, it hurts and is irritating and the baby cries. We can put medicine on the teeth or rock the baby to soothe the symptoms, but this does not stop the teeth from growing once it has started. Kundalini transformation is a biological process similar to teeth coming in and it will not stop until completed. With kundalini transformation, if we choose to treat the symptoms rather than transform the cause, then we channel our growing force toward strengthening the personality rather than strengthening our higher-self. What we focus on expands.

In the earlier awakening stages, it is easier to suppress kundalini energy. After full-blown kundalini transformation, radical changes have been done to the mind and body, and there is no going back to the old structure of personality. The choice we are left with is how much transformational pain we are willing to accept daily.

In any stage of evolution, if we suppress the kundalini force, it will continue working and what we will notice is increased tension and stress building in the body and mind, and eventually pain will motivate us to surrender control. Evolution is like being between a rock and a hard place. If we resist the growing force, we experience pain and if we surrender to it, we experience pain. Pain however does not have to be experienced as painful. When we resist the growing force we only experience pain, it cannot be reduced if we resist it. When we accept the growing force, we change and experience pain from transformation of tissues. However, we can take it a step further and surrender to the sensation of pain, in that way we do not experience it as painful.

The easier, less painful way to evolve is always to surrender, accept our current reality and not resist the growing force. The state of non-resistance is surrendering the mind and being quiet in the meditative state. Our evolution to enlightenment is about learning to be our higher-self as pure awareness in body. The choice is to let go of control as the personality by surrendering to our higher-self. When we practice like this, we are guided and it is easier and takes less time. After we have experienced unity with our higher-self, we know there is a blissful location that is free from pain, and we can return there whenever we want.

It comes down to a personal choice, either to work with the growing force or to try to suppress it. The kundalini growing force continues whatever we do; what is important is how that energy is channeled. What we focus on expands. If we keep our focus on our personality, it will expand and personality itself is a resistant solid form that causes pain. The larger the personality gets, the more rigid we become and the more our survival is jeopardized.

Enlargement of personality is the path of disease, stress, hatred, violence and all kinds of destruction of self and others. If we rather divert energy from personality, then higher-self expands and our self-realization grows. The personality reduces in influence, we are more flexible and our likelihood to survive increases. As personality reduces, it is the path of joy, happiness, abundance, compassion and absence of pain.

Even after a spiritual awakening if we do not continue to surrender and instead resist the growing force, our density will increase, our awareness level will drop and we will reverse the progress we have made. The growing force is still going on, but what is occurring is our focus is expanding the personality rather than transforming it. If we continue like this, the old way of responding as conditioned personality and losing ourselves in thinking and emoting will happen again. This happens because the structure of personality was not fully transformed, and then it physically gains weight as we lose energy. Eventually you will see this clearly and understand that if you want to completely transform the structure of personality and overcome the force of gravity, you must consistently work to get more energy on a daily basis. Otherwise, we tend to remain the same. This must be done each day, until there is nothing left to transform. The secret to continue to grow, transform or heal is that we need more energy than our normal daily levels. We can get a boost of energy in various ways, but the largest boost comes from quieting our mind.

Suppressing the growing force causes more harm than good. Pain is going to be experienced either way, so we might as well get used to it, and learn to go beyond the sensation and grow. Knowing our evolution is at stake, I cannot advise someone to suppress their growing force, as they may never get another chance to evolve. We have to latch onto the opportunity to grow when it is available, and that time is always now. The growing force is the same as the ever-present force that is expanding the universe, if we accept it and grow with it we move along and change with it. If we reject it, we do not grow and eventually it will be too strong for us, due to our inflexibility and it will destroy us. Our choice is either to adapt to it, or to reject it. See this clearly; do not wait to start the process of self-realization. If you keep putting it off until tomorrow, it will leave you in the dust.

Wanting To Quit - Fear Of Losing Control And Going Further

A common reason for wanting to stop kundalini transformation is we have intense fear of losing ourselves, which is directly related to fear of losing control. Another reason we want to stop is that we have fear of experiencing strong symptoms that happened before. If this is the case, it may help to understand that higher-self is not afraid of the symptoms, as these symptoms are signs of higher-self coming to life. This fear comes from the personality, from the one that is afraid to be obliterated. Yes, the symptoms will return but know that they are not hurting us; rather they are healing us of that fearful self. Probably the main reason we want to quit is we cling to the way we know ourselves and are afraid to enter unknown territory.

When we stop the mind-chatter, it feels like death because we cannot hear the familiar echo of our voice that confirms we are alive. When we stop the mind-chatter completely, a huge force of energy arises, that is astounding yet frightening. At that moment, we feel there is nothing to latch onto, everything is foreign and fear grips us. Feeling we are dying and losing ourselves, we grasp for the known and start the mind-chatter. The intense fear comes from the mind-voice, so it was already activated. When the mind-voice dominates, our higher-self has been stifled. It takes many tries to face this unknown, to overcome our fear, stay still and not react and allow our higher-self to rise. Each attempt to let go makes us stronger. Eventually, we are strong enough and trust it is okay, and will not react with fear. A full let go is not done in one attempt; rather it is a gradual process of building strength, so by trying we eventually get used to it.

5. Can I Go Crazy In Kundalini Transformation?

Craziness has the cause of overactive mind-voice. If we suspect we are acting crazy or someone we trust tells us we are acting crazy, then we have been given valuable information. To cure our craziness, we must first understand we are crazy. To know we are acting crazy is the first step to become sane. Of course, it will hurt the pride to discover we have been acting crazy, but to take a step beyond the mind we have to know what the problem is. There are many pitfalls on the path of awakening and it does not matter which way or technique we use in regards to the pitfalls we will face. The craziness comes from our strong identification with the story we are telling with our thinking and responding emotionally to life out of that story. We fully believe 'our story' is truth. Craziness or mental illness develops when we are stuck in a reactive circle of thinking certain patterns of thought habitually and respond emotionally according to the undertone of those thoughts. The thoughts charge the bodies muscles with the undertone of our thinking pattern. When we are thinking anxious thoughts, the body is anxious and prepares to take flight and the vibration of fear and anxiety in the body's muscles triggers more thoughts that are anxious. We think anxious, we feel anxious, we are anxious. Our story gets confirmed as the truth because of how we feel. What we cannot see when this occurs, is how we have created the anxiety ourselves. At this point, we are stuck in a reactive circle and are acting crazy. Once we are like this, the personality is strongly activated and it is nearly impossible to observe our thinking, which is the cause of the problem.

All these thinking patterns happen unconsciously and have to do with how we learned to get identification and confirmation from the world and people at an early age. As we progress in our spiritual evolution, the unconscious thinking pattern becomes visible as craziness. Unexpectedly, we have anxiety or panic attacks and it becomes problematic to function normally. Now we have a mental health issue. What we need to know is when mental health issues surface it is a healing reaction and is an opportunity to take a step in our evolution and increase our awareness level. Before spiritual awakening, craziness is present in everyone. It is merely hidden inside. When it becomes visible as a mental health issue, then it can be observed and we can question our reactions and heal the cause of the craziness.

I think all seekers have to pass though this 'crazy step', so it cannot be avoided. It occurs in several flavors at various times, which all precede the full-blown kundalini transformation. Fear of going crazy is understandable, yet to go beyond a fear; it must be confronted head on. If we can accept that every spiritual seeker must eventually confront our craziness and go beyond it, then we will be more willing to face this challenge. What I am saying is do not blame craziness on the practice, the person, the method or the technique, or on anything in the outside and feel like a victim. Craziness is something we create ourselves and is likely already there. It is merely hidden under the surface, below our current awareness. To find the cause and go beyond it, it is necessary to do daily meditation, which gives us the skill for self-observation. As we practice meditation, we gradually get better at seeing our thinking and seeing how it traps us. When we are ready to face it, look inside to see where those crazy thoughts come from and in this way, we will take another step.

With the full-blown kundalini transformation, there is an emotional and physical cleansing of the body during the first weeks, where it is difficult to act rational but this soon passes. Getting lost in crazy mind is not likely once we have reached this level of self-realization, because we have already dealt with the problem. At this stage, we can discern clearly between the thinking and not thinking state, and can control our mind and stop the mind-chatter.

6. Do I Need Help With Full-Blown Kundalini Transformation?

In the early part after full-blown kundalini transformation is triggered, the mind is reorganizing and is not reliable, so having an assistant or helper can be a wise choice. In the first few weeks we can ignore doing things we should do like eating, drinking, exercising, bathing and eliminating. An assistant can prepare broth or drinks for us, give a massage, and encourage us to take fresh air, exercise and bathe, wash our clothes, and take over our chores, to check in on us each day or ask if we need anything. It is likely we will not be hungry and will choose to fast during this period. It is a period of profound organ cleansing and because many changes to the nervous system are occurring, eating can make us feel nauseous. I think it is wise to ask for help from a trusted friend when this event triggers for the first few weeks, as they can see more clearly than we can. After the initial stage, our higher-self is stronger and guides us. Of course, seek out others who have been through the transformation and ask for advice. Other than that, we do not need much help, as we are prepared and ready for this.

7. Is Kundalini Transformation Easy Or Difficult?

I think it is fair to say that everyone will find kundalini transformation challenging. It takes a long time and is similar to an intensive physical therapy. It challenges us on all levels: mental, emotional, spiritual and physical. Another reality is because of its physical nature, it cannot happen without a clear decision and active engagement and participation. It does not happen by wishing it to happen. To rehabilitate or to rebuild the body into a new shape, it takes many hours in the gym with focus on the task. Along the way, emotions release, concepts drop and our belief system goes through a housecleaning.

Some people will find kundalini transformation easier and more difficult for several reasons. First, it depends on where the person is in the kundalini awakening. It is easier at the beginning, harder in the middle, and easier at the end. It also depends on the person's true ability to surrender control of mind and body to higher-self. The more fully a person can surrender, the stronger the transformation forces. People that are fearful of transformation and of pain, will not be able to surrender fully and can report 'how easy it is'. This is undoubtedly true, but it may possibly mean they have not let go deeply yet. Presuming the full-blown kundalini transformation is underway, the following applies. Difficulty is directly proportional to the number of injuries in body, congenital defects, current health and agility, emotional traumas and beliefs and concepts we need to heal and unload. The more baggage we need to unload and the more physical problems we need to heal, the harder it will be. If we have much to clean up, we should not take it personal and feel like a victim! This is ourselves after all, all that we own is part of our past, it is who we are and what we valued and did not value.

In my case, I have a congenital deformity that affects all joints on the right side of the body, as well in the neck, skull and spine. This is similar to cranial facial microsomia, where one side of the skull is smaller than the other side. Because it is an old injury from before or around birth, then the part where the sutures open was difficult. I had extreme pain many times and became skilled at going through it. The stronger I got, the easier it was. If we do not have such tight joints, adhesions or physical defects, then this part can be much easier for us. On the other hand, I did not have much emotional trauma, beliefs, and concepts to unload, because I had been working on healing these issues for many years before the onset of this event. Another person may find this part more challenging. In any case, we can know and trust the challenge we receive will be designed for us, and we will grow strong by facing it and going through it.

Kundalini transformation is about releasing energy from our personality and using that energy to create the new body. Our personality is an accumulation of pockets of energy all over our body and mind. To reach enlightenment all energy stored in the personality must be released and transformed.

8. Can Pain Be Avoided? Is There An Easier Way?

The reality is that transformation is like an intensive physical therapy. Growing a new body is physical and we will have to endure transformational pain, the same as someone does when they have to rehabilitate a broken leg. It is a metamorphosis, a slow long growing in the existing body, thus it is physical and does not happen magically in an instant. The kundalini transformation causes various types of pain. We are naturally pain avoidant and the reason we do not change is that we avoid the experience of pain. Now we see the problem of being caught between a rock and a hard place. To go further in this transformation it is IMPERATIVE that we learn how to allow the transmutation of energy.

We Need To Learn How To Transmute Pain

Transformational pain[5] is perceived as painful when we resist the healing process. When we relax and have a quiet mind, we do not experience healing as painful. In the center, it is neither pleasant nor unpleasant, it merely is. While transformation of the personality can be painful, it does not have to be EXPERIENCED that way. When we are in the center, we can observe the healing but we do not feel pain because we are no longer identified with our form. This center state is ideal to promote healing. After we have experienced that transformational pain does not have to be experienced as painful, then we are secure in the state of quiet mind. While there watching what is going on, we understand that we are eternal and will never lose ourselves. We see that life is transformation and we know that allowing ourselves to change increases our prospect of survival, then we allow changes to happen to us whenever needed.

Pain Is Always Felt Past Tense

Being in a living body, tissues are always transforming according to the 'vibration of energy' represented by the body. When we learn a new thing, this changes our vibration and later our body will change to reflect that. Pain is real and we feel it often. What we can control is our identification with 'what is past'. This depends on where we set our focus. If we are in the observation state, then energy is flowing through our body and there is no resistance to change. We watch the vibration and see what is occurring. We notice pain like it is a memory. If we are in pure observer state, we are as one with the locus of transformation of the tissue changing shape. We are watching the energy moving back and forth, we feel a sensation like a vibration, but it is neither pleasant nor unpleasant. When we declare it to be painful, we have identified with the body (past reaction) and are no longer watching. We pulled out of that state and now we experience pain. The longer we stay in the state of feeling pain, the harder it will be to distance from that sensation and go back to simple observation again.

Pain felt from transformational energies is mostly due to mental or emotional resistance to what we would prefer versus accepting what is. When our mind is quiet, we are as one with our higher-self. That is the point where life unfolds, that is where the growing

---

[5] For more information about transformational pain, see Chapter 4.

energy is, and where we let energy pass through us. We are then in control of not being resistant but not in control of the physical change itself.

Resistance To Change Is What Is Causing Pain

The experience of pain is mostly caused from resistance to change, and when we let go of identification with the past reaction, pain is not experienced. Some people die easy and go out softly; others resist it fighting to the end. Some cancer patients are so happy even they are dying; others fight and experience extreme pain. The more we resist change, the more pain we experience. We resist change by identifying with past forms. We resist change by 'being as the personality'. When we identify with past non-existent forms, (they are memories) then we are in the state of resistance, we are using our mind and not letting go.

I hope it is clear it is not about controlling the pain; rather it is more about controlling our attitude. Pain can be a signal we are resisting and can remind us to stop the thinking and return to our center. When we do that successfully, we will have the experience of healing and feeling pleasure versus pain, in whatever transformation we are facing. Pain can come and go, depending on our identification and focus on what is changing. Prolonged pain is a sign of prolonged resistance to change.

Transformational pain as a symptom coming from an effective healing will change nature being slightly different after three days. We see signs of healing even though it seems to be going slowly. There might be pain each day as larger areas of tissues in a body heal, but it is not the same from day-to-day, slight differences can be detected. This then can be a positive confirmation we are successful at not identifying and learning to let go.

Learn To Transform Pain

Learning not to react to the sensation of transformational pain helps us to grow, because when we can do it successfully we are not identifying with the personality. Pain is a big motivator for us to surrender control, because the sensation can build when we do not. When we do let go, the pain goes away and we feel bliss. That is beautiful!

Part of kundalini transformation is learning to quiet the mind and relax the body and be in center, no matter what is occurring, even if it feels painful. Pain increases as the vibration and transformation accelerates. This is all good, because through the sensation of transformational pain we will learn to transform and drop our resistance to change and to let the energy flow through and heal us. By learning it, we become more skilled at dropping all attachment to our old self and grow stronger. The more we do this, the more we heal and the less pain and tension we will experience.

All physical pain is real. As a practical advice, whenever we feel a strong pain we can try to feel the pain and use the pain to DISIDENTIFY. Instead of dreading pain, we see it is teaching us to quiet the mind and be in the center as our higher-self. We only have to feel it, we do not label it or judge it or deny it or want it to be anything other that what it is. If we can do this successfully, healing will happen exactly as it needs to and we will not experience pain. As we practice like this, we notice healing and changes are occurring, which then is the feedback we are getting good at quieting the mind. The side affects of bliss, contentedness, healing, reduced pain, expansion of light, increased self-confidence and insight, gives us motivation to continue to seek our center. Soon we enjoy being quiet more than being mentally active.

Warning: If pain is not going away in the meditative state, is extreme, and is persisting whatever you do, then another action is quickly needed! It is then possible the pain is not of the transitory kind, and pain sensors will continue to fire, as a warning to do something because your survival may be jeopardized. You should deal with pain like this immediately! This may be as simple as changing the position of your body if you were in a session or you might need an immediate trip to the hospital. I am reminded of the sweat lodge incident a few years ago, where three people died. For sure, they went beyond extreme pain to attain a higher state and the result was a tragedy. Do not be extreme with matters like this. To repeat: If the pain is not resolving, a different action needs to be taken as soon as possible!

9. How Can I Work With Kundalini Transformation?

There is no mind-directed technique helpful for kundalini transformation, but there are ways you can practice. Animating your personality uses all your energy, so encouraging transformation is practicing with various techniques to learn how to divert energy from doing that and allowing your energetic vibration to get stronger. The more you practice the better you get at it and your rising vibration, growth and insight will be evidence to you that you are doing the right things.

Quicken Touch

This is my Reiki acupressure technique that was partly inspired from visions during the hardest part of the onset of the kundalini transformation. I experimented with the basic principles in the first year and came up with this method. I feel this technique is very effective to raise energetic vibration and help move out energy blocks. I still use it today. Full details on how to do it are on my website at http://phoenixtools.org.

Let Go Of Body Control

Stand in a relaxed way and start the simple meditation of feeling the energy movements in your body. As kundalini transformation progresses, spontaneous body movements become stronger. Allow your body to fold and move according to the energetic charges building, but do not decide to move in any way. Keep checking that you are not preventing energy from working in any area of the body, noticed by painful sensations or resistant thoughts. When you notice this, try to relax the area and thinking and allow energy to enter it and practice 'melting'. Keep practicing letting go of body control and trusting higher-self will move you safely without you having to do it. This is useful in later stages, to start clearing out larger blockages owing to skeletal misalignments. It is like using your body as a lever to open joints and bones to release stagnant energy. This ability grows stronger as you progress, and you will eventually know how to do it. Full detail of the 'Moving as Awareness' meditation tool is on my website at http://phoenixtools.org.

Learn To Meditate

There are different meditation techniques to help quiet the mind. You should try various ones until you find one that works for you. However, do not go into the game of learning many and being the master at none. Try one technique for three months, and if it is not working for you then try another. You can use more than one technique per day, but keep it consistent. It takes consistent practice and time to get good at meditation. Because you start out in meditation heavily identified with your thinking, you can get lost in a thinking loop or technique and not be getting a result. Therefore, it is good to have your meditation checked by someone who is more advanced, so you can be sure your meditation is effective. I have full directions for basic meditation on my website at http://phoenixtools.org.

Learn To Relax Areas In Body With Strong Muscle Tension

Rather than resist strong muscle tension, merely become the observer of this feeling and more energy will flow through, open and change the area. When you feel strong muscle tension, it can be a sign your mind is active and you are resisting the transformation energy. I have full directions for a body relaxation tool on my website at http://phoenixtools.org.

Accept This Is A Long Process And Don't Do Too Much

In the beginning when I felt a strong reaction, I felt I had to stay still until the energy work finished, often sitting for many hours on end with the hope to finish. Long sessions are not necessary and know the energy continues to work and will pick up where you left off next time. One hour to one hour and a half is the most effective session and taking breaks between. On average, it takes forty-five minutes for the body to activate all energy centers. The strongest healing happens around the forty-five minute mark.

Trust Your Breathing Will Happen Spontaneously

The breathing sometimes goes into apnea (no breath) for very short intervals, while energy is changing critical areas in the body, such as in lungs, trachea, heart or brain. Know that this is natural, and try to relax with this strange sensation and trust you will be okay. The longer you resist this feeling, the longer it will take to change these areas.

Easy Meditative Focal Points To Encourage Transformation

No matter what technique you use if any, it is helpful if you try to keep your focus on a vibration felt in the body, such as in the root chakra, lower abdomen, bottoms of feet, or in your legs. Only feel it, do not try to make it be in any way by visualizing it somehow differently. Another simple technique is to use your inner vision, to look at the area where your 3rd eye is during the session. It is common to see various colors and points of light, as energy works in the mind and is an easy focal point. When focused strongly and intently there you are getting strong visuals, and know energy is working in the mind, super effective! I find it effective to listen to the inner sound and simultaneously look with my inner sight. Techniques such as this can help you stay meditative and the kundalini transformation will be more effective.

Experiment And Be Open To Hear Intuitive Messages

If you need something special to help you along, trust that if you ask for help you will receive an answer from your higher-self or others. Be open to receive such messages, try various techniques, and experiment until you find a routine effective for you and fits into your life in the least obtrusive way.

10. How Long Does The Kundalini Transformation Take?

At the time of writing this book, I do not know this answer. I have asked it of many people and have not heard anything that makes sense yet. My current theory is it can finish in as little as seven years. I do not think it can finish faster than that. I do know the more you work with it the faster it goes and vice-a-versa. Therefore, it depends much on us. Several people have reported their kundalini transformation is still going on twenty-five years after initially awakening. I do not like this answer much.

11. How Can I Regulate The Kundalini Symptoms?

The higher our energetic vibration is, the stronger the kundalini reaction and symptoms will be. Conversely, the lower our energetic vibration is, the weaker the kundalini reaction will be. If we are working with transformation, our energetic vibration gets higher each day and overtime the reactions get stronger, but as we get stronger it is much easier to control the reaction. As we progress to transform our personality, we get stronger and can better handle strong reactions.

Thinking back over all the years I have been in this transformation, I do not recall a moment where I could not control a reaction while in public. The main thing I would experience was increased muscular tension in a certain body part and had the desire to release the tension by stretching, but I could have relaxed instead. Muscular tension tends to resolve eventually, but it takes much longer this way and can be uncomfortable. I feel it can be comforting to know we are always in control of the transformation. The stronger kundalini reactions mainly happen when we are sleeping at night or in the quiet mind state where we decide to let go of body control and allow the healing reaction. Stopping a reaction is as simple as making the quiet mind state go away by activating our mind-voice and deciding not to allow transformation.

The more meditative sessions and healing techniques we incorporate into our daily routine, the higher our energetic vibration will raise. The higher our energetic vibration rises, the stronger and more intense are the healing reactions. Each mini-healing raises our energetic vibration over time, so with each session we start stronger than the previous. These reactions happen predominately in our sessions. Eventually the deeper issues heal, such as opening tight bones or releasing old stored emotional energy. After these harder things heal, we have much more energy in reserve, we get stronger and eventually it is like coasting for the remainder of the transformation.

To raise energy, do things such as meditate, stretch and exercise, eat whole grain and uncooked foods, eat little or no meat, give energy healing to yourself, get a massage, dance, draw, write, take walks in nature, do a fast or body cleanse, and don't do addictive substances such as sugar, alcohol, tobacco, caffeine, or drugs. Any change in habit by adding in a new health routine compared with what we did before, will raise our energetic vibration. If we want to lower our energy, then do the opposite recommended to raise our energy.

However, I do not recommend establishing any habit that will keep our energy low on a daily basis. I state it this way so we understand the principle operating here, and leave it up to each of us to find the correct balance that works in our life. If we feel a strong reaction, then we can lay off the meditation for a day or two, eat some heavy food difficult to digest, such as meat, or do not exercise. If we decide to use these measures, we should use them sparingly and be careful that we do not get addicted to the bad habit of keeping our energy at a low vibration level. It can be difficult to start if we let our energy get too low, and can be a strong setback to further progress. If we decide to use drugs, we can get addicted to them believing it is helping us to feel normal and later it can be difficult to get out of this dependency. I do not recommend using any addictive substances or mind-altering substances, as this keeps us far from higher-self.

I think the best middle-of-the-road thing to do is at least one meditation session per day, so our awareness level and healing continues to progress. How many minutes we meditate each day is a way to regulate the effect. I think it is much better to put up with some reaction, versus having none and risking going backward, or gain density and stay at low vibration and low awareness level. The lower we keep our vibration, the lower the reaction, the lower our awareness and the longer the transformation will take.

It depends on how much time we want to devote to this, and what other things we have to do in our life. I encourage experimentation with various routines, to find the right pace of increasing vibration that keeps us moving forward, but does not cause too much reaction. For my journey, I decided to work with it full-time, as I had the cash and a private retreat space. I did twelve hours each day for many years and thus experienced strong reactions, because I was in high vibration and high meditative state most of the day. At the time of writing this book, I do a meditative freestyle and Reiki acupressure session each day. This keeps my transformation going, but it is much slower than I would like it to be. Having to go back to work was a necessity and I had to find a new balance.

12. What Are The Abilities Of The New Light Body?

Many people are spiritually awakened and seem happy with their limited abilities. They still need to do daily meditation to stay alert and continually monitor their tendency to revert to reacting as the personality. Many people are keenly alert only a small part of the day, and to do that takes effort. Some people cannot be aware at all, and unfortunately believe they can do it. Do not get me wrong, it takes many hours of meditation to get any result, and to become enlightened it has to be done. What I am saying here is do not be happy with a mediocre result, there is much more possible.

It is obvious that the transformation is reorganizing my brain and nervous system, with what seems an infinite number of new nervous system branches all over the body. My body and mind are gradually filling with light, and everything in my body is connected to each part in a fast and new way. At the time of writing this book, I have not completed this transformation, so can only guess about the final abilities. I have many benefits now and presume others are possible given my understanding of this transformation. The strangest thing is there is no perceptible change in my outward physical appearance, despite the thousands of hours energy has worked in my body and mind. I believe the physical change and full abilities will manifest when all energy is recovered from the personality. When more people complete the kundalini transformation, the benefits will be more widely known.

I think some benefits for human beings are feasible today and some will not manifest for hundreds of years. It seems logical that if I have healed myself of personality, then I should never need to sleep. I feel sleep is necessary in our evolution, to give our higher-self access to heal us before we can do it on our own. Because healing is always going on once kundalini is awakened, it seems logical we should never have disease or grow old. It seems the structure of personality and the mind-voice will persist until the brain is rewired. I guess one structure will be replaced by the new one in the blink of an eye. I think when the last energy has been recovered from the personality; all that energy will form as a strong vortex and will go up the spine with orgasm and then complete the final changes to the brain. I have heard that is like the tree of life expanding in the brain. That vortex will be like death when the soul leaves the body, but this time because there is orgasm it will produce a new life. After that, the new body with the new features will grow and the physical outward changes and new abilities will become obvious. I presume.

Benefits I Am Experiencing

Frequent momentary occurrences of heightened hearing, sight, smell, taste and touch

Healing of congenital defect and all adhesions in all bony structures

Increasing flexibility and elasticity in the body

Rarely get sick

Keen insight and intuition

Happiness and sense of joy, rarely down and not for long

Increase in extrasensory abilities, such as distance healing and insight

Increased compassion and love for others

Easy to control the mind-chatter

No longer walking in circles in life

Learning how to create my vision in the world

High energy levels all days

Theoretical Benefits

Not needing to sleep

Total disappearance of mind-voice

Spontaneous reactions and adaptation to events

Thinking capacity beyond any IQ level recorded in normal human

New organization of brain and body into one mind and body

Ability to transmute toxic substances

Extraordinary sensory abilities

Super efficient digestion, perfect metabolism without toxic buildup

Ability to adapt body to hot and cold, not needing heat nor cooling systems

Ability to regenerate any damaged body part, including growing new teeth.

Ability to self-heal and maintain proper equilibrium and homeostasis in body

Ability to communicate telepathically with others of same ability

Not needing to be reborn on Earth, moving on to another life form

Not aging, keeping a youthful appearance

Free from misery and suffering

Elastic, adaptable, strong, flexible and agile body, alive and energetic

Compassion for all life forms and loss of fear

Full restoration of sexual reproduction ability

Maybe none of these benefits manifests. At the end of the transformation, we simply physically die and exit to another dimension.

PART IV – MY KUNDALINI JOURNAL

Chapter 8: Spiritual Work Before Kundalini Awakening

Beginnings: A Brief History

For many years, I meditated twice per day, used various transpersonal tools, and noted my reactions to people and life to discover, "Who am I?" In August of 1999, much energy released while in a deep meditation and I had a spiritual awakening with strong kundalini awakening symptoms. I had high sexual energy, changed my diet, lost weight, had vivid dreams and visions, felt tingling and electric shocks, felt the uterus thumping, increased body vibration and heightened senses. These were like the kundalini symptoms I experienced later. The symptoms were strong for three weeks and gradually tapered over six months. In the first three weeks, my energy vibration was very high, I did not need to sleep and my thinking was super fast. The knowledge about enlightenment was revealed and I had many insights. When I walked, I felt I was in a three-dimensional world. I felt different and alien but was thrilled and elated. Then I heard the thought, "Betsy must go". That thought I did not like much. After this experience, I knew I would never be the same and had awakened. I call this experience the crown opening, and think it is often confused with the full-blown kundalini transformation.

After spiritually awakening, my life changed dramatically. I quit my job and became a full-time student of personal transformation. Feeling myself as intense vibration energy for those three weeks, became my beacon in the darkness. After that, I never believed I was enlightened, because I did not feel like that. I would not stop until I was vibrantly alive like that again and this desire motivated me to keep doing the work to unravel the layers of my personality.

Mental Body: Escape From The Mind-Trap

From August 1999 to February 2003, I meditated twice per day, learned yoga and tai chi, studied spiritual books and kept an eye on my responses, learning from them about my conditioning. Soon after the spiritual awakening, I went into a head-trip of believing I was a reincarnated person with an unbelievable story and after some time crashed back to Earth when I finally saw the head-trip. Writing was my main vehicle to gain self-knowledge about my unconsciousness. I would review what I wrote and note how people reacted to what I wrote and how I reacted to them. Many times, I thought I was enlightened when I received a new insight and would attach to my accomplishment. Eventually experiences would show me I was not awakened after all. Then I would crash and feel disappointed, yet humbled and would return to the work of unraveling my conditioning. This lasted years. I went through phases of creating a new spiritual self-image and the conceptual games of the personality, such as trying to live a concept, criticizing others, writing in spiritual forums, acting as an authority and teacher.

From March 2003 to March 2004, I did the sungazing protocol as popularized by Hiram Manek. In sungazing, you stand barefoot and gaze at the sun at sunrise or just before sunset when the ultraviolet levels are low. You start at ten seconds of gazing and add ten seconds more each day until you reach forty-four minutes of gazing at the sun. When I reached thirty-five minutes of sungazing, I had the insight the emotional state of my body had a stronger affect on my experience of reality than my thoughts did. This was a great insight, which helped me take further steps of self-realization. During this time, I experimented with and studied various alternative healing methods, did organ cleanses, did a raw food diet and several fasts.

From April 2004 to March 2005, I did my daily meditations, worked with self-enquiry, and did much writing in the Internet. I focused on helping others and it was a long period of acting as an authority, feeling I was qualified to help others awaken. In March, I received a compliment on my ability to see how others were trapped, and they asked had I ever used my skill to analyze myself. This slap in the face was a wake-up call. It turned me back to my source and work to uncover more layers of my conditioning. During this time, I became acutely aware of the persistence of the internal dialogue. I was aware of my childish behaviors, dramas I was creating in life, and was having strong emotional reactions. I felt I was walking in circles. Eventually I saw the root problem of all these troubles and it was the storytelling self. Then I understood the storyteller did not know anything and could never know anything, it was purely a reaction. This understanding took me out of the conceptual trap of the mind. All these years I had done the transpersonal work and my awareness gradually rose, to the point where I saw the truth, I needed to see to get me out of the mind trap. I had no idea there were two more steps to complete until they happened.

Emotional Body: Healing The Inner Child

From March 2005 to June 2005, I started looking closer at my emotional reactions. As providence would have it, I began menopause with periods of strong emotional outbursts, night sweats and hot flashes. I was having a conflict with a friend that gave me many opportunities of 'emotional outbursts' to scrutinize. I went intensely into observation of my emotional state and used new tools. I saw how difficult it was to control emotional reactions, even when I had an eagle eye on my thinking and feelings. It seemed impossible not to emotionally react when somebody pushed my button. I instinctively knew I needed more energy to boost my momentary awareness so I could nip it in the bud, and I needed more information about the emotional reaction.

I practiced the present moment techniques of Eckhardt Tolle in the book Power of Now and I used the enneagram to determine the emotional passion of my personality type so I could detect how I got my emotional kick. I did Qigong, barefoot walking and used techniques to increase my sensory awareness. I did the sungazing again and increased the length of my meditation. Near the end, I was pushed to my limit and cried like a child for days on end. I had done the same in 1999, after my first spiritual awakening. The same scenario was repeating, but this time I heard what I told myself that made me cry so hard. It was like the voice of a child repeating the pains of childhood, feeling alone and unloved. With hindsight, I knew I had completed the step of healing the inner child. Cleansing the childhood traumas and crying jag had happened twice. The first had cleansed the cognitive parts of my survival strategy and the second had cleansed the emotional parts. There was one more to go.

Deepening Meditation

From June 2005 to October 2005, I was watching carefully in my meditation for what worked to help me achieve the no-mind state. It was helpful for me to tune into listening to the inner sound I have always heard inside since I started meditation. I would become one with the sound, which felt awesome. I focused on increasing my sensory awareness whatever I did in my life. I had to work harder to achieve present moment awareness.

I became acutely aware of the storyteller, and how my story created my emotional state. I changed my attitude toward life conflicts, and saw them as creative opportunities to practice gaining control over my emotional body. As I practiced like this, it started to work and I was elated. I became fascinated with energy and learning how to get more of it. My momentary awareness started rising and I became sensitive to my energy and the energy in people, animals, plants and minerals. I wrote this poem then, which expresses my increased sensitivity.

> Bamboo stalks swaying
> song erupts from clacking leaves
> merging with the wind.
> Recalling what I have seen
> the past stays alive inside.
>
> Have I ever seen
> a still bamboo in the wind
> refusing to sway?
> Human's great ability
> guarding our separation.
>
> Smiling at my dog
> he smiles back and wags his tail
> being one with me.
> Dropping all our facades
> the barriers fall away.

On October 19, 2005, I did my meditation while focused on feeling the vibration in my body and suddenly I went very deep. When that happened I realized the vibration energy I feel in my body is CONSTANT, it was always there. This was a profound revelation and a big smile arose on my face. I understood then, that there was nothing more to find. I was done with seeking. I had found my true self. I knew another step remained, to manifest this vibration in the flesh, to become one with it physically. I had another insight then, that what I focused on would increase. I could clearly see what was most important to increase, so my focus shifted to increasing my energetic vibration. I was determined I could do it and nothing was more important to me. From this day onward, I did six hours of meditative work and experimented with various techniques looking for ways to deepen my awareness.

Reiki Self-Healing

November 1, 2005: A Little About Reiki

For the last five years, I had explored alternative healing methods to help people and what I had not done in all those years was focus much on my healing. At the time, I was feeling the effects of aging and my body would ache when I woke in the morning. I was successful to increase my awareness but my body was breaking down, it did not make evolutionary sense that awakening comes so late in life. I wondered if it was possible to have high awareness, agility and good health simultaneously. With this thought, I decided to try Reiki and to do the important step of giving LOVE TO MYSELF through self-healing.

There are three main symbols used in Reiki, which establish a pattern of resonance in the body by either saying the name of the symbol or visualizing it. These symbols are ChoKuRei (power symbol), SeHeiKi (emotion symbol) and HonshaZeShonen (long-distance symbol). By visualizing or saying the name of the symbol, your body will resonate with the same frequency represented by that symbol. This is due to the principle of entrainment. After your body is resonating with the symbol's frequency, you put your hands on your body. Then you focus on the vibration you feel moving between your hand and the body part. The focus on feeling quiets your mind and further accelerates the vibration in your body. The vibration acceleration is partially due to the principle of oscillation and how nerves respond to stimulus. As the vibration in your body rises, it creates the ability for your muscles to do work and has a healing effect. To explain more about this topic is beyond the scope of this book.

November 2

I experimented with Reiki. The first thing I did was to see if I could notice a difference of resonance in my body between the power and emotion symbols. I did this by intoning and visualizing the symbol and did a meditation to watch how my body responded. Because I was already sensitive to energy, I felt a distinct difference in my body between the two symbols. This experiment convinced me there was power in the symbols.

November 3

I did two hours of experimentation with the Reiki symbols. After my vibration was strong, I put my palms on the bottoms of my feet. As I gave a treatment there, it was affecting other parts of my body. My hands got hot at times and it felt good to receive this energy. I almost fell asleep with the feeling I was receiving strong energy all over my upper chest and rib cage areas. My right body has much less energy than the left.

November 4

While doing a Reiki session I tired and the energy was not flowing. I think this happened because I used too much effort to visualize energy moving a certain way through my body. When I understood that, I trusted the resonance pattern was established and I could drop the visualization. Then I put my focus on the feeling in my hands at the point of contact with my body. Immediately I went into a state of pure awareness with total silence, the tone in my ears rose and my hands grew hot and warm. The energy I felt in those warm hands felt wonderful.

Insight about drop the technique once the resonance pattern is established in your body through entrainment, you do not need to focus on 'the technique' anymore to keep it going. The body is resonating with that frequency, so merely switch your focus to feeling the vibration and this alone will raise it higher.

November 5: Deepening Meditation & Signs Of Healing

About noon, I did a Reiki session with the power symbol in the woods under a large tree, placing palms on all the chakras, which felt good. In the evening, I used the emotional symbol to treat the chakras and spent a long time on the heart and solar plexus chakras. I drifted into a deep meditative state while treating those chakras. I still need to work with meditation, spring boarding off the Reiki sessions. Next, I did the power symbol and intuitively placed my hands on several chakras while doing meditation.

After the chakra session I felt energy going up and down the spine differently, it felt wide open and my tongue moved strangely. I felt a hollow open space in my throat. My right hand gets warmer and I feel tingles in my toes and ankles on my right side. Something is happening with my teeth. After having done Reiki for a week I notice healing in my body. I had a cold sore erupt under my nose, it quickly burst, there was a scab on it and the next day and then it was gone. I could not believe this happened. I have an eczema patch in my ear that has been there for a year. A pimple developed on it, which hurt for three days. Then it burst and it seems healed. The bunion on my big toe is loosening and I can flex the toe more. My meditation is deep and often I am in the state of feeling myself as a breathing vibration for a few rounds of breaths. It is still puzzling why I cannot fully let go and allow higher-self to take over. I know it is a non-doing. Reiki healing is helping me because it releases blocked energy in my body and my overall body vibration is rising, which seems the same as rising awareness. I wonder if Reiki symbols represent a different energy. I think Reiki self-healing works to amplify our own energy. I suppose it works in any physical object or body. The Reiki technique excites energy in the area where the hands are placed.

Insight about formation of ego I think the ego forms because people are mostly growing in a world of unconscious human beings. This means there is an extreme lack of unconditional love, the love we need to thrive. The ego develops as a means to protect the individual in a hostile world. If parents were beyond the ego, they could give the child all the unconditional love it needs and there would be no need for the child to develop the ego to protect itself. Maybe the next step of humanity is to awaken and children will not have to go through this if the adults can do this step. I think most human beings are sick in some way because we did not receive enough unconditional love. Because we did not receive it, we are holding defenses in our body to prevent getting hurt again. Keeping this defense in place is what causes the energy to stop flowing to certain areas and prevents access by our healer to get to those areas to heal them. If we can relax our defense then our healer can heal it for us.

I do not know if energy blockages can be removed if the psychological reason we are holding a blockage is not cleared up. To let go of a blockage we must first be aware we have a blockage and to understand what value it gives us to keep it in place. To remove it we must be convinced we no longer need this protection, and then we can let it go. When I try to 'be as energy' in meditation, then the thoughts start up. There cannot be any resistance or any holding on to past forms. When meditating I scan all over for any resistance. It is difficult to see how a 'thought' is resistance but it must be so.

November 6: Referred Pain, Work In Spine

Tonight I used the long-distance symbol to treat the chakras. I was not sure if I could use that symbol for healing and often felt I should have used the power symbol, but it seemed to work. Energy worked strongly in the throat chakra and simultaneously, my right toe hurt badly. I worked that chakra until the toe no longer hurt, it was painful at times. It is strange the toe hurts when I treat the throat chakra. Energy works in the spine.

Healing Circle Treatments

November 7: Energy Rush, Tingling, Numbness, Shoulder Pops

I looked closely at the Reiki long-distance symbol and see it means, "One Love". I used it tonight and thought to use it on people distantly, but what came is that it is more important that I heal myself first. I have decided to use this symbol with my meditation. While using it I felt waves of energy moving up and down in my body, and a few times, I fully forgot myself. I try to keep my focus on feeling the vibration inside my body while putting my hands on the chakras. I am amazed by my increase in energy and quick progress. I want to heal and be a healer!

I found a Reiki healing circle that gives free treatments. At this point, I want to heal so badly I will take everything. I signed up and found out I will be sent long-distance Reiki healing tonight from thirteen people at once and they will do it for six days in a row. They give a great gift. I will use the long-distance Reiki symbol and be in meditation just before they start sending the energy healing so I can observe what occurs and elevate my energy so I can better receive it.

Group session 1: I used the long-distance Reiki symbol then put my hands on the sacral chakra. I meditated like that for about twenty minutes before the appointed time. While receiving the Reiki my entire body heated up. Before I only felt heat in my hands. Distinctly, I heard my inner sound change pitch, as if I heard other voices join it. Soon after this, my right big toe was throbbing with pain and I had to work hard not to identify with the pain. Soon I felt a rush of energy move through the chakras on the right side, and then I felt strong tingling in my toes on both feet. My left side went numb, which has not happened before. I felt it went numb to force energy through the right side of my body. After the session, I used Reiki to treat my shoulders and neck. Then I felt popping in both shoulders and felt extreme pain in my right big toe with pops in the toes and ankle. I had to breathe through that a few times. With each pop, my shoulders relaxed more. Afterward, it seemed all chakras were open another notch. After that, I was tired.

November 8: Menstrual Cramps, Hands And Palms Activated

I slept long and feel tired yet energized. I have bad menstrual cramps and back pain. After rising, I gave myself an hour-long Reiki treatment. Now, the soles of my feet and my palms activate and my right hand is stronger.

Group session 2: I gave Reiki to my crown chakra for fifteen minutes with the long-distance symbol before the session began. When they started, the inner sound increased and sounded like a train coming toward me. I did not hear distinct voices this time but it grew loud. The energy seemed much more powerful than the night before. When I felt that rise in energy and knew I was connected with people I laughed. It is amazing to connect with people in a way I did not know was possible. I felt strong energy was sent for the entire session. At moments, I felt I could surrender and forget myself for eternity. I must have been successful with this at times, as I do not recall much of the session. My hands were activating strongly. I felt a few pains as things released and felt warmth building all over my body. After a break, I did another session and fell asleep while doing it. I slept long and soundly. In the last weeks, I sleep a few hours each night, and it feels more like resting than sleeping.

November 9: Pain In Right Body Joints

I did a Reiki session in the large acoustic dome lying on my back under the middle in the sweet spot. This was my first session in the dome and the dome amplified my vibration much. I went through the chakras and noticed each felt stronger today. Then energy worked strongly in the throat chakra, and I felt pain in joints on the right side of my body, which went deeper than last time. I wanted to stop but felt the pain was necessary to heal. I did not identify with the pain and continued the treatment until it no longer hurt. Each day it is easier to surrender and let my vibration pulsate and become one with it. It is all about having no resistance to whatever is occurring, which includes my thinking and feelings. After the feet chakras opened, every part of me is receptive to energy. Indeed, there is little difference; the boundary of the body is mostly mind-made through identification with it and is limiting.

Group Session 3: I began a Reiki session thirty minutes before the group session, giving treatment with my palms to various areas on my head. Then I moved my palms to the crown chakra and went into a meditative state. When the Reiki group session began, the inner sound rapidly grew stronger and I felt waves of energy moving in my body. I then used this time to treat all the chakras. After three sessions, I cannot tell when they stop sending the long-distance Reiki. It seems it boosts my energetic vibration. The vibration and louder inner sound stay elevated for hours after. After the session, I gave myself a full Reiki treatment.

Dream Of Vertebrae Bones & Sound Symbols

November 10: Kriyas, Bliss, Stinging Prickles

Dream of vertebrae bones & sound symbols during the evening I had a repeating dream about bones with sound symbols. The bones were identical cross-section

 pieces like the ones with the marrow inside and looked like the **figure**. There were four syllables etched on the side of each bone comprised of two letters each. When you sang the sound syllables while holding your lips above the center of the bone and blew on it like a flute, then the sound resonated in the bone. In the dream, there was a campfire and many bones like this were spread on a plate. Two friends were there. One friend picked up a bone and showed how to play it, and then we were all playing with them. When I sang the first syllable and blew on the bone, the resonation was unbelievable.[6] Then I woke.

I have been doing Reiki for eight days; it seems as if I have been doing it for months. The progress has been so fast. During the dome session this morning, energy worked strongly in my right shoulder joint while I was treating my throat chakra. I felt much pain in the shoulder and continued. I felt pain in my hip joints and jaw for the first time, as if the healing is now reaching there. The shoulder and arm felt strange at times, like it was morphing and the arm would jerk spontaneously. I felt this was a healing reaction. After this, I treated the rest of the chakras using the heaven symbol. I ended by connecting the crown and root

---

[6] I did research and discovered that the bone in the dream looked nearly the same as a cross-section of the spinal column. With hindsight, I understood that the dream gives information about how resonance can be established in the spinal column through sound as the voice box is on top of the spine.

chakras. When I did that, I felt I was held by my Creator, like a baby in hir arms, it was comforting. I want to return to that feeling repeatedly.

Group session 4: I went to the big dome at 7:30 pm, and sat with the soles of my feet and my palms together. Then I sang the long-distance symbol about five times. Next, I gave Reiki to my palms and soles of feet for about twenty minutes. Then I lie down and intuitively put my hands on my sacral chakra and entered a meditative state. I could tell when the long-distance sending started, as the inner sound got loud and I felt waves of energy moving up and down my body. Later, my body and palms felt warm. There were two notable things. I sensed that someone else joined in the healing circle later and the intensity went way up. I felt a sensation like stinging prickles between my eyebrows, which rippled back and forth. It was like the tingling I felt a few days ago in my toes. Near the end, I decided to send distance Reiki to a friend. I imagined I was my friend and followed my intuition to tell me where to place my hands. Doing this was interesting because my vibration was stronger.

November 11: Joints Opening, Uterus Pain, Weight Loss, Twitches

I dreamed much. When I woke I was vibrating strongly with energy, I curled in a fetal position and felt the energy massaging my body. I feel zapped. I put on black clothes and want to lie in the sun and soak up the heat and be in nature.

I find what is happening fascinating, I am full of gratitude, and each day I feel better, lighter, healthier and happier. Lately, my mind-chatter is strong with delusions of grandeur. I have to be more vigilant to dismiss the chatter and not let it go on so long. Fooling myself is a concern, but when I feel the increasing vibration, I trust it is real. I trust what I am feeling much more than the mind-chatter. The increasing vibration gives me a new confirmation. I am strongly drawn to dive deeper into this mysterious, loving, all knowing and generous energy.

My big toe bunion, neck and shoulder have loosened considerably and the joint mobility increases. I have to stretch parts I could not before. I sat with my legs folded under me in the yoga child pose. I could not do that for a long time. I washed some dishes outside while in a deep squat position, another position that is nearly impossible for me because of my ankle, hip and toe problems. My menstruation continues strong and I have pain in the uterus. During the group session last night, energy worked in the uterus and I felt pain in my ovaries. My bowels have changed to be more solid and I have lost weight. I am fifty-four kilograms now. This weight loss began spontaneously about a month ago. I wonder if everything in my body will be healed.

Group session 5: I did Reiki with the long-distance symbol and was in a deep meditative state when the session began. I set a timer to know exactly when it started. After 8 pm, my hands warmed, the inner sound increased and my body grew hot. I could tell the difference in my energy before and after they began sending. I let myself fall into the vibration and moved my hands to places I felt I needed healing. While doing my heart chakra I was relaxed with no resistance and it felt wonderful to bathe in that energy. At times, I felt twitches and pulses in areas, as if my body was reforming or moving toward proper alignment. The elevated body vibration lasted some time, which I took advantage of later, by doing more sessions. I was getting tired while giving myself Reiki so I switched to distance sending to a friend. When I did that, I was amazed at the increase in vibration and went into a deep state of no-mind. Then I allowed the Reiki to flow and felt as if I were observing myself from a distance, which lasted about thirty minutes.

November 12: Strong Abdominal Pain, Uterus Pulsing, New Tones

I gave myself a full-body Reiki treatment in the dome using the power symbol. I began with palms and feet together and meditated for ten minutes. It is difficult to put the soles of my feet together due to stiffness in my hips. During the session, I had much pain in my abdomen with thumping in my uterus that I nearly passed out. I continued with it for an hour. When I had my first spiritual awakening, I also felt the strange thumping in the uterus. At 6 pm, I felt strong energy activation in the body so I gave myself a Reiki session lying. Two tones sounded, one was a high-pitched 'eeee' sound and the other was a low sound like a train. The two sounds were different. I have heard this three times this week and wonder about it.

Group session 6: I did Reiki with the long-distance symbol standing with my palms together singing into the dome. It took a few minutes before my hands were warm and I felt the energy like waves going up and down my body. Then I lay down and used Reiki palms to various positions on my head. When the group sending began, I moved my palms to the heart chakra. Again, someone enter the session later, which I hear as a distinctive high-pitched sound. I do not recall much different. It was a strong session and a few times, I surrendered but not as much as the night before. Afterward, I treated the rest of my chakras, and sent a distance healing to my friend. Again, I surrendered deeper while doing the second session. I fell asleep while sending the Reiki and slept long and deep.

November 13: Strong Vibration, Neck Snap, Increasing Quiet

Energy visualization technique: My current practice is I sit upright with palms together with some pressure and with my soles of feet together with my eyes closed. Then I visualize the Reiki symbol over my crown chakra and sing it three times. With the in breath I visualize energy is coming from above down through the crown chakra and into belly button area. With the out breath I visualize energy is radiating from there into all parts of the body and exiting at the palms and soles of feet. I continue this until my hands and feet are warm. Then I lie down and drop the visualization, trusting the vibration is established. This raises my vibration strong and energizes all parts of my body making me feel hollow. After doing this for three days, I can relax my legs enough to sit comfortably with soles of my feet together.

I did Reiki with hand positions on the head. Energy went to various parts of my body, my hands got warm and the sensation of warmth and bliss was relaxing. It felt especially good on my heart chakra. I tried to send the Reiki with my mind to where I felt pain or stiffness in my body and it seems to work. It seems when I am in the surrender state I can send the energy with only my intention. However, if I do healing this way, then I am treating the symptoms, I am doing pain relief. This might not be the most effective way to heal, as it requires my limited wisdom about what might be best for me.

Insight about 'I don't have to do anything' then the thought came that my higher-self is vastly more intelligent. I only have to trust that my higher-self knows how to heal me. I do not have to do anything except to get quiet and allow the energy to flow. I tried it and the moment I was quiet energy zoomed around all over and worked efficiently. I am convinced that I do not have to direct my healing and clearly see the limit of my knowledge.

While surrendered a bone in my upper spine audibly snapped. This event confirmed the surrender state was the best way to heal. It seems I can put my hands anywhere on my body to get the same effect. Tonight I think to do the heart chakra and sit with the bliss. Now I see what the sages mean when they refer to the gap between the breaths, the energy sits there in the openness. I am learning to be one with this gap. I read something from Osho that said if you can sit for forty-eight minutes in total quiet, then you are 'done'. The quiet intervals get longer. The purple light I see in my 3rd eye is pulsing strong. All of this looks real, I am happy about the healing.

November 14: Sustained Quiet Mind, Energy Waves, Orgasmic Intensity

The inner sound is changing. There is a high-pitched sound and a low-pitched sound like a train and I hear various sounds between. When I listen to the inner sound, I sink into waves of vibrating energy. When I woke, energy was slowly working up and down my body, as if a healer had been released and was looking for problems and working on them. I think the energy boost I received from the healing circle is enough for me to go on with self-healing. I think it will be like most transformation and will take twenty-one days to complete. I started Reiki on November 1, in one more week the healing should be mostly completed. There are still problems in my body, but every day it is better. Each day I stretch and it feels good to do it.[7]

I did Reiki all morning. I stood in my room under the dome's sweet spot and held my hands together in prayer position, and felt strong energy in my feet chakra that seemed it was coming up through the earth. I did some hand positions on my back and felt energy work in my spine. I laid down and felt pain in the uterus, and treated the sacral and root chakras for a long time. It was similar to orgasm and was so intense I wanted to stop, but did not because I felt I needed to open this chakra. Reiki on the root chakra reduced my fear of letting go which helped me stay in quiet mind for a long time. During this time, I felt my body as an awesome single vibration. I still feel intensity in the root chakra much later; it is as if the entire area is alive. After this, I did the other chakras ending with the crown. Once I tried to warm my eyes, as I did with my hands. When I started, purple light appeared strongly in my 3rd eye and I went into a deep meditation. A big thunderstorm with hail occurred outside the entire time and I felt as one with the energy releasing outside. I felt I was entraining to it.

---

[7] Wow, thinking the full healing will only take 21 days!

I did an awesome Reiki session where I went into outer space for a long time. My energy is getting stronger. Tonight I sent distance energy one-by-one to all my loved ones; some had stronger energy than others did. What worked well was to focus on my breathing pattern and let everything else go. When I did that I went beyond which I find interesting. The inner sound is strong and constant and sounds like a train most often. I feel waves of energy in my body continuously working on healing me. This is unbelievable! When I lay down my neck and shoulder hurt badly. Eventually I found a comfortable position, put Reiki hands on my body, and fell asleep quickly.

Insight about 'When 2 or more gather in my name' the primary power of energetic healing is on another level, as was done in this healing circle. The energy of many people combine and is directed at someone to heal them. This is now my focus and how I will continue. Each human that reaches enlightenment can then pass it on through entrainment. What is wonderful about long-distance healing is there are not physical or geographic limits.

November 15: Teeth Pain, Weight Loss

When I woke in the morning, I was in the identical position I fell asleep in last night, with my hands in the same place. I must have received healing all night! I am buzzing. I did several stretches and will do more as it helps to open my stiff joints. I often feel pain in my teeth during the sessions. I am not sure what is occurring with them. My pants are falling off and my stomach flattens. Tonight I gave my first physical Reiki session to a friend and learned I need to read the part about giving Reiki to someone else. I felt tired afterward, mostly because of uncomfortable positions I was in. At times, when I looked with my eyes where I had my hands; it was as if someone else was looking. It seemed the Reiki worked better if I was looking. It was harder for me to keep my mind quiet while I worked on someone else.

Start Of Organ Cleansing

November 17: Body Healing, Tingling Rushes

Yesterday, I was sore in the shoulder joint and tired and did one session. My shoulder is healing! There is inflammation under the clavicle, near the shoulder joint, the muscle knot in the trapezoid is shrinking and I have pain in the right breast. The inner sound is melodic with rich sounds. The middle finger on my right hand is straightening, which hurt much yesterday. This is amazing! I want to do more Reiki to heal everything. Last night I heard a message to be patient, "Every healing session raises the energy vibration as blockages are released. This will wake you up. You don't need to do more than this."

I did Reiki for four hours this morning. I gave myself empowerment using the Reiki master symbol. I wanted to treat all my chakras but did not move beyond my crown chakra, which I treated for a long time. Afterward, much healing happened in the sacral chakra and I had intense pain in the kidney region for about an hour. Now there is less kidney pain and more pain in the bladder and uterus. The uterus feels as if it has a heartbeat inside. From the uterus area, I feel a connection to the pain in my right breast.

At the end, I worked the lower chakras and that is when I felt energy going to my head with tingling rushes. I think this symptom occurs when blocks open and the nervous system somehow makes a stronger pathway through the body. The Reiki was strong, maybe the self-empowerment worked. When I treated my face and lungs, drainage started and I was coughing hard. I had to sit and stop. After this, I did the sacral chakra and fell asleep. Later I woke, did a position on my shoulder, and fell asleep again.

Insight about Reiki symbols while watching my breathing I felt a difference between the energy vibrations of the in and out breath. The in breath was like the heaven symbol, expanding and filled with light energy. The out breath was like the power symbol, heavy, relaxing and dark. Then I thought the long-distance symbol is like the vibration of the universe, the cosmic pulse and that is why it connects you to others. I think there is something to the symbols, that they represent physical cosmic energies.

November 18: Lung Cleansing, Chakras Open And Spinning

On awakening, I have strong energy but am tired. Yet, my desire is strong to reach my full potential. In the evening, I did two Reiki sessions in the dome and worked the chakras. The chakras feel open, with a circling vibration pattern on most.

While standing, energy quickly activated my body. I felt it shooting around doing work and going up and down through the chakras. It felt like my body was circling. I did my crown chakra and meditated trying to go quiet and sink into the vibration. This worked well and I could have stayed like this forever. I felt healing going on in several parts of the body. Then I worked down through the chakras, which feel open!

At the heart chakra, I switched to long-distance sending and the energy increased when I did that. Distance healing is interesting. It feels as if I am the other person, out of my body, not thinking and the Reiki happens spontaneously. My hands get warm and the energy is drawing strong. I then did the other chakras all of which were drawing much energy. In the sacral chakra, the draw was strong, it was as if my hands were on fire and I could have stayed there forever. Then I switched to the heart chakra, imagined I was anther person, and asked what they needed. I put my hands on the jaws to do the teeth and continued like this for about ten minutes. After I finished, there was much drainage and pain in my throat and lungs with much coughing, A few times something cleared in my throat and air rushed in.

Insight about distance sending there is no distance separating me from the being of another person. It is not 'sending' it and there is no time factor. The limit of body, space and time is illusion. Energetically there is no distance between physical objects. You can reach to the ends of the universe directly and all times exist simultaneously!

Pulsing In Root And Crown Chakras

November 22

In the evening Reiki session, I gave myself self-empowerment using the four symbols all to crown chakra. The session was deep. After this, my crown opened and I felt a heartbeat in the fontanel and in the root chakra. Near the end, I felt air suck in behind my right cheekbone. After this, I sent long-distance Reiki to friends and fell asleep while doing it.

Dream of having another person's dream I woke at 2 am, with strange dreams as if I were having experiences from my friend's viewpoint. I remember while dreaming wondering what that had to do with me. It is their story. This is not mine! I did not try to recall the dreams; I only wanted to get out of it. This is why I woke. Having another person's dreams and experiences did not feel good! Later, I realized I was still connected with them and I need to break the connection after I do something like this. Strange stuff, there is another dimension that has different rules.

Lymph Cleansing

November 23: Shooting Pain In Arms

I am tired and sore in various spots, a vein hurts in the left knee and I have a bad headache. I am doing chakra balancing and it is strong. I intone the power and heaven symbols then tone the sound for the chakra. The lower three chakras open much.

When I did the sacrum chakra, I felt intense pain everywhere and it was hard to take. Then my body got hot and I felt strong pains shooting up and down the outside of my arms. Once a neck vertebra adjusted and I kept hearing a popping sound in my left cheekbone. My eyes, ears and teeth hurt badly and the area by the belly button down to vaginal area was burning. I used the pain to go beyond otherwise I could not have done this. I thought the lymph was cleansing or I had bone cancer. I have no idea. I tried to watch but could not tell what this was. I was in that session for two hours. I am tired and there are four chakras left to do. I am sad when I see how much healing has to be done and how much pain it causes to go through it. I suppose many people would want to stop here, but of course, I will not do that. I took a break, did Reiki on the heart chakra for a long time, and fell asleep.

November 24: Shoulder Pain, Dolphins Singing, Waves Of Bliss

When I woke, I felt I was submerged in the music of dolphins singing. It was a pleasurable experience, as if each breath was a symphony of music filling my entire being. I guess this is what enlightenment will feel like. Now I know what the mystics are talking about, when they say waves of bliss fill their being. I did Reiki in the dome on the root chakra for about an hour. It was intense. I still have much pain in my shoulders and they crack and pop when I move them. I need to stretch these joints.

November 26: Neck Crack, Right Body Tingling, Lung Healing

It has been two longs days with pain in my lungs and shoulder. I still have not made it through all the chakras in one session. I stay on one chakra when it draws much energy, then I fall asleep. Two days ago, menstruation started with strong cramping and flow as when I was young. I wonder if I am healing. Perhaps I am attaching to 'waves of bliss' and tuning everything else out or going into a fantasy world. I need to look at the possibility. I am not working to quell the mind-voice as before. Today and yesterday, I have strong power in my hands and energy flows out of them by touching something.

In the evening Reiki, I intoned all three symbols plus the master symbol. I followed my intuition and did the crown chakra for two hours. Later I felt a crack in my neck and tingling on the right side of body with strong menstrual cramps at the end. I still have a heavy menstrual flow and especially after Reiki. I think there was a lung healing. When I coughed, gunk came up and my breathing was clear afterward. I recall feeling something in my ear and the brain and left eye was painful and tearing. I felt my entire body was worked.

Insight about energy follows focus I realize something simple and profound: energy follows my focus. If I concentrate on feeling the vibration in my body and hearing the inner sound, my vibration rises automatically and I feel like waves of energy. This is all I have to do.

Copper Ring Oscillator Dream

November 27 To November 30

I have been treating four pets every night before my treatment. I am not sure if it is helping them but I keep doing it. I have not been taking notes but this evening I remember well. While doing Reiki in the last sessions it felt as if I had stalled. I have pain and soreness in my right body, which makes it difficult to treat, as my arms tire and my right hand is weak. I was doing Reiki, pondering this dilemma and drifted off to sleep during my 8:30 to 10:30 pm session.

Dream of wire oscillator I was dreaming I was in my room and walking around in it with many things lying on the floor. There was wire on the floor that kept catching my foot, which I then had to disentangle so I would not trip. Then I was looking at all the things in my room and felt someone had placed things there and moved things around. On my desk, I saw a plastic male doll lying with a block of wood under his head. It seemed he was lying giving himself Reiki. I stared at that a long time. Then I reversed to go the other way back in my room and again the wire was wrapped around my foot. This happened about three times, then I was annoyed and decided to deal with it. I reached to get all the pieces of wire to pick it up. When I had it in both hands, it was a coil of medium gauge wire like those in every tool shed. When I stood with it in my hands, immediately I felt a strong energy going through my hands and body. Then I raised my arms toward the ceiling with the coil of wire in my hands, feeling the strong power in it. Then I woke.

Immediately I remembered the dream and felt it was significant. I went directly to the tool shed, got a similar coil of wire, came back, and did a standing meditation with it intoning the Reiki symbols. It was unbelievable! I felt the energy going around in circles on the coil and reversing directions going back and forth, and it was energizing both sides of my body. I pondered it some time during the night and concluded that it empowered me. I used the wire coil many times in the night and each time the energy rose quickly in my body.

December 1

I discussed my dream about the coil with a friend and she said something about people working with copper. Then I thought that copper is what they have in electric wires and perhaps it would be a better conductor of energy than the steel wire. I found a heavy-duty copper wire cable the electric company uses with eighteen wires in it and took it apart. I made six coil rings with the pieces of wire I had of several sizes. I made a small ring, four of eighteen inches in diameter and one huge ring, three feet in diameter that can be used by multiple people. I made each coil with at least seven wires from the center of the utility cable, and used extra copper wires to bind the coil together. Of the two coils I made, the one with looser wires works better. I have used them in various ways, on my body to fall asleep and keep my vibration high and to energize before a session. The latter seems the best use of it. It amplifies my vibration to a higher level than I could achieve without it. It is a self-empowerment tool.

December 2 To December 3

I went to the dome after my walk and did yoga. I have to do something to move this body; the Reiki alone is not enough. I need to attend to my diet. The food they are cooking here is too rich and I am not getting enough liquids. I am constipated and do not feel well. The physical work is demanding for me and I am thinking about a new line of work.

December 4

Dream of old men in wheelbarrows: I had a dream where I was walking toward a park and ahead there was a bridge over water and beyond it I could see some tables and chairs. I started walking toward the bridge. While on the bridge entering the park, I saw an old man who looked like Santa Claus lying naked in a wheelbarrow and basking in the sun. This was amazing to see and when I looked at what else was in the park, I saw the same man in identical wheelbarrows all over the park and all of them were sunbathing. While I stared at this in amazement, I felt someone come behind me and put their hands on my shoulders from the back. I immediately felt strong energy enter my body. Feeling this, I responded energetically and melted with the other person. Then they said, "I like your energy". The person felt alien, I could not see them and they felt thin, wiry and strong muscled. Then I woke. The energy coming from this person was so nice, I tried to go back to sleep to pick up the dream again. I think about making a metal bed and sunbathing in it because I feel this information is a way to boost my energy. I am becoming a channel for energy, including the sunlight and the heat from my stove.

December 5 To December 16

I cannot find any notes for this time.

December 17: Reiki Level I Empowerment

My Reiki Master sent me a long-distance empowerment at 8:30 pm. It boosted my energy markedly. My energy has been low. My entire body heated and this has not happened for some time. I could achieve the quiet mind state much easier.

December 18: Increased Energy Sensitivity

I feel the energy of the big tree by putting my hands on it. It is strong and healing. I pause to get a dose and thank the tree for its gift. I feel energy coming from the heat from my stove as I sit next to it and from the sun. I think my body is changing, I become much more sensitive to energies of all kinds including people's negativity, emotions or whatever energy they are emitting. I will strive to tune into the energy field of things around me.

Dropping The Storyteller

December 20

The last week has been challenging. I have allowed my personality to energize strongly and when I let that happen it takes a long time to calm. Usually, the trigger is from a friend and I strongly believe that how I see things is the truth. My story goes constantly inside me. The trigger this time was somebody not asking me for my opinion and informing me about a matter I felt was important. I felt I saw anger in the eyes and heard it in the voice of my friend, which seemed unwarranted. I reacted out of my view with anger. It is difficult to hold my anger, and not burst out with it.

Dream of cards with monster faces I had a dream of a teacher, showing some cards that were an ancient Korean teaching. He showed one card to a Korean woman and asked her if she knew it. She said yes, and opened the one card and made it into three cards showing how simple it was. I am not sure what was on the cards she opened. Then he handed the card to me. I spread open the card and it split into six or seven cards, each card had the face of a horribly ugly monster with teeth. It was as if I saw my face on each of these cards. I did not like what was revealed, I closed them and reopened them several times, and the same happened. The teacher laughed when he saw my distress. This dream bothered me much and I was glad to wake out of this nightmare.

At first, I did not want to record the dream and recognized not wanting to accept this ugly aspect of myself. This is how the 'lie' of ego hides; we do not want to see ourselves how we are. My physical healing has slowed, probably because emotional and intellectual elements of personality are healing. This has not happened since I started the Reiki. I suspect it is a healing reaction. Many things rise to the surface to heal, including how my ego stays alive.

Reflecting on the dream, this is how I see people. My head is full of ugly pictures of everyone. I do see mostly the negative in people; it is a main way I get my confirmation to feel superior to others. Today, my thinking is full of negative thoughts of everyone without provocation. It is good that I see this, because I do not want to be this way. When I judge others, it insulates me from looking at myself, and keeps me stuck in the trap of the personality. I know this mind-chatter has nothing to do with reality, so I must work harder to stay aware so I can divert energy from the storyteller.

December 21 – Winter Solstice

I need to know exactly what technique I use to defend my personality, so I can stop the behavior. I think it has to do with being hurt and not trusting anybody because I fear getting hurt again. That is my armor. I do not want to drop my defense because I feel it protects me from experiencing that pain again. Then I see this armor keeps me from getting love and from being love. Is my armor finding everything wrong and bad in people? Do I look hard at others to find the faults because I am looking close to see if they can be trusted? Have I a difficult time accepting a friend's betrayal because I trusted them? Probably this is it and why it is difficult to break my bond to them. I am sensitive to how others react to me, I pick up every nuance and watch like a hawk looking for anything I can react to. I am empathetic to them, feeling hurt when I see how they feel about me.

The negative views I have about everyone, do not allow me to see their true being. I want to see people clearly, unfiltered as they are without my clouded perception. I will practice doing this with all energetic life forms. Perhaps if I can learn to do this with animals and plants then I can move on to people and not be sucked into the reactive energy of their ego and mine.

I have to acknowledge my reactive tendency and not react. The way I am practicing this is by accepting my negative response when it occurs and defusing it by redirecting my focus out of thinking to feeling and awareness. I understand if I divert energy from the old response pattern, it will gradually lesson and eventually go away. I want that badly. I want to take the next step and obviously too much energy is wasted reacting as the personality.

Lately I have heightened sensitivity to people's unconsciousness. I talked about this topic with a friend and learned how I get my good or bad feelings according to how others respond to me. I have a new lesson to face and it is accepting the unconsciousness of others and not reacting to it. I have to remind myself when others react; it is not because they are out to get me. It is not personal. Rather it comes from their need to provoke to react strongly to keep their game of personality going. People in relationships know how to push each other's buttons and it can become a habitual way to get the fuel they need to keep their personality activated. I do not want to play that game anymore with others and I do not want it for me. Once the personality activates strongly, it can take a long time to settle the energy and return to inner peace. I want peace.

How To Shut Up

December 26, 2005

I awoke and noticed the mind-chatter immediately. Then I wondered if this is going on while I sleep and is there when I wake, then what hope is there ever to go beyond it. Pondering this, **I felt my energy rise, my feet started pulsating and I heard the inner sound of dolphins singing. Then I saw clearly that there was 'no way'. I only have to avert energy from the mind-chatter, and then higher-self is there.**

Chapter 9: Full-Blown Kundalini Transformation

Prologue To The Journal

After the full-blown kundalini triggered, I was given instructions as teachings, dreams, visions and insights about how to raise my energy so the transformation was effective. At first, the vibration is low, the body does not move much spontaneously, and I relied heavily on the techniques. Each day the vibration in the body gets higher. As the vibration rises, higher-self takes over stronger and the techniques are needed less. Kundalini transformation then takes on a life of its own.

It helps to understand my journal by knowing about my sessions. A kundalini session is a time where I was meditative and surrendered control of my body and allowed any reaction to happen. On average, sessions were ninety minutes long. From the beginning, I understood I did not have to figure out what to do. I only had to follow my higher-self. When I quieted my mind, and merged into the vibration, my body would move spontaneously. At first, it moved a little, later it moved much more. The transformation work going on in my body determined what kind of session I had. Sometimes the energy was calm and I meditated, watching the reactions in the body that were either freefall or the growing phase. When I moved, I named the session according to the main position my body was in the duration of the session. I would choose my start position depending on where energy worked to make it more effective. The sessions naturally evolved out of the activation pattern of the body and my increasing awareness. In the beginning, sessions would concentrate on one body area and over time would work the entire body from toes to head, in lying or sitting positions.

I had the prevailing belief the transformation would finish soon. This belief kept me going full-time for three and a half years, always with the hope to finish and see the result. I had the savings to live on and the space to do it, so that is what I did. Other people in kundalini transformation may not notice the observations I did, because they were not dedicating as many hours to it and thus have lower vibration. I worked with this full-time averaging twelve hours each day, and kept a high energetic vibration. I do not feel this dedication is necessary or even desirable, as you cannot live a normal life! I think a benefit of my doing it like this, is I have these detailed notes that I can share with others. After my savings ran out, I went back to work and reduced my sessions to two per day. The kundalini reactions tapered when I cut back, but my vibration continues to rise daily.

Another prevailing belief was I thought I was transforming into a male. For many of my notes, this belief biases my observation of what is happening. Today, I believe most of it was due to interpretation, but as this process is not finished, I am not certain. It is strange this happens so late in my life. I wonder what benefit it has for humanity and our continued existence as a species. I can understand the benefits for the individual but not for the whole. How is enlightenment passed to future generations? Perhaps by becoming enlightened, a change will happen to the global consciousness and it may have an effect energetically. Maybe kundalini transformation will start earlier in each generation, and eventually it happens to young adults who then can pass it along in the genes. Maybe it is a onetime thing that has to be done by everyone in his or her last physical life on Earth. Maybe it happens to all people in a short period, like a species wide metamorphosis. Maybe the only value is when a person goes through it then they can write about it and encourage or help others.

I still have many unanswered questions and until my transformation finishes I cannot answer them. I am not attached to any result and am sure I will love the result. I want it to be clear that what is written herein is not necessarily, what I believe today and I am not seeking approval for any of my theories. I am interested in the truth and can let go of my current theory when something better comes along.

Acupressure On Meridians

January 3, 2006: Copper Ring Bracelets

I felt I needed more energy and Chinese meridians kept coming to me, which I knew nothing about. Finally, I looked up the meridian charts in the Internet and printed them. A meridian is an energy pathway in acupuncture and Chinese medicine. The Chinese call the energy chi that concentrates and moves along these paths in the body. The fourteen main meridians are the lung (LU), heart (HT), pericardium (PC), triple heater (TH), small intestine (SI), large intestine (LI), spleen (SP), kidney (KD), liver (LV), gallbladder (GB), urinary bladder (UB), stomach (ST), conception vessel (CV) and governing vessel (GV) meridians. Along each meridian are spots called acupoints, marked and labeled in meridian charts. On the acupoints, you can excite energy flow in the meridian either by using slight pressure with your fingertips (acupressure) or by using an acupuncture needle. Many acupoints can be felt as a light pulse once you are accustomed to feeling energy. The meridian charts I like are from YinYangHouse.com and can be printed online.[8]

This is what I needed. Using Reiki with acupressure is stronger than only Reiki. I started sessions by intoning the Reiki symbols and did acupressure on various acupoints. Today, I felt angry and noticed how energy was building in my muscles all over. I started with the liver meridian because I heard it is related to anger. I used acupressure with Reiki on the liver meridian and see the area inside my knees is blocked. While feeling my anger, I used acupressure on the liver meridian acupoints by the knees. I felt my leg meridian open and bliss drew me more than anger. I still wanted to think and be angry, so I sat with the emotion feeling it wherever it was.

During the treatment, I felt much tension in the back of my neck near C7 and the right shoulder. I continued until the tension and anger dissolved, which took about forty minutes. I still feel some tension and anger. I think my shoulder tension is related to how I express anger, which I have been doing for years. Reiki with acupressure is a way to heal this. I am looking for a quick way to discharge my anger before it builds too high. I think to do a body scan and note where energy does not flow or where there is pain. I think to feel around to find those acupoints and write them down. I have to work on my reactive tendency. I do provoke and then people respond and I am caught in the ping-pong game. I talk too much and do not listen well nor feel the other's energy. I aim to keep a keen eye on my body tension, so I am aware when the mind-voice is too active.

I am very sensitive to energy now, maybe because I am wearing copper ring bracelets I made. I went outside and felt an energy vortex everywhere on top of the hill where I live. The source of the strong energy in my room comes up through the floor from this vortex. Before, I thought it was coming from the potbelly stove. The tree mystery is solved; the strong energy comes through the ground from the roots. I will check out these things more. Many insights come now.

January 4: Body Scan Checking Meridians

---

[8] http://www.yinyanghouse.com

I spent time with each meridian experimenting with using acupressure on each acupoint along the path. I would see if it was open or closed and what affects I felt in the body by applying acupressure to that point. Details of these notes are in my Reiki healing journal. I worked with the liver, gallbladder and urinary bladder meridians.

January 7: Liver Meridian Experimentation

I experimented with acupoints on the liver meridian for a long time and noted the effect of each point. The most significant thing I noticed is the LV1 acupoint at end of long toe were effective to activate the entire meridian. I observed how energy opened higher in the body as I moved along the meridian. My sinuses opened and my nose cleared. The liver and gallbladder meridians had similar side effects and I think they must connect. I discovered that treating the same meridian on both sides of my body at once was stronger than doing one side of my body. I discovered that working acupoints on either side of an energy block was effective to open the blocked area. I spent a long time working on opening various blocked acupoints. Then I thought, instead of working every acupoint on a meridian it may be more effective to find my main energy blocks and work to clear them. When I stopped, my liver and spleen were tingling strongly. I think this is good for all the organs.

Vertical Meridian In Legs Opens

January 8: Kidney Meridian Experimentation, Opening Blocks

I feel pain in my right knee, liver, gallbladder and shoulder. I wanted to write as I have many ideas but my body is saying do this now! I experimented with acupoints on the kidney meridian, and noted points blocked in my body. When I pressed acupoint KD4, it caused strong pain in my shoulders, lungs and kidneys. When I pressed acupoint KD5, I first felt much pain and then bliss as energy poured in. My upper body and neck spontaneously moved all over, it seemed to move energy through my shoulders. After that, the shoulder pain was relieved! Energy works in my body even when I am busy doing other things.

While working acupoint KD10, I felt pain and discomfort under lower ribs. I felt tingling in bands running horizontally in area of lower ribs just below sternum and above waistline. After this, I heard a new clear inner sound like Ah or Aw. When I rested, energy moved strongly into my shoulder, which felt great. My right leg hurts on the outside edge of the knee. I am grateful of this healing.

Later, I worked an acupoint for an hour. I felt energy going back and forth across my abdomen and often I wanted to stop because it hurt. Once I felt a meridian in my legs open,

then the back and stomach pain stopped. Then the energy switched to a vertical direction and energy worked above the navel. When I stopped my kidneys were tingling, especially the left one. A while later a buildup of gas caused pain. My sinuses opened and my nose dripped. When I worked acupoints KD18 through KD21 and up, I felt intense pain. I was trying to raise my body to an upright sitting position but could not because there was much pressure under my lungs. Once, energy worked across my forehead **(see figure).**

Dream of doctor in bar I had a dream that awoke me. I went to a place like a bar with low lighting to meet a doctor. The doctor was a beautiful woman who looked like Sharon Stone. I sat at her table and she never spoke. Then she stood, walked over to me and put her hand on my body. When she did that, I stumbled across the room as if I had lost control of my body. Then I fell on my back to the floor with my armpit pointed up and my arm pointed to the north **(see figure).** I thought this was my diagnosis. Then she walked over and I understood a silent message, "Look at what you are protecting. Go to the center, that's the problem". I thought she meant the problem

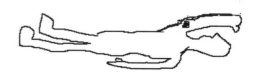

was in my armpit. Then I was standing and she touched me and she was surprised to feel the strength of my energy. When she touched me, I melted. Then with her left hand, she made a motion like flicking water off her fingertips toward that area. I felt or heard the sprinkles with dolphin music and ting, ping, ting sounds. Then I felt blissful energy waves inside, which I felt was her gift to me. She did this three times. I did not want her to stop. When she stopped, I looked at her and she knew I wanted more. I answered her: "Yes, I know it's enough. Thank you". Then she was gone.

Arm To Spine Energy Circuits, Passing The Threshold Of No Return

January 9: Meridian Experimentation

I experimented with each acupoint on the pericardium meridian, starting with PC1 and doing all acupoints. Energy first worked in right lung and right head, and then moved to left side of body and I felt tingling in fingers of left hand. Then I felt tingling in both lungs. When I stopped, I felt much tingling in right skull and fingers of right hand.

I experimented on the heart meridian and worked with the lung, triple heater and small intestine meridians from finger acupoints. While working the triple heater meridian, energy works in a horizontal direction across the shoulders. A rod of energy was ramming through the right shoulder to open it.

While working on the liver and small intestine meridians something happened. First, I felt a strong pull, clearing something vertically through the head and shoulders. After this stopped, I felt a right to left wavy energy between the arms. Next, the energy started down, like seeking an energy circuit to ground. Then I clearly felt energy coming up through my feet and legs, I think it was by the top of foot by the middle toe. It was interesting that doing the finger acupoints had this effect.

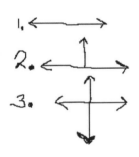

After this, energy worked strongly. Again, I felt pulling and tingling in other areas of my arm (index finger) up through the head and into sinuses and my nose started dripping. It seems like the laws of electricity. First the shortest distance energy circuit is made from arm to arm (1), then it goes up to make an energy circuit to crown chakra (2), then it goes down to Earth to complete the vertical circuit (3) activating everything **(see figure).**

I felt the energy circuit working left to right and soon felt all the arm meridians activate. Then my left hand activated, then the left arm and then left skull with draining sinuses. Next, the left leg activated. Then it was like all activated energies on the left side of the body joined as one force and worked my right shoulder, TMJ and somewhere above that in my skull. Later I felt work in my throat on both sides under the tonsils. My nose runs like crazy.

Then I let go of body control and my upper body gradually lowered to left front, a notch at a time toward my chest with my neck stretched **(see figure).** I was drooling and my nose was still running. I heard a few cracks in my spine by the neck and felt some rotation in my shoulder. I felt some pinpoint pains above my ear in my skull. After a while, I had to sit up. Then my right leg activated. Again, all activated energy forces were pushing at the right

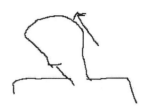

shoulder, then it went up into my head on right side and I stopped. I just coughed a large gob of hard phlegm with blood in it; I think this came from my right lung under my shoulder. Wow! I never expected anything like this. It is so amazing! I think I can use the principle of combining forces to discover a way to increase vibration for healing. Next, I will do all meridian endpoints to see what happens. The endpoints are the beginning or end of the meridian, numerically as they appear in the meridian charts. For example, the liver meridian has fourteen acupoints, the first is called LV1 and is on the toe next to the big toe, and the last is LV14 and is on a rib midway on front of body. The endpoints are LV1 and LV14.

The energy continues to work strongly; it is working to open the right side of the body. I think this reaction means I have reached some threshold and cannot stop it even if I wanted too. I think my energy is high enough, so I only have to relax and get quiet and healing will continue. I have taken a break, as I do not feel too good. My throat is swollen, I am sneezing and my nose is stuffed up. I wonder if I can overdo this.

I did another intense session. At the beginning, my buttocks got warm and the thighs felt tingly. I guess these areas are activating. Then energy went up the spine and I felt deeply relaxed, as if I could fall asleep. It is difficult to stay awake now. This time my neck went far to the left, then to the right and down between my knees. I was drooling again. There were several snaps and pops in my neck and maybe one in a vertebra on the back. The energy felt like a spiral going up and down the spine. I want to try all meridian endpoints before bed.

While doing the liver meridian acupoints LV1 on both feet my head lowered to my legs. I am blocked along this meridian and it is hard to work on it. I felt the energy spiral on my spine still working. I will activate all vertical meridians to check if it is more effective. It seems a single acupoint should connect the conception and governing vessel meridians.

When I did acupressure on the CV1 and CV22 acupoints on the conception vessel meridian, energy activated strongly and did not stop for thirty minutes. Energy worked in upper regions of lungs that now tingle. This is a strange feeling. I recall my breathing opened and my body temperature rose strongly. I am so sleepy.

I did acupressure to the governing vessel acupoint GV28, and the conception vessel acupoint CV22, simultaneously. These are the two meridian endpoints. Much energy spirals in my feet and energy works along the liver meridian. Energy is zooming all around and working on everything. Much work is happening on my teeth. Energy moves to my head. It is difficult to breathe so I will do the gallbladder meridian.

Insight on doing identical acupoints on both sides at once: Giving acupressure to identical acupoints on both sides of body at once is powerful. The strong push-pull force may be due to the distance between the acupoints or because both circuits are activating.

January 10

For over a week, I have been giving Reiki treatments to a friend. The first time I gave them a treatment, their energy nearly floored me. I had never felt that much energy in any person I had given a Reiki treatment to before.[9] I have been experimenting with activation of the meridian endpoints from fingers and toes on people and animals. When giving the next treatment to my friend, meridians I worked before are still open at same level as last time. The back-and-forth energy movement between the feet (while working the same acupoint on both feet), creates a strong force to clear blockages and make new energy circuits along that meridian circuit.

Insight about how energy healing works: Lying on of hands heals by increasing vibration of body part or meridian you are touching. I think it is possible that healing happens electrically in all the body parts, tumors can break apart, veins can clean and everything heals in the same way. To heal you only need to increase your rate of vibration, then your internal healer will use that boost in energy to heal what is most critical for your survival

---

[9] With hindsight, I know that the sessions I gave my friend were also very beneficial to me. Sharing of our energy likely was a catalyst for the full-blown kundalini activation that followed. It is a form of shaktipat.

When I give acupressure to another by pressing the acupoints on a single meridian on both feet, this meridian activates in them and me because it is at the same frequency. It is as if the meridians in both of us join as a single energy circuit. As our unique vibrations merge, I feel entrainment and healing as a back and forth movement occurring between them and me. Because the same frequency activates in each owing to entrainment, energy works along this channel in both bodies to clear blockages. Where I feel energy work in my body, energy is working in their body in the same place.

When an energy block is near to clearing, energy speeds up with waves going back and forth very fast. When the blockage clears, the back and forth waves stop and the energy circuit feels calm with the sensation of running, pulling or drawing energy. When an energy block opens a circuit, both people experience an increase in vibration. The new vibration is stronger and immediately energy will work on the next blockage. The healer within always has the purpose to 'get more energy' to achieve the goal to become enlightened.

January 11: Gallbladder Meridian Opens, Right & Left Body Circuits

Small Intestine (SI) meridian experimentation

I spent two hours working individual acupoints on the small intestine meridian to clear blockages. Energy worked in several blockages in neck muscles. I have two nodes at the back of my neck at base of occipital on right side of cervical spine. I feel they are a large blockage on right side of body. They have been there for as long as I remember. When I felt the gallbladder meridian open, I switched to working it on skull acupoints. It opened more but did not work to relieve my congestion. Next, I checked the stomach meridian for blockages and found another big block in the neck. I wonder if I have a cervical vertebra out of alignment.

On break, I doubled over with a sharp pain in my gallbladder and feel gallbladder acupoints in the head clicking. After this, I started working all acupoints on all meridians, which could affect my neck. Many of them helped to open my neck. Then I had the idea to send as much energy in the up direction as possible. I did all the vertical circuits: the kidney, conception vessel and governing vessel meridians. I did the horizontal ones across my face, alternating between vertical and horizontal. I activated every circuit and kept trying to open the gallbladder between these. On the governing vessel meridian a vertebra popped. After this, I did the gallbladder meridian a long time and something finally opened.

Then the energy rocketed when a circuit formed between right and left sides of body. This is interesting! I went to sleep and awoke two hours later thinking it was morning, and was disappointed I was not healed. I feel rested. My sinuses are still plugged but I have less pain. I think the gallbladder meridian has to open for the congestion to drain. One finger activates strongly and emits tingly energy when I use it with acupressure. It relaxes everything inside. I will experiment to see what I can learn to move this healing along.

I think I need to heal the organs and give acupressure where I feel pain on the cord of personality. I worked the liver meridian, which is removing the block. I felt openings in both ankles and shoulder joints and my head started to clear as energy moved up the gallbladder meridian. Energy is working in right hip so I will work higher acupoints. I felt the right shoulder open with click sounds, then I felt pops in neck, and the sinuses cleared some. I cleared a block in a joint working LV8 on the liver meridian. After this energy shot up and started working on neck and shoulder. The gallbladder and liver meridians are connected especially at the liver meridian acupoint LV13. Working the liver meridian was opening the gallbladder meridian.

Discovery Of Drain For Lymph

January 12

I am looking for a 'liquid drain' to clear the fluids that backup as is obvious due to my blocked sinuses and gallbladder pain.[10] I decided to work the urinary bladder meridian because its vertical, relates to urine and may help drain the lymph.

On the urinary bladder meridian, acupoint UB67 activates the meridian channel and acupoint UB60 feels great, maybe this is the pump to drain the fluids. Acupoint UB59 opens the sinuses. It seems acupoints UB60 through UB58, could drain the fluid if these acupoints were open. The left side of my body on the urinary bladder meridian is open but the right side is blocked.

---

[10] My experimenting all over was clearing blocked paths and caused drainage of lymph. It could not drain because the lower circuits in my body were blocked. I was desperate from the growing discomfort and good for me my intuition gave me the answer.

Insight about hand meridians: Pressing the acupoint on the base of the nail in the center of the middle finger activates energy in the upper back and lung area. This is not an acupoint of the fourteen main meridians. If I use acupressure on both acupoints on either side of the nail bed of the finger, it is stronger than doing one acupoint. All the meridians make a circle in the body; probably there are other energy circuits as well. Thumb on palm chakra after doing finger meridians keeps all the meridians in the hand activated and pulls the energy together causing energetic work to happen in upper quadrant and arm of body. Probably you could start with pinky fingers, move to lung meridian, and note the connections occurring between these to determine the connections between meridians. The same experiment could be done on the feet. There is obviously an order to energy movements, body activation and flows.

Internal Rain, Big Body Spiral From Head Down To Toes

January 14: Full Moon & Reiki Empowerment

The gallbladder meridian goes up left side along flank of body and outside the legs and down the right side. It does not seem to matter which side of toenail you press. The middle of the toe below nail also works. The stomach meridian moves up front of leg, then up under ribs close to midline of body. The liver meridian moves up inside leg to groin, it goes up long bones of leg. The Spleen meridian goes up inside leg under rib cage in front more to outside torso than the stomach meridian under rib cage. The kidney meridian moves up inside leg and circles ankle, and I feel it on the inside knee near the back, and I feel it near the spine. The urinary bladder meridian travels up to outside foot edge, and goes through heel and up back of leg.[11]

The urinary bladder meridian feels blocked, so I stayed working it until it felt clear. While giving acupressure to outside little toe on urinary bladder acupoint UB67, I felt the big toe ache and later I heard crackles in my skull above my right ear. Body activation is

---

[11] The torso meridian paths are shown on standard meridian charts. Here I was experimenting without the charts to feel where the energy went through my body, trying to discover the connections and relationships between the different meridians.

happening from the toes. The urinary bladder meridian is opening vertically on my head on front and back of body, and up and over top of head. When I felt that open, I switched to working on the gallbladder meridian. Around 9 pm, when I was getting a distance Reiki empowerment, I felt the gallbladder meridian open as a path that goes around in a circle on outside edge of body.

It feels like it is raining inside my body as the fluids drain. I feel the energy flowing down the left kneecap. I feel drainage behind the right armpit. Energy spontaneously activates along similar meridian paths in my arms as the urinary bladder and gallbladder meridians. A circle forms around my chest through my armpits. Energy is spiraling down my legs and energy circles the knees and cleans them. Energy increased momentum. It feels like it is raining everywhere in the body and I am very cold. I think I have reached a threshold! The fusing begins and with it an unbelievable healing. It seems my entire body is gently healing![12] After the cold internal rain, my entire body was tingly, like the nervous system was changing. Then it seemed the circulatory system was worked and last it felt like energy worked on the bones and I fell asleep.

I awoke at 12:30 am, because energy worked strongly in my intestines. I noticed several things about the energy flow. First, always the left side activated first: fingertips, hands, wrist to shoulder, and energy worked one body side at a time. When energy finished working on one side, then that side would be calm and the other side of body would be worked. It was as if it was done in halves. At some point, energy would reach a certain level and my entire body was worked.

I am not sure if my personality is gone after that. Energy is still working strongly in my body. I was not sure if I should continue with acupressure on the toe meridians. Several times my heart jumped and stopped beating, which frightened me much. Energy works in the lungs now. I think energy is moving up to work on the brain. D-Day is near!

Energy is working in my head with fine adjustments made to the bones. The internal music is strong, as if it holds all the notes of the scale. I feel tingles here and there in my body as if something happens to the nerves. The bones are moving gently.

---

[12] This was my desire speaking here; based on a belief I was holding of the possibility of being spontaneously healed in an instant. Fused refers to full enlightenment.

Energy went up and down the spine and works in left and right shoulder with much internal rain occurring. My right shoulder is rotating and popping which feels great! The neck was worked, a vortex forms inside and there is an increase in intensity. For more than an hour, my neck rotated and was stretched to the limit on one side and then on the opposite side. There is much pulling and stretching of tissues. This is intense I have to take a break.

I have been through hours of excruciating shoulder and neck work. The left shoulder was stretched in many ways and then the left side of spine was stretched. This felt nice. Then there were neck rotations with right shoulder for about one and a half hours. My shoulder is sore. Now energy is working strongly by C7. Near the end of the shoulder work, I sighed with relief to be rid of this pain, which I feel has been with me since birth. Stopping, I see sparkling lights in the air occasionally. Now fluid is draining out of my head on right side. I cannot straighten my neck now. It is 3 a.m. and I do not want more, but I am not tired.

Acupressure Sequence To Rise Energetic Vibration

January 15: Clockwise Spin In Body, Meridian Experimentation

I continued to work on the urinary bladder and kidney meridians. Again, I felt drainage of liquids and felt the kidneys tingling. I feel a clockwise spin in my body. I have been sitting for many hours with work in the shoulder and the pain is nearly unbearable. I took a break and then worked the conception vessel and governing vessel meridians. The energy along the conception vessel meridian seems much softer than energy on the governing vessel meridian. One feels yin the other yang, it feels right to do them together. Energy worked all over the body and my sinuses drained. After this, I felt swirling along the spine and it was like all the open meridians joined force with the energy on the spine.

I think I will try these meridians because the shoulder and neck work is difficult. After doing it, it is effective but I have no relief from the pain. Maybe I can make it easier. Yeah! Now, there is an open circuit through my shoulder. Mostly I felt joint pain with much pressure. Maybe my right shoulder is dislocated or has a congenital defect? Maybe my lungs were what hurt, because I cough and the lungs feel inflamed. I have a bad headache, so will continue.

Stimulating the middle toe creates a peristaltic action in the intestines. An afterthought, perhaps the undocumented middle toe acupoint, works on pancreas and digestive regulation. I tried pressing and holding the acupoints on each toe, first the right foot, then the left foot. On the middle toe, I can detect one acupoint in the middle at base of the nail bed. All toe meridians activate the entire meridian circuit. I do not know much about the arm meridians yet. Maybe I need to do them first, because activating them might boost the energy in the body to help boost the feet. No! Doing the feet first is the DRAIN I was looking for! Toxins drain from body from top to bottom, so lower part of body that contains the elimination organs must be opened first!

If I do one toe on a foot, it activates the circuit on the other toe in the foot. I think this is ideal because it is more effective; it works a smaller quadrant of the body and is gentler. The best so far is to go from little toe to big toe, then to do the kidney acupoint on the bottom of the foot. This brings all the energy together as one force. I work the kidney acupoint as long as I want to clear blockages.

I feel the wavy right side to left side sensation in every meridian I work. I hold the same acupoints until the waving and tugging between them stops and I feel the energy has calmed down. This can take a long time. Then I move to the next acupoint. If the energy starts moving up then it is time for me to move my hands higher, otherwise it is too forceful and hurts and is not as effective. After the feet, I activate the root chakra, and then move up doing acupoints on the conception vessel meridian. After each acupoint is done, I feel an increase in my vibration. This is stronger energy and always at the correct frequency to heal the corresponding organs at that conception vessel meridian acupoint level. This is the most effective way to do it. This is fantastic! Organ healing occurs along the conception vessel meridian and the spine. I think the energy travels from front of body to back of spine, which makes this easy to do by myself from the front. The spine acupoints are difficult to reach. Maybe I can heal myself this way without getting energy from another person. As I clear blockages, my energy keeps rising and each time I am stronger. It is a snowball effect.

Rewiring Of Nervous System –Start Of 21 Day Fast

January 16

I slept long. The pump in my legs is still activated. I am coughing stuff from my lungs and blowing my nose much. My lungs hurt but with each cough, I breathe better. My right ear popped once and the inner sound is like a chamber orchestra. I am excited; I know I will have acute senses after this finishes. People and animals look different today. I "see" them. It is difficult to contain my happiness, but I must or people will think I am crazy. I will do the gallbladder meridian next because my head is still stuffed up. That was my last entry in my journal on this day.

January 16 To January 24

During this period, I had a strong reaction and stopped taking notes. Most of the following notes are recalled from memory. I was not hungry, laid up a stash of boxed pineapple juice and water to fast on, and went into isolation in my room.

Working Gallbladder Meridian

I worked a long time on the gallbladder meridian and did the Reiki acupressure sequence.[13] I recall there was another event where one meridian after another connected to the next and set off a cascade of events. I recall that an energy vortex formed at the base of the spine and went roaring up the spine into the brain. After that, the number of energy circuits made all over the body exploded into the stratosphere. I fell into this reaction and was deeply relaxed in body and mind. I think I successfully quieted my mind long enough for energy to enter my brain. When this event happened, it was as if my normal consciousness was overridden and 'I' was out of mind and was led the entire time.

Light Showering Down From Heaven

After the energy work was done in the body, I recall there was much work going on in my head for about thirty minutes. I remember seeing a view of the galaxy in my 3rd eye clearly at one time. I felt it was important to hold still while energy worked in my head. When the work stopped, I felt a rush of energy, heard internal music, and felt sprinkles of light showering down on me from heaven. Then waves of energy were showering down on me from a bright light like the sun, in descending circles (**see figure**). Then I felt a vortex form in the body and heard the sound of a windstorm. A little later, this stopped and everything was quiet and my eyes automatically

---

[13] Once I had knowledge of the body activation sequence, then I was ready to take the next step. This sequence evolved over time and the final version is on my website as Quicken Touch.

opened and were pointed to the outside **(see figure)**. Then they slowly settled to straight ahead. I did not open my eyes or do any of this. At that moment, I felt I was awake.

Body Full Of Springy Light Energy – Following The Leader

I remember after the first series of energy circuits formed when I stood my body was full of springy light energy. I felt alive as higher-self. To facilitate moving as higher-self I would raise my energetic vibration by giving myself the Reiki acupressure sequence, then would stand and allow my body to be moved. In this way, I continued the entire time, moving how I felt I was led to move, whether it was stretching, lying, or doing a long hold. At the time, I called this, "following the leader".

Tons Of Energy Pouring Out Of Hip Joints

It is difficult to move as higher-self. I do well while I am standing but when I bend and go toward the floor, I lose that feeling and it gets painful fast. In most freestyle sessions, I quickly go down to the floor and I am folded into awkward positions to open the hip joints. Many times my leg folds and I feel pressure on the hip while lying, which can go on for hours. The hips were torturous. Each time I dreaded having to stretch the hips and it would happen again. It could not be avoided.

Eventually it got easier and once, there was an amazing event. It was as if a spring was tightly coiled deep in the hip joint and a ton of energy poured out of it. Energy poured out of the hip for hours, moved over to spine and down to the tailbone. It was like a huge machine removing energy from the joint and sending it down the spine. I felt a huge vortex forming in the pelvic bowl. While this happened, my awareness rose rapidly and I no longer felt pain in the hip, but still felt extreme pressure on it. Then I clearly saw the symptom of pain is due to the healing process. Shortly after all the energy rolled out of the hips, there was an important change to the spine.

Crisscross Pattern On Spine

After the hip work finished, I remember sitting with my legs to the front and was bent over for eight hours while energy crossed back and forth across my spine in an X pattern like a tennis shoe. I thought new energy circuits formed in the spine.

Nervous System Rewiring

After the energy circuits on the spine completed, then the nervous system rewiring started. I think after this my mind blanked out and it is why I do not recall these events nor even had the thought to write them down. I guess because the brain is part of this complete overhaul, then my thinking was not so reliable. It was as if higher-self took over and I was purely following my intuition. This period was like being in a dream that went nonstop for days, where I moved my body as directed from one session to the next. Then I was taught to move my body through various positions, which helped to complete the work under way. I recall I stopped doing the Reiki acupressure sequence, because my energy was so strong I felt I did not need it.

The Sequence I Was Taught

Disoriented and not knowing what to do, I kept asking, "What should I do next?" Then I would wait to hear the answer and do that, trusting it was right. I would always stand and allow my body to move. I would often be held in a cramped position with strong energy working on various body parts. It would eventually get uncomfortable and then I would ask what to do next. In this way, I was taught a sequence of body positions to move through. I knew I had been taught a sequence after I had moved through it a few times and saw the pattern. After that, I repeated it and went through the remaining time like this.

1. Stand and allow your body to move as it will, down to squat or any poses between.[14]

2. Once on floor, sit with legs together to front and allow spine and head to lower toward the feet. When I did this, I felt energy moving down the spine and building in the pelvic bowl accompanied by an increase in sexual energy. Sink into the freefall feeling and focus on the

---

[14] Standing is the position of maximum starting energy moving along the spine. Your body will naturally fold through stretches of spine and this position activates the legs and tailbone strongly as you move down to squat position.

building sexual energy to help quiet the mind. A common result of freefall is a rising sexual energy that sometimes results in orgasm.

3. After the freefall, and when I no longer felt energy moving down my spine, I would sit with erect spine for a few minutes to change body position. Sitting straight allows energy to go up the spine.

4. Next, I slowly lowered my spine backward, to lying on my back with my head and spine straight. If a spontaneous orgasm did not result, I masturbated which brought energy from root chakra to the crown chakra. After orgasm, I would feel the sensation of fireworks in the skull as energy worked in my brain. After this, I felt energy go down my spine and felt shivers and intense cold. Then the growing phase would take over and I would relax in the lying position. In the growing phase, the long periods of numbness and stinging prickles on various body parts would happen.

Pattern Of Remaking Nervous System In Body

After the growing phase started, I would notice energy concentrated in a certain body part. Then I would feel stinging prickles, which would turn to total numbness. I experienced the stinging as very painful and tried hard to sit in center to distance from the painful sensation. This would often go on for many hours at a time before the reaction subsided. As I was in the follow the leader mode, I saw no reason to try to stop this reaction or to do anything else. I felt everything was happening as it was supposed to, so I laid there until it finished.

Body Activation Pattern

I watched the pattern of body activation before the numbness would start. First, the left leg would active, then the left arm, then the left body, and then it was as if energy of left body was used to activate the right body. Energy would then activate right leg, then right upper body would activate. When both sides of lower body were activated, I would feel a rotation in the pelvic bowl and energy would move up to chest and go back and forth between the arms. Then the energy would go down spine and into pelvic bowl and a larger vortex would build and go up spine to skull.

Programming Of The New Light Body

The numbing of a body part would go on for many hours, as I felt energy passing over that area repeatedly. I would often hear pings and different tones sounding in the brain during this process and would often go into altered states. While this numbness occurred, I had a clear image of the area morphing into a different shape. When the sensation ended, I would feel a huge rush of energy flood into the body part and felt it expand or elongate. Then I had a visual image of that body part with the new shape. I would rise and look at the part and be disappointed that nothing looked different. My intuition told me the transformation was programming a new DNA pattern into my body. It was as if instructions were laid down to complete later. The visual image of the body part was so clear, that I was certain I was physically changing appearance right then.

The numbing started in the feet and slowly moved up the body. Each time I would enter a numbness phase it would pick up where it left off last time. If the feet were numb last time, it would start there and then numbness would rise higher in the legs. Eventually the numbness reached the groin and hips. Most growing activity happened in this body area. After that, energy moved up and worked in chest and shoulders and the last time was in the arms. I do not recall this sensation occurring in the skull and face. The groin was the hardest. After a while, each part of the body was worked in one session so I would have to pass through each area repeatedly. Each successive time a body part numbed, energy flooded in stronger and the feeling the part had physically changed was stronger.

In this time, many of my beliefs were questioned and I was surprised at how many I still had and how they strongly affected my life. Some issues were similar to, 'What is God?', 'Am I God?' and 'Am I Protected?'

Legs And Heel Pain Pricks

Often pain would increase all over my body to such a crescendo I did not think I could endure it. Then I would feel pain pricks on my heel bones with an irritating frequency. I thought nerves were stimulated by my higher-self teaching me how to sit in center as the observer of pain versus identifying with it. This was a skill I needed to master.

I can remember a time when my legs were worked and it seemed they were getting consecutively longer. It felt like my heels were moving closer to the edge of the bed with each elongation. I swear I felt my legs go off the end of the bed near the end. I remember looking close to see if I was shifting my body by noting where my head was on the bed. As far as I could tell, my head was stationary and my legs were creeping off the end of the bed. The legs felt much longer. I felt the leg muscles get much larger than they are now; it seemed they were forming the size and shape of male muscles. When it was over, I would measure my height and see no change. It was all very strange.

Work In The Groin – Image Of Becoming A Man

Eventually the body numbness reached the groin and after that, each session of body numbness would spend longer working in the groin, the most dreaded part. It was difficult not to identify with the stinging prickles in the genitals. I worked hard to quiet my mind and to distance myself from pain while this area was worked. I think early on, an image popped into my mind of an erect penis, from the viewpoint of it being on my body and I was looking down at it. The image of the penis filled my frame of view. Then there was a flash and change of perspective and I saw a man sitting with the same erect penis. I recall he had shoulder length blonde hair and no facial hair. I was perplexed why this image flashed and what it meant. After this image, changes to the sexual organs started. Later I thought the image told me I was going to turn into a man. This was my belief and effected my interpretation of the transformation for a long time.

Going OBE Into Ceiling With Images Of Faces & Geometric Patterns

I think after there was work in the groin area, energy would move up the spine and would work in the brain. Because the groin symptoms were painful, I worked intensely to go to that space outside my body so I would not feel anything. I was often in altered states of consciousness during this stage.

I can recall how I went out of body. The numbness would start in the feet and as it rose higher, pain increased and skyrocketed when it hit the genitals. I knew this was coming, so I was preparing for it by working hard to focus on a spot of light with my 3rd eye so I could distance myself from the pain and get through it. The pain would be increasing and I would focus harder. I remember the first signs I went into altered states would be amplified hearing like being in an echo chamber. Next, I saw images of faces or a geometric pattern all over my internal field of view, like a ceiling above me. Then I would be traveling up and through that maze of faces, going through the ceiling to another side. After passing through the ceiling, I felt I was in a space that was devoid of all feeling, time and space. I felt so far away, yet could still sense my body was way down there with work occurring in it. Once I was up there, I was safe and did not have to focus anymore. I knew with a simple decision I could return. That spot became my refuge. However, I could not always escape; sometimes I had to be in my body for various stages that took me to my limit.

Balls Of Energy Move Down Inguinal Canals

A repeating sequence happened and worked in the groin and genitals. After the stinging prickles, large strong energy balls went down the inguinal canals[15] starting at the ovary position and slowly moved down toward the groin. This was one of the hardest things; it was extremely painful as that energy ball moved down. It was most intense at intersection of pelvic floor and inner thigh. Often my hip would be held open at an angle and I would feel intense energy pummeling at that intersection. It was much like giving birth. Often there were strong spontaneous pushes that seemed to have the purpose to move this ball down through the canal. At the time, I thought my ovary was moving down, turning in to a testicle, and making a tract for the testes to descend. I thought a testicle might pop out any minute. I would go through these strong pushes having no idea why I was doing them and feeling I was surely crazy. Then I could see no physical change from doing it. The energy ball moved further down each time. I recall this first happened in the left side and later in the right side.

Making Of New Genitals

I think after the inguinal canals completed, the next stage started and was mostly energetic and out of this world. I guess it was a nervous system reaction and what occurred is highly subject to interpretation. I presume new DNA instructions were programmed in my body. I remember feeling drops of liquid running down through my body. They were like thick drops of honey in a narrow tube, coming one after the other in circuits, which were all over my body. All these drops were coming down through the body and landing in the genitals, especially by ovaries and inguinal canals. Later I wondered if it was a large release of hormones. I felt this sensation many times in repeated episodes. It was strange and something I never felt again.

---

[15] The energy balls may have actually been moving down a different area, perhaps to open the hip girdle.

Light Beams Full Of Souls From Heaven

Then I remember many sparks all over the body and feeling narrow beams of light shining on me from above. Simultaneously, I felt I was receiving messages and blessings from The Creator. The light was focused on both areas where testicles would be in a man, and it felt like thousands of souls were entering my body the entire time light shined on that area. It seemed the light streamed for hours, and I had the feeling each soul was blessed by The Creator.

Sensation Of Penis & Testicles Growing & Morphing Into Man

After this, each time the groin went numb, it felt like a penis was growing and testicles were forming in the groin. Each time this was more distinctive. While energy worked in the genitals, I felt changes happening to the breasts. The breasts felt like they were shrinking and breast tissue was pulled down the body and used to build new genitals. I felt the chest get larger each time, with decreased breast size. I distinctly felt how it was to be in a man's body with a large chest. In addition, the lengthening and expanding sensation was progressively stronger in all body parts. I had the sensation of huge legs with thick muscular quadriceps and calves, large hands and narrowing hips. With each successive pass as the penis and testicles grew, it felt more like being in the body of a man.

Numb Arms & Pinned To Bed – Taking Control

The arms were hard and the last area that was done. I was lying in my bed and as I rested, the arms grew numb with the stinging prickles. It hurt much and I did not want to continue but I did. At the time, I thought the transformation going on all over my body was growing new bones. The arms hurt more than anything that had gone before. It lasted many hours and then I needed to go to the bathroom. However, I could not move my arms or shoulders. I was surprised to discover I could not raise myself if my arms would not move while lying on my back. I was effectively pinned to the bed. I was cold, nighttime had arrived, and I had no fire in the room. I could not get the covers over me. I was thirsty and could not reach my drink. I needed to blow my nose and could not do it. Like all the previous sessions, I thought I was supposed to stay unmoving until it finished. I was waiting for it to stop.

The hours grew and I struggled with this problem all night and part of the next day. In my mind, I kept hearing the message pounding out to me, "Surrender, surrender, surrender". I was desperate. Nobody could enter my room. I have a strong door and it was locked. In addition, I did not want anyone to see me like this so calling for help was not an option. Then a notion arose, that I always had had the power to rise. I only had to focus on what I wanted and it would happen. I needed to take control. With all my intensity I focused, it worked, and I rocketed out of the bed dangling my numb arms behind me. It only took a few minutes for the numb arms to return to a normal feeling. This might sound trite reading this or even that I was insane, but I believe it was a lesson taught me to learn how to focus and realize an increasing power. When I arose, I inspected my arms and saw peculiar gray indentations like channels running down my arms. I suspected nerves were stimulated. I felt this episode was about my higher-self teaching me how to surrender and take control. I saw it in an instant right after I leaped out of bed. I laughed to see it with a new perspective.

Chapter 10: Tension Release From Joints, C7 Opens

Organ Cleanses

January 25: Coming Out Of Retreat, Fasting & Organ Cleanse

I was nearly dead. I ended my retreat and exited my room. When I got outside, I realized how sick I was. My left kidney hurt. I felt as if I had to vomit for two days. The last two days I had nothing to eat or drink save a few drops of milk. I had the vomit sensation and I could not eat today. My large intestine was full of hard round balls of matter, which I could palpate from the outside.[16] It was like a row going down the entire intestinal tract! Earlier, the toes on my left feet were numb and some on my right. I thought it was because it was cold outside but after my walk, the numbness was still there. Once I had a fire in my room then I activated my body by pressing acupoints. My body was shutting down and my energy was so low. I decided I needed to continue fasting until all these toxins were out of my body.

The acupressure quickly rose my energy, my feet warmed and I did an enema and moved some hard balls. In the middle of this, my body activated strongly and my body expelled more enema material spontaneously. This alone was a meditation. After this, I stood and allowed the forces in my body to take over. There was a long session of learning how to move with the new capacities of the changed nervous system

Sitting, I watched the path of energy movement inside working through the digestive system. First peristaltic waves were happening in the large intestines, and then energy moved from here into my gallbladder, next energy moved to liver and went up body and came across the shoulder and went down the esophagus and into the stomach. From here, it traveled over to small intestine where it worked all over it. Then energy would go to large intestine and continue moving in this big loop. Later energy pounded hard on the gallbladder and liver and I felt gases forming in the small intestine. Then I started passing gas and belched. I feel like vomiting. I still have the balls in my intestine.

In the evening I did several sessions where there was long hours of work on C7, I could distance myself from pain and time passed quickly. Much neuron growth happens around the joint. I was tired from sitting and soon after I lied down, there was a sudden

---

[16] I had not had a bowel movement in about nine days; I was not paying attention at all to things like that.

buildup of force on the joint, and I heard a SNAP in C7. After it snapped energy rushed into my head, soon came back down, and started working on spine again. After the work in the spine finished, the inner sound was like a storm with strong winds. Then it felt like billions of neurons were making connections in my body in a patterned sequence. I watched the energy coursing around in my body for about an hour. It felt like my entire body was coming alive with a warm and tingly feeling. I fell asleep getting the best energy massage I have ever had.

C7 Opens, Billions Of Neural Connections, Spine Helix Forms

January 26: Tornado Vortex

At 1:30 am, I suddenly awakened and a few seconds later, I felt a whoosh! Internally I could detect an energy vortex rising into my head and it closed with a loud sucking sound of wind. Then I felt strong work occurring in the intestinal area and kidney. The energy feels different, like it is not limited to the paths of the energy meridians anymore. It is like waves of energy prickles moving up and down and massaging my body. It feels very good.

I think I was very sick a few days ago. I remember I was feeling my heart jump and it felt like it had stopped. This happened about every thirty minutes yesterday.[17] My kidney still hurts and energy is working on that area. Everything in my body is cleansed with these waves of energy. It makes me feel sleepy.

Around 6 am, I woke and energy is still working, the kidney pain is gone. Energy is working in the intestines. My stomach feels fine, the small intestine has shrunk and I am not so bloated. Since the cleaning started on the intestines, I have been belching strongly. I think this is due to the gallbladder working and gases moving out of my intestinal tract.

The energy waves in my body start to spiral. As I view it from the inside, it is counterclockwise. They are waves that come from two angles; it is like a double

---

[17] Later, I experienced more episodes of the heart stopping and jumping, and think it is a symptom of healing, it was not an indication I was sick. In this phase, all the organs are being healed.

helix creating a crisscross spiral on the spine (**see figures**). This spiral pattern differs from what has happened before; it makes connections in the body in many directions. Before there were energy circuits connecting the vertebrae in the spine to other joints, such as C7 to shoulders, etc. These connections seem to give the capability for each vertebra to move spontaneously. The neck and tailbone can energetically rotate creating an energy vortex that goes up and down the spine. Before this, energy went up in a singular line on either side of the spine. One line went up and one down.

I feel sleepy, and then notice the energy moves to my head, the internal music stops and all is quiet. I hear outside sounds with amplified hearing, as if roosters are all over the valley. As the skull work begins, there is an acceleration of tingling in other body parts. There was work for hours on C7, inside brain, and making energy circuits from spine to body. During this time, I worked to quiet my mind. I did not have much pain, mostly I am tired. Around noon, this process finished and I felt I was supposed to surrender somehow. I tried various things but nothing worked, I need a break.

From 6 pm to 1:30 am, there was a long healing session along the cord of personality. I started with a freestyle session because my intestines were still blocked. I had one bowel movement but felt it was not enough so I did an enema. Then I saw how plugged the gallbladder meridian still was. I did another enema and much material came out. As the gallbladder meridian opened then my energy rose strong. I did another long freestyle session after this. Then I was tired and when I arose, I grabbed the ladder to bend over and stretch my shoulders without thinking about it. Then I realized I had never done the shoulders and knew they held much tension.

Tension Release From Shoulder

It was curious after all this work on the joints, that I still had the same problems in my body, albeit everything was better. Many times, I thought I had fixed them, yet later I worked on them again. Therefore, I did not want to do the shoulder but it was a new position. I had never tried standing with my arms forward leaning on the ladder to support me. Okay. I started with it and saw how much tension was coiled in the shoulder joint. I stood there about three hours with energy coursing through the shoulder and releasing tons of tension energy. When I got to the end of that large release, it was a relief I cannot tell you. However, quickly I saw this was not the end. I was then led on a long stretching path through my body. I stretched down the back, to the spine, to the hip, back up, to the shoulder for a few more releases, up to my jaws, down my neck, back to the shoulder, then to my spine, up and down the spine, across the back, back to shoulder and ending at the C7 vertebrae.

As I went down through these coiling stretches, I felt strong pain mostly under the right scapulae bone and energy that released from the shoulder was amazing! I was amazed at how much there was. It felt like an endless release of energy from the joint, like a river of water flowing out and returning to the root chakra. As tension energy released, I felt searing hot pain and pleasure simultaneously. I felt I had found the root of my problem and endured to the end wanting all this pain to be released.

When that was done, I did a freestyle session and it was unbelievable how many pops and cracks happened in the body. The pops and cracks did not seem to release tension energy. The stretching passes through the body are repeating. I kept moving my right hip joint to a new position with intense pain, but it keeps going back to the old position. It is the same with my jaw joints, with the gallbladder and the knotted shoulder. With the gallbladder meridian running through the shoulder then it would always plug again. This explains for me my recurring sinus and ear problems for years.

I think it is important to keep going with this healing until all the pain is released and everything is healed. I am guessing there are many layers of healing to go through before you can release all the energy of this cord. The big muscle knots are still there around the shoulders, on the back and along the sides of C7. When I put my finger on the sore area near them, they dissolve. I feel the meridians opening when I do this. I am wondering how to release this cord. Perhaps the root of the cord of personality is a childhood injury or trauma. What is clear is that this cord of personality is what keeps me identified with my material aspect of self. The energy in the body cannot rise through C7 to heal and open this area. Many people have crunchy sounds and cracks when they move the C7 joint. I see this joint as the gateway to the head and the link to the lower body.

After energy work on the spine, it felt like my neck was freely rotating in a physical full circle! People tell you not to bend your head backward in exercise, maybe because of the C7 limitation. I feel this part is not finished. I have spent many hours trying to surrender and it does NO good. I have to let go of identifying with the pain. I did a quick stretch and my upper body feels free! The shoulders rotate. It looks like the right hip still needs some work. Manana, I am tired.

Tension Releasing From Joints

January 27: Vortex Rises Into Head

It is 4 am, and I cannot sleep. I am skyrocketing because the energy is moving so fast. One-half billion more neuron connections are forming. My face is tingling and my ear opened. I feel getting through C7 was significant. There is a vortex in my neck going up into my head. I feel when it reaches the brain I will be whole and will have no need for this mental surrender crap. You surrender enough by going through the pain. Your reward equals more energy. In short, when you let go of pain it transmutes to energy. You free the block. The personality exists as energy held in a fixed form in the body. When you find it and let go of the pain then you are free.

I slept well feeling refreshed after a few hours. My body is still in a growing phase with the energy massage feeling, which I think is neuron growth. The body feels great; it is difficult to describe how good it is to have a relaxed posture.

I just did one and a half hours of stretches that went for miles all over the body. Tension energy is pouring from joints and muscle knots. My energy is getting strong. I feel springy in my body. I want to stretch out the rest to be free of this pain. Later the work got difficult and there was stretching work in the jaw joints and going down to open the hip. Still, I am happy to feel my body this way; it is SO ALIVE and flexible. In the last stretch, my neck circled around five times and I could hear small cracks in my spine.

At 2 pm, I did a freestyle session and it feels great with no pain. I can move in two or three directions at once so it goes fast. There is a tight vein or muscle down the inside back of my legs. I just moved freestyle for another twenty minutes. Wow, it was intense and fast! There is much pain in the right hip. The joints that released all that tension now rotate energetically.

At 3 pm, I was so tired that I went to lie down and immediately I fell asleep. I woke with another vortex rush in the head and my body position was like a mummy with ankles crossed and arms folded across my chest. Then I felt energy sweeping down my body and next it felt like it was rebuilding the bones in my feet and ankles. It was so painful, I wanted it to finish and rise. I tried to move and I was numb and felt I was stuck there. Then I was thinking a sustained surrender for full metamorphosis might be next. The feeling of being a larva in a cocoon was strong. Then, I said, Okay, but not now. I shook it off and arose.

At 8 pm, I did an enema and more stretching, many more miles of tension released from hip, back, shoulder and jaws. My intestines are still sluggish, so I am going to do a fast on liquids until this clears up. At 10 pm, I was stretching and doing more cleansing; my intestines are blocked and need to be cleared.

Insight about caricature of personality: I asked a friend to show me how another person reacts when angry. My friend has an uncanny ability to mimic people. She closed her eyes, then her body formed into the exact picture of this person with their right arm raised and finger pointing and their elbow turned in with their back arched. In this demonstration, I saw clearly the physical pain profile of the cord of the personality. Then I asked my friend to show her posture and she gave me another exact cord of personality profile. All our life we habitually express our defensive postures in our face and body, and over time it accumulates tension along that posture line from contraction of the muscle groups used. From the body shape of the 'anger posture', you can find the beginning and end of the energetic cord of the personality. The cord of personality appears to follow the defensive body posture and always goes in a line through the main joints connected directly to the central nervous system, which has a special link at the C7 vertebrae. If a person were enlightened there would be no cord of personality, all energy would be balanced all over the body. I predict the majority of held tension energy exists on the side of the body the person uses most, re left or right-handed and that that side will tend to get more injuries because it is less resilient.

Bodily Reliving Childhood Trauma

January 28: Tension Release From Paired Joints, More Cleansing

At 1 am, I did a freestyle session and there was hip and shoulder work. I get a better idea of what it means to allow my body to move spontaneously from the charged muscles. I have not been doing that. I will rest and let the energy build and try to go through the hip again, trying to stay focused on feeling the energy. This room is too small for this workout; I need a big area full of padded mats. Tomorrow I will try to find another location.

At 2 am, I worked effectively on the hip and shoulder and most tension is gone. The joints are somehow malfunctioning as a pair, and had to be worked together at the end. Near the end, there was a continuous torrent of energy releasing in both joints for about two hours. At 3:30 am, I went to bed.

From 8 am to 2 pm, I relived a childhood trauma that was intense. My body was moving spontaneously, widely jerking around for hours on end and as it did, memories of the trauma came into my mind and it was as if I was living it again. I went through the same scenario physically many times and it provoked the pain that happened then. I was crying much. I never knew I had this experience until today. Once I tried to rise and was pushed to the ground. I felt I was being squished during this process. Near the beginning of replaying my trauma, I observed injuries that happened long ago to places I currently have problems. I cried because it hurt badly.[18]

The replaying of the trauma lasted hours. At the end, my body was like a rag doll, but through this, I learned how to relax and sit in the center and allow the violent jerking body movements. While sitting in the center as the observer, there was no pain. I still feel sad, but the energy is massaging me and I am resting. I am sure I will feel better soon. I hope this is over; I do not want to go through anything like that again. Perhaps there is still something repressed that waits to be replayed. I do not think it is all unrolled yet. It surprised me that the cord of personality would have the trauma in it. I guess I needed to be energetically strong enough to heal the memory. I suspect to transform all energy of the personality one has to go back to the baby and probably fetus, so probably there is more of this left to do. Meanwhile, I will build my strength to make it easier to release it.

I took a nap and arose because I felt much pain in my ankles, feet and lower legs. Now it is not bad. The energy worked on the abdomen and I had a dream about gallstones. Sitting, my chest is expanding out.

---

[18] I believe this was emotional cleansing of the body and was related to various traumas recorded in the tissues.

Second Spontaneous Liver And Gallbladder Flush

It is 3:30 pm, and I finished another enema and tons of stones are coming out. I will continue this until it is clear. At last count, there were sixty large liver stones ½" wide in diameter. At 6 pm, my digestion is working so perhaps the gallbladder is clear. When I sat, I felt a chill followed by the internal rain symptom. Great, because I do not want to stretch. My hip is sore with some swelling and my right forearm is sore. At 7 pm, many more stones came out. The intestinal action gets strong. I feel a block between the liver and the gallbladder. I feel a hard lump. Therefore, I will keep going. One stone was hard like a crystal and was around ¼" in diameter.

From 8 pm to 1am, I will get long-distance Reiki empowerment at 8:30. My hip is still blocked and I cannot clear the gallbladder meridian. I did a little stretching and exhausted went to bed. While sitting I was sleepy and higher-self was taking over. That would be a gift.

January 29: Feeling Springy, Cracks In Spine

When I arose at 6 am, I had a springy feeling all over the body, which I still feel. From 7:30 to 8:45 am, there has been much work in the head. Doing the freestyle session, I feel alive and tension knots release. There were many cracks in the spine and many loud cracks and pops in the back and neck. At 10:45 am, I lay down and the energy sped up. I feel stinging prickles here and there but it does not hurt badly. My mind is relaxed. In the afternoon, more of the same goes on, only stronger. From 1 to 6 pm, I did several stretching sessions with difficult work in the hips. Ouch!

January 30: Organ Cleanse Continues

There has been much work in the right hip; it seems it is mostly done. At 8:30 pm, the hip, shoulder and neck tension released. I have fasted three days on pineapple juice and I have done water enemas, stimulating the gallbladder and liver meridians with Reiki and doing a stretch between. This works good, I passed around one cup more of large stones, a few of them at least ¾" in diameter. I just did the oil and grapefruit liver cleanse protocol to provoke the bile release to see if it helps clear the gallbladder. At 9:30 pm, the green liquid of bile passes. I do not see any more large stones, only small ones. I hope all is cleared now. I think all the digestive organs are cleansing. I am going to sleep.

January 31: More Gallstones & Liver Stones

At 1:30 am, I woke with belching and did another enema. At 3 am, there were more large and hard brown liver stones and the bright green small stones from the gallbladder. At 3:30 am, the meridians are opening. At 6 am, I did Reiki on several meridians and worked a long time on C7. The digestive system seems calm for now.

There was much work on C7 with large releases of tension. There is no pain, I surrender and let myself be stretched. Problems are tension in neck from base of skull to shoulder. There is still a big knot in my trapezious muscle and I have pain in my entire arm from forearm up to shoulder. At 8:45 pm, there were many crunching sounds in the shoulder joint. The bicep muscle of the left arm is sore. The ligaments in the legs feel tight. I did another enema and many more green gallstones and monster liver stones came out at the beginning. Each time it is clearer, I will keep going until it is clear. I ate some rice and an artichoke. The food sits okay so far but I do not want to eat much until the liver is clear. I had a dream about a problem in the pectoral muscle on the chest. I think that is true. All the tension is around this area. The other dream was to take rosemary tea. I will try that as I am getting tired of pineapple juice.

February 1: Release In C7, Energy Vortex From Skull To Tailbone

At 12:30 pm, C7 released and energy can now move it in another direction. This should result in more power to help open the rest of the body. I woke at 3 am, with an energy vortex going from my head to my tailbone. A little later, I leaned forward with my head relaxed and healing is occurring in the body in all places at once. My arm relaxes and the gallbladder meridian clears. It is somewhat intense but welcome!

From 4:30 to 7 am, I think the work in C7 is done.[19] I hope I do not have to do that stretch through the hips again. It took hours. There is rapid energy work occurring all over the body. At 9:30 pm, the energy is high and there is work on the bones and ligaments that hurts if I identify with it. I am sweating profusely. At midnight, the intense stuff has passed but I am still hot.

February 2: Looking For Easier Way

---

[19] Years later, there is still work in C7.

From 2 to 4:30 am, I have been stretching. The tension is gone from spine and is now in the shoulder. Energy worked in hips and shoulders. I am exhausted and need to sleep.

From 10:30 to 11:30 am, I did one long stretch through the hips. It was difficult to do but what a relief. Much tension released from the hips, lower back and shoulders.

I am exhausted; its 6 pm and I was outside working for hours. My energy is low for physical work. Earlier, I sat and cried while the tension poured out of my neck and shoulders. I feel as if I want to die, because it seems impossible to release this coil of tension.

At 8 pm, I will seriously try to let go of body control. I can follow a sprinkle energy path when I have no resistance in mind or body. It is like finding the path in the dark. When I am on this path of following, I feel no pain and gain energy instead of getting tired. By trying to force the tension out of my body, I tire myself and it has little effect. With twenty minutes of doing this I feel great! 9:30 pm, Great, but it is a little tiring as I am not perfect at following and the tension is real.

Insight about easier way is following: The way through this is to unite with the higher-self, done with a complete surrender of mind and body. I need to follow the bliss feeling and I will be led through the pain. I need to get better at surrendering the body.

February 3: Increased Body Heat, Dying Would Be Easier

It is 12:45 am, and I cannot sleep. The heat is intense and the energy is active. Then there is my anticipation, I do not want to miss anything. I am surprised this much time has gone by. Old traumas and memories of times when I had stress and conflict in my life surface when the heat is high.

I was interrupted all day with outside work. In the middle of the day, I did an awesome stretch through my body. Afterward at 7:30 pm, I was brought to the position that I knew was one of my early traumas. I was lying with all my joints smashing into the ground, for about twenty minutes. Then I cried and got angry and arose and forced myself through all the pain, wanting more of it so I could let it all out. I went way beyond myself for hours with much crying and pain. Then it was late and there was not enough time to rest afterward, as I had other work to do. Finally, I got back to my room and I am still crying and tired. I feel ill and sore all over and the internal music plays strong inside. I feel alone and at the end of my rope. I do not want any more treatments or stretching. I feel like dying, it is close to that. My ear is still plugged up. I feel as if I am between two worlds. Higher-self wants to be, yet I resist feeling I prefer my pity-party or something like that. I will rest and see what is next.

Loud Neck Cracks & Release At C7

February 4

Much tension was released from the neck and I am sleeping much lately. While I slept, it seemed my body was repaired. I started using Reiki and the coil ring again. These tools helped me to clear two meridians, the small intestine meridian across the shoulder and the gallbladder in the shoulder section. Using Reiki on these seemed to boost the capability to move energy through the neck. Last night I had the idea to apply Reiki to acupoints near my ears on small intestine meridian, by cheek and ears. This worked well to move energy in reverse through C7 downward to loosen my shoulder.

After this, I could stretch my neck turning into my shoulder and up to free the tension on both sides of C7. I had passed through work in C7 in front and back and did not realize the sides were left. After this, the shoulder released through the neck. Then the C7 vertebra cracked with a loud noise. There was no pain, only a huge relief. After this the neck near the base of the skull felt free, then stretches were easy with loud crunching and popping noises in upper spine with much tension releasing. At the end, the neck felt free. After this, the stretch went down the spine and cleared things down the middle of the back. Exhausted after this, I slept long.

Pressure Both Sides Of Neck, Stretches & Sudden Collapse

February 5: 21st Day Of Fasting, Difficult Work

Lately, there have been unbelievable stretches through the back, shoulders, hips, legs and arms. Each time after the stretch, I sit on the floor with legs to front and lean forward relaxed. In this position, energy moves down the spine, as if it is working in reverse bringing energy down from skull into the pelvic bowl. At a certain point I automatically sit upright, all sense of tension disappears, and it feels as if I am gently floating as energy moves up for the next round. I went through many repetitions of stretches before I understood how to complete the process. I was usually so tired after a session that I often skipped this other step. One stretch forward and one stretch sitting upright.

When I arose at 6 am, I did a standing stretch where work happened in spine down through the hips and lower back. It was difficult, but once done then my hips started rotating energetically and I felt energy flooding into my body. I went back to bed from 10 am to 2 pm.

I have been doing chores. The growing phase continues strong. I am hot. Energy works in spine behind neck and moves up into skull. I will see what I can do to assist this, but still am tired. Perhaps I am tired because this is difficult physical work and because this is the twenty-first day of fasting for me. I have eaten only two days in all this time. I think I weigh around a hundred pounds, which is light for me. The pain seems mostly behind me so that feels good, but I am left wondering what is next. My mind seems quieter. I will check if the personality is still there.[20]

At 6 pm, I did a three-hour session in the dome, lying on my stomach with intense pain until it dissolved. I am shaking and tired. I still feel much pain. I want to cry. From 6:30 to 7:30 pm, I did another stretch, with concentrated work in the hips. I cried much from the pain.

After this, I went to bed because there was a reaction of a gentle neck stretch and I needed to go backward. It resulted in one hour of sitting upright with intense pressure on both sides of my neck with my head and spine stretched to the limit. I was holding that awkward position until the tension gave. Then my spine and neck collapsed with much force and it went as low as possible on both sides. This was all painful. Then I was back to sitting in upright spine position for more stretches. Finally, I lay down and I did not want to move and had strong pain in the neck. Soon after, the energetic vibration patterns started in the body with neuron growth all over, and I fell asleep.

February 6 To February 7: Repeated Passes Stretch Joints

A new day dawns, its 12:30 am and energetic work is still occurring in my shoulders and skull. At first, I could not rise because I was frozen from numbness. I feel sad and am tired of this. I need to participate in the work around here tomorrow and the transformation is not finished. I have no clear idea what will come next and that bothers me. There is much

---

[20] Hahaha

stretching and healing work seemingly to get these knots out, yet I still have all the same problems. It looks like all this work is focused on building a new spine. Perhaps I will unfold when that is complete. The ear seems clear on the right and the gallbladder and liver meridians remain opens. I hope I finish with all this cleansing soon.

At 3:30 a.m., it seems a bone correcting stage. Energy work started at toes with pain in big toe and moved up to pelvis with pain in hips, back of hips and sacrum. I wonder if it is easier to take this sitting and if it is still effective to do in this position. Lying is difficult to do now.

From 8 am to 4:30 pm: In the morning I did a freestyle session, I was moving easily until the work was in my hips and lower body, then I lost it. I sat discouraged and decided: "NO! I'm angry about this hip and I will do it as best as I can!" Therefore, I did, I think I got through it okay. Later in the day, I did a standing session in an unbelievable posture. I went out of body and surrendered, as there was much pain. I was determined to surrender and I think I did well. Afterward a big force rose and I cried to feel it, but still this was not the end as stretching continued. I feel I surrendered, yet the personality is still here. Much work was done in the skull and something was starting in the legs when I stopped. I did sessions continuously the entire time.

Its 6:30 pm and it has been another exhausting day, stretching through hip joints, lower back and on up to C7 and neck. I cried much this morning; it seems impossible to get through the hips and shoulders. It is all twisted together somehow through the lower back and upper neck. I presume each time I am stronger and there will be less to do. I feel desperate. Surrender, yes, I do it for hours on end in these endless stretches pushing against my neck, hips, back, etc. I do not want any more!

At 11pm, I felt higher-self take over or I allowed it about two hours. Then I was lying on the floor with my hip against the ground and tension was pouring out of my body, but I only felt pleasure as energy released. I laid there for an hour, then arose and went to bed.

February 7: I Quit

I slept through until 8 am, with much healing occurring in my body during the night. I remembered the insight that 'I don't need to do anything'. This makes all this 'work' I have been doing seem as if I have been in a big head-trip. So then, I sat and surrendered and I thought I did well for two hours until I found myself in the head between the knees position in the chair. This hurts much in the hips and legs. I stopped after thirty minutes, as I could not bear more pain. It has been twenty-three days and I quit and will not do more sessions. I will go outside tomorrow and live normal and forget this. That is how I feel now, that none of this is real. The forest is real, my dog is real, and the outside work is real. I want the normal world. If something happens tonight, okay, but I am not staying in isolation in this room anymore. I am at the end of my rope and do not see that I can do more. I feel the energy strong inside me, but it is like in the background and my head sits in another world distant from it. Tonight I will try to allow this energy to be; otherwise, my practice is to surrender.

Neck Cracks, Spine Vortex Forms

February 8

I slept many hours until 10 am. I felt energetic work occurring in the body all night. There were many cleansing dreams. I did a few hours stretching but stopped at the hips. I went outside, did some work, and went for a walk in the forest with my dog. There in the field with the sun I had a good stretch through my body. I lay on the ground for about thirty minutes. Later while walking I had an idea about how to loosen my shoulders. With anger and strong determination, I worked them and knew I had loosened them much. Much later in the day when I sat then I was taken over by higher-self and soon put into this sideways stretch on my neck and shoulders feeling pressure in all the bad parts in hip, shoulder, neck and jaws. I held that position for two hours watching as tension continuously released, like it was rolling out all along the cord of personality path.

From 6 to 11 pm, I continue with the transformation. I have to let go of body control, as there is no other way. I get desperate for relief from the tension and surrender is the only thing that works. Energy is working at C7. Near the end, there was a loud crack in the neck, then some movement in my shoulder and I felt energetic power assist me to rise. Then I felt freefall, but it did not last long. I did an hour-long hold in a bent over position with painful tension, as all the joints were worked rapidly. I arose and took a break even knowing how near this is.[21] It is 11 pm and I rest, and while sitting upright there was a strong snap in the neck, the strongest so far.

---

[21] I believed I only had to release one more joint or muscle and there would be instant transformation.

February 9: Skull Drainage, Skull Energy Circuits, Skull Pressure

I slept long and did sessions all day. The neck breaking feeling happened three more times. Always I am trying my best to surrender, always there is more to do and what I want does not happen. The energy inside is strong but I cannot be it, I tried hard to allow spontaneous body movements. At first, it went good but eventually I lost it.[22]

I boosted the energy in my body with Reiki on the root chakra. Afterward my energy seemed much stronger. Later I felt much despair; I do not know what else to do when even my attempt to surrender does not work. I cried much yesterday and today too.

At 4 pm, when I sat after a session in the forest I felt strong energy working in the skull and felt liquid coming down. Then I felt strong pressure at base of skull with many neuron connections made there. Then I was forced to stretch my neck strong in two directions, first to one side, then the other. I think this was done to make an energy circuit. Then energy went down the spine, between my legs, to hips and feet. I felt like all the body tension was taken away. I cried not believing it was true. After this, energy built in pelvic bowl, went up spine and more energy circuits formed. I felt a spiral of energy go down from my head, circling my body along the spine. That was the first time I felt this.

After this, I felt strong energy in the genitals and wonder what changes are made to them. Lately I feel certain about nothing and see I lack trust. At times, I feel split, feeling that my higher-self is luring me with these nice feelings of bliss then I am sitting for hours doing these painful stretches. Yet, I notice progress in the spine and the energy keeps getting stronger. My skull is ready to split open there is pressure all over. I stretched before sleep. There is high sexual energy and a strong growing reaction in the body.

Energy Ball At Base Of Skull, Opening Cervical Spine

February 10: Ear Popping, Skull Tingling, Cascade Of Energy

I slept in until 10 am. I wonder much about the changes going on, and fantasize about transforming into a new body. I have no idea what is possible and what comes from my imagination. I was strong while doing the freestyle session and stayed surrendered while

---

[22] At this stage, many nervous connections are made in rest phase. As connections are made, there is increased capability for spontaneous body movements. When I say, "I lost it above", I was too critical; this capability to stay as one with the body movement slowly increases.

stretching through the hips. Eventually I lost this feeling while lying on the floor with back pain and tension releasing from the hip. I think I often make the mistake of holding a position, uncomfortable and enduring more pain than is necessary. I feel like a failure when I have to stop. This time I decided to rise and do a freestyle session and that worked to release tension in the upper neck.

There was much work in the neck, which released much tension with many cracks, pops and crunches. It is incredibly difficult requiring centering or it hurts. There is still much tension on the side of the neck and at the base of the skull. My head feels ready to explode. There is a funny feeling ball[23] at the base of my skull for the last few days and now it is strong. My ear opened with many big pops. There was much tingling in the head and the body energy grows as the skull opens. After strong tingling, I was cold with shivers as energy coursed down. I hear pings and feels muscle twitches here and there going down the spine.

After getting through work in the upper most neck vertebrae, an awesome strength pulls my body exactly where I need to go. The urge to stretch does not settle down. I had to stop after a long session twisting down from base of skull to tailbone. After that, there was another stretch up and another strange one with shoulders hunched the entire time while holding that energy ball at the base of the skull in position.

Next, I stretched down through all the same things again. However, this time there was an intense burning feeling along the path of stretch. I had to follow perfectly or I would lose the energy ball and it would hurt badly, I knew that somehow. I went like this with searing pain for maybe an hour and then had to stop. When I stood, I felt tingling, and stretched slowly down all the way through the legs to the floor with the sensation of freefall. I stood and felt cascades of energy falling through my body. I am resting, I am physically drained but I want to continue. From 8:30 to 10:45 pm, I did a stretch and ended in a position where I felt I needed to surrender. I gave up after a valiant try. It was difficult. I tried to surrender three more times and failed.

I feel better knowing how to respond to the stretch reaction. I do not have to tolerate any more excruciating painful positions. If it hurts, I can try another position or stop and rest if I feel I need it. The transformation will pick up where I need to be next time; it seems obvious now. I cried feeling like a failure that I cannot surrender fully. This has more to do

---

[23] This is an energy ball

with my expectation than what it means to surrender. Higher-self has been taking over often. I think I am not strong enough to do it yet. I have enough energy to go as far as I can. Each session of releasing tension gives me more strength. Finally, I see that. Surrender is the act of allowing the transformation, and while the fire of transformation is happening, it feels painful. I think when all the pain is gone then I will be enlightened. As far as I can tell, my awareness rises as I convert the old energy body to the new light body. All these endless stretches along the cord of personality finally make sense. All this time I have been converting energy held in from to higher awareness. I have two days left of my retreat and hope this will finish by then. Wish me speed.[24]

---

[24] I was fixating on releasing the 'cord of personality', which I thought could happen any moment. This is not how it works. The truth is that the stretching movements themselves are doing the work, and there is much more to go.

Chapter 11: Physical Death, 4th Dark Night – Surrender

Chest Expansion Cycle, 1st Cranial Suture Crack, Right Spine Opens

February 11: Energy Swirl Up Spine, Energy Ball Down Right Spine

It is 1am, and I am afraid I will die, that is it. When the energy moves up and goes into my chest, it expands and I feel I cannot breathe. It feels like death. I panic thinking I will die and lose it. I will look at it and try again.

It is 9:30 am and I slept lightly. I felt a large vortex form in the root chakra and then with a big swirl it went up and out my crown chakra. Later I felt the growing reaction, this time only in the left leg. Next, I felt much pain like menstrual cramps in my lower back and abdomen. I tried to surrender. I did better. Higher-self took over more and energy moved up through chest, lungs, and throat and partially into the head. The last effort went well as I was much calmer. Then the reaction stopped. Perhaps each effort, builds on the previous one and I get stronger each time. I must stop thinking, as the failure feeling is heavy. Sitting, there is strong swirling energy in the buttocks. It is difficult to relax.

It is 11:15 am, and my friend will do my work today, so I can relax. I hope this is not a head-trip and something concrete happens today. This is my last day of retreat and I want my Sunday free to enjoy the outside. The marching music is strong and the energy swirls in the tailbone all morning. I will sit quietly and see what is next.

It is 2:10 pm, and I have been lying for three hours going through the chest expansion cycle. The cycle: I hear pings and the inner sound of marching music and feel wave-like sensations going though my body changing tissues. This is like the freefall feeling, it relaxes me and quickly my thoughts settle down. While relaxed, energy increases and my chest expands, and I go as far as I can before I am gasping for breath or exhale deeply. Each time it is easier to keep my mind quiet and stay relaxed. I think there were nine cycles. I feel each attempt makes me stronger and I go further each time. Once I felt close to being through, my body felt warm and sensual which would motivate me to try again. The lower back and uterus hurts much like being in labor, when I sit the pain lessons.

Sometimes I think this pain is about forcing me to let go of body identity. Then I get angry! I work on trusting all is exactly as it should be. I work to quell my failure voice and tell myself I am doing the best I can. Finally, I remind myself, 'I' do not need to do anything except to surrender. Sitting, I felt a strong force descend in my body that sounded like a windy storm. While this happened, I was pressed to the Earth with a strong gravitation pull.

4 pm: I have been stretching and it was intense through neck, hips, lower back and legs. 6 pm, I did a two-hour surrender session with the chest expansion cycle. It is still difficult. I hope I am truly getting stronger. From 8 to 9 pm, I did a stretch and almost came alive it felt so good, but when I lied down I lost that feeling. I did several long surrender sessions. The last surrender was good and at the end strong energy moved into my head. After some work was done in the head, I felt a crack line in my skull on the right side. I think the right side of my body opened much more. Then a huge energy ball came roaring down my body setting off a strong growing reaction on the right side and raising the body vibration. I kept on surrendering and the sensations in the body got stronger and stronger. At 9 pm, I felt I was 'truly awake'. There was a sudden quiet and that is when I heard the dogs howling outside. I did not hear outside noise before because the inner sound was melodic and loud. After this, it felt like physical changes were made all over the body. I felt spiral patterns of energies in skull moving down the body. Then a strong growing reaction started with intense tingly bubbles in the genital area and strong work in right toe joint. At 10:50 pm, I feel I have surrendered my body and mind well and it is easier to do it. I hope something happens in the body tonight. I want to be as HIGHER-SELF!

Spine Vortices & Pelvic Pushes

February 12: Drops Move Through Body, Energy Rush Into Skull

At 1:10 am, I used Reiki while standing in the dome, which raised my energy quickly. Then I did some stretches and went to bed. While standing meditatively, it seemed energy worked to release the cord of personality. A spiral of energy formed at the top of my head and moved rapidly down my body. Then my hips moved in the same direction of the spirals. I felt the spiral action inside moving from root to crown chakra. Then I folded down and felt energy building in the root chakra while simultaneously energy sucked upward. Then I felt the same from back and shoulder, through neck to crown. Then I felt energy moving down and building in the root chakra. Afterward I was directed to lie down.[25]

---

[25] When I write that "I was directed", it means that I started each session in a bodily surrender stance. I could tell

While lying, I decided to use Reiki on the root chakra, this worked well to raise energy quickly and then growing phase started. It is getting difficult to remember what happened. I felt the drops of liquid moving through my body down to the genital area with strong intensity in the genitals. I was holding my hands there and must have fallen asleep. It is 1 am, and I am tired and not sure why I woke. The body vibration gets strong, when I stand on the floor I feel it vibrate back, it shakes. I am sweating and feel warm when energy rises. This is similar to hot flashes but much hotter. My head hurts much.

From 1 to 3 am, I did a difficult physical pressured stretch, which worked the spine from neck on down, with many crunches and cracks. I stretched through the same circular paths in the body and I felt the spiral vortices. I was exhausted and slept deeply afterward.

From 6 to 11:30 am, I did long stretching sessions through the spine. First, there was a long painful session, with cracking and crunching going down the cord of personality. I think the cord has been removed. Then there was a different stretch, which felt like it pulled me apart in all directions. I think this work is enlivening the spine. I went until I was numb and exhausted, at the end I was deeply surrendered and allowing it.

Then an energy circuit was made after some intense holds in the neck. There were a few strange positions and pops. Then my head felt clear and I saw purple light in my 3rd eye. Then I felt internal rain and had a nice feeling of freefall.

From 1:15 to 3 pm, I did a long stretch while sitting. There is a pushing action occurring similar to that of having a baby. After that, I sat in the upright position with legs to front and felt tingling bubbles in the genitals. Then there was surrender work that was difficult because it was noisy outside my room. I plugged my ears; closed my eyes and tried to visualize purple light. At least I understand what the purple light is now, it is 'my light' and I see it when my mind goes quiet. I was trying hard and crying.

4:30 pm: Rest. I wonder why I write all these notes. At this moment, it is strange to see my hand moving and writing this. I feel hyperactive, as if I can move a mile a minute. That is how I worked outside, doing yoga, washing dishes and singing simultaneously. I am amazed at how much I did in a little while.

From 4:30 to 5:45 pm, when I sat a huge force overwhelmed me, I naturally relaxed and surrendered to it. It was so strong there was nothing else to do. It is difficult to allow

---

from the stretches when they were leading to a lying position.

higher-self to take over; it feels much like death and that I am losing myself. I know I am in the process of being reborn which I want very much, but still difficult to let go of the 'me voice'.

10:30 pm: Maybe I was successful with having quiet mind. I cannot tell for sure. I used Reiki on the root chakra and did two sitting sessions to try to surrender without success. My neck and hips were sore, so I lay down and did more Reiki on the root chakra, which I held a long time. The feeling is difficult to describe, but it helps me to go beyond the pain. From 10:30 pm to 12:30 am, I did a stretching session. I want to finish, but I am too tired.

Higher-Self Takes Over With Lightening Fast Body Moves

February 13: Chest Pop & Expansion, More Chest Cycles

1 am: I went to bed and immediately a strong growing phase started. I felt my chest pop and expand, but nothing was physically different. Then my legs got warmer than ever with strong swirling energy in the genitals. I said aloud, "You entice me with the promise of this new body, but there is still the dying gasping surrender thing to get through." I responded to myself, "Okay, but I'm not interested in doing all this for that." I was tired and shortly the dying, gasping for life, choking thing started. I thought I had "made it through" but later found out it wasn't true. I had enough and slept until 6am.

Awaking at 6 am, tension exists in the body in all the same places. Why doesn't it go away? I am sure the power of higher-self can remove this tension from my body.[26]

It was strange last night how the stretches were going through all those parts again and for so long. Is it that I am not strong enough or awake enough to complete this? Vacation is over; I have to take over the work outside. I have to start dealing with the chaos and the reality of people. I do not feel ready to do that.[27] The growing reaction feels strong this morning; I might do a session, maybe not. At this point, I am discouraged and disappointed.

Giving myself Reiki treatments works well for me to quiet my mind as it boosts my energy[28]. I will work with that more and give others treatments. Soon I need to go outside and

[26] A common societal belief is of spontaneous and instant healing. The reality is we are made of flesh and bone, and healing takes it is time, we cannot grow a new tooth overnight.

[27] It is hard to carry out your normal duties when this transformation starts. The best scenario would be a total retreat of at least a year and having the support of others.

[28] Many times, I quit giving myself Reiki because as my energy grew, I felt I did not need it anymore. Today I still

try to act normal. The Reiki on root chakra worked well to help me surrender. Higher-self taking over seems a gradual thing, as my vibration increases, higher-self gets stronger and takes over more. It is more like merging into your higher-self. After the session, I went out to work and took a walk. On the walk, I started feeling strange and so happy. I saw things differently and was walking with a spring in my step. When I was walking, I could hear the marching music, so I started walking to the beat of it. It got stronger. When I stopped, higher-self took over with the most amazing spontaneous stretches so far. I moved so fast and was twisting and twirling all over for about an hour. I found out the bone in my leg that joins to make the hip socket is on the wrong side of the joint. It is as if I have to lengthen tendons in my legs to pull the joint around to the front.

When I went to my room at 3 pm, higher-self took over with such force and afterward the genital growing was so strong so I went to bed until 6 pm. It feels like a penis is growing but I do not believe it. I was not sure about surrender; near the end I tried it and realized, I must keep doing this every time. Higher-self then gets stronger and takes over more each time. To enliven myself I have to keep surrendering.

8 pm: there was a beautiful moon; it was blood red with the sunset on it. I prepare for another round. I think it is near now. I keep on doing what is indicated and surrendering as much as possible. The last few days I am going so fast inside and outside and I hear the marcher music strong. Still the personality is dominant; I guess that is the case until this completes. I will do a session with Reiki working on surrender. Energy swirls in my head and in the genitals, feeling it is changing things. It is strange that what I visualize changing in my body in the long growing phase is not physically evident afterward. I guess a change is made to the energetic form, which can unfold when higher-self takes over. Like when a flower unfolds from the Earth and grows so fast.

From 8 pm to 1 am, I practiced surrender with stretching. If I stretch without surrendering, it hurts. After this, I stood with ring in dome for two hours, practicing surrender. Later, I lay down with hands on root chakra using Reiki. It was intense. Next, I moved my hands to the crown chakra. I feel I did well with longer periods of true surrender. I think it counts in the end. I need sleep now.

---

benefit each time I give myself Reiki, you can never have too much energy.

Key Insight: I'm Not The Observer, Higher-Self Doesn't Think

February 14: Rib Cage Release, Skull Work Starts

It has been a day of torture having to push down through the pelvic muscles and with many stretches and neck crunches. The cord of personality seems to be opening but I am stretching for three hours in the same loop. I am angry and crying much. I do not want to do anything more, dying would be easier.

8:30 pm, I am over my resistance streak. I did the Reiki standing in the dome and it was strong. Right away, I had to stand with head tilted with neck bent. It was painful. I had to keep lowering my head and going back up. After this, there was excruciating neck crunching and work in the back. All the time I worked on surrender but was not successful to distance from the pain. During one of the stretches, there was something new. I have always felt pain under my right ribs while stretching, like there is a bubble or tight tension in there. Tonight after many stretches, I felt a knot of tension move under my ribs, up the middle of my chest and over to the spine. Then there was intense neck stretching and crunching in the back. There was another loud crack in the neck and work on sides of neck and at base of skull. After this, I lay down and gave Reiki to root chakra and fell into a deep sleep. I woke near midnight, feeling gentle healing waves in my neck, back and shoulders, the spine and skull are more open. There was much work in the skull, in sinuses, eyes, ears and jaws.

Insight about the observer is the fake one Then it came that the 'observer', the one who watches what is going on is the 'fake one'. This is the thinking one who thinks they are alive. All this time I thought this was higher-self and I would be transformed via the new electric circuits in the body. Tonight I see that this 'observer' is what is hanging on. Higher-self has no thinker, it is direct awareness, there is no reflection, and there is no thought! I think I am afraid to let go of this old thinking habit. It seems the way to be as higher-self is by feeling, which does not need thinking, and the Reiki helps me do that. Seeing this illusion was good, I know what I am NOT aiming for.

February 15

There was strong energetic work in the body during the night and I could easily surrender. I need to take some friends to the airport today, I feel it is near and I worry it will happen in public. Then I will be left as an unknown person outside these walls. If I return, people will not know me. Probably none of this will happen; I need to be alert.[29]

When I returned, from 3 to 5 pm, I did a long session. My energy was strong but I was tired at the end. I barely remember what I did. I recall stretching, and energy building in pelvic bowl and rising up the spine to skull. Energy worked in the skull for a long time while in deep surrender. After the skull work, I rested and I saw purple light in my 3ʳᵈ eye and it was easy to be quiet while energy worked in the body. After awhile, I arose and did a stretch with long stretching pulls through neck, chest and back. This stretch enlivened the spine.

From 6 to 11 pm, I did several sessions. In one, I had an orgasm and observed energy moved up strong to the head afterward. Then it comes back down with the tingling feeling of growing and elongating and the genitals tingle. I did a few holds working with surrender but got too tired to continue. I still wonder if it is a problem because I have not completely surrendered. For sure, I have sustained quiet mind. I am still confused about what happens here. It still feels like a penis is growing. Now that I am working again, I need to set up a schedule and make my sessions more effective. I did many sessions and the Reiki acupressure sequence. The marching music is strong now.

Insight about "I" releases energy to higher-self I had the thought while I was stretching, that when I am surrendered the "I" releases energy to higher-self. My higher-self releases 'energy held in form' as the 'I' and uses this energy to make the light body. Before I thought I was moving tension energy out through the path of the spine, but I have to ask moving it where? It is my energy trapped as tension energy as the personality in the body. The transformation of the body happens during the surrendered state, transforming the old to the new and always getting stronger.

February 16: Deep Tones, Blanked Out View, Pings In Head

5:30 am, last night the growing reaction was strong when I lay down and I felt tension moving out of my neck. It continued all night and I still feel it. The vibration in my

---

[29] I believed at any moment I was going to transform into an entirely different person, which I thought would be a man. I can laugh about it now.

body has doubled and I feel tingly. I feel internal stretches with waves of energy filling the stretched part. A vortex works around the spine.

From 6 to 8 am, I did a standing stretch that relieved the tension and pain in the body. I felt surrender was total near the end. At the end, I felt energy built in the pelvic bowl and after this energy rose to the skull and came back down again. When it came down, I felt as if I was sinking, stretching and growing. Each time the energy building in pelvic bowl gets stronger. Then suddenly both ears had a deep tone in them and my internal field of view blanked out. This lasted for some time but I do not know how long. I was very still. I have shivers, hear the marching music strong, and feel a downward spiral along the cord of personality.

I am tired of surrendering, sitting waiting for something to manifest. Perhaps the step I need to do now is to take over as the higher-self. It sure feels much better than sitting in these cramped positions. I have been working all day and feel angry. I think this is because I am suppressing strong energy. When I sit the energy quickly increases in intensity. Twice I came in to sit during the day, and once there was strong neck stretches with crunching. While sitting I heard three pings in my head, and after this, I felt my right side open. I need more energy.

6 pm: Finally, I have space to do a workout. The days are difficult. I am irritated with people and I am tired of living here. I want to move but this is difficult because I am weak. It bothers me that I do not know what is occurring with me and I do not trust my mind. I feel alone with this. I worked my toe joint and I did a standing stretch. After this, the neck opened, growing phase started, and I went to bed.

Vortex Shaking Spine, Drips Of Water, Skull Crack, Surrender Practice

February 17: Energy Balls In Legs, Buttocks & Groin

All night the growing reaction was strong. This morning and last night higher-self was taking over powerfully with a springy feeling, stretching the body when needed. I took some time off, arranging for my work obligations. I walked in the forest and did a very long stretching session outside. I stretched from toe to head until all tension was released and the energy reversed downward. It was difficult to sustain to the end, but I endured not wanting to do it again. I am sure the cord of personality was released and the full change will happen soon. After this, I retreated to my room and did a stretch.

It is the afternoon, and I have a fire and will relax and see what I need to do next. I have strong shivers. I did a relaxing, melting stretch down to hips and felt energy building in the root chakra. Then my neck and back hurt and later energy went up the spine into the skull and came down and I felt tingling in root chakra, which lasted some time. I felt increasing energy build with heat and it felt like male genitalia was growing. Every time the energy increased, it felt like the genitalia was at a different stage of growing. This time it felt complete with the sensation a scrotum was made. It felt like growing with a constant stretching, burning and tingly feeling in the genitals. When I arose, there was nothing there. It is strange; it feels real and hurts. I sat awhile and energy worked in other body areas. Soon all was quiet so I arose.

4:30 pm: it has been unusually quiet in the body. Sitting, there is energy moving in the spine and shaking my body and I hear the marcher music strong. I feel movement in the left buttock. I have shivers and an energy ball is going down my neck, across my shoulders and back, and down the spine. The muscles burn and my shoulders are rotating energetically. Next, I felt energy balls pummeling my left leg. It started at the big toe, moved up inside leg to the groin, and then went down doing the leg. Then I felt energy balls in the buttocks, which were going around in circles until the left buttock was thumping. It was intense in the groin. It felt like something was growing in the genitals; it was painful and difficult not to identify with it. Then I could see it might go on for a while so I went into intense concentration to distance from the pain. The pain intensified in the groin and both legs and I heard the message shouted: "Surrender". I took it while I could and arose. Again, there was nothing there but it feels real. This is blowing my mind.

I am disappointed that I used an entire day for these sessions and there is no result. I have been doing sessions for five weeks and I cannot keep going like this. I asked my higher-self to tell me what I need to know about this. Does the transformation pain give me the opportunity to learn how to surrender? There was nothing enjoyable about that last session. I hope this was actual work because I do not want to do that again, it burned much.

8 pm: Something new is happening. I feel drips of water here and there in my body and there are cracking sounds in my skull. The vibration increases and strong gravity is

pulling me toward the Earth. There is burning in the genitals and it feels like something grows there. The body heat is high.

At 10 pm, I lay down with the growing phase and decided to try harder to surrender. Trying it, I see what it is. It is being completely still in body and mind. I can do it for some time but when the breath starts, I lose focus. I can surrender easier in the gap. I arose and tried holding my breath and higher-self tries to take over. While in this quiet state it is strange, I can observe the beating of my heart and the breathing is in the background. Then a feeling comes as if I am going to be swallowed and I panic. It looks like this would only take a minute or so of stillness. Yes, it is about learning to surrender.

I am sweating. Surrender feels impossible now. I tried it sitting, when my chest rises, I panic and identify. I tried it many times then it got to where I could not feel the groove of being still. Perhaps I could try different things every ten minutes or so to see what works. It is difficult to know when my mind is truly quiet. Relaxing on the out breath helps to get me in the zone. Looking to the right in my head with my inner sight and eyes closed is the best so far to still my mind. Yet, possibly these all are techniques and not truly quiet mind. Still the observer is there 'maintaining' the focus or technique and it does not work. It seems like a big out breath and deep let go might be best.

I still hear the marching music and feel swirling in the root chakra. I hate to go to bed feeling I failed and facing another long day. I want this to finish. I was successful at surrender for short periods in my last session and feel I am better at it. I know I have surrendered before in meditation, but I guess higher-self was not strong enough to take over then. It is difficult for me to relax when I fear being swallowed.

11:45 pm: I tried the dot meditation, where I gaze at a dot drawn on white paper. That seemed to work good to stay surrendered for longer periods and I had no fear with gasping for breath. It is easy to tell when my mind is quiet as well. While I did this, the energy vibration increased dramatically. The buttocks are humming and there are stinging prickles that hurt in the genitals. I do not understand this! I will go to bed, as I do not know what else to do. The growing reaction in the groin hurts!

Insight about eternal transformation of form: I thought about a fetus growing in the womb and wondered if it experiences these growth cycles. It is another thing to go through it consciously. I guess no other life form can do this. Only man has the potential to transform his body to another form. I guess after you have done it once, then you could do it again to whatever form you wanted. That is a thought difficult to fathom. If you have this transformation ability, you would never grow old and would have eternal life in body. You would no longer be subject to the growth and death cycle of lower life forms.

February 18: Spiral Forming From Crown To Root Chakra

3:30 am: What is new is both legs feel like they are growing. Getting out of bed, my calf muscles are stiff. There is a clear inner sound sounding constantly, it is a high-pitched melody like dolphins singing. There are slow undulating waves of energy that pull and stretch the legs. Energy works in the buttocks and groin and the intestines rumble.

7:30 am: It was difficult to sleep with a strong growing reaction and pain. My energy is strong with humming in the legs, buttocks and groin. Shoots of energy continuously go up my back. It is difficult to walk, as the leg muscles are stiff. When I sat, it was as if I was pulled down. To stand is like going against gravity and takes effort. I cannot imagine doing much and likely people here will be upset about that. At 8:30 am, I went out, walked the dogs, and had a normal workday.

6:30 pm: all day I have felt hyperactive. There was much work in the right neck and shoulder. One time when I sat, my mind blanked out for thirty minutes while energy worked. Tonight I get distant Reiki, maybe something happens. That would be welcome as my life feels on hold until this is complete. All day there is pain near the pubic bone; I hope I do not have to go through much more pain there. I notice that the growing reaction happens in my body all day without me doing anything. Maybe the growing is not like a leaf quickly unfolding. I still do not know.

My spine, back, shoulders and neck are healing in an important event. While sitting, energy balls keep rising up the spine to the neck. I think these balls are collecting as a force of energy to loosen adhesions especially in the neck area. After the balls move through, I feel tingly energy in the path they went through. There is no indication to stretch, yeah! I will make a fire and relax. I sat and then the entire body went numb except my skull, and I felt a vortex forming from crown down to tail.

7:45 pm: I stood with the ring in dome and intoned all the Reiki symbols. I went through a long stretch to ground ending with hip on the floor. I used the opportunity to try to surrender. I almost did it, but when higher-self takes over, I panic and lose it. I feel the sensation of energy rising higher in the body each time. This time it made it past the heart and lungs but I lost it when it rose into the throat. I wonder if this phenomenon has anything to do with prior changes made to my body. It is strange to fight with myself this way. Logically I want this transformation, yet panic when it happens as if I am dying. I know a new beginning is always better and there is no such thing as death, there is only transformation. The absurd thing is this transformation is done by my higher-self, so why do I not know how to do this? The best thing so far is a deep let go, total relaxation and being extremely quiet. When I convince myself the breathing will happen spontaneously, I can relax into it.

I have done sustained surrenders before and I went to a place of total stillness without the sense of time. Then the mind is still and there is no sense of the personality. I would think higher-self could take over from this state, that it is the same. If I am identified with the mind-voice, I will have conflict or fear. With various meditations I have tried, most require too much mind involvement. Watching is the best with a simple focal point and deep relaxation. I will try to go to that place in simple meditation.

Now the energy is swirling in the root chakra intensely and energy balls move up my spine again. There was a big release of energy in the previous session from the hip. Energy was collecting from all body parts at once and moving up in a big spiral. The tension release was melting my body. It was pleasant. I think I need to accept that I do the best I can. Thinking about it is what is creating the problem.

Low Point – Wanting To Die And Not Able To Do It

February 19: Skull Work, Burning Pain All Over Body

3 pm: I had to go outside to do something normal. I did chores, took a walk in the forest and fed the animals. It occurred to do a stretch while I was walking, but I did not want to, so I did not. I do not even want to sit still and face another torture session of pain, failure and insanity. This is bothering me. "Surrender", but when I try I cannot do it. I feel caught in a difficult situation and want to cry. I wish there was a way to escape this feeling of limbo. Sitting, the marching music is strong. There is much pain in my skull with work in jaws, teeth and nasal cavities and the groin growth goes on. It looks like the changes are moving up.

6 pm: It's Sunday and I had no break it was much of the same. I spent most of the day doing various stretches through legs, and up and down through spine. I almost completely surrendered a few times. My head is moving more. From 6 to 7 pm, I sat for over an hour. A growing reaction happens stronger than before and affects my entire body. It started in the left leg and moved up with a burning pain felt in most places.

9:45 pm: It has been hours of sitting and lying with growing phase and working with surrender. I started giving Reiki to facial acupoints, which helped reduce the head pain. 10:30 pm: I feel terrible. I tried to "die" and even I cannot do that. Nothing works. I cannot surrender and higher-self cannot take over. I do not want to be like this. I will try to sleep, it is my only refuge until this resolves. My body hurts all over, emotionally I am a wreck and mentally I am a nut case. At this point, I pray to The Creator for mercy and grace to relieve my suffering, because I understand there is nothing I can do to save myself.[30]

Pelvic Pushing, Energy Balls In Inguinal Canals

February 20: Energetic Rotation Of Hips

4:45 am: It was a long night. It felt like my head was opening along lines in my skull. It started on right side of head near top but not in the middle (**see figure**). This occurred until I fell asleep much later, if I slept at all. I remember after an hour it felt wavier and not so painful. I do not recall if the left side was done like this. Next, it felt like my facial bones were changed. I look the same. I guess it is near given how changes happen in the head. I do not feel any strong pain only discomfort. I felt a stretching sensation from skull down to body near morning, I was not awake only aware of it. There are numerous energy balls in my neck from base of skull to shoulders mostly on the right side.

7 am: I am up and I feel better, the growing reaction is strong but not painful. My lower back is warm and tingly. All body parts are in a strong growing phase, except the arms and hands, which have a light tingling. The most intense work is in the back, shoulders, neck, head and groin.

---

[30] When we approach a strong transition point, we feel desperate and want to die, as this is the maximum point of pain. When we feel like this, we are close to a break through. Just hang in there and work to quell the mind-voice.

8 am: I did around three rounds of pelvic pushes and the sutures are opening. 10 am: I have been working all this time to open the pelvic bowl, but I am not sure what I am pushing, I feel an energy ball moving down the inguinal canal. I used Reiki on acupoints in this area to make it easier. Without Reiki, I could not have done it. 10:45 am: I cannot take more. I need to take my aching head, sore hip and neck full of energy balls outside and do my daily work.

2:30 pm: I am back after working. I still have difficulty accepting this is happening. 3:30 pm: I had to do more work outside and I am getting tired. I slept for an hour and feel better. I need more sleep. I sent a letter off to my friends and family telling them what is going on with me. I called it the new body and I took the risk of being labeled crazy[31]. Well it is possible, but at this point, it does not matter to me. I feel the transformation is near, so it is better people have some clue about it before it happens. At 8 pm, the stretch felt different and softer. Energy is building strong in the root chakra with a swirling feeling.

10:30 pm: I ended in a position with the legs open and it took a long time to move energy through the right leg and hip. I felt a big ball of energy moving along the line of the inguinal canal toward the perineum area. Strong energy was pushing this energy ball down. Eventually I felt it move down, then I turned over to the other side and the left hip started rotating energetically. I was in a painful hold for about thirty minutes. Then the entire genital area was full of energy and it felt like something was growing there. Then a big energy ball started moving down on the left side. I had pain on both sides combined with energetic rotation of the left hip. Then a growing reaction with intense burning pain started in my left leg. At that point, I knew I could only continue with a full surrender. I moved the growing left leg and all the energy suddenly stopped. I need a break and then I will give it my best try to surrender.

From 10:40 pm to 12:45 am, it was difficult but I did not identify so the pain was not so bad. I could not breathe through my nose, which made it difficult to relax. I fell asleep and awoke with sweating and a strong growing reaction. I was having irritating cleansing dreams so it was nice to awaken.

February 21: Energy Balls In Inguinal Canals, Spontaneous Mantra

---

[31] The reason I sent the letter was to forewarn people they might not recognize me. At the time, I believed I was going to suddenly look very different. When the skull sutures opened, I thought this miracle was very near.

5:30 am: There was a sleepy, wavy growing reaction, in the night. Something came in a dream like the message, "You are doing a good job". It gives me some reassurance that I am doing what I need to do and it progresses. I feel rested. I dread the reaction of people to that letter. Yet, I feel confident this is occurring or I would not have sent it. I see why it was necessary to tell people what is possible before it happens so they are prepared if suddenly I appear dramatically different. I hope this happens soon as I grow anxious to see the 'new me'.

10:30 am: I did a long grueling session with the energy ball going down the inguinal canal. At first, it went down the right side then after this down the left side. On the left, I felt the energy ball move down and then I knew that the work on the right had not been completed. I guess multiple passes are needed. It is intense when this energy ball moves down through tissues of hips and pelvis. Once, there was intense pleasure and I almost passed out from it. I have never felt anything that strong before. I worked outside and now I rest, I am tired.

From 3:30 to 6 pm: I slept deeply. Some work occurred and when I woke, there was a strong spontaneous stretch with yawning. I had to cut it short and feed the animals. Its 6:45 pm, and I want to get on with this. I think to do a freestyle session and work with the right hip to help the energy balls work easier on the right side. Having my leg open is painful which makes it more difficult. My ovaries are pulsating.

From 7 to 10 pm, much tension was released out of the hip; it was intense but felt good. I stayed centered well. Once, I was spontaneously repeating a mantra, musically with my breathing. The words were, "Personalado ende". Then I thought 'The end of the personality'. This is possible as much tension energy released.

This time the work went deep into the center of the hip and there was much work in lower back and hip girdle. I felt the energy ball going into groin through there. Near the end, there was a spontaneous stretch along the spine and that is when I lost focus. I still think the shoulders and upper body have to be released with the right hip, which is still out of alignment. Arghhh, this is so difficult. At midnight, I finished stretching the upper body from the hip. The energy never let up, but I had to quit. I will try to go down through leg before bed.

Strong Spine Vortices, Energetic Rotation In Shoulders & Jaws

February 22: Chest Expansions, TMJ Opening Starts

From 2 to 2:30 am, I feel I finished with the hip but there is always more to do. Everything hurts. I finished with a downward stretch with a killer neck-crunching episode. No more!

8:30 am: I am awake after a restful sleep. From 9 to 12 am, I have been stretching along the cord of personality, which feels great. I am shaking with a strong vibration and it feels impossible to go outside now. My bowel movements finally are regular.

At 1 pm, I shook for about thirty minutes with shivers and a spiral of energy going up spine from tailbone. This upward moving energy worked my arms, back and shoulders.

It is 6:30 pm, and I have been stretching easily almost the entire day. Much tension releases from my body. When I stopped, an energy spiral was moving up my body. When I first noticed it, it went around my shoulders and neck. As it moved upward, I felt both shoulders energetically rotate. With this energetic rotation starting, I observed that I could sit doing almost nothing while the energetic rotations above and below were doing work in the body. Many new pathways in the neck and shoulders formed and there were many cracks in these areas. It felt great to have tension release from the shoulders, head and jaws. At one time, I had to open the jaws as far as possible for energy to work in the TMJ joints and there was one loud snap. This is difficult to do. I think my skull will break when the tension goes against the jaw deep inside my skull. My personality is going strong, I think because there is much tension in my body. I want it to go at this point, surrender is a beautiful space compared to this 'mind-voice'.

From 7 to 7:50 pm, I did a fantastic stretching session! Tension all over my body is removed by energy spirals that move up and down the body simultaneously changing it. This happens with my head bent to one side without me moving. My vibration is quickly rising with strong tingles in the groin. Fifty minutes flew by.

9:30 pm: Wow! The tension releases and simultaneous changes are occurring with increasing speed. While my neck and head is worked, other areas in the body are worked. There is the sound of a big windy storm inside. Each time something opens, I feel increasingly like one energy unit going in a vortex from toe to head.

Work was just done on the left TMJ and the right
TMJ joint. My jaws traveled across my face in a horizontal
circle and then each was held open and worked **(see**
figure). Once open then energy went down the spine to

release all the tension on the left side of the body. This was intense, but bearable. I suspect I
will have to open all the joints down that side but I am not sure. I am happy there is a finally a
change!

From 10 to 11:45 pm, I did a surrender session. At 11:15 pm, the energy reversed
with the root chakra activating and heat rising with some twists of the body. Then there was a
holding pattern and chest expansion started which I still find difficult. I do not have fear of
losing myself anymore. I can go for a few breaths with sustained quiet mind, and then repeat
it for some time. I do not know if this is enough.

Passing Threshold Of Chest Expansion, Tension Release From Body

February 23: Surrender Work, Both Sides Of Body Activate

It is 12:30 am and I am exhausted; I will try to surrender in bed. At 2:30 am, a
different type of growing reaction is all over the body. First, heat started in the root chakra
with a swirling feeling and then energy radiated to all parts of my body. I am tired but will do
more.

It is 9:20 am. In the night, it occurred to surrender but I am still confused what it
means. Sitting, the growing reaction is strong, the buttocks are humming, the root chakra is
swirling and my stomach is rumbling.

11:30 am: I did a surrender session. I started with Reiki, which helped me to relax
and feel less identified. Later I switched to holding my mind still, which quickly led to the
sensation of higher-self taking over. I felt I stayed with it long enough to pass through some
threshold. Later I felt tingly energy moving up through my body and then energy went
downward with stretching and freefall. Tension releases from the cord of personality on the
right side of body. It appears there are two cords of personalities, one on each side of the
spine.

From 12 to 1:30 pm: much tension releases and is pleasant. I often use my mind-
voice to chatter, so I need to stay alert to keep going back to quiet mind. If I am busy with

mind-chatter, the release of tension is less effective. Suddenly, pain was intense all over the body. The hips and shoulders rotated energetically and my neck was stiff. I went into surrender space, which seemed longer and easier than before. Energy activation started on the right side of body, then the left side activated, and then both sides together. Both sides of body activating together is what hurt. Later I did a freestyle session with stretching and moving as higher-self.

From 4:15 to 5:30 pm: The marching music goes on inside. I did a standing stretch interspersed with growing phases. I used the 'Personalado ende' mantra. From 6 to 9 pm, I did a sitting session with legs out to front and slowly bending down. At end, there was increasing pain in right pelvis and right hip. I took it for about one hour and collapsed. Then I lay down and worked with surrender.

From 9:45-11:45 pm: The marching music is strong which I think means I should stretch. There was intense skull work and a killer session of opening the TMJ's. Then I did a stretch on both sides all the way down from head to toes. I can see that the energy goes out from the jaws. It seems all joints have to be in alignment all the way down to release tension from the cord of personality. I did a few upward stretches where I felt balanced in the spine. It felt amazing. There were many stretchy twists and crunches in the right shoulder, which dropped afterward with a huge relief.

Chapter 12: Energetic Joint Rotation, Joint Vortices

Energy Circuit Through The Joints

February 24: Hard Palate, Frontal Bone Work; Skull Vortex Down Spine

1 am: I did a sitting session with tension releasing as healing waves. From 8:30 to 9:30 am, I did a freestyle session with much stretching. At noon, I took a walk in the forest, did a freestyle stretch through right hip, down, and back up where my body moved freely. There was much work in the jaws.

At 2 pm, I did a sitting session. The jaws opened and after this energy started working on many cranium bones, especially in the hard palate and the forehead.

From 4:30 to 5:45 pm, I did a sitting session that released miles of tension and felt great! Once, there were long spirals of energy on each side of the spine going endlessly downward with an awesome feeling of bliss. Near the end, I felt a spiral of energy around the top of the skull like before when it was on my neck. Energy works on joints and spine as it travels downward. This was intense; I stopped when all joints on right side of body were worked at once. First one side of the body is worked and then the other, presumably to line up the joints equally. Energy continues to work as I sit here.

From 6:30 to 10 pm, I did a long and intense session with work from jaws down to hip. At the beginning, I opened my mouth as wide as possible and heard the message: "Hold this". Therefore, I did while the head rotated around for some time. Then a strong force started working in the central part of my hard palate near the back. Then the mandible and maxillae bones were lifted together and brought forward with my jaw protruding to the front. I then held this position, as my head, neck and shoulders moved spontaneously. There was a strong force pulsating in area of neck, shoulder and on right side of body.

After this, I heard loud pings in my head and a vortex formed in my skull and moved down the right side of body, pummeling the head, neck and shoulders and some in the hip. After the energy arrived at the hip, energy started building in the root chakra and soon thereafter shoots of energy were sent upward in body to various directions: straight up spine, to shoulder points and then in a circle around the body. At 9 am, I did a freestyle session.

From 11 to 12, I was pummeled with strong energy and it felt like my head was breaking apart. Strong body movements happen now.

February 25: Neural Connections In Neck, Twitching Muscles

It was a restless sleep; I arose once to stretch, though I was mostly sleeping while I did it. I did a session at 11 am, and then a session at 6 pm. Sitting, I hear a cracking sound around my left ear; like the ear is opening and I hear pops in the skull. Next, a strong stretch started moving down from head, to neck and shoulders and my body feels springy in the stretched areas. Now, the head and neck are stretching spontaneously with energy whorls in these areas. There is much activity in the skull, much different from anything I have experienced so far. I feel burning lines in the skull.

At 7 pm, I opened my jaws wide and there was stretching of them back and forth and left, right, left. Then my chin dropped and rotated and it felt like the maxillae came up and over the jaws and settled down. My jaws remained closed, there were a few more twists, and then my head dropped on my chest with the chin tucked in. At this point, neural connections formed and then all joints energetically rotated and I felt the growing reaction all over my body.

From 8 to 12 pm, while lying there was one strong stretching session with spine and head alignment. Then I did a sitting session and my head slowly lowered. It was difficult because my nose was stuffy and my body was sore. Lastly, I lay down and there was the sensation of popping and twitching of muscles intensely all over the body. I felt the energy ball move further down the right inguinal area, but I did not feel any pain. Lastly, I felt strong activity in the root chakra for about thirty minutes and while observing this, I fell asleep.

Energy Rays From Spine To Torso

February 26: Muscle Twitches

2 am: I woke but there was no urge to stretch. There is a soft melodic melody and everything in my body feels tight. I feel as if I am expanding, gently and slowly. There is a pulling feeling, mostly in the shoulders and back. I went back to sleep. At 5 am, I woke and I am extremely thirsty, the same continues. Spaced widely all over the body are small muscle twitches with the feeling they pull the flesh. The body feels heavy, like I am pulled to the

Earth with a strong gravitational force. While sitting, the activity gains momentum. Now, my right foot feels numb, warm, fuzzy, and light.

At 9:30 am, I did a stretching session with a sleepy feeling while it happened. Lately, my urine smells strong and I urinate frequently. I guess a cleansing occurs in the urinary system. At 10:30 am, I did a spontaneous stretch. I need more space and a large soft mat for the spontaneous movements as I move everywhere. I did well to let go of body control.

From 1:20 to 2 pm, there was an intense session with work in jaw and stretch through hips and shoulders. My head feels ready to burst. From 3 to 3:30 pm, I did a standing stretch that hurt this time especially in the skull. I feel like a bag of broken bones. A circular ring of energy moves down the body, mainly going to areas of joints. Energy is around the top of my chest and shoulders and is moving down. It moved down very slow over one hour and I mostly felt work on the right side. It felt like changes were made to the tissue in all directions as I stretched down.

After this, there was a cascade of energy from the top of the head down the spine, where I felt fingers of energy moving from the spine out to the sides of my body, neck, shoulders, chest and back *(see figure).* It felt like energy circuits were made. Then energy amassed on the spine and went down to the tailbone. Then energy rose up the spine a few times with changes made to tissues on both sides of spine at once as it went up to my head. As energy entered the skull, I felt it working in the nose and sinuses on each side. Then energy made a long descent down and it felt great like my spine was straightening. I am tired but I want to go on. The truth is that it causes more discomfort not to stretch than to do it because of the building tension.

From 6:20 to 9 pm, I did a standing stretch down to hips. It felt like higher-self had taken over from the center point at the hips; I felt in the groove and bodily surrendered. I observed then that my higher-self was making these changes to my body. This insight made it easier to be still and not engage my mind. Daily the reaction of thinking seems less.

Midnight: I did an athletic freestyle session, where my body moves so fast the only thing I can do is surrender. With the fast movements, the bones are shaken loose. After this, I slowly stretched to the ground and then twisted around and ended in the position in the **figure**. I held my hip in this bent position, which seemed like forever. After this, I felt a strong sensation of growth in the center of the left hip. I hope I do not have to do another long hold in the hip as it hurt much. It has been a long day!

February 27: Energy Whorls On Skull, Joint Circuits Made In Torso

I slept a long time; after awakening, my head hurts near the right sphenoid wing on the side of the skull. The growing phase continues. From 9 am to 1 pm, I did a freestyle session with difficult stretching and much neck crunching. Next, I was sitting with my legs to front, bent over and in freefall for a long time, while energy worked in right shoulder and hip. I did another freestyle session, stretching down through both hips, first the left and then the right. Once, all joints were aligned together as one on the right side, and the stretch went through all together. I held this body position of joint alignment, which seemed like forever, and felt energy circuits were made between them. After this, it felt as if I was holding my spine straight while connections were made along the length of the spine. Often I am sitting without moving while these changes happen.

Then the growing reaction started and my body felt like a circle swirling out from the center with energy in the root chakra increasing. After that, energy moved up the spine and cranium bones moved with crunching sounds. Now, I feel the marching music strong, gravity pulls me to Earth and I am shivering. Staying in the surrendered state is easier and the feeling I am doing the transformation myself is stronger.

5 pm: Strong growing phase happens with small energy whorls all over the skull. I still feel pain above the TMJ joint near the sphenoid wing. From 5:45 to 7:30 pm: The session started with twisting my jaws around and there were cracks in my skull with strong tingling. Next tension arose strongly on both sides of my neck and my head tipped to the right. Then

my left shoulder was worked for a long time with extreme discomfort. After this, energy worked in the right shoulder and then worked in both shoulders. Then the shoulders energetically rotated together and this energy then moved up the neck. This caused great discomfort, as if I was pulled apart with strong pressure on my breastbone and across collarbones.

After this, with a posture of a straight spine, the energy went down and work was done on the back, hips and legs in sequence. The tops of my shoulders on up to the neck are sore. Once my head, shoulders and parts of my upper chest felt like one unit of energy, strong and united. I did not feel tension anywhere, I felt hollow and it was nice. My skull cracked much and there were many strong shivers.

From 7:30 to 9 pm: this session started with a little work on jaws and then the right shoulder lined up with the right TMJ as a single energy circuit up side of neck and front of shoulder under clavicle in the transverse part **(see figure).** After this, there was a long hold with excruciating pain as changes were made along this circuit. As the hold progressed, my head was tipping more and more to the left. I had to surrender deeply to get through this. At the end, there was a big pop in the head, shoulder or neck. After this, the energy moved down to the hips, my left arm and buttocks went numb, and the neck hurt like hell. Then I had to stop. My body temperature rises and some work happens in the hips. Later I was disappointed because there were two more passes of work in the jaws and shoulder. It seems there is no end to this.

From 9 to 11 pm, I did another sitting session, bent over while the right hip in the lower back was worked. It was intense. 11:30 pm: I am sitting feeling as if I am expanding while tissues are changed. My personality is still active; I hope it goes, as it is a tiring and irritating habit. I got out of bed to shut myself up for a while. Later, energy balls moved down both inguinal canals at once. I tried for some time, but had to stop, as the pain was too much.

February 28: Surrender Is Clearer, Energy Balls In Inguinal Canals

There are still energy balls in the inguinal canals and the pressure is so strong I can barely rise.12 Noon: I stretched in my room, and went for a walk and stretched in the forest. It is obvious that not all tension has released from my body. Another thing is obvious and that is what is meant by "surrender". We surrender every night when we stop thinking to fall asleep.

While our mind rests, our healer goes to work on our body to make repairs and release tension. The question remains, "How to go to sleep while awake", to allow more healing to occur. This is my current challenge. Today, I am full of resistance on many levels. I am wallowing in self-pity with the poor me story with broken bones.

From 3 to 4 pm: I have been sitting and relaxing, there is much activity in the groin. There is the urge to push down through the hips and tailbone. From 5:45 to 9 pm: I sat and

did a few stretches then put the soles of my feet together **(see figure).** Then energy balls moved down the inguinal canals and simultaneously I felt pain everywhere in my body. It felt like all bones were worked at once. Then the hips energetically rotated with excruciating pain in hips and lower back. I went into deep surrender and prayed for help from The Creator. Finally, I found a quiet space amidst all that pain which lasted three hours. It is hard to endure all this pain when nothing seems to change. I have pain in my hips and legs. From 9 to 11 pm, I did another session with intense work in hips and shoulders.

Sphenoid Crack; Shoulder, Neck, Ear & Torso Vortices Form

March 1: Energy Balls Down Neck Sides, Floating Head Sensation

I woke after a long sleep with work occurring in the jaws. Then I felt skull bone movements of hard palate, frontal bone, and a bone moved deep in my head. Then there was a loud crack in the skull, which I intuited would allow the bones of the skull to move. It was a long session with energy work in the jaws and then energy circuits formed between the jaws and the shoulders while these tissues pulled up together with many cracking sounds. Next, energy moved to the spine and made more energy circuits. Then it was like a big circuit opened in the spine on right side and tension started rolling out from all areas at once. It was intense and I had to lie down. When I lay down spontaneous body stretches started and it released the tension from my body. Yawning has the function to open the jaw muscles to align the spine and cranium bones.[32]

---

[32] You can notice by now in the notes, that every time there is an opening in the hips (yesterday), then it ripples up and there is a corresponding opening in the skull thereafter (today). This repeats, where the time between hip and skull movements gets shorter and eventually the body becomes elastic as one stretching unit. Then corrections in

Noon: energy has been working in the TMJ joint non-stop; it is difficult to stop the reaction. Just now, the entire neck opened and an energy vortex formed in the neck and is winding downward which releases tension as it goes.

3 pm: I continue to do sessions with work in jaw, hips and shoulders. I am tired but it is difficult to stop. I did a spontaneous stretch outside. My skull is like a jigsaw puzzle with pain everywhere. From 3:30 to 5:30 pm, I did a sleepy sitting session with strong energetic work occurring and came to with strong energy building in root chakra.

From 6:30 to 7 pm: The first thing that happened was my jaw spontaneously opened widely and both sides of it were worked. Then energy moved up to center of skull and down on right side and I felt intense pain like striking a nerve. Then energy worked down while my head was in a held position. Then two energy balls moved down the sides of my neck and went into my shoulders on both sides going along the sternocleidomastoid muscles. Then the balls came together going across the collarbones to the U area of the breastbone. It felt like my shoulders were energetically rotating around this area of the neck. Then the energy went back up and my jaws energetically rotated. Then my left ear was worked, and I felt a spiral going from the inside to the outside of my ear. Then the right side of my face was worked. When all this finished it felt like my head was floating. Then the energy started moving slowly down and I sensed it was intelligently directed. Next, there was freefall with energy zooming around all over inside, which felt great like getting an energy massage

From 7 to 8:15 pm, the left shoulder, left jaw and left side of face were all worked together. The energy worked in a patterned path moving through shoulder joints and muscles, across clavicle, inside of neck and on backs of shoulders. It felt like being stretched while in a hold and sometimes was painful. Then there was a long hold with the neck bent to the right side. After this, the energy moved to work on the right shoulder. The jaws were held open loosely the entire time.

From 8:20 to 9:20 pm, the right shoulder work was nothing like the left. It was mostly jaw work and lining up energy through the joints. There was a long and painful hold while much tension released. After this, the left side of the spine opened with the inner sound of wind and I felt a big rush of energy going up that side. My body felt frozen and my left ear felt like it was in a cold wind.

---

hips and skull happen simultaneously in one stretch.

From 9:20 to 10:30 pm, there was much work in the right shoulder and neck and then I felt the right arm open. Right after that, the shoulders energetically rotated with the chest to create an energy vortex. This immediately rose and then an energy circuit was made from the spine to some place in the shoulder. I think these energy vortices that form are due to new neural connections and will result in powerful transformative capability.

From 10:30 to 11:30 pm, work just finished in my spine after profound alignment with the spine and the skull. I felt pain for a few minutes when there was pressure in the jaw. After this energy worked in my lips and they quivered and moved which felt strange. Body heat increases and I feel like I am melting.

Falling Asleep With Brain Work

March 2: Opening Of TMJ Joints With Extreme Leverage

Last night much energy swirled in the genital area. I arose and stretched to escape the sensation. When I lay down again, the growing reaction increased strongly and I fell asleep.

8 am: I am tight all over with stiff muscles. When I arose and walked, I felt a sharp pain in my right rib cage, in middle on back near outer edge. This is still there. I felt another pain in my right inside upper thigh. My right shoulder joint is popping mildly at the top. There is still strong growing reaction with a slow and wavy rocking feeling. The activity in the root chakra is strong. There is no indication to stretch or move.[33] At 9:30 am, there is strong pain in the groin and my left leg is numb.

At 1 pm, I did a freestyle session with stretches on left and right sides of body, which felt great. The right side was stretched twice and feels near to lining up the spine. I feel alone with no support for what I am going through. I tell a few people a little about it but they do not understand. The only thing I trust is to follow the leader and see where it takes me.

Form 8 to 10 pm, it started with stretches in right body and then I went quickly to the ground and released hip tension where it felt the joints lined up. Energy worked in jaws most of the time with some work on facial bones. My jaws were opened wide and I was drooling and felt energetic rotation above the hard palate. There were long holds while the right jaw muscles were worked. It is clear that I could never figure out how to release this tension from the personality to transform it. The only way it can be done is for me to surrender my mind

---

[33] The symptoms of groin tingling and pain in lower body, indicate a hip movement is imminent.

and allow the body to move spontaneously. It is complex. I do not think the best scientists could figure out how to do it.

Once, I was amazed when my left jaw at the TMJ joint was pressed hard to the mat and I tried to lift my head but could not. Then my head was turning from the left TMJ toward the right. The pressing force was using leverage to open the TMJ joints. I watched close to see how it was done. I clearly saw I was not choosing to do this, intelligence was moving my head this way. That was a difficult session with much drooling and my mouth is dry. My left hip aches and my head and jaws feel like they are broken.

From 10 to 11 pm, the session started with a big yawn to open my jaws wide and then there was work on the left side and some work in the head. The head feels free of tension and energy is moving down gently. I feel energetic rotation in the jaws, adding to the energy flow going down neck and spine. After this, I blanked out. This happens often lately. I get sleepy but am still aware and can observe myself sitting. I think this happens when changes are done in the brain.

March 3: Heat Rises Into Skull, Cold Wind On Both Sides Of Spine

3 am: I had a dream of somebody lying on the floor sleeping and I was telling her she needed to rise. In the dream, I realized the message was for me. The body heat is high and I am sweating.[34] From 3 to 5 am, I did jaw, neck and shoulder crunching. I am exhausted.

From 9 am to 12:15 pm: It has been continuous non-stop twisting through neck and shoulders. I have obligation to work, yet feel I cannot stop this.

From 3:30 to 5:45 pm, I returned from work, sat, and had much head and neck pain. I worked with deep surrender to release the pain. There was difficult crunching work in the neck and something opens in the shoulder crook. I hope the transformation completes soon as it is getting difficult to function like this.

From 7:45 to 10:30 pm, I did a long surrender session while sitting with barely any body movement or crunching. It was as if everything was in the background. I worked to quiet my mind and feel sleepy. I think I did well. Once, the body heat rose and it felt different because it rose into my skull. I allowed this sensation knowing it would heal me although it felt uncomfortable. There were many stinging prickles in shoulders and jaws. I think there

---

[34] I surmise at times when there is critical work to be done in the nervous system such as in the neck, then there is no let up in the energetic reaction and you have to continue until it is done.

were five cycles of energy going through head and body. I stopped when I heard strong marcher music.

I was using the copper ring with Reiki and acupressure, which helps me to quiet my mind and accelerate my vibration. Several times while treating the same toe acupoint on both feet with each hand it felt like that meridian was starting to make a complete circle in the body. Once I felt a cold, windy, rushing feeling on both sides of my body.

It is 10:45 pm and I am resting. There is a strong reaction occurring with energy pummeling my body all over, without pain. My head feels better and shivers occur often. I hear pings and little cracks as the energy courses around. I feel like a big circle of energy and my thoughts stop when I tune into this feeling.

11:45 pm: I was sitting by the fire and energy rose from root chakra in a circle and I felt my chest expand as it slowly moved up with pressure. Energy worked in the shoulders and head. I feel sleepy. Energy circuits are forming all over the body. It is difficult to lie down because my nose is plugged and I cannot breathe easily.

March 4: Horizontal Stretch Across Shoulders, Intense Skull Work

2 am: The high energy continues. I do not know what happens. My mind is still noisy even after long and deep surrenders. I keep pushing it down. I guess there is nothing more to do about it. Its 9 am, I slept well. Tension is rolling out of my body and I feel warm and tingly with stinging prickles in the groin.

1:30 pm: About noon, I took a walk and did a stretch. Now, I am doing a sitting session with neck crunching. Energy is working on a cord, in the back of my skull on right side about halfway up. This area is sensitive and painful. After a while, the neck stretched and then the area of spine between the shoulders filled with energy. Then I felt stretching in a new direction, horizontally across my shoulders. In general, each time a stretch happens tension is released and new neural connections are made, resulting in higher overall body vibration and more power to transform the next thing.

5:30 to 7:30 pm: I am sensitive and when I am around people, I have strong reactions. If I had the choice, I would be in total isolation. I feel like a caged animal, full of pain, loneliness and uncertainty. I am sure it will pass, but now my heart hurts. It has been endless neck and shoulder crunching. If I completely surrender bodily to the stretch reaction, it is much more efficient. I was repeating another spontaneous mantra this week: "Petrilatus Erle".

I have no idea what this means, I could not find it on the Internet. The spontaneous mantras help quiet my mind when the healing is intense.

From 7:30 to 9:30 pm, I did a killer neck and shoulder crunching session. Once, I felt a cool rush of energy in right side of body. I felt work deep in the right TMJ. Once, energy worked on two nerves on the back of head and another in side above ear, which was painful. My head feels broken. Once, there was pain everywhere in my body and it felt like the entire body went into one big spiral. I am sad because I no longer believe this will finish soon, my body is a twisted mess. I need something to lift my spirit; I want to cry because it is so difficult. About 10 pm, while lying I felt energy align on the spine and fell asleep while holding the copper ring.

Counterclockwise Energy Spiral In Body With Joints

March 5: Liking Surrender State, View Of Healing Myself

5 am, after rising, I feel a strong wavy growing reaction, with no urge to stretch. Later I did a long stretch and nothing more until the afternoon.

6:30 pm: A strong growing reaction happens that feels great with warmth and tingling and deep relaxation. I did an hour meditation and lay down for an hour. There is no urge to stretch. From 7 to 8:30 pm, I did a long sitting session with legs to front and head bent to chest. I like the surrender state now. When I have fear, I know I am resisting transformation. To clear an energy block, the brain must change and that is why the quiet mind is necessary to progress and heal. You cannot heal the brain if you are using it. While centered, I see that I am transforming my brain. There is a noticeable increase in energetic work in the skull when I am deeply quiet. I understand that each second of quiet mind counts and has a cumulative transformative effect.

In most sessions lately, body heat rises quickly and then energy moves up spine from tailbone to the skull. I observe a big loop in the right body going through the hip, flank, shoulder, neck and jaw, along the line of the cord of personality. All is energetically worked without stretching. I feel less energy pummeling on right side and a spiral of energy is forming through my body.

As this transformation goes on, my personality is weakening and my higher-self is getting stronger. I think I will eventually reach the point to take full charge and my full potential. At this moment, I see the beauty and wisdom of this transformation. The most painful thing I experience lately comes from identification with the personality. I want to heal this split.

From 8:45 to 10 pm: Sitting, energy is forming into a counterclockwise strong energy spiral from head to tail. As it forms, I feel neuron growth made in the same pattern in the body behind the energy flow. After this, I stretched my neck with some new cracks and energetic feelings. I observed when I was in quiet mind state that tension held in body was releasing along path from back of head, through TMJ, then down to hips, then back up to shoulder joint. I have the insight I am holding this tension in body as the personality and only with quiet mind can I release it.

From 10:15 to 11:20 pm, I sat for more than one hour in a hold with extreme tension on both shoulders, up sides of neck and into skull. I went as long as possible until I could take no more. After this, all the joints started energetically rotating as a spiral formed with them and I felt pain everywhere. When I am caught in the pain sensation then it is difficult to distance from it. The sacrum by the tailbone hurts now.

March 6

Last night I had to rise to stretch, which I did sleepily. When I arose, I had to stretch again, which I did for two hours. I felt a long stretchy pull through the muscles and ligaments in the sides of my head and neck, which connect to the shoulders. Energy works deeply in the TMJ, shoulder and hip joints on right side.

From 11:30 am to 1:45 pm, I have been sitting bent over for hours in a stretching loop that went up and down the body. It starts with energy building in root chakra, then the spine straightens and energy goes up spine and I feel tension releasing from back, shoulders and neck. The energy moves laterally from the spine toward the flanks. Then the cycle repeats. Near the end, something popped and moved by my lower back and right hip, which I think was a separation of the suture of sacrum and hip. I felt it release to the outside and afterward felt tingling energy whorls all over my back, shoulders and head. I rested some and did another session. There were strong pops in the shoulder, neck and head. All seems quiet for now.

10 pm: All day I have been stretching the neck and shoulders. I have decided to move away from here. I cried as it is sad to leave and not a good time for me to do it. I allowed

more pain in my body and a deep surrender because it drowns the emotional pain. A strong growing reaction happens on the right side after an opening in neck and shoulders.

March 7: Neck Lifts, Rapid Spontaneous Body Movements

9:00 am: A slow wavy growing reaction occurred all night; there is not an urge to stretch. From 2:30 to 4:30 pm, I have been doing other things, not much need to stretch even while walking. Driving in the car, I felt my buttocks humming and I heard the marcher music. I took a long nap while strong energy work continued and my entire body went numb.

From 5:30 to 7:30 pm, I did a long stretching session with quick movements, ending on the ground and lying on my back. Then my neck would lift up and the head would bend back and move around. The last three twists were strong, with two in the shoulder and the last in the skull, which felt like it broke the skull somewhere. Are these strong twists of the head done to align the spine? After this, I lied down and there was the strong pinging sound of neuron growth in the brain.

From 7:30 to 8:30 pm, I did another hour of fast body movements, and unbelievable neck and spine maneuvers. After this, my head and jaws hurt and my teeth feel out of alignment.

Stinging Prickles And Neuron Growth In Stretched Tissue

March 8: Strong Work Between Shoulders By Spine And Neck

11:30 am: The energy is strong; it is difficult to stop because of the neck tension. The pattern: Neck crunching, brainwork, then energy goes down, and it starts all over.

9 pm: I spent the entire day cleaning and going through my things and checking ticket prices to move. The strong growing phase continues. From 9-11:15 pm, I was lying on my stomach with energy work in back, neck and area between the shoulders and neck. Near the end, there was a stretchy crunch through skull to top with face pressed into mat most of the time, which frightened me, and I did not know what to do. I felt many energetic changes occurring in the backs of shoulders toward neck and the broad area of upper shoulders and down to lower back.

From 11:20 pm to 1 am, I did a sitting stretch through neck, TMJ and shoulders with different angles and paths while in deep surrender. A new phenomenon is energy prickles and a burning sensation with neuron growth occurring immediately in stretched tissue. This feels good as tension is released. Energy went deep into the center of my ear, which felt good. The inner sound is richer and not so wavy and melodic. While sitting, ripples of energy rise up the neck and make changes. There was a significant right TMJ adjustment and some big pops and cracks in the skull. New areas are cracking, one in shoulder and one in the neck by the clavicle.

March 9

I did a short stretch in the forest and a longer one for about one hour into TMJ, shoulder joint and neck. Energy is opening things.

From 4 to 8:15 pm, I did two stretching sessions working in neck, shoulders and TMJ's that opened the areas. In the second stretch, I ended on my back with much work on the spine. I felt energy building in the root chakra, then rising and going up the spine and working with great force on the lower back, shoulders, neck and jaws. Some work done on head and shoulders was difficult for a short period. It was a long period of surrender, allowing the body to be worked in this way. I waited until the energy shifted to the freefall feeling before I stopped. The neck and jaw areas feel different, like they are aligned. I went to bed early.

March 10: Intense Skull Pressure

I slept deep and arose about two for a sleepy stretch. I did not do much today, feeling I need to prepare to move.

From 5 to 6 pm, first, I stretched and then there was a hold lasting forty-five minutes while a different area below the ear was worked. This felt like a tendon was stretched, from the position under the ear, down to the trapezious muscle in the back of the shoulder. After a release here, energy filled the newly opened area, which felt great.

From 7:30 to 9:45 pm, I am exhausted. I have been endlessly stretching through the same body parts, seemingly getting nowhere. Tonight energy worked in the right hip and worked high in the TMJ. This was painful. This time I felt a physical rotation of my shoulder together with my hip, while lying on my right side, so that is new.

From 9:50 to 11:45 pm, it appears that I am changing my brain and transforming my body. This thought occurs often. I see when I do not think energy works in the skull. At this moment, my skull feels ready to burst; there is too much pressure to sleep.

Energy Spiral Forms Between Jaws And Shoulders On Both Sides

March 11: Weird Dreams And Mind-Chatter

From 3 to 6 am, I did what I could in bed. I could not keep my jaw open wide when I needed to. I sat and tried a few things but then I lay down exhausted. Sleep was restless with weird dreams and constant mind-chatter. I woke up with much body tension and went back to bed with more weird dreams and mind-chatter.

From 8 am to noon, it has been four hours of continuous stretching of TMJ's, neck and shoulders. The energy does not calm and I am exhausted. This is the worst my head has ever felt. I went outside and did some chores with head pain the entire time.

From 2:30 to 5 pm, finally, I lay down and it was exactly what I needed. When I arose, I felt good. From 8 to 9:45 pm, I did a freestyle session with ring and long-distance Reiki symbol working on jaw more. I felt some stretches going through all joints on one side of body and then a hold while energy worked in these joints. Then there was work in hard palate which seemed to bring the energy to center there. There was work on left TMJ and shoulder and then all seemed calm. When I heard the marcher music, I arose.

From 9:50 to 11:30 pm, I was sitting with stretching in jaws and neck with much work on right TMJ. Once there was a strong crack in the TMJ, followed by a rush of energy and a downward spiral of energy moving through jaws and shoulders on both sides. Lastly, I did another stretch down following a different path of stretch through the shoulders.

Maxillae Rays With Electric Teeth, Chest & Neck Lifted

March 12: Pain In Skull By Squamosal And Lamboid Sutures

From 12 to 2 am, I did a long stretching session mostly through the shoulders and the back, and a little in the TMJ. There was painful tension in the shoulders and I went to bed.

From 7 am to 1 pm, I woke feeling rested with growing reaction and no urge to stretch. I took a long walk in the forest and did a freestyle session outside on an energy vortex. I enjoyed it very much. The energy goes deep into both shoulders, which rotate energetically. The purpose seems to align the joints of the shoulders with the spine. There is strong pain at times but it feels good to allow energy into all these sore spots. There was a strong pop in my right shoulder somewhere. The energy is strong now. I love sitting in surrender. It is peaceful and blissful. Energy work occurs across my upper back and shoulders, and periodically works in the TMJ. My right leg feels more energized and energy builds in the root chakra.

From 1 to 6 pm, I spent the entire afternoon outside stretching with strong body movements with work concentrated in the shoulders. A loosening occurs at the back of the neck and shoulders. The energy works laterally across the back and up the sides of the neck. There was a little work in hip and near the end, the TMJ joint lined up with the shoulder. Then I felt a rush of energy with sudden absence of tension in those joints that has been there for so long. That felt great! I sunbathed in the forest for about forty minutes. It was nice. I am exhausted. The root chakra energy is building.

From 6 to 8:30 pm, I have just experienced the strongest growing reaction so far. It felt like everything in my body was worked at once, where heat and the growing reaction encompassed me. Near the end, I felt energy work in each tooth of maxillae moving from one to the next in a ray-like pattern. The ends of the rays were centered at top of head near the fontanel and radiated down through the head and into the teeth. Then energy went around each tooth one at a time with an electric buzzing feeling. Then higher-self took over and my chest and neck lifted.[35]

From 8:30 to 9 pm, I did a sitting stretch through neck and shoulder muscles. I become aware that the stretching of neck, shoulders and TMJ's are stretching muscles, tendons and ligaments between these joints. I noticed three main areas: the side of neck, front right of neck and back right of neck, which seems to connect and end at a point high up in the back of the skull. There is a dent in the skull about halfway between vertical midline of back of skull at same level as top of ear where I feel intense pain. I feel a dent like this on both sides of skull, which is the junction of squamosal and lamboid sutures. There is a pain near my appendix. The skull work was painful.

---

[35] I think this ray pattern is new energy circuits made from hard palate to maxillae to top of skull and results in a new capability to lift the chest and neck by the central nervous system. The teeth are not changing here; the tingling is felt in them because they are part of the energy circuit pathway.

Lately, I no longer have a cross-bite in my teeth and when I open my jaws there is no loud popping like I had before in either TMJ joint. This is a defect I have always had. In addition, it seems that the top teeth in front come out more with a larger gap between bottom and top teeth. One of the tight muscle areas in skull goes through the lower right molar, up behind the ear and to the TMJ. My right ear opened more with loud pops and feeling of drainage.

Moving Facial Bones, Vortex Forming In Skull

March 13: Learning How To Release Tight Ends Of Skull Muscles

I arose a few times in the night to stretch. I did four hours of continuous sessions with work in skull, shoulders and hip joint. I feel pain in the skull at the ends of the muscles and cords from the neck and shoulders. One end was inside the right sphenoid wing near the bone. The path of stretch goes from there down through TMJ to jaw and lower right molar, then down side of neck and into shoulder crook and then across to shoulder joint. This has been a main area of work lately.

From 5 to 6 pm, my jaw, maxillae and nose bones feel like they are moving around on my face when I lay down. Much work occurs in the skull with many tender points so it is difficult to get comfortable without lying. When I took a rest earlier, I could have stayed there forever; it was warm, tingly and relaxing as tension rolled out. My mood gets better and sitting in surrender is welcome. Lately in the lying sessions, energy in my head forms into a vortex and my mind goes blank with total silence for a few seconds.

From 6:30 to 9 pm, I did a long sustained surrender of about an hour holding head to left side, while work was done on tense cord on side of neck. I adjusted my position and there was another hour of work going on in the skull with tension on this cord. It was painful most of the time. It is clear these neck cords connect somewhere in the skull. I think tension accumulates on these muscles over our lifetime owing to habitual patterns of thinking and facial and body expressions. I notice different thoughts pop up while energy works on various cords. It seems true these cords can only be relaxed at the end in the skull by having quiet mind. The quieter I am, the more the cord relaxes and tension releases. I have increased ability to sustain surrender as the skull work progresses.

March 14: Painful Vortex Forms In Top Part Of Skull

I slept long. From 9:30 am to noon, I did powerful stretches down back and up through neck and shoulders, then there was much skull work with pain and intense burning at times. Then there were strong stretches in skull, neck and shoulders with work in TMJ that went in circles around the head and laterally worked the jaws. The shoulders have a tingly stretchy feeling across them and the left shoulder popped. The growing reaction is stronger today.

At 8:30 pm, I have been stretching most of the day but not too effectively. The pressure of moving does not help. I know I am identifying with 'my sad story'. While packing, I feel sad about leaving my friends and have some fear because I do not know where I am going.

From 9:30 pm to midnight, I worked to quiet my mind and eventually it settled. There was work on neck, shoulders and back ending with a long hold with head bent to left side. When I was in deep surrender, energy worked in the skull. I feel intense pain in small areas of the skull, which correspond to the cords stretched in the neck, back and shoulders. Later body heat rose with burning pain as a section of my upper skull was worked on the surface. After this a circle formed in top section of skull, I think the direction was counterclockwise. This is the most painful thing I have felt so far.

I go into deep surrender state and cannot remember well what happened. I am not interested in knowing, I only want to get through it. I hear sounds outside far away when I am quiet. There was a big snap related to a long cord on side of neck somewhere in line of shoulder. There is a similar work in left shoulder that is easy compared to the right shoulder. There was another alignment of TMJ joints with squishy sounds in the skull and my head hurts.

March 15: Fast Head Movements, Neck Crunching, Intense Skull Pain

10 am: I slept long and have little desire to stretch. When I went to walk, my toes and fingers were numb. I spent thirty minutes meditating under the tree near the energy vortex. Then my left shoulder crunched loudly and something gave. After this, there was a period with quick bobbing and moving of the head. These happen fast and I do not like them but they usually open something.[36] There was stretching on right side of body through hip and

back up through neck. When I returned to my room, my head hurt with growing reaction, so I went to sleep. From 5:30 to 6 pm, when I arose there was a strong force in shoulder crook and I could not move from this position easily. Then there were strong neck crunches and work in left shoulder. From 11 pm to 1:30 am, I did a long session of stretching on all sides of neck and with sides of neck to both shoulders. It was painful. There were stretches into skull and TMJ's, with pain in all these parts at once. It was the most skull pain I have experienced so far.

March 16: Big Crack Behind TMJ Joint

1:30 am, the neck and shoulders open much. I would like to do more but I am exhausted. From 2:30 to 3:30 am, I did one more session and slept. 6 am to noon: I had to rise and stretch. I have been stretching all morning. From 3 to 9 pm, I have been stretching in neck and shoulders. There was one strong stretch in both TMJ's and a big crack in the head behind that joint. Now, it is pleasant to sit in surrender with quiet mind.

March 17: Vortex Forms From Base Of Skull Down Neck To Shoulders

I awoke once to stretch and needed to stretch immediately after rising. Later in the day, I took a walk and did a freestyle session in the woods on the energy vortex. From 4 to 9 pm, it has been almost non-stop stretching. It occurs to me it is important that I work harder to stop the thinking so I do not energize the personality strongly. The work is more effective when I am quiet. My head hurts badly and I feel I need to get it together better. There are about two weeks left before I leave. My personality is strongly activated which makes it harder. I like the surrendered feeling much better. I see this clear and know I have a choice of either holding onto my pain or letting it go. Letting go gives pleasure.

There is physical lateral stretching of muscles and tissues in the back of the neck and both shoulders. It is like the infinity sign across my upper back and twisting around the C7 joint. There are many popping sounds in the neck and shoulders while this happens and the stretched area feels tingly. Once there was a lateral move in two directions (one to right and one to left) at once, through the neck and the top edges of shoulders across upper back

---

[36] These are spontaneous movements (kriyas) with quick movement of the head; it is comparable to an epileptic fit, and later it will affect the whole body.

circling around C7. There was a big release after it happened. I felt both shoulders had to change enough before this could happen.

After the path across my shoulders, energy moved rapidly down the spine about halfway down. The pattern forming in the back was like a circle. Then my head moved around in a circle and I felt a circle of energy moving from base of skull, encircling the neck that went down to shoulder crooks and then just below the tips of the shoulder joints.

I did one more session sitting and then lying with the ring. Next, I used Reiki on my legs and worked with surrender. Just before I fell asleep, strong energy went up spine and into base of skull and something cracked with excruciating pain. Thankfully, it was brief. Then I thought, "That did it" and fell asleep.

March 18: Cleansing Dreams

I awoke recalling dreams of old traumas and wondered if this was a cleansing reaction. I thought about the purpose of dreams and it came that our internal healer cleans our memories and emotions when triggered elements are brought to the surface. There is much tension in the neck.

From 8 to 10:30 am, I took a long walk and did a stretch in the forest. I have been rolling my head around most of the day, opening something in the right side of the neck through the TMJ joint and across the shoulders. This is starting to feel endless.

From 8:30 to 10:30 pm, I received a long-distance Reiki healing. I felt my vibration rise and used it for a surrender session. It took some time to quiet my mind. I am stressed and agitated because of moving. To accept my move I need to see it as a new beginning. The door is wide open to do anything I choose to do and I like this idea much.

March 19: Loud Cracks In Skull

I did one short stretch and nap because I need to leave soon, and want to calm this reaction. I was on the computer and packing my belongings for most of the day. I have strong energy, feel good with a sense of adventure and newly found freedom.

From 11:30 pm to 12:30 am, I just did a neck stretch with intense pain in the skull and shoulder crooks with lighter pain all over the body. I stretched for fifteen more minutes and strong cracks started happening in the skull. After this, the tension released and I slept soundly.[37]

March 20 (Vernal Equinox) To March 22

On the 20th, my neck was stiff which I felt to be a sign of healing and did not do any sessions that day. The next day I did stretching in neck, shoulders and TMJ's. A few shivers happened and the TMJ on right opened more. It feels like my teeth are moving around. In the evening, I stretched with crunches until my head hurt bad and went to bed. On the 22nd, I slept long and deep. The root chakra is energized and I have premenstrual cramps. My neck is stiff and I am not getting much time to work out; preparing to move takes all my energy.

Elastic Sheets, Throat Muscles Balloon Like A Puffer Fish

March 23

The energy works deep in the bony part of the shoulder joint. I have soreness, swelling and tenderness in the neck. When I arose, I yawned and did a spontaneous stretch with bones cracking in the hips and shoulders. It felt good. My toe joint hurt so I bent it and it cracked.

For two hours in the evening, I did freestyle and sitting sessions. There was a long period of lying on my back while energy worked strongly up the side of my neck and face. My toe joint hurts and the right side of the body opens more. Circles of energy work around the C7 joint, in skull, TMJ and shoulder. The area under my chin in the throat balloons like a puffer fish and work is concentrated near tonsils. When my neck and head turn, it feels stretchy. Energy work stretches through new pathways in shoulders, neck and skull. I looked up the anatomy of the cervical spine and shoulder. This is very complex and it does not surprise me it takes many passes through these areas. The root chakra is active lately and this is the second day of a light menstruation. I would like energy to work more in lower body, because my lower parts are stiff. I did one more sitting session before retiring.

March 24

I did not do any sessions all day not even a walk; I was busy with painting and cleaning! ☹

---

[37] I think the head pain is due to pressure building in the skull to open the cranial sutures. When the crack happens, the suture opens and the pressure is released.

March 25: Reiki II Okuden Distance Session, Chest Crack, Skull Pain

I did not stretch or walk in the forest, instead I painted my room. From 8 to 9:30 pm, I did thirty minutes of stretching with Reiki symbols and the ring. At 8:30 pm, I received Reiki Level II Okuden from my Reiki Master long-distance. When he started sending the energy the stretching stopped and I stood still. Each time he gave one of the three empowerments, the stretch was more effective.

Later I did a strong session lasting until midnight with no break. Notable was a loud audible crack in my chest with the feeling a bone shifted afterward. I think it was deep in the front. Perhaps it was a rib by the breastbone or perhaps the collarbone. Later there were two more cracks, which felt to be deep in the shoulder crook. After these cracks the C7 area opened much and energy went deep into the area of the trapezious muscle and up through the TMJ's. Then a new path was worked much from shoulder crook and under right jaw, two molars forward, then on up and behind the eyeball.

I decided to call this new phenomenon occurring 'elastic sheets'. Many stretches had the elastic sheet feeling that encompasses larger areas of the body. There were some painful holds and numerous burning lines along various pathways. My toe hurt and the right hip was worked at times together with the other joints. There was work on left shoulder and both shoulders together. The majority of the work concentrated in the cord on the side of the neck. My head hurts much now.

March 26: Energizing Connective Fascia

3 pm: I am still stretching. I feel I cannot stop. It occurs to me, what this elastic sheet feeling is. Before the stretches in the body went along a narrow path with energy pushing along it, now the paths are wider bands. So I become like elastic woman. On the backside, it is the back of head, neck and up to the shoulder joints. There are fingers of this feeling starting to reach down on the back and some in the front. Lately, I feel an energy vortex forming inside my head.

From 3:30 to 4 pm, on front of body, the elastic sheet is below the mandible and throat and goes down to the top of the lung area below the collarbones. The skin in the throat visibly puffs out especially where the tonsils are. I do not feel this in my face or on sides of neck. I think the formation of elastic sheets means I am getting stronger. The elastic sheet sensation feels like a massage and being ironed out. My head hurts.

March 27 To March 28: Corkscrew Spine Movements, Wild Head Swings

It is the afternoon, and I cannot stop stretching; I have had little rest since Saturday night Okuden. I have much to do to move, but this is strong so I decided to devote the day to it. There is much work going on in neck vertebrae, by C7, and with energetic rotation in the shoulders. There were energetic rotating movements around C7 that felt weird, with cracking all the way around it. There is much crunching, popping and cracking all over. I feel much energetic rotation behind neck and shoulders when I lie down.

Often there are spontaneous body movements, which happen strong and are hard to endure. There are wild swings of the head and corkscrew like movement down the spine. I think these happen to align the spine. I hear amplified sounds outside, the ear keeps popping and my head hurts badly. When I rest there is a loud melodic inner sound with much body tension, so I need to stretch even when lying. There is no rest now.

From 8 to 11 pm, I have been stretching and gave a Reiki treatment to my cat. I gave myself a full Reiki acupressure treatment on the meridians and treated the chakras. The Reiki really helps. I refused to stretch and it felt good to do that. At times, I heard a high-pitched sound and felt moments of total silence, which has been occurring over the last few days.

March 29

It was another day of stretching and of having a big headache. I saw full surrender is needed to release something in the skull to relieve the head pain. I worked with that. Later in the day, I gave a friend a two-hour Reiki session using my Reiki acupressure sequence.

March 30

It is 7:30 am and I slept long. I feel slow wavy energetic movement with inner sound. There is less tension in the neck area; it is nice to have a break. My personality seems calmer too, I am more aware of the thinking and it is easier to stop it. The rest did not last long; I spent most of the day stretching. I am not getting anything else done. I work with the transformation, as it is what I want the most.

March 31

It was a day of many stretching sessions with many spontaneous body movements. Energy moves deep into the shoulder joint with crunching. Energy works in right hip, pectoral muscles and armpit. Often my shoulders hunch and the neck drops and I feel intense pain while an alignment happens through the shoulders. This is followed with a strong force on both sides of the neck and skull at once, which I cannot take long.

Energy Vortex Forms In Shoulder Crook

April 1: Loosening Of Scapulas, Cracks In Shoulder & Base Of Skull

From 8 to 11 pm, I started with a Reiki session and went until exhaustion. My ear opened many times and the cord that goes through lower molar down to neck loosened. Vortices form in the shoulder crook, which shows the purpose of the shoulder hunching. Frequently I heard high-pitched sounds and had amplified hearing and smells. There was much work in the TMJ and skull. Near the end, there was a big pop in the cord deep in the neck with a huge release of tension from the neck. Energy spirals are forming in the head and when they first form there is intense pain. I feel a lateral alignment of the jaws and energy moves down to neck and shoulders. There is crunching in both scapulae and the right scapula feels loose. 11:20 pm, the energy does not settle down. Just now, there were cracks in the shoulder, neck and at base of skull. The body heat rose many times up into my head. The inner sound is noisy, I felt shivers and fell fast asleep.

April 3: TMJ Popping, Energy Balls In Skull, Neck & Shoulders

I leave here in two days; the time goes by too fast. I did many stretches in neck, shoulders, hips and TMJ's. There is much energetic rotation with crunches in the shoulders and loud pops in the TMJ's. I hope I can release the neck tension before travel. Yesterday while talking with someone I had to open my jaw to release the tension. I do not like the thought of being on planes and in airports for almost an entire day without stretching.

From 7 to 10 pm, I did a long session stretching in the neck with unbelievable movements. I felt energy balls in many places pushing ligaments around in the skull, neck and shoulders. There was much crunching all over the body and the neck tension released. The yogic fish pose head moment was prevalent which happens while lying on my back and twisting my body. It seems lying allows the neck to be more relaxed because there is no weight on it. I rarely hang my head anymore; it is all this horizontal work.

There was high body heat during this with sweating and intense pain in various places in the skull. Energy worked deeply in the skull on the ligaments and I heard skull cracks in numerous places. I found it easy to surrender for this. Many of the movements were rapid and included the entire body. There was much work on the energy vortex in the shoulder crooks with shoulders hunched. Each day my body feels more like a physical spiral. I remember some infinity sign patterns but cannot recall where they were. When I am completely surrendered, I do not remember much.

April 4 To April 5: Moving

I spent all day yesterday preparing to leave. I left early in the day at 6 am. I did not hear my alarm clock. I am very grateful my friend woke me. There was no time for anything except running to the airport. During the day on planes and in airports, I found places to do short stretches. Twice in bathrooms, I did thirty-minute sessions and I worked some stretches in while sitting on the plane with a blanket over my head. Probably people were looking at me as if I was weird but I did not care, I needed it much. I arrived at 6:20 pm in the states.

April 6

I spent most of the day getting my computer configured. Later in the day, I gave a Reiki session to a relative. His energy was strong and he seemed receptive to the treatment. I was surprised how strong the whorls of energy felt in him. Afterward, he said it felt like being engulfed in a cloud of energy. I took one walk and spent time under a big Banyan tree. I want to return to outside sessions, the energy under large trees is awesome. However, there is not much space around here to walk and be in private, there are people everywhere.

April 8

I did many short sessions, I am feeling more relaxed and the energy returns.

April 9

Lately, I am working harder on my sessions trying to regain my energy. The work in the body is much the same: TMJ's, head, neck and shoulders. Later, my right shoulder felt looser with rotation in the joint. In most sessions, there is substantial cracking and popping of bones and ligaments.

April 10

I did many sessions. I am more relaxed and the stress of moving lessons. There is a remarkable reduction in my anger, so it was good for me to change my surroundings. I feel an openness that I am free to do whatever I want. I had an insight about the strong energy I feel when giving energy treatment to some people. I think it is because the person is desperately in need of healing, so their 'inner healer' strongly draws energy when I give a treatment. I feel like I am not progressing with the shoulders, neck and jaw work, nothing is moving. I did the full Reiki acupressure sequence yesterday and that worked to move something. Last night I could barely sleep, I was alternating stretching sessions between short naps. Though my neck was bent, it felt good.

April 11: Long Cord Moved Vertically Across Spine

From 6 to 7:30 am, I did a session early because my neck was stiff and the force of corkscrew like tension was strong on the right side of my body. I sat in a chair with the copper ring over my head and resting on the C7 joint, then moving it to different places on the shoulder crook. This was strong but still nothing was moving. It occurred that heat helps to move things. Later in the session, heat naturally built and it was more effective to make movements in the head, neck and shoulders. For the stretching sessions to be effective, I need to build the energy beforehand and to stay in the surrendered state.

I am still surrendering my body for the movements, not doing it with my mind, yet over all these weeks it barely moves anything. From now on, I will do the Reiki acupressure sequence before stretching to raise the energy and build heat. The acupressure raised energy in the lower body, which I need because I am so stiff there. Energy worked in my toe and hip. Near the end, a long ligament was moving vertically across my spine, almost like a flexible stick, I felt this twice. So something different happens.

I am trying to find out how to move energy up through neck and shoulders to head. It helps to do acupressure on the joints on the back of the neck, the area between the nose and eyebrows and at the back of head at centerline and top of head.

April 12: Opening In Neck, Elastic Sheet In Shoulders

I did three or four sessions. I did the full Quicken Touch[38] sequence starting with the toes on up to the skull. I am experimenting with acupressure on the joints. So far, the Reiki with acupressure on the meridians is the strongest routine. Something opens in the neck, there was one shiver and the growing reaction is strong all day. I had the elastic sheet feeling deep in the right shoulder.

It is still difficult going through this twisted mess in my joints. I guess its part of my process to discover how to continue to progress. I am no longer satisfied with stretching, as this obviously is not enough. It works well to use acupressure on the neck vertebrae and on acupoints in areas of shoulder and TMJ.[39]

There are slow, wavy energy whorls in the root chakra now. Lately, I rarely hear the inner sound. I sense the marcher music, but far away in the distance. In addition, when I do the bodily surrender, it feels like my mind moves me rather than my higher-self. I guess this is starting to feel normal, that it is growing on me. Yet, I miss the springy feeling and the music and arising of higher-self. Maybe my awareness is reduced because of the change of environment and because I have not established a regular routine.[40] I am determined to make the transformation my primary focus. I think about doing an extended retreat.

April 13: Experimentation And Getting Side-Tracked

I read about cranial sacral therapy and have enough information to know how to palpate along the cranial sutures. Combined with detailed anatomy of the skull, I am using the sensation of energy movement along the sutures and when I feel irregularities then I apply Reiki there. This is effective. There is much to explore and it is interesting to know the structure of the skull and see how it affects other parts of the body when energy is applied to it. Energy works in neck vertebrae above the C7 joint and at the base of the skull on the right.

I did something where I had three fingers on all the sore spots: at base of skull, back of skull on right and along side of right temple. This revolves around the sphenoid bone that is mostly deep in the skull and is the only bone that articulates with all the skull bones. The squishy sound I hear in my head I think is due to the movement of the sphenoid bone. There

---

[38] Quicken Touch is the name I give my Reiki acupressure sequence. Full details are on my website.

[39] I am getting off-track here, going into intellectual solutions versus surrendering and following. I even say it; I am no longer satisfied with just stretching.

[40] The latter was true; it was due to reduced awareness and energy levels. I had several episodes like this, which happen when the mind chatter becomes dominant.

were many cracks in the head and neck from doing this treatment. I am excited because something moves.

April 14: Cranial Sacral Treatment

I had a cranial sacral treatment, which was fantastic and moved something. The entire day I was reacting from it, stretching stronger and something in the skull opened.

April 15: Circle Around C7, Ears Popping, Sinuses Opening

There were many kriyas in the night. Energy works in skull and deep in the shoulders. I am using cranial sacral techniques on my skull and using Reiki on the sutures in the skull and at the base of neck. I am tired and the skull hurts much. I felt a release in neck by C7, which then filled with energy and felt great. My ear is popping and the sinuses drain. It feels good to have some progress and a new tool to work with.

Energy Tracing Around Edges Of Skull Plates

April 16

For most of the day I was stretching. I have integrated a new technique on the skull combined with the stretch. While I am stretching, I use Reiki on the acupoints in the skull, neck and shoulders where I feel tension or pain. This is effective. The pulling sensation in the skull is owing to energy tracing around the suture lines of skull plates. I think the intention of this activity may be to loosen this bone so it can move. The neck and shoulders open much.

April 17

I used the new technique on the skull and it is working well. My neck and head are sore. At 2:30 pm, I catch a flight to Reno, Nevada. I hope I can settle into a routine quickly and start writing. I feel I need to commit full time to this transformation, otherwise I have too much tension. I do not want to do anything else. The day on the planes and in the airports was horrible. On the planes, I needed to stretch and sleep but they were such small seats and there was no way to get comfortable. I had to stretch in public while sitting and for sure people thought I was weird. There was no possibility to stretch in the Atlanta airport because all the bathrooms had people standing in lines. When I arrived in Reno, I had heavy bags and could barely move them. I called my Dad and waited outside in the freezing air for him to arrive. When I got to his place, I went to sleep immediately.

April 22: Shoulder Examination & Aura Healing

It took time to settle and start again. I started a few days ago. I have been working with manipulation of the cranial sutures and doing my Reiki acupressure sequence. I did stretches and there was energy work in the shoulder. After this, I felt my shoulder to find the sore spots. I found big muscle knots in trapezious and under scapula on right side, so my shoulder girdle does not have much range of motion. I started applying acupressure to the sore spots. A strong sore spot was just under the end of the collarbone at the breastbone. This tightness went across and ended under my shoulder on one of the ribs right under my armpit. The knot in the trapezious affected three areas. It was tight from in the skull area near the TMJ joint and down the neck under the collarbone and to an area in the rib cage by the breast. It was tight from back of head down back of neck near C7 on right side and then when down to middle back and right hip. The movement of my shoulder is restricted both vertically and horizontally in the front and back. I worked all these points and afterward I felt the shoulder loosening. Then I went back to working on skull, back and shoulders.

My current routine is to do the Reiki acupressure sequence and to do the joints in the same way and then I do a freestyle session applying acupressure on spots where tension is felt. Then I sit and meditate. After that, I lie down and allowed spontaneous stretches. Since I have been working like this, my energy increases. I try not to be carried away with too much stretching; instead, I focus on being still and surrendering. I feel I am doing endless stretches in the body, but it seems to move something. I had an aura healing done. The person said that my aura was too much to the front and he balanced it and moved it back into center.

Later that day I had a strong session with big movements in chest and shoulders. There were flexible stretches with my back arching and once my chest pushed out. When that happened, I felt a big pop in the rib cage in front and felt the shoulder release. There was much crunching transversely under the collarbone and the shoulder.

April 23: Constant Neck Tension, Fetal Healing

I slept a little but feel rested. The growing reaction continues strong. I would love to get relief from this constant need to stretch my neck. It is difficult to do daily things with awareness because I have the constant urge to stretch. There were many shoulder stretches and releases and energy worked in skull in the morning session. At the end, I decided to do regular yoga stretches because my muscles feel powerful to open the chest, ribs, shoulders and neck joints. This felt good even though it hurt. I feel as if I have much power to stretch the tight shoulder. Lately while doing freestyle sessions, my body is in a fetal position when I feel areas of strong tension. I guess the healing goes in reverse order, of how the personality was laid down, the oldest layers are healed last and now I am healing the fetal layer.

Ear And TMJ Vortices

May 7: Mandible & Sphenoid Release, Ear Vortices, TMJ Rotation

Since I last wrote, the stretching continues non-stop and gets stronger each day. About a week ago, I started sitting in the sun with a large flat quartz crystal under my feet and holding a large crystal in my hands.[41] This raises the energy effectively in the body. I have been sitting about thirty minutes to one hour, meditating without movement allowing the energy to course around my body. I have been giving my father energy treatments. In the last two weeks, there has been much movement of the sphenoid bone and much work in the right shoulder.

My first rib on the chest, which goes into the shoulder, holds much tension; I am trying to release it by using acupressure on acupoints by it. The mandible released with a loud snap and after that, many cranium bones shifted with notable movement of the sphenoid. Then I felt large vortices form in the skull. For the first time I felt energetic rotation like I feel in the hips and shoulders occurring in the TMJ's, which hurt when it first started. After this energy moved down to neck and esophagus, then back up under roof of mouth, into nose, behind eyes, in temples and worked in most of the cranium bones. Then it went back down to shoulders, back and hip.

The time it takes for energy to move in spine from root chakra to crown chakra is getting shorter and I experience shivers often. I have little motivation to do anything except meditation and stretching. I cannot sleep long and awaken with strong tension or compression that needs to be released. Tension builds during the day too. I feel my energetic vibration is finally at the level of a few months ago. The growing phase happens each time all over my

---

[41] I call this a sun session.

body starting with the toes and moving up. There is a pain in my bladder. The inner dialogue increases when I have too much tension. I am happy because I can easily turn off the mind-chatter and go deep in meditation.

Description Of Vortices

I want to map all the internal energy vortices that are formed as I can easily see them. I think this information might help open adhesions of the skeleton. I observe vortices form when the tissue of the body in that area are loose enough. When they spin, they are super effective to accelerate healing. I notice one from the eardrum into the depths of the brain, going half way on each side to the midpoint of the skull. A vortex moves from the shoulder crook and circles the side of the ear. There is a horizontal one across the shoulders like an infinity sign, which create energetic rotation in the shoulder girdle. I guess this infinity sign pattern will form in the skull to connect the mandible joints. There are more. Lately, I recall memories of being born. I had the sensation I was pulled from the womb by a doctor pulling my right arm.[42]

May 9: Hand And Feet Numbness, Ligament Snaps By C7

I did a Reiki session on the gallbladder and liver meridians combined. Quickly my hands and feet went numb and I could not feel them. I sat like that for more than an hour. There was intense pain from the left TMJ down the side of the neck, across the back of the shoulder and ending at the top of the left shoulder joint. Later on there were little snaps in the spine near the C7 joint at the base of the neck. I was dripping with sweat most of the time.

I have been doing Reiki on the toes, combining certain meridians, and treating them as a pair. The other night I did the urinary bladder and kidney meridians together which make a strong combination. I cannot tell if it is significant or is due to my stronger energy. There was a strong growing reaction in all parts of my body.

---

[42] I discovered forceps were commonly used for women giving birth while in twilight sleep. My mother had that and she cannot recall my birth. In twilight sleep (1945-1960), the mother was injected with morphine and scopolamine to induce a state of semi-consciousness, without feeling pain and with scant memory of what happened. Women were restrained and strapped to gurneys for their protection as they thrashed around in bed, freed from their inhibitions by the drugs. I feel it is likely I was pulled out with forceps or possibly by my arm.

Occipital, Sphenoid, Parietal & Temporals Release, Facial Bones Open

May 10

I have to rise several times at night to stretch and release tension. After rising, it takes an hour to release the tension. Apparently, tension cannot be fully released in a prone position. In the last days, I need to do a session every three hours. There are big releases in the jaws, neck, shoulders and down the back into the hip. I find that doing the Reiki acupressure sequence and freestyle stretching is effective. Energy has been working in the TMJ joint. There is sensitive work by the sphenoid wing. I feel a ligament moves deep in the head. There was a big crack above the right TMJ by the sphenoid wing and afterward many cranial bones shifted. The elastic sheet feeling was along the occipital bone edge and then it moved with a squishy sound. Then there was much movement of facial bones, I could not believe how much they moved.

In the freestyle sessions there were many twisting body stretches and I felt cords moving across the spine. One cord released and the right shoulder suddenly dropped with huge tension release. There is work on the left shoulder with a similar problem as the right from the tip of the shoulder joint on top, across the trapezious muscle and into the neck and on up to the left TMJ. Many times both shoulders are worked together that does not hurt as much as it did before.

This is a slow process. It takes a long time to reposition everything; the parts of the body do not magically go to a new position. Even after something releases, it tends to return near to the previous position. Continuous effort is needed to transform the body. The most effective work happens while I am in the meditative state. Often, my hands or feet quickly go numb and I feel as ONE unit of energy. When I feel like this, the transformation is more profound.

Lately I have conflict between doing this full time versus establishing a new career. I am far from being able to 'go with the flow'. I have everything I need but it is hard to enjoy it and not feel like I should be doing something else. I wish I knew what would happen with all this. It is much work so I cannot help but think something great will come from doing it. I suspect after all the skeletal alignment work is done it will still take quite some time before the new body is fully grown, if it even works that way. I have many unanswered questions and still do not know what to do next. I will work another meridian before going to bed.

May 11: Throat Unzipping, Parietal Moves

While doing a session, I had the sensation of zippers opening all over the throat area. There was strong movement of the parietal bone moving laterally with the left shoulder. It felt like stretching in two directions at once. After this energy moved down to the sternum and rib cage and I felt releases there. I am happy.

May 12: Stretching Cranium Bones, Snapping Around Temporal Bone

I did a sun session, which is strong and effective. There was much stretching of cranium bones. Fine bones snap around my ear and jaw joints[43] and I feel open spaces here afterward. My right ear pops much. I experience frequent sweats. Strong energy currents come up muscles of body into neck and ear, like a huge spiral pushing upward. Energy worked in back and chest, which open more. I did freestyle stretches of shoulders to back, alternating stretches of shoulders and doing both shoulders together. I feel I cannot stop. I frequently need to lie down and when growing reaction starts, I fall asleep. I frequently experience sustained quiet mind during the growing phase. The inner sound is like the night air full of crickets. I rarely hear the marcher music. It was not an easy day and my head still hurts. I am tired of this constant neck tension. I will do more hoping it will help me sleep.

May 14: Parietals Open, Energy Balls Bombard Neck, Palate, Nose & Eyes

There was much crunching deep in the skull at the back of the neck, with cracks and ligament snapping. Afterward there were vortices at top of the skull working to loosen the parietals. Huge tension released from back of skull, throat and my neck. Another time I felt strong energy balls push up center of the neck and move to the hard palate. Then it felt like the entire hard palate was massaged with an upward force from these energy balls. After this, the energy balls rose through my lips and nose. My lips quivered and went numb. Then the energy balls moved to the eye sockets and last to the top of the head. Later energy moved down and worked in ribs, hips and pelvis. My toes, hands and all body parts vibrate strongly, and the bed shakes when I lie down.

May 15

---

[43] This is likely snapping around edges of temporal bone.

I did a strong freestyle stretch into trunk and hips. The neck and the cranium bones continue to move around and crack. Daily I feel more like a single vibration in the body. I can easily watch the patterns of energy flows inside my body.

Spinal Circuits Form (CV & GV)

May 16

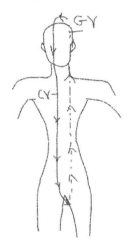

There has been continued work all over the body, each day the vibration gets stronger. Tonight I felt an energy circuit form up and down the spine from root chakra to crown chakra. It seemed to be the same paths as the conception vessel and the governing vessel meridians. The circuit went up the back and down the front of the body **(see figure).**

I worked specific acupoints using acupressure with Reiki to try to loosen the trapezious muscles. The following worked well to release tension there: small Intestine meridian SI19 acupoints near ears on both sides of the head works the upper shoulders (trapezious muscles) in back and the jaws. Liver LI20 acupoints on sides of nose and triple heater TH23 acupoints both work the trapezious muscles. All these pairs were effective and quickly I fell into quiet mind state.

Insight about healing is done first in brain: It came that healing in the body is done first in the brain and this change echoes down afterward into the body.

Chapter 13: Cranium Bones Open

Cranial Sutures Separate

May 17: Right Body Energy Spiral, Whiteout

In the sun session, I saw when I have the galaxy view, I have gone out of mind and this state allows maximum healing to occur in the brain. I seek a way to relax my mind on command so I can enter this state readily. It is related to falling asleep. I tried a conscious focus on area of pituitary gland and on the 3rd eye region. It seemed focus on the 3rd eye area readily induced the sleeping state.[44] I then thought of an epidural, how certain points when stimulated can numb areas of the body. I will research acupoints that induce anesthesia, numbing or sleep. In auricular acupuncture, the tranquilizer point is near the small Intestine meridian acupoint SI19, which I used a few days ago.

All morning, energy worked strongly in right side of body, while the left side hummed but did not move. Often I am put in a long hold with my jaws open to the maximum. A large energy vortex is forming in my body where the right side is half of that whole. I felt uterine contractions and it feels like my menstruation starts.

Tonight I felt the cranial sutures on top of my head separate. There was movement in the hard palate, the right teeth and the nasal bones. The ear continues to pop. I worked in a sweat continuously for more than an hour. Near the end, I felt the energy circuit along the right spine activate strongly all the way through the neck. This is the first time I have felt energy going straight through the neck. When I lay down, energy worked on a circuit going through the neck to the skull and then a total blankness and quiet happened that lasted a few seconds. Later it happened again, that quiet is awesome.

I went to bed about 1 am and woke at 3 am. I was having many cleansing dreams. I had to stretch my neck, shoulders and jaws to relieve the tension. I do not feel good now; I am tired, have head pain and the dreams were depressing.

---

[44] Mirror neurons are located in the frontal lobe of the brain behind the forehead. Relaxing this area of mind settles the self-reflection ability. I think we intuitively do this when we fall asleep; we relax this area with our mind's eye.

Insight about vortices for healing it is interesting that most meridian paths are vertical running along the skeleton. There are vortices of rotational energy. It seems it should be possible to produce a rotational vortex in the body by pressing the right combination of acupoints. Rotational vortices are much stronger healing forces of energy than linear circuits. Movement of the joints produces energy rotation. The body is one whole and all points connect in some way to each other. I experimented with this idea and had some success to generate vortices in the joints.[45]

All Cranium Bones Move

May 20: Changes To Extremities

There were strong movements in the skull, jaws and down the body. It gets close to an energy vortex forming in my entire body. I did a long session with skull work. I feel empty spaces where I have had tension for so long in neck, jaw and right side. One time it felt like all the cranium bones moved at once. I never expected that would happen. I see the skull as a joint and all the cranium bones need to loosen. I am feeling the same releases in joints on the left side of the body as I did with the right side earlier. Increasingly the movements down the spine affect the joints on both sides of the body. Often the body vibration rises high and I feel work with pain in the extremities down to fingers and toes.

I guess millions of pathways need to change. I feel when the neck is clear it will set off a reaction. Often I feel many reactions happen at once. My mind often blanks out and I continue to sweat much. It is easier to stay quiet and allow work to happen in the brain. When I do this, it is similar to leaving the body and explains the galaxy view, the deep meditation and the blue light experiences I have had in meditation in the past. I often practice to achieve this state on command. It helps to speed up the transformation and gives me a pain free place to ride out the storm.

My Current Meditation is to feel my body as a single unit of energy and watch the movement occurring. I try to feel drowsy or like I am falling asleep which fully relaxes me and facilitates this state. Everyone knows how to fall asleep. I merely do that. I imagine myself as sleeping and then go out of body to observe my body sitting there. When I

---

[45] The details of this technique are in my Reiki healing journal under notes for May 17, 2006.

successfully do this, energy zooms around freely in my mind and body. As 'I' am not there, there is no resistance to impede the energy and it speeds up dramatically.

May 22

I did a long freestyle session this morning with mostly skull work. I started with standing and stretched down though legs and hips. Then there was energetic rotation in the hip and a power arose to move the spine and after this energy rose to work in the skull. Standing seems the most effective work out. It seems a high energy is needed to make changes in the skull and the lower body workout builds and collects energy into the root chakra. Then this energy moves up the spine to work in the brain and after this change is done, energy ripples on down the body to carry out the new change.

I did many sessions. I found other good acupoints for working in the skull. One is the horizontal line in the skull where the arm of glasses goes across and above the ear. Another effective acupoint is the indentation behind the ear toward skull at widest point of ear. A third point is the back of the skull where midway there is a triangle.

3rd Eye Opens, Cranium Bone Crunches, Rocketing Body Vibration

May 24

In the morning while doing a sun session, I had three images come while in the sleep state. These images appear like a picture on the screen of my 3rd eye. The last one was of me holding a glass of water using the cup I normally use. I knew it was a message to drink more water. I am sweating much of late and know it is important to stay hydrated. Today, I see that moving to the impulse I feel in my body is not always the best thing to do, especially with skull work. A strong force is needed to move these bones, so letting the force build without moving the body is also effective.[46]

After the work in the skull, there was much energetic rotation in the jaws and later I felt energy paths opening in my head, which facilitated movement of the cranium bones. I felt I knew how to move and crunch the cranium bones. I guess the crunching is a progression

---

[46] The best way is to surrender and not think and then you are moved when you need to be moved, you do not need any technique nor have to think about what to do.

after the prior work of loosening the cranium bones. When I lie down, the energy vibrates my entire body and while it happens, it feels like neuron growth is going on all over my body.

May 25: Intense Tingling In Toes

I did a freestyle session with the ring stretching down to toes. There were strong spontaneous movements, with pulling stretches in areas of chest, shoulders, neck and head. After this, I did a sitting session. When I first sat, I felt intense tingling in the toes that moved up the body. There was much skull crunching with work on sides of neck and hard palate. There was more work in the left skull this time. I almost cried a few times, the work is intense and the more the skull moves the more I have to move with it. Around the clock, I have to do a session every three hours to relieve the tension or it hurts. The energy is incredibly strong today and the inner sound is high-pitched.

Energy Balls In Throat, Hyoid Bone Moves, Cranium Bones Release

May 29: Spine Alignment, Long Hold In Hip, Skull Pain

I have been giving my father Reiki treatments on a regular basis. He had a strong healing reaction in the first weeks and feels better. I practiced trying to feel his energy while giving the treatment. I would project my inner sight toward his body and found I could see where the energy worked in his body. The energy traveled on a circular path from my right hand up the left side of his body to the skull, then over and down the other side until I felt it at my left hand. I observed energy worked in my body identical to where it worked in his. I think this has to do with entrainment. As energy worked, I described to him where it was and what he should be feeling. From numerous replies from him, it confirmed what I felt.

My energy continues strong. At least once per day I do a freestyle session, stretching down through the hips and legs. The last few times there was a strong crack in the big toe, which alarmed me because it was loud but it did not hurt much. The skull work continues with much movement of the cranium bones. Much work happens in left side of skull with intense pain yet I can endure it in surrender. At one moment, energy balls were pummeling the throat area up to the back of the skull and across the spine. In addition, a bone moved in the upper throat and later I found out there is a bone there.[47]

---

[47] This is the hyoid bone.

I did a freestyle session, which lasted a long time that felt like the entire spine aligned. After this energy slowly moved down to the hip and there was a long hold with intense pain lasting about twenty-five minutes. After this, I did a long sitting session using Reiki on the toe meridians, which I continued until my legs were numb.

I took a three-hour walk; tension mounted the entire time in my upper shoulders and neck. When I returned I was exhausted. My ankle and toe hurt but the tension in my shoulders and neck was worse. I lie down for two hours and did neck and head crunching. My head hurts much. The jaws or some bone in the head needs to move and until it does I will not be comfortable. Before bed, there was much work in the TMJ's. Once I felt the cranium bones opening like magic, then there was an energetic rotation of the head.

Dream about raw potatoes: my father told me of a vivid dream with detailed description of a village that was primitive. In the dream, he was shown how to treat infants after birth to clear them from viruses and rashes all their lives. It sounded like it might be a traditional Native American treatment for the immune system. It uses raw potato slices, fried just until the skins start to loosen. It was important to stop cooking the potatoes at that point. When they are warm to the touch then all are placed on the skin covering the entire body and the infant is wrapped in a cloth. After some time the potatoes are removed and the infant is washed in seawater.

June 1: Skull Popping, Rib Release, Atlas Bone Moves, Leg Tingling

In the last days, there were loud popping sounds deep in the skull and intense short bursts of pain as small cords moved in my skull. Tonight it felt like a big bone inside my head moved vertically, maybe it is the top of the spine? After this, there were strong stretches along the spine and right side of neck, which felt they were done to align the spine.

Lately, my legs are tingling intensely starting with the toes. Sometimes I feel it in my hands. It is not like the numbness I feel from lack of circulation that goes away when I move and blood returns. This reaction goes on a long time and moving does not make it go away. The movements in the head and spine are foreign and scary and at times, I worry about something breaking or a nerve getting pinched. However, I let go of my fear and allow whatever movement to happen. Several times a rib bone shifted in the chest. I do not feel well. I have constant head pressure and there are pimples along the sides of my nose. I have pain in the uterus and ovaries. I am getting tired of this and wanting it to be over. It is unbelievable how much time this is taking. I do not have time left to do anything else.

Atlas Bone Released With A Pop

June 4: Physical Rotation Of Hip, Entire Body Numbness

Since my prior journal entry, the healing continues with much movement of the cranial bones and intense tingling and numbness in the entire body. I need to stretch and release tension often. While standing yesterday there was a fast movement with physical rotation of hip and strong energy in the root chakra. I stood with knees slightly bent and went with the movements for about thirty minutes going beyond comfort, which is normal lately. Later, I gave my father a Reiki treatment and I felt explosions all over inside my body like fireworks were going off. I have never felt this sensation before.

Something different happens. The stretching was the most difficult physical work I have done so far. It felt like the spine ended in the skull at the tip of the head where the whorl

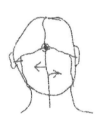

is. Then there was popping of a vertical structure, which felt to be the spine. It was popping laterally repeatedly from right to left (**see figure).** It was not comfortable yet it did not hurt. At the end, there was one more movement with a loud audible pop. After this energy zoomed all over my skull, concentrated in the TMJ's, and then went down the neck and into the shoulders. I sensed energy traveling along pathways never traversed before in the skull causing intense pain. There were many facial bone movements, in the hard palate, nose and behind the eyes. I felt the top of the spine had been reached and a large vortex was moving down the body versus the left body and right body energy circuits of the marcher rhythm.

June 5: Ligament Moves In Skull With Pressure On Wormian Bones

I slept four hours. My body hurts in the right hip and the head and I do not want to move. It was a long difficult day with much stretching. My head hurts badly and not much gives relief. I cried a few times. The most effective thing was using acupressure and Reiki on the toe meridians. I feel I need more energy to move something. I suspect the spine is ready to move. I feel the most pressure at the whorl in the back of the head when there are pops deep in the skull. A ligament is repositioning vertically across the spine. There is a popping of a ligament like this by the C7 joint at the back of the neck. I think it might be the same one.

June 7

I did a freestyle session and stretched down through toes and the big toe keeps cracking. I feel much resistance in the entire right leg in all the joints. Later I did a sitting session with Reiki. I notice it takes much energy to move the cranium bones. Work is done to loosen ligaments of spine attached to skull. There was work done in the throat, the trapezious muscles, in cranium bones and the TMJ's.

June 9

Lately, I am using a healing technique that I call multiplying forces.[48] Later I used acupressure on the urinary bladder meridian up the entire path from the back of leg up and over skull ending near the eye. This opened the back of my neck along the spine. I blanked out while doing it for about one hour and then fell asleep. Later in the day, my shoulder and neck opened the most so far. The energy worked deeply in shoulder crook and trapezious muscles. Later I used acupressure on the stomach meridian with many reactions in my body, and while doing it I fell asleep.

Occipital Bone Pop, Energy Spiral In Skull

June 11: Energy Whorls Down Spine, Inner Sound Like Katydids

Last night and this morning, I felt prickles in the head, upper shoulders and neck. It felt like I was cracking open, like a butterfly emerging from a chrysalis. The cranium bones have more range of movement and move deep inside my head. In the afternoon I felt energy move down as strong force from the TMJ's into the shoulder crooks and it felt like the spine straightened as this happened. I then felt energy whorls descending starting at top of head and going down the back to the bottom.

There was strange snapping of fine cords around the right TMJ. Many times, I lose identification with my mind and feel any moment I will 'take off'. I chemically burned my fingers using bleach and immediately felt energy whorls on my fingertips starting to heal

---

[48] This technique is in my Reiki healing journal, under June 9, 2006.

them. In the last sessions, my body is coming alive as a powerful energetic force and feels like higher-self is strongly taking over. I do not have a word for it. Changes are occurring all over my body all day. I feel over the hump of last week with much head pressure. I guess it had to do with shifting cranium bones that is now done. The spontaneous body movements feel like powerful yoga, and they 'hurt good' when I do them. My spirit is up because I progress and I move out tomorrow to get my own place.

Once in the afternoon session, I instinctively scrunched my nose and eyes together to allow facial bones to shift without hurting. After this, there were strong crunches in the bones around the TMJ's and loud pops in the back of the skull[49]. A few times, it felt like some cranium bones were aligning in parallel with the TMJ. Afterward I felt large spirals forming inside the skull. I have a slight discharge from the eyes. The inner sound was deafening at times and now sounds like katydids in the August night. This transformation has been going on a long time, it is now eight months. In the last eight months, my average work per day is six hours, so that is one thousand four hundred and forty hours of sessions so far.

June 17: Moving Again

I have been busy moving. Yesterday, I got back to normal workouts. Most work was physical movement of the jaw joints that work to align. Several times, there was a squishy sound at the right TMJ endpoint. I am back to weird bending of my head and opening my jaws often, which makes it difficult to be around people. I have my menstruation in the last two days. Later in the day, there was a huge energetic rotation in my entire head and I felt much movement of skull bones.

Energy Traces Around Edges Of Skull Plates

June 18: Movement Of Hyoid Bone, Sweats With Skull Work

In the session, there were three sweats all having to do with work in the skull. The final sweat lasted a long time. The energy work on the cranium bones was done in a sequence. First energy went around the TMJ on right around the ear, and then it moved up the side of the head doing the suture across the top to the corona suture. Then the frontal bone was worked, next the cheekbone, then across and down to back of head to parietal. The most

---

[49] This is likely a pop of the occipital bone.

intense work was on the parietals. A few times the energy moved across to the left side of the skull and made some adjustments. I felt small movements as energy worked along the edges of one skull plate on the suture line for some time. After this, I would feel small crunching sounds with the feeling the plate had loosened and then energy moved to the next plate.

After work in the skull, energy worked in the front of the neck more than ever before. I sense the hyoid bone is now worked. My jaws ache after a three-hour session. I still cannot believe how slow this process is. I work long and hard on these sessions and the changes are by microns. I am getting tired of the incessant need to release the tension. It is difficult to drive because I cannot turn my head well over my shoulders with all the tension in my neck.

I wonder what abilities this transformation will give me. Will I grow new teeth, will I have a youthful appearance, will I be free of disease, will I transmute poisons, will my metabolism be perfect, will I have to sleep, will I reproduce again, will I have completely quiet mind, will I have open access to universal mind and will my physical appearance substantially change? At this point, none of them appears true. I wish I knew the truth.

June 20: Many Energy Balls Rise Into Shoulders, Neck & Skull

Last night I felt I needed to do something different so I returned to my idea of modifying my Reiki acupressure sequence to include the joints.[50] It was awesome! This experience reminds me to keep exploring especially when things feel stuck. I did this session before bed, going into an altered state many times. The main effect seemed to activate all meridian circuits. The second was that energy gathered into an energy ball as I worked the technique up the legs toward the spine.

The big surprise was when I put my finger on the pubic symphysis. Soon after this, all the energy balls rose and were in my shoulders at the base of the neck going up through the spine to the skull. When these balls moved there were strong spontaneous movements in my shoulders, neck and TMJ's.

June 21: Skull Plates Traced, Cool Breeze, Body Swelling Starts

Last night I was too tired to do anything, I slept long and deep. There were many reactions in my body all day yesterday. I still feel it today. A few times, I heard the high-pitched inner sound with total silence. There are energy whorls in my right trapezious muscle

---

[50] The details of this sequence are in my Reiki healing journal under "Technique through Joints", June 20, 2006.

and shoulder area. I do not feel much compression in my head. My foot is swollen near the big toe; and there is much pain in it. I was going to take a long walk today…

It felt wonderful to do the sun session. I was meditating and energy worked in the right skull. Energy traced around the edges of the right temporal bone, and then energy traced around the right parietal bone. I felt all sides of a skull plate were loosened. Then I felt stretching in the skull, could hear small crackle sounds, and had the feeling these plates shifted. After a plate shifted, energy would go down the spine and there would be a combined stretch of the TMJ joint with some other part of the body such as back of neck, the shoulder, side of neck and even the hip joint! After the body stretch, energy would concentrate in the skull moving on to another cranium bone. It was going efficiently. After the right side of head was done, the left side was done in a similar way. Sometimes the right side of skull was worked in tandem with the left side forming rotational paths of energy in the skull. I observed energy spirals in both hemispheres at top of head and a link between the TMJ joints as a single infinity sign shape that moved down the skull in a vortex. I was sweating much and this would alternate with cool breezes in the body.

When I came in, I did a freestyle session. The power I felt in my body was incredibly strong. It felt like higher-self took over and aligned the spine by stretching spontaneously down through hips and feet. After that, I sat while energy worked in TMJ with body stretches that included the shoulders and hips.

I then did a deep meditation until 11:30 not wanting to move more. After a short break, there were more strong crunches in the right TMJ and C7. Near the end, I felt a cool rush of energy on both sides of the spine. At the time, it felt like the spine almost lined up with the skull. This is the first time this has happened. I can easily sustain deep meditation. The sessions are spanning hours. There was pain under my right arm in the rib cage area, the first time I ever felt that. I went to bed early and fell asleep while working the liver meridian.

Insight of cranium bone relationship to body I had the thought, "twenty-two skull bones", and that maybe each corresponded to movement of an area of the body. While watching the cranium bones shifting and stretching with a certain body part, it was obvious there was a direct relationship and I clearly saw it in the TMJ to Hip connection.

June 22

I slept long and woke with strong tension in the spine, shoulders, neck and skull. I started with the Reiki acupressure sequence through the joints and after three hours, I still have not completed it because I blank out when I touch areas where I need the energy. I did another session working both sides of body at once and fell asleep doing my ankle. Then later to bed to continue and I fell asleep again.

June 23

I slept long and rose early. The jaws and neck feel near to releasing. I did a long session starting with freestyle and noted I still have many blockages in my right leg and they radiate all the way up to the TMJ joint. I did Reiki work on the liver and gallbladder meridians working them on both toes together. Later I did another freestyle stretch with strong twisting down through my ankle. Afterward there were spontaneous movements with excruciating positions going through the body. I feel I need to do more freestyle sessions now, because much charge is building in the large muscles and stretching is the only way to release it. I need a better balance in my workouts; doing the meridians is not enough.

I think I did some effective work but feel depressed to see how much work is left to do and how difficult it is. At 12:30 pm, I needed another session because of strong skull pressure. I did acupressure on the finger meridians, which helped to release the skull pressure. There was high body heat with sweating when energy worked in hip and spine. I feel the growing reaction all over my body.

I felt my left foot rotating energetically and heard popping in the left jaw with each bite of food I ate. Lately, my shoulders are worked in combination with the neck. There is much pressure on the occipital bone behind head, my head hurts and I am tired. While I was walking, my right hip feels more balanced in the joint, it felt good to feel a new swing in the joint. The swelling of my big toe joint is mostly gone. I went down through this joint a little and stretched it during a sun session. I fell asleep while giving acupressure to my finger meridians. I guess it is not sleep; rather my mind is going quiet for healing in the brain. This is occurring often. I just blanked out in a hold while energy worked in the body. Later I blanked out while there was energetic work done on trapezious muscles, neck and TMJ's.

June 24: Energy Surge, Rib Cage Rotation, Energy Whorls On Skull

I slept long and there is not much pressure now in my head, yeah! I did a thirty-minute sun session. Later I did a freestyle session stretching down through the right foot and worked ankles and toes with Reiki on meridians while in stretch. Later I worked the liver meridian and felt strong work in right shoulder, along neck and up to TMJ. While I worked this meridian up into the torso, the energy got stronger. I think to do each meridian again to look for main blocks.

I did no afternoon session. I got home about 8 pm and it was hot so I sat outside with the crystals. Strong energy was zooming around all over working various parts of my body and I barely had to move. I felt it coming up the liver meridian and working in the rib cage more than ever before. I now feel my rib cage rotate. Many times the cranium bones cracked and moved apart. I felt work directly on the knots in the trapezious muscle. Many times, I thought insects might be biting me but they were pricks of pain. I sat in a meditative state most of the time. I still observe the body worked as one unit, with skull work occurring simultaneously with work in the body or at least up and down together. It is not like in the past where a change would be made to the body and later in the head, it works together now. It was a nice break to sit in meditation. I think much work happened in those two hours. The inner sound is strong with right ear popping and energy whorls on top of my head in many places. The energy still courses strongly through me.[51]

Floating Skull Plates, Amplified Hearing With OBE

June 25: Shoulder Girdle Work

I did continuous sessions from about 7 am to 2 pm, and took a break. I did the next session in the evening. I had my feet on the crystals and held another crystal. I meditated and moved slightly. Near the end, my hearing amplified and I could hear children talking and playing far away. This lasted for a long time. Meanwhile my head was tipped back in discomfort while work was done in the sternum, collarbone and shoulder joints. There was work in trapezious muscle with a strong sweat while that happened. I will try the urinary bladder meridian next as it seemed ready to open. I will continue the meridian work going

---

[51] I think a strong growing reaction often follows a high-energy surge, after a major energy circuit is opened. It is time to rest when the growing energy takes over. Eventually I came to recognize this and could just relax with them.

more into my body parts. The urinary bladder meridian work was good. Once, it felt like I was not in my body and felt the skull plates floating and moving around. It was a strange sensation.

June 26: Amplified Hearing, Insect Biting, Cool Breeze Rises From Feet

I had to get up twice in the night and rose at 5 am. Much tension released from the spine during a sun session. I did the complete Reiki acupressure sequence. I blanked out while working on the stomach meridian, while energy worked under the jaw by the molars, on the bottom line of the mandible, in the rib cage and by the clavicle.

In the evening, I did a sitting session outside with crystals and Reiki. It is amazing how strong the energy gets. There was much work done in the trapezious muscles by shoulder blades and on up to skull. For me it was easy tilting of the head and feeling tension releasing. Again, I experienced amplified hearing. It has an eerie feeling to it, like being in a ghost town or a dream world and hearing sounds and voices 'of the past' echoing around all over. It reminds me of a movie I saw or something. The sounds were startling; my body was reacting and shaking from them.[52] There were many small pricks of pain feeling as if insects were biting me. There are no mosquitoes here in the desert. Once I felt a cool breeze rising around me, coming from my feet on up. For sure it was not from outside, it is almost one hundred degrees.

The majority of the work is loosening the rib cage, trapezious muscles and scapulas. I want to go to this space of no thought and never return allowing the healing to happen until it stops. I am strongly drawn to go into deeper states of observation, like out of body experience and merely watch the healing happen. This is much nicer than the difficult stretching sessions.

June 27: Loud Cracks In Skull, Elastic Stretch In Ankles

I arose a few times, but then went back to bed. I had a dream about red versus brown leather and something about using the correct color or energy for meridians. I think the dream is related to the rocks I used last night. I think each mineral, rock and crystal has a unique frequency that should match what you are working on. It seemed a warning that using the

---

[52] I suspect this symptom of amplified hearing may be due to going out of body while work is done in the brain.

wrong one was not good. I decided to stick with using my hands, as these cannot be the wrong frequency.

I did acupressure on toes, ankles, knees, hips, rib cage, shoulders, elbows, and last on my hands. Then I did a little on the C7 vertebra. This order makes sense to me. After this, I meditated and allowed skull movements to occur. Then I was lying on my stomach and higher-self took over with spontaneous spine stretches. Later there were strong movements in the skull with loud cracks, it is alarming how hard and loud this is. Later in a freestyle session while in the squat position, I felt my ankle and toes turn like they were suddenly elastic. I could stretch them easily beyond their normal range of movement.

Later I sat and did the finger meridians on both hands. I kept blanking out and when I felt sleepy would observe fine skull adjustments were made. At one moment, I felt I would take off and never return. When the energy gets strong, my mind goes suddenly quiet. I feel anytime the energy will get high enough and set off a long chain reaction of healing.

Insight of my new power: I have a new power in my body owing to the new neural connections that have been made. I only have to let go of body control and the work will be done through the spontaneous body movements. It is crystal clear I need to do more freestyle sessions.

Skull Plates Separating, Spontaneous Movement Sessions

June 28: Regular Spontaneous Movement Sessions

I did a long session. I started with feet on crystal and then put my palms on upper thighs with the idea to bring energy down to my feet on right. I did liver and gallbladder meridian acupoints in the knees. This did not seem to work because the meridians were not activated. Therefore, I did liver plus gallbladder meridians on toes. This did not work well; it did not feel like enough energy was building. Therefore, I started with little toe and moved toward big toe. I stopped and worked the middle toe for a long time. This meridian energetically rotates the joints, not only the feet. Once energetic rotation of joints starts, then it is like a domino effect, as each joint rotates it affects the one above it. Therefore, I held this for a long time until the jaw joints were energetically rotating. After this, the energy in my body was strong and I thought to do the liver plus gallbladder meridians together.

Instead, my body signals told me to stretch now that all the joints were activated. I started a freestyle session with the idea to hold various positions like postures, starting with the head and working down through my body. Soon after I started higher-self took over and I understood it would be better to 'follow the leader' meaning to let go of body control, so I did. There were various stretches while standing, then quickly folding down to squat, through hips and toes. Afterward the toes were nice and warmed up, I stretched my legs, and my feet were all tingly. My feet were much more activated with the stretching than I had accomplished with the acupressure. Stretching and moving my body with the force of gravity, activates the vibration stronger than any other technique. Albeit, starting the energy is low so activating the meridians and raising the overall vibration helps to do the next step.

When I sat with legs to front, work was in the upper body and especially in the spine and skull. This was an effective session this morning yet long and difficult. At the end, the cranium bones felt loose and soon after this, my head moved spontaneously around with terrific crunching sounds in the skull. It felt like my brain was the Earth and the skull plates were the crust of the Earth floating on top. The crust was in upheaval and moving around. It was scary at times that the skull plates can move this way. I could have went longer with it but stopped because I was tired.

Moving as Higher-self Technique, Freestyle Session

1. I activate all meridians with my Reiki acupressure sequence. This elevates my vibration allowing higher-self to easily take over.

2. I start standing, and relax my body and maintain a meditative state by focusing on feeling a vibration in my body. One of my focal points is to feel my body as a single unit of vibration and tune into the pulsation felt which alternates between left and right sides of body. When I tune into feeling the natural energy flows it quiets my thinking. Another focal point is to imagine I am at center and not moving and that my body is moving around this center point. I visualize a dot of light in my 3rd eye. Then my direction is to follow this dot of light by turning my inner eyes toward it. I then trust that the body will follow behind the movement the head is taking. It is the same

principle that you can control a large animal by controlling the head. Both of these focal points require no thinking, thus allowing the body to move spontaneously.

3. I let my body move spontaneously. During the session, I scan for body tension or pain. If I find tension, I relax that area to allow energy to enter it. With this stage of the kundalini transformation, the nervous system is advanced and spontaneous body movements easily happen. A typical progression of the session is standing, stretching poses on way down to squat, holding and stretching in various squat positions, then sitting and finally lying on either stomach or back. Yoga stretches occur in every position. In some freestyle sessions, I stand or lay down the entire time.

4. After spontaneous movements stop, I rest and allow the growing phase for a little while. When the tension in body builds then I start over with 1.

Chapter 14: Spine Vortex & Sphenoid Release

June 29: Urinary Bladder Experimentation

In the morning, I worked the urinary bladder meridian. The urinary bladder meridian is interesting because of the two vertical circuits. Energy activates with the sides of the body marching in step; it is a right-left-right pumping action like when you walk. After the vertical circuits are activated then energy connects laterally across the sides of body to create an energy spiral. The spiral then moves to the top of the head, then goes down the body to the toes, and repeats a few times. I feel tingling in the lower abdomen once it is strongly activated near the bladder area. It is effective to work on the muscle adhesions in my upper neck and shoulders by the spine. Because it runs vertically through the entire body, it has much power. During this session, energy mostly worked the trapezious muscle. I watched many cycles where energy would go up and work through the TMJ vertically on both sides of the skull and then movement in the right TMJ movement would cause a movement in the left TMJ. Then I would feel the cranium bones adjusting and then energy would move down and open something. I blanked out while energy worked in the brain for more than thirty minutes.

I think to go through all the meridians again to see what they do. Last night before bed, I did the heart meridian for one hour. There was work done in my heart and now I remember I have a heart murmur. My chest still feels tight so I work to open the rib cage and heart area.

Everything is connected and all paths have to be cleared. I went through all the meridians and I have problems in each. After I worked the urinary bladder a long time it activated the kidney acupoint KD1 and around the right ankle. The urinary bladder meridian helps move fluid in the body and connects to all main joints except the TMJ's. I think there must be a connection to the TMJ's, because energy travels sideways in the skull to activate them. The entire time I worked both the left and right urinary bladder meridians from the toes energy never worked in my left body. After this, I worked all toe meridians for about forty-five minutes. Then I sat upright and put my hands together with my feet on the crystal. Energy continued to work in the meridians for more than an hour after I stopped.

I did the urinary bladder meridian last night for more than two hours because I wanted to do it until I felt energy come down the left side of the body. Near the end, there was intense work in the shoulders, then it went through on the left and then I blanked out. I think I was like that for more than two hours and do not remember what passed. Then I went to sleep. There was a deep pain in the crease of the leg where it meets the body. I will do this tomorrow and see if I can get a complete circuit to form in the body.

Insights on meridian paths follow the bones: in the anatomy book, I do not see an obvious reason for the urinary bladder or kidney meridian paths. I asked the question, "What path of energy are the meridians?" and the answer came, "The energetic path of bones". This makes sense because bones are the densest tissue in the body, resonate with vibration, and carry high energy. Bone marrow is a source of growth in the body and makes red blood cells. The meridian acupoints are points of high energy in the body and are palpable with your fingers. All are near a bone. By stimulating an acupoint, it causes a resonance in the bone. Because all the bones are connected, resonance in one bone affects the next. A meridian path represents a main flow of energy along the bones and muscles that attach to the bones, which corresponds to a way that group of muscles and bones can move.

Rib Cage Vortex Forms

June 30: Cleansing Dreams

I had many cleansing dreams. There is much body tension with a torque on the spine. Often my rib cage expands and opens. In freestyle sessions, there are stretches in the left side of the neck, at lower edge of occipital bone, in trapezious muscle, down front of my throat, in the hyoid bone and muscles going down to the sternum. I still have knots in the right trapezious muscle and look for a way to get energy to move horizontally through it to open the shoulder. I will put acupressure on the knots and see which meridians activate. Using acupressure on the upper knot, I felt the ring finger (triple heater) and the front of the leg (stomach) meridians activate. I will try these together and see what happens. A quote comes to mind, "It's natural for people to put their hands on the places they are sore."

I used acupressure on the stomach meridian acupoints on both toes for a long time. Eventually I felt a big circle going around the lower rib cage. At first, it hurt much and I felt like throwing up. I sensed it went around the edges of the diaphragm. Energy worked there a long time and then slowly moved up front of the body to the skull. When energy passed through the clavicles I felt the back, scapulas and TMJ's activate. After energy worked in the skull, then it came down the backside and I sat upright. This was a huge relief. Once, I felt the spleen meridian on my big toe tingle. After this, I did acupressure on the triple heater meridian acupoints on the fingers. During this, I felt a release in the scapula. I kept feeling tingling in my pinkie finger on the inside meridian so I started applying acupressure to that acupoint.

That was effective and soon I felt many whorls of energy moving in a ray pattern from point of sternum to points on shoulder tips, to edges of rib cage and projecting to the TMJ's **(see figure).** After this, the entire rib cage rotated with a strong vortex. Next, I felt this vortex connect with lower part of body below the diaphragm. I was sweating profusely, especially on the face. I am soaked. It was a strong session. Later I did a stretching session. The right lower part of my rib cage feels stuck.

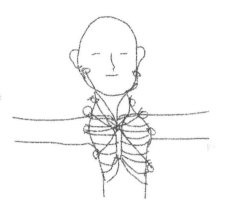

July 1

Early today I gave acupressure to all the acupoints around the mandible and between all the sutures in this area. When I did that, I felt the cranium bones move. Later I did the entire Reiki acupressure sequence, trying to stay quiet and to finish. It takes too long and needs to be simplified. Last night I spent hours stretching and got no relief. I have to raise my vibration before I stretch or it is not effective. There was a big release in my shoulder and TMJ. I had strong pain in my head many times as the bones moved. I cried when it was difficult.

I hope the transformation will finish soon. I am tired of having so much tension that I can barely move my neck. It is difficult to be around people or go anywhere for long and I rarely enjoy walking. Now, the energy is strong and higher-self keeps taking over. I do not want more, yet I know I will not be comfortable sleeping. This is the difficult part, when the big energy does not let up.

Dream of making a book: Last night I dreamt I picked up a book. When I opened it, there was an envelope inside with money in it. It was as if a surprise was hidden in the book. This dream came again tonight. Perhaps it means the book I will write will bring money so I do not have to worry about how to survive. My savings draw down fast.

Energetic Rotation Of Shoulders With TMJ's, Strong Feet Tingling

July 2: Shoulders Open, Wavy Undulating Energy Movements

I did a sun session and then a freestyle session with much stretching and many openings. I found an acupoint on the large intestine meridian at point on the shoulder (LI15), which activates the shoulder joints. It is right at top of arm bone, front and back under scapula bone between arm bone and scapula.

In the afternoon, I did several sessions with painful face crunching. There was much work on TMJ, shoulders, spine and the rib cage on right feels near to release. The entire shoulder opens with cracks in many difference directions at once. This feels good. The energy is still high.

In the evening, I did a long session. I started with acupressure on the articulation points of the clavicle, in sternum under clavicle and just before shoulder tip on clavicle where it meets the scapula. This seemed effective to loosen the shoulder girdle. Later I activated the lung, triple heater and large intestine arm meridians from the fingers. During this time, I blanked out many times for long periods while my shoulders and TMJ's were alive with energetic rotation. After this, I stretched through a multitude of pathways connecting the upper body through the neck to the head. This was challenging with much crunching, cracking and popping. The TMJ's were shifting as energy worked deep in the joints. Sporadically higher-self took over with a high energy charge building in the muscles, then a strong spontaneous stretch and then back to a working pattern. In the last week, the growing reaction feels wavier and glides across the body transversely through swatches of the body. I often feel myself elongating. I lack vocabulary to describe these symptoms.

July 3: Opening Of Knees

I slept long and woke at 6 am with much tension in the shoulders. All morning I did continuous sessions. In the sun session, I put my feet on the crystal with hands together to raise the energy as quickly as possible. By pressing my feet into the crystal and with my fingertips together, I could activate the hand and leg meridians. I sat like that and did stretches until the sun was too hot. Then I went inside and did a freestyle session. I applied acupressure to my toes while at the lowest point in the squat. This worked well to activate the legs but was awkward. Then I sat upright with feet to front and my feet were tingling strong. I had the idea to bring this energy up the body, by giving acupressure to various points in the joints not necessarily on acupoints. I started with the kidney meridian acupoint KD1 and then did the sides of the ankles. The rest of the time, I worked the knees, which block energy from going up. The inside and front of my knees are the worst. I stayed on the point in the knee right below the kneecap. It is good to open the upper body and I think it is connected to the diaphragm. There were strong chills many times near the end as something in the spine opened.

In the late morning I did another freestyle session, "Let's get physical" was the message. I need the force of my body to open larger blockages. There was a painful crack in the big toe joint. The energy does not settle down. In the afternoon, I took a walk and now I am zooming inside. There was strong tension in spine, on C7 and skull so I did a freestyle stretch. After this, I took a nap while energy worked in the body.

Next, I did a two-hour acupressure session outside with my feet on the crystal. I did each toe meridian for two minutes each. Then I held the stomach meridian acupoint on the feet while in a long hold while energy strongly worked around rib cage and under shoulder girdle. After this, I sat and gave acupressure to the finger meridians. While doing the heart meridian acupoint, energy worked strongly in the trapezious and around C7 so I held it longer. During this time, energy went into head and worked the TMJ from front to back of head. It was as if C7 was the center point and energy was moving between the TMJ, scapula and trapezious muscle. An energetic rotation pattern formed between the shoulders tops.

From 10:30 to 11:45 pm, I worked the urinary bladder meridian until both sides of my body felt open along it. I then worked the gallbladder meridian. This meridian activates energy to work in the joints. In the skull, I felt the gallbladder meridian acupoints open and my sinuses cleared. After this, I felt many cranium bone movements and then energy went down the body to align something with the cranium bone movements.

Spontaneous Meridian Activation

July 4: Trapezious Work, Back Ligament Snaps, Cervical Spine Work

I arose at 2 am, did a session, and fell asleep while doing it. I woke at 4:30 am and decided to stay up. Its 9:30 am and most of the morning I did a sun session. There were strong openings along the spine and I felt five strong shivers. Then there was a forty-minute hold with excruciating pain. I had my head tipped back and chin toward ceiling, while energy worked in both trapezious muscles and all cranium bones. I was sweating profusely on my head and upper body. I breathed deeply and used every skill I had to endure it. It felt like energy worked to line up the sides of the shoulders and TMJ's with the neck. While this work occurred, the meridians were activating spontaneously from one to the other. I would notice the marching rhythm of energy moving up the back along the urinary bladder meridian. Then this would stop and another meridian would activate. This was occurring last night too. I am happy something moves but I still have much tension.

From 6 to 9 pm, I took a three-hour nap. I woke and did a freestyle session with deep stretches into the TMJ joint, which 'hurt good'. The TMJ's and cheekbone were moving around and sometimes my eyes shifted with a popping feeling.

Later I stood outside and easily activated my feet meridians by standing on tiptoes. Then I quickly folded into squat, with stretches in big toe joint, ankles and right hip. In freestyle stretch, I feel the charge in the muscles combines with the weight of my body and these together creates a force to activate my ankles and feet. After this, the energy ripples up and activates the joint above the activated joint with an energetic rotation, on up to the top. Then I am led through a body stretch, which seems to have the goal to straighten the spine. I am tired and my head aches.

Later in the day, I had just touched an acupoint on the right urinary bladder meridian and instantly there were hundreds of small snaps, prickles and energy whorls all over my upper back. At 11:30 pm, I continued working the urinary bladder meridian and I felt the KD1 acupoint of the kidney meridian activate on the sole of my foot. After that happened, I decided to combine them and gave acupressure to both these meridians for more than an hour. While doing it, my lower legs went numb. I think this is an effective combination because it is activating two vertical body circuits with the urinary bladder meridian going down and the kidney meridian going up. Near the end, there were brief sharp nerve pains along the sides of the cervical spine. I felt this about six times on the left and a few times on the right. After this, I continued giving acupressure to the toe and finger meridians and fell asleep about 2 am.

July 5: Multiple Cracks Across Right Parietal Bone

When I rose, work was going on in the TMJ with intense pressure so I did a freestyle session right away. Later I did a sitting session with heavy pressure in the sternum, as if energy is rotating around a compressed or dead space. It feels like a stuck rib. I went down through the rib joints next to the sternum working them with acupressure and found a sore spot, which I think was the fourth rib down and under the right armpit. Next, I worked the urinary bladder meridian a long time and then did the spleen meridian. After this, I did the kidney acupoints along the rib cage while lying and fell asleep. After waking, I did another session.

In the afternoon, I used acupressure on the feet meridians. I did the inside acupoint of the big toe which seems different from the spleen meridian acupoint on outside of toe. It seemed to do an energetic rotation vertically from back to front, going up through all the main joints of ankles, knees, hips and TMJ's. The liver and spleen meridians are blocked. I will continue to work all meridians until they are clear. I do not know what else to do.

From 8 to 10 pm, I worked the small intestine meridian a long time. This goes through all the blocks in the trapezious, neck and TMJ's. It never cleared after working it for more than an hour. It always reaches the point where it is difficult, like I am forcing the work because I use the energy of only one meridian. I laid down and fell asleep doing the hand meridians.

Multiple Cracks In Right Parietal, Rib Cage Release, Vertebrae Work

July 6: How To Move Spontaneously: Don't Think, Just Be

I slept long until 6 am. I rose once but went back to bed. After rising, there was much tension so I did a freestyle session. Then I did the full Reiki acupressure sequence[53] in a sun session. I was sweating profusely on the head. From 9:40 to 11 am, I did a Reiki acupressure session.

---

[53] The full sequence is recorded in my Reiki healing journal under this date.

Sometimes I move rather than hold a position when there is much pressure. I cannot tell when to hold still and when to move. I decided to hold still if I felt twisting tension. I did this in four or five positions and it was difficult and painful to do. After strong pressure, the area eventually releases and I can relax into a new position. After doing this there was a series of cracks following a ridge above the occipital bone and below the parietal in the back of the skull on the right. This happened about twenty-five times. The cracks moved from midline at

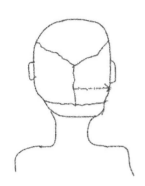

back of skull to the right. I guess it is a bone deep in the skull or ligaments **(see figure).** After this, energy worked strongly in skull with cranial bone movements.

In the afternoon, I did a freestyle session trying to determine when I should move and when I should not move and received the answer, "Don't think, just be". When I am as one with higher-self, my body is tingly and electrified. This was probably the most effective thing I have done for months. The energy rose high like when this started. Then I wondered if all this meridian work was a waste of time. It seems allowing higher-self to take over is the strongest and best thing to do, as it requires no thinking, no manipulations and no technique.

I did a freestyle session with twisting and turning of the ankles and toes while in a squat position. While doing that my left lower rib cage twisted and enveloped. This was painful. After that, I was sitting with legs to the front and very slowly, my spine lowered forward. Energy worked each vertebra slowly up to the head. I did this until I could not take more. Then I lay down and there was strong activation of my legs and root chakra. Once again, energy came up the spine. Then there were intense holds of my head while my jaws and cranium bones moved around feeling like my head would break. When I could not take more, I sat up. Then I blanked out and was in a freefall sensation for about fifteen minutes. I am tired; I fell asleep while doing the arm meridians.

Feels Like Head Is Reshaping

July 7: Both Trapezious Muscles Release, Work In Pectorals

I slept through the night. First thing, I did a freestyle session to release the extreme tension. This was not working so I did meridian work from 7 to 9 am, in a sun session. I started with the arms and then did the urinary bladder and gallbladder meridians together. After this, the energy was ramped up.

From 11:30 am to 1:30 pm, I did a laying session and worked foot and hand meridians. I was drawn to work on the gallbladder meridian pressing all acupoints upward. When I was pressing acupoint GB29 (in lower hip girdle) and acupoint GB25 (Mu, on last rib) then it felt like the twist in my spine started to come out. Pressing the spot under my arm worked to release shoulder tension. Acupoints GB22-23 and GB20-21 are effective to release neck and TMJ tension. At the end, I did the beginning points of the gallbladder meridian at acupoint GB1 at the temples on each side in the skull. There was excruciating pain when bones moved behind my eyes. While this occurred, I cried and felt I was releasing emotional pain from past relationships. I stopped when I could not take any more. Afterward the line from my shoulder up through the neck had a clear path; it was a strange feeling of not having that big knotty muscle on the side of my neck.

In the afternoon, I worked the gallbladder meridian for an hour with painful head and shoulder crunching. From 5 to 6 pm, I did a freestyle session with intense body crunching. From 8 to 9 pm, I did a sitting meditation outside. A big shiver happened. Most of the time energy was loosening cranium bones and working to release a muscle connected to the skull in the neck and shoulders. The work was intense but I easily distanced from the pain. There were many head rotations and energy zoomed all over my body. There was much work on the ribs and pectoral muscles under the breasts. I do not recall that sensation before; it felt like having a breast massage.

From 9:20 to 10:20 pm, I continued and the same type of work happened. Near the end, I was blanking out and sweating profusely for a long time while energy worked the trapezious muscles near top by neck on both sides together. This hurt much. Then this area opened and it was as if two energies merged. There is a big energy vortex moving down in the head now. It feels like my head reshapes with the pressure of the bones shifting but it does not hurt. Later I did a short freestyle session to relieve the tension before going to bed.

Spiral Circuit Made Around Vertebrae

July 8: Cranium Bones Move With Neck & Shoulder Stretch

From 7:30 to 9 am, I did a sun session working the meridians. From 9 to 11 am, I did a freestyle session with stretches while sitting. Notable was spine, rib cage and right hip work. There are strong rotations and bends of my rib cage that shift it. There is continual twisting and release of tension from the scapula and trapezious muscles on right side like last night but stronger today. I felt all cranium bones move together from left ear to right ear. It felt like my head was forming a new shape, a strange feeling.

Tiny vortices moved down starting at top of skull and twisting around each spine vertebrae. I think a spiral energy circuit was made all around the spine (**see figure**). When energy went through the TMJ's and shoulders, I had to twist my body around with it. It is not done, it continues while I sit here. Now there is work deep in the skull with crunching.

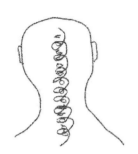

From 3 to 6 pm, I lied down and stretches moved the skull bones for an hour. Then I blanked out. After a while, I came to and was in an intense hold, but do not recall the position. I felt I needed to assist and that is why I woke. I held the position until I could not bear more. I decided to move and sit in the chair and continued to hold tension for another hour. I kept blanking out. It was difficult to stop.

At 8:40 pm, I think to do the gallbladder meridian after observing what is going on inside my body. My head compresses and cranium bones move with a muscle in my shoulder and a sweat rises. The cranium bones shift constantly now in tandem with stretches in muscles of upper neck and shoulders. The cranial bone movement with stretch of body part keeps going lower; sometimes I feel it all the way down to the toes. There were big cracks in the skull earlier, like some bone in the center of the skull moves. There were thud-like bone sounds around the TMJ as it popped. My sinuses drain and my ears are popping. I feel healing pain in my right armpit, big toe and ankle.

From 9 to 12 pm, I did acupoints GB1 to GB6 on the gallbladder meridian. While I treated the GB6 acupoint, I felt intense pain above right TMJ deep in skull and sweated heavily. I continued working the meridian and eventually it opened on both sides. Mostly the work was holding positions for a long time. There was one hold with my head tipped back with much pressure in the shoulders and head at once. I went to outer space to endure it. After a long time, my head dropped forward with chin to neck and then I felt my mouth scrunch up. Then my head came up quickly stretching backward and then went back down again. When it did this, there was a huge crunching sound just above my right TMJ joint. This surprised me when it happened. After this there were several more held positions, I was falling asleep during them and do not remember what was worked.

Rib Cage Vortex, Body Vortex Forming

July 9: Rib Cage Vortex, Birth Memory, Dance On Toes In Squat

Awaking at 5 am, I have much tension in the right body. From 6 to 9 am, I did a sun session to release the tension. I used acupressure on the urinary bladder and gallbladder meridians on toes, and then did the other meridians from my knees. It is nice to work the meridians from the knees because I can sit comfortably. While working the urinary bladder meridian, energy strongly worked in the upper spine. There were more rib cage maneuvers and various openings in the arms and legs. From 9 to 10 am, I did a freestyle session, stretching down through feet and then lying. While lying there were many head crunches, spine stretches and rib maneuvers. The rib in front by the sternum near a gallbladder acupoint is a sticking point as well a rib under the arm.

From 11 am to 2 pm, I did a session lying. There was a long interval where it felt like the bottom part of the spine was strong and was held rigid while the upper body and head were worked. There was strong work in sternum, collarbone, scapula, ribs and shoulders. After this work, I felt a strong vortex form in the rib cage. While walking my right hip feels 'seated', like it has energy inside and rotates like the left one. It was a strange and good feeling.

From 7:45 to 9:45 pm, I did a long freestyle session. Energy worked a long time in cranium bones, TMJ, neck and upper shoulders. Later, energy built in the root chakra, legs and feet and then I felt it rise as a strong vortex to the skull and then slowly move down. Then I very slowly stretched down and felt the vortex distinctly travel down through head and upper shoulders. I guess there it is stuck. When I finally stretched down through the ankles, there was so much tingly energy that I could not feel my feet. Then I could easily stretch into sore parts of hip, knee, ankle and toe on right. I sort of danced on the toes in a squat position, which opened my hips and caused movement in the lower rib cage. Then I moved down to floor on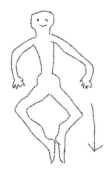

left side with body crunching on right side. Next, I was on my back but this time with hips apart and slowly the knees lowered flat onto the floor. There was much work then in the lower parts: hip, knee, ankle and feet **(see figure).**

This session takes be back to the ones in February, which were difficult. I had to deeply distance to endure it. I observed a big vortex forming in my entire body at times moving in a clockwise fashion. When I stopped, I had difficulty to rise as everything was stiff, but in ten minutes, I felt normal again.

I almost forgot about the session on the floor! It seemed like I was reliving my birth and it came to me that my shoulder was damaged due to a delivery complication. At times, I

felt my arm moving around my body. The hurt position was my arm across my neck with my shoulder pressed flat to the floor **(see figure).** My arm pulled around my neck as I rolled on the floor. When my arm was in the position of resting across my neck, it stood out because I do not recall ever doing that in my normal life. Now, I cannot lay either arm across my neck as it was in that session. Maybe it gets to the end. I hope.

Cranial Sutures Open, Horizontal Healing Plane Goes Down Body

July 10: Spine Circuits Join In Skull, Energy Circuits Front & Back Of Body

From 2 to 3 am, I rose, did a sitting stretch, and then fell asleep. From 6 to 9 am, I did some stretches in bed before I rose. Upon rising, I felt a strong pulling sensation between the hip and right shoulder. I did a long sun session where I worked the urinary bladder meridian. There was strong work in spine, upper shoulders and C7 vertebra. Near the end there was a strong marching feeling alternating between sides of the body. It took a long time for the energy to rise to the head. Once it did, I sensed the energy of both sides of spine joined there. Then it felt like the cranium bones along the urinary bladder meridian path were working to align. After this, energy came down both sides of skull together. Then I felt it descend down through neck a little way then do some work in both shoulders together. Then it arose and made more skull adjustments. This cycle repeated many times. Then the energy went down to the toes. A few times, I felt work done in the upper spine. Then I felt the stomach muscles get strong and then a contracted muscular force was used to hold the spine at the bottom and then energy ripped up the back and front in a straight pattern. Then the back of my neck popped a few times and after this, a strong sweat arose. I felt droplets on the head seemingly on the suture lines. Then I felt all skull sutures open and sweat poured off my head.

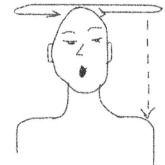

Soon after this, a vortex of energy formed in my head and started moving down slowly. It reminded me of a science-fiction medical treatment, like from star trek, where your body is in this intense energy field and it goes from head to toe and heals everything. As this vortex of energy moved down it felt like the bones were falling into alignment. It moved down through tops of shoulders and back up a few times. I sensed the energy was beyond the edges of my body, like in the aura. The energy pattern was a narrow horizontal plane that moved down. It felt like my body was sitting within this energy field and the entire body was healing **(see figure).** I would like to stop but cranial sutures are cracking and opening, so I will continue.

From 9:40 to 11 am, I did a freestyle session. I stretched down through the toes into a squat and did a dance on the toes, which opened the hips, rib cage and spine. Then I stretched down through knees, ankles and toes again. I did some sitting stretches and lying positions with neck crunching with head tipped to right side. There was a long period of holding this position while the trapezious and TMJ's and shoulders were worked. I held this until the work was finished. Then there was strong body activation with fast movements of my head whipping around and crunching bones in the skull. From 11 to 12 am, I did a sitting session.

From 12:30 to 2:30 pm, I took a walk and did a sitting meditation in nature by a river. At one moment, I felt one with everything, the insects, the wind, the river, the trees and the Earth. I felt the rhythm of nature was flowing through me and I felt no separation from anything. I was beating to this rhythm and it was so beautiful that I cried. It is 9 pm and there is not much urge to do anything since my walk. I worked the right urinary bladder meridian until it felt clear, and then I worked the gallbladder meridian for a while which felt clear. I felt a strong relaxing rhythm in my body and heard a high-pitched inner sound. Then I fell asleep.

July 11: Meridian Experimentation, Shoulder Crook Release

From 6:30 to 7:30 am, I worked the urinary bladder meridian with the stomach meridian. Next, I worked the gallbladder meridian with the liver meridian and last I worked the urinary bladder and gallbladder meridians. From 7:30 to 9 am, I did more meridian work on the endpoints of the triple heater meridian with the urinary bladder meridian. Then I did the triple heater meridian endpoints with the governing vessel acupoints at crown and back of head. Then I did the cranial sacral technique. The triple heater meridian is not open. It is stuck in the muscle at the side of neck and scapula. This area when open has an eggbeater type of

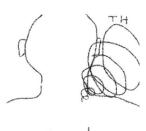

circular pattern. This meridian may be the one responsible for the vortex funnel at shoulder crook **(see figure).** I think the muscle is the sternocleidomastoid, which goes behind ear and attaches to occipital and then down to clavicle. It connects to the temporal bone. Contraction of both muscles flexes the cervical column and draws the head forward. Contraction of one muscle rotates face in opposite side of contracting muscle.

From 9 am to 12:30 pm, I blanked out doing the small intestine meridian. I am not sure what work this does. I recall watching energy go down to the stomach after left side activated which took a long time to happen. There was a strong pain along the inside of my left leg. After it opened, I recall a chain reaction of other meridians opening. Lastly, I felt strong healing work on the path of the muscle from clavicle to knob on occipital bone (triple heater meridian path); my neck and shoulder were all scrunched together while it worked. There was a loosening under my right shoulder pit. I feel it working there again.

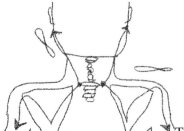

The pattern of the small intestine meridian was mainly across the tops of the shoulders. It creates a marching pattern between the shoulders. I guess this corresponds to urinary bladder meridian and its marching pattern. In addition, it works the mandible in some way. The point it hooks to on back of spine is C7. This is like a pivot point for the shoulder girdle. This causes the shoulder blades to move up and down creating a horizontal working pattern like an infinity sign across the tops of the shoulders. In the TMJ's it is the opposite direction and goes up and down vertically as a figure eight **(see figure)**.

From 1 to 2 pm, I worked the small intestine meridian and then the triple heater meridian acupoint TH23 at end of eyebrow. I then did acupoint TH23 combined with urinary bladder meridian acupoint UB2, Wow, what a combination! I can reach the small intestine acupoint SI19 with three fingers and can do all these meridians at once **(see figure)**.

From 6:30 to 7:30 pm, I did a freestyle session. It was strong and difficult to do because I was standing without moving for a long time. Later I bent at the waist and went down to squat through toes.

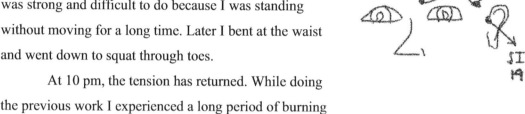

At 10 pm, the tension has returned. While doing the previous work I experienced a long period of burning pain in my skull. It was in the upper right quadrant, under the parietal near the top and above the temporal. This is where I have felt there was an injury in the skull. I did a long session. There was physical rotation of my shoulders and then a hold with much tension on muscles at shoulder crook, which I held until it released. After release, the shoulders really opened and strong energy went through them in amazing ways. I felt the trapezious muscle knots melt. I cannot express how great that felt. I cried and laughed when that happened. I think right before this, there was a flash of lightening inside then deafeningly quiet for a second, which startled me. I fell asleep while working acupoints of the urinary bladder meridian on my face. When I lied down, strong energy was zooming around all over inside.

Energetic Rotation In Left Wrist

July 12: Shivers, Birth Memories, Energy Whorls On Fontanel

From 4 to 4:30 am, I woke with strong tension in the shoulder but I feel good. Something moves and things are opening. I can put both shoulders back now with my hands clasped behind my back. The trapezious knots seem smaller. There is a pain in my right elbow that tells me the arm and shoulders are in new positions. My right ankle is loosening; I can rotate it freely and there are cracking sounds when I do that. The big toe is tender. Last night, I stretched the foot and hip strongly. I wish I could remember more about the sessions last night as much was occurring, but I cannot.

At 4:30 am, I worked the stomach meridian for a few minutes and immediately the energy went to the area of the C7 joint. There were several cracks then work on muscles in the shoulder crook. From 8 to 9 am, I worked the urinary bladder meridian while sitting. I felt nice crackly openings in neck and trapezious area. I blanked out for about fifteen minutes. The blanking out seems like higher-self takes over and then I feel intense work occurring at a fine muscular level in the body and or brain. When it is done, I return to consciousness. Soon after this, there were strong spontaneous stretches through the long muscles of the spine, which occurs often. I had a shiver episode afterward. I think these shivers are due to a rush of energy flowing through the body after neural connections are made. In the last weeks, I have the sensation an insect is on my skin, usually on my legs.

From 10:30 to 12 am, I did a freestyle session ending with lying on back in a hold while something was worked. I felt energetic rotation in the hip, knee and ankle, which felt to be working to straighten my leg, while my leg was lying on the ground. I felt pain by coronal suture near top right quadrant. There was another body roll with shoulder and arm going across my neck again. I picked up sensory images then which were natal or pre-natal. I feel like a squirmy worm coming out of a cocoon with no idea of what is happening and having no control over it. I am flopping around and being squeezed, pulled and stretched apart. I felt strong shivers and got so cold that I went under the covers.

From 6:30 to 7:45 pm, I did a sitting session with the crystal. Energy worked all over my body in the heart, lungs, rib cage and digestive system. I burped loudly and felt a rush of air with an intense feeling on both sides of the neck at once. Then I felt burning pain in the skull. Next, I felt energy whorls at top of skull by fontanel. Then I felt burning go down left arm near the wrist and felt energetic rotation forming in the wrist. I was not moving at all. There was a big shiver at end. The sounds at times were loud outside with amplified hearing. I have the strong feeling insects are crawling on my legs and arms. That was a difficult session. From 7:45 to 9:30 pm, I did all the foot meridians while strong energy worked in the head. I went to bed at 10:30 pm, and while doing the arm meridians I fell asleep.

Abdominal Muscle Activation

July 13: Skull Pain, Movement Of Rib Cage & Shoulders, Many Shivers

Dream of lining up joints: Last night I had dream that I needed to line up all the main joints of the hips, shoulders and TMJ's. Another part of it was that I should turn my head all the way around.

I slept through until 7 am. When I arose, I did a two-hour freestyle session. From 9 to 11:30 am, I have been trying to free the shoulder joint. I am looking closer in the sessions to determine where the big restrictions are. I see them in big toe, outside right ankle, inside right knee, right hip outside, lower back, connecting to hip and up to trapezious. The rib cage is stuck, so I started working the conception vessel meridian to move the energy up. I felt around the rib cage, using my finger on acupoints until I found a spot that felt it was holding much tension. This spot was my finger on the coracoid process, the projection of the scapula in front to which the muscles attach. Perhaps this is the LU1 (Mu) acupoint on the lung meridian. I cannot tell the exact acupoint this is from the acupuncture chart I have.

It is 1 pm and I am dead. I tried to roll my head all the way around a few times and it was difficult. The thought comes, "The body will follow the head". I am tired but will try this later. All the hours before I worked on releasing the shoulder and hip joints and now my head feels like it will explode. It has been six hours straight and it is enough![54] This session was one of the hardest I have had so far. The pain was so bad in my head at times that I cried and prayed for The Creator to help me. I guess she heard me. ☺ Now it is not easy but the head tension has released.

In the afternoon, I sat outside in meditation with the crystal. At first, I felt strong peristaltic action with release of gas from the intestines. The entire abdomen from pubic symphysis up to diaphragm and between the hipbones contracts in a rhythmic action. While it does this, it generates a strong force that ripples up the body. It feels like the entire abdomen activates. First, this force worked to open the spine and then it worked to move ribs, shoulders and then moved up to neck and skull. It has been working amazingly strong since, like it is

---

[54] Often when stuck in the kundalini transformation, your higher-self will relay a message telling you what you need to do. I received messages like this often, and always trusted in them and acted on them.

rolling out all the twists in the body. There is increased skull crunching and work in the TMJ's with thud-like sounds as bones release. There were many shivers. I guess all this work with the ribs in the last weeks has been about freeing the spine. This surprised me to see this. I can turn my head with more freedom and the neck rolls all the way around. It is strange how I could do that at the beginning and then could not do it later. It puzzles me how earlier changes do not stick. I did another short session before going to bed hoping it would help me sleep.

Energy Circuits Made In Skull In All Directions

July 14: Chest Contractions, Stinging Prickles In Chest & Skull, Birth Memory

I had five hours of sleep but it was deep, rising with much tension in the body. I feel strong bowel activation and the abdominal muscles are strong. I did a freestyle session from 6 to 8 am. I am certain that higher-self can control my body using the central nervous system and knows how to use leverage. A full leverage position of the body is going down on tiptoes in the squat position. I go down to this position often and it quickly activates all the meridians. While I was down in the squat on my toes, the energy worked to open the pelvis and the hip joints. I took it until my feet started to hurt, then slowly the feet and ankles energetically rotated and I was lowered to the floor sitting on the buttocks. Then I felt an energetic rotation through the hip with the tailbone as a pivot point. Next, the energy moved up the back working one vertebra at a time until I was gradually lowered to the floor on my back. Lastly, neck adjustments were done. I let this go for a while then moved outside. I was getting shivers and wanted some sun to warm up.

From 8 to 9:30 am, I did a sun session. The sweating started right away and energy worked in the skull most of the time. My feet, hands and arms were numb. I worked to quiet my mind to allow energy work in the brain. At times, it was difficult because I felt I could not breathe and noticed the chest and rib muscles were contracting. I overcame this hurdle before when it felt like I was dying. Breaths happened in a gasping way between the rhythmic pulses so I could relax.

From 9:30 to 10:30 am, I did a session. There was work, which seemed to be lining up muscles in the skull with corresponding ones in the body. I felt the creation of energy circuits in the skull with rippling muscle activity. It is clear the charge in the muscles is moving my bones but what orchestrates that is still a question. I felt energy traverse almost every muscular path of movement there could be in the head in all directions. There were quite a few paths moving down the body combined with the skull. Energy worked much on the TMJ's. Then my head tilted forward hanging from the neck in a hold, which I held about fifteen minutes. Energy worked to make a path through the C7 joint. There are many stinging prickles all over my head and chest.

From 10:30 to 12 am, I did a freestyle session. Much happened but I remember little of it. I spent much time on the floor, with strong energy and pain that pushed me to my limit. I went through amazing body twists and there was a strong scrunching of facial bones. During this, my arm went over my neck at least three more times and then I was curling into the fetal position with arms and legs tucked. I felt like my body was traveling through a repeating loop of my birth trauma and the fetal position. Then several images flashed in my 3rd eye. One was an image of an obstetrics table and the next was a photo of my mom showing how she looked when she was young. I think I sustained an injury to my shoulder during my delivery because my mother was in twilight sleep and they either used forceps or pulled on my arm to make the delivery.[55]

Later, there was strong pain in a right rib in front that poked into my body for about ten minutes. Then I focused hard to quiet my mind and relax with the energy because I was concerned this might hurt me if I did not pay close attention. In some longer sessions, I get the feeling I should stay with the reaction and not stop in the middle. I remember I had a problem before with a nerve when I stopped too early. Sometimes there is delicate work and I feel it is important to be quiet and relaxed. My head feels broken.

From 1 to 11 pm, I did several more sessions with skull crunching and shoulder stretches. I did a lying session and gave acupressure to various acupoints. My energy is low and the work is ineffective.[56] There is much tension in the body focused on the C7 joint and both of my ankles hurt on the inside. I am convinced my central nervous system can move my body spontaneously and it happens often. I only have to relax and allow it. I guess it took all these months to be convinced of that!

---

[55] See footnote on May 8th

[56] Maybe I did a stretching session when it was not ready because I was in a growing state.

Vertebrae Snapping In Cobra Pose

July 15: Energy Circuit Through C7

From 6:30 to 11:30 am, I did a sitting session and sat for an hour with my head tipped back while strong energy worked by C7. I held it until it released. Then I did a freestyle session with work on spine. There was a long intense stretch down through the ankles and toes with loud snaps in the big toe, which hurt like hell. Everything still hurts. Then I did sitting and lying sessions. The right side of spine was worked while I was lying on the left side. There was a long intense hold while lying on the stomach while energy worked all the vertebrae from bottom of spine on up to C7.

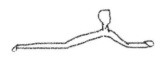 Then I moved spontaneously ending in the yogic cobra position **(see figure).** The sternum, rib cage and abdominal muscles and hips were contracting and somehow pushing on the vertebrae to snap them. These snaps continued up and down the spine, sometimes with head turned left or right or toward the floor. Some challenging holds without movement occurred. The energy slowly moved up the spine to the C7 vertebra and when it reached C7, I felt a strong stretching force. I turned to my left side feeling a stretch go through the C7 area and heard crunchy squishy sounds. Then I felt the vertical trapezious knot release and then energy started working on the horizontal knot. Then energy went to the head, and worked to align the TMJ's with the spinal column. I felt cranium bones moving and then the energy went down and out of the skull. I stopped here.

From 6:30 to 10:30 pm, I did a session sitting outside starting with acupressure on the urinary bladder meridian toe acupoints and later did acupoints near the eyebrows. This was effective to work on C7 and relax areas in the skull. Then I did all arm meridians. I could easily observe the energetic path of each meridian. I finally felt what it was like for the urinary bladder meridian to be open on both sides as a complete circle through the body. Tonight, I felt much pain near the C7 joint, the right shoulder and TMJ's.

Strong Abdominal Contractions Push On Sternum

July 16: Floating Head, Amplified Hearing, Ear Popping, Sweating

I will go through all the meridians and take notes about which muscle groups activate and what is the pattern through the body, because I can easily see it. I think this is a special skill I have now and may not have later, so feel it is important to document.

I slept long and I think about going back to bed. There is much tension in the usual areas. Energy is working in the rib cage on front right and under my arm. The root chakra activated quickly. In the morning session I used acupressure on the small intestine meridian, the notes are in my Reiki healing journal for this date.

From 11 to 1 pm, I did a freestyle session with work in spine similar to when I am lying. There were releases in the left shoulder and right shoulder crook, which were painful. There was much crunching in the skull, TMJ and C7 joint. It is 1:30 pm and I am exhausted. Now, a big vortex forms in my entire body and my head is dripping with sweat.

From 1:30 to 2 pm, I stretched through the neck, head and shoulders and I feel better. I have to stop for an appointment but I do not want to go. From 6:30 to 8 pm, I did acupressure on meridians. I spent a long time on the urinary bladder meridian, while energy worked on both of the knots in my trapezious muscle and then they released. The energy gets strong in this meridian. Then my head started to feel weird, like it was floating or full of air, maybe because of the trapezious release.

I worked the gallbladder meridian and noticed the energetic pattern is like an eggbeater going back and forth between the joints. Something loosened in the hip area in front by the ribs. My abdominal muscles contracted strongly many times while working this meridian and a force pushed up my sternum several times. There are amazingly strong forces now. Then I did acupressure on the middle toe and stomach meridian acupoint on long toe, which is a vertical path up front of body. I felt strong dimples on the acupoints, which tells me energy works strong in the meridian and I need to work it more. My stomach rumbles. I guess the gallbladder and liver meridians open and this stimulates digestion. My right ear pops and moments of total quiet are occurring frequently with amplified hearing. Working the large intestine meridian acupoint LI1 was strong. I fell asleep while doing the hand meridians.

Sphenoid Release, Vertebrae Releases, Energy Coil On Left Body

July 17: Releases On Lower & Upper Spine, Stinging Prickles On Body

I slept a long time. I have many cleansing dreams lately. From 6:30 to 9 am, I did the full Reiki acupressure sequence in a sun session. From 9:30 to 11 am, I experimented more with the meridians. There is a spot on underside of knee on outside edge near the tendon that strongly actives the entire knee.

After this, I did a freestyle session. My abdominal muscles activated. It started under the diaphragm and then moved down through the pelvis and the legs. Then I bent at waist while energy worked in spine and was in a prolonged hold in full squat on my toes, I stayed like that until it felt my feet would break. I felt the hips and rib cage open on right side. Then I went down to floor and stretched right side of body while lying on left side. Then I was lying on my back with neck crunches. While on my back, the neck area suddenly felt like a snake. Next, I felt the area stretch up, twist and turn and then felt vertebrae settle to the left. It was a strange feeling!

Next, I was spontaneously turned from lying on my back to lying on my stomach! After that, there was intense work in the shoulders, spine and skull. I felt something release in the spine near the tailbone. There was much crunching deep in the skull and work by lower edge of occipital bone. The skull work was intense so I was pressing on acupoints in the skull trying to assist the process. The spot in the temples, outside eye orbit at zygmatic and frontal bone, urinary bladder acupoint UB2 and the gallbladder acupoint GB1 were helpful.

At 1 pm, I lay down and my spine was worked the entire time. From 6:30 to 8 pm, I gave long-distance Reiki to two friends in sequence. When done I felt as if I was one rotating ball of vibrating energy.

Form 8 to 9:30 pm, I did a freestyle session. While standing, there was a backward bend in the spine, while my head went around in a circle. This was difficult to do and I think it moved a lower vertebra. Then I stretched down through toes and ankles and energy worked to open hips and lower rib cage. Then I was lowered to floor and sitting with legs out to front for ten minutes, then slowly lowering the back and eventually with head on floor on my back. Then energy worked in the neck and it felt like my head came alive and was moving powerfully with my neck. Then I felt cranium bones loosening with a strong muscular action that also worked in the neck. Eventually something opened and my energy soared. I felt energy waves go down my body with many stinging prickles all over the left side of my body.

Then energy went to the toes and my left body went numb. Then I felt a thin line of energy like a wire, coil in a spiral on the outer surface of my leg going from my toes to the hip. Then the same happened in my left arm. Then I felt the same a little later in my head. I slapped at it thinking it was an insect. Then the right side of my body was worked mostly in the head and neck. The energy work was strong and moved fast and kept building momentum. The focus of this work seemed to be working to align and fix the problem in the right TMJ. The energy work was so intense that I could not divert any of my attention to observe it. I focused on being quiet and relaxing and lay like that on my back for about an hour.

I felt something painful in the occipital bone area while in a ten-minute hold, with neck arched and back of head on floor. There were horrific sounds in the head with movements. I think the sphenoid bone released from the occipital bone. There are prickles in the skin all over and rising body heat. I lightly scratched my arm and it hurt after. From 10 to 11:30 pm, I sat outside and did a sitting session with more crunching of cranium bones.

Chapter 15: Sphenoid Directing Body Movements

Horizontal Skull Vortex, New Circuits From All Skull Bones To Body

July 18: Energy Pummeling Left Skull, Head & Spine Whips

It is 5:30 am; I had many cleansing dreams. Many nights do not feel like sleep, my lungs, heart or mind is worked which makes resting and breathing difficult. I still feel rested when I rise. I have much tension at base of skull.

From 6 to 10 am, I did a freestyle session. Energy worked mainly in hips and right sacrum suture, which feels tender. Many times the hip stretched on both sides. Later I did a sun session giving acupressure to the urinary bladder and gallbladder meridians. Most of the time I was in a hold while energy worked in the hips. Later there was a strong sweat on the skull sutures. Then I came inside and did twisting stretches through the spine and hips.

Later I was lying on my right side with compression in the right pelvis and energy force in right body was used to work on shoulder, hip and TMJ joint and skull in left body. The left side of my body has more energy than the right and wonder if this is why work has mainly been in right skull so far. Is it because I now have enough energy on right side of my body that now there is enough to work in left skull? The energy was pummeling the left side of the skull and it is the first time I recall this occurring. I stayed in a hold for about forty-five minutes until I could not take more. Near the end, I felt energy form into a large horizontal vortex of energy, working both sides of skull together.

Sitting, my head hurts and there is tension and pain in left top of shoulder and down the big muscles at sides of the neck, on back of skull near occipital bone and suture line of the parietals. There was a large release in the right TMJ, and then energy worked in left side of skull. I think the transformation will not finish soon, which is disheartening. It is nine months and I am tired of it.

From 10:20 to 3 pm, there was work in the skull, neck and shoulders with many releases in the jaws. Much tension released from the right TMJ and the area heals. After the jaw released, the lower right molars knock together and on the other side, the bite does not meet.

From 7:30 to 9:30 pm, I did a sitting session outside on the crystal that was different. Starting out, energy worked in right side of skull with tiny muscle movements moving around the cranium bones. Then I felt a slow stretch go down in body connected to a certain cranial bone. Different stretches went to all parts in entire right body, starting with neck and shoulders and moving down until all were done like that. After the legs were done, energy moved up and worked the right and left hip together. Then energy would return to skull and come down again, and work on connections with right skull and other body parts. Sometimes the body parts were in left body, or in right body and sometimes in both sides of body always with the energy returning up into the skull. After all this was done, energy worked both sides of the skull, as if it was hooking together various parts into one unit. There were several strong sweats and at the end, my body felt like one energetic whole. Then the root chakra activated intensely. Energy then moved up the spine and my head stretched with it. It felt like all bones were in alignment, even the TMJ's. Then there were spontaneous quick whipping movements of the spine and head. At 11:30 pm, I did a sitting session and there were small pops in the neck. I am tired.

Front To Back Vortex Opens Rib Cage, Coronal Sutures Open

July 19: Left Body Work, Legs Go Numb With Intense Stinging Prickles

I decided to work the inner leg and arms meridians that start on long and big toe, index finger and thumbs. When I did the stomach meridian, much work occurred in the right shoulder and neck before it activated. I felt strong pain under left rib cage and then felt an energy vortex moving from front to back and working the left rib cage. Then the energy vortex moved up and worked the left shoulder area going from front to back. Then the vortex rose into the skull and worked the eye socket[57] with all muscles around it. There was a large energy ball in the eye.

From 12 to 1:15 pm, there were strong spontaneous stretches in the neck in all directions with crunches. Mostly, I was lying on my stomach moving up and down to cobra position with lower back bends while energy worked in lower spine. Then there was a hold for about thirty minutes with pressure on the lower back. From 8 to 10 pm, I used acupressure on the acupoints on both feet of urinary bladder, gallbladder, middle toe and stomach

---

[57] The back lateral wall of the eye orbit is partly composed of the sphenoid bone.

meridians for about one and a half hours. My left arm, leg and body went numb. When I started, there was strong PHYSICAL rotation in the shoulders, which is new. I have only felt energetic rotation in the shoulders.

I did several sessions. In the first, there was intense work in left shoulder along the path of the stomach meridian, which I worked earlier. In the next session, there was much energetic work in hips while I was bent over while sitting and giving acupressure to the toe meridians. Energy worked in both hips with premenstrual pain and my legs went numb. When the numbness in legs recedes, it is like millions of bee's sting me. My left leg slowly came back and energy moved up with intense healing in the body as the stinging prickles rose. This has been occurring often in my legs.

After the stinging prickles receded, energy zoomed around in the body. Later I felt energy whorls on the fontanel and energy moved down my nose and then to the maxillae. Then the left coronal suture opened followed by the right. Then there were intense movements in the spine, shoulders and head. I took a break. From 11 pm to 1:30 am, I did a freestyle session ending with lying in a long hold with all joints on right lining up somehow.

Insight about layers of muscle enervation: I think the transformation starts by enervating the smallest layers of muscle tissue. Over time, this gradually expands to affect larger muscles and body parts as the energetic vibration grows. Lately, it feels like body parts come alive, such as my shoulders, abdominal muscles, legs and head. While these movements seem repetitive, I think they are slow growing the body and making changes. Now energy is strong enough to move the larger muscles.

July 20: Long Hold With Intense Pain On Alar Ligament

I slept well. I did a long session with acupressure on the large intestine meridian[58]. From 9:30 am to 3:30 pm, I did a long session that lasted nine hours! There was intense pain on a ligament along backside of neck going up to skull on right **(see figure).** This area was stretched and moved to the left or to the center. Often I wanted to cry because the pain was strong. At the end, the spine and neck were opening.

From 6:30 to 8:30 pm, I did acupressure on the large intestine meridian acupoint LI1 and on another acupoint on the finger of this meridian. Work on the large intestine meridian eventually sets up an infinity sign pattern that works across the tops of the shoulders. It creates a vertical vortex around lower part of nose and upper teeth **(see figure).** In the back, the energetic movements of scapulae activate muscles, which go up either side of spine to the occipital bone.

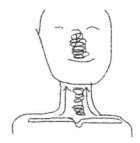

From 8:30 to 9:30 pm, I did shoulder crunching which hurt! Then I did acupressure to the pericardium and lung meridians and fell asleep while working them.

Right Skull Energy Spiral, Lifted Rib Cage, TMJ's Circuit

July 21: Large Release In C7 And TMJ, Parietals Open

I did not sleep well. I rose twice to stretch and had many cleansing dreams. From 7 to 10 am, I used acupressure on the urinary bladder meridian for two hours. Work was mainly in the right shoulder and rib cage with several pops in vertebrae. I had several shivers after a squishy crunch in C7.

From 1 to 2:30 pm, I did a freestyle session with stretching while lying through spine, hip, neck, skull and TMJ's. The stretches in the TMJ's were the most intense so far. I pray this will end soon. After this, I took a walk and had to do mini-stretches during it. Later while sitting, something popped in the TMJ joint, I felt a big release of tension and the constant tugging feeling was gone.

---

[58]The notes from this session are in my Reiki healing journal under this date.

At 8:30 pm, I did acupressure on the urinary bladder meridian and it felt open when I started. As far as I recall energy opened in the neck and then the parietals opened. Then I felt a strong internal spiral with bones moving deep inside my head and it was turning around **(see figure).** Then my neck was held strongly in a fixed position while energy worked various sequences of bones, moving down and covering the entire right side of head. I felt drops of water landing on my skin in various places and stinging prickles all over. Then energy worked in both sides of my head at once, which is new. Then energy went down the center of face. I distinctly felt a line of energy go down the frontal bone to the maxillae, then down to mandible and then up and around the temporal bones. I felt a stretch from my jaw going down throat to clavicles.

A big thunderstorm started when I sat. The skull work lasted a little longer in both sides of skull but was not as strong on the left side. At moments, the entire skull was energized and undulated.

From 8:30 to 9:30 pm, I was lying with the right body joints lined up while energy worked through them, the spine and chest. Once, energy went down the sides of my neck and then went across the shoulders and lifted and twisted my rib cage such that I felt something was lifted over it. This movement released energy, which rippled up and adjusted the TMJ and shoulder. It felt like joints were lifting and moving. I have never felt anything like this before. This is not easy to do and it hurts but there is much power to do it. My part in this is to sit in center and allow the spontaneous body movements. When pain increases, I work to go to deep center by putting myself into 'sleep mode'. At times, I tensed parts of my body and worked to relax them so energy could work there. When I relaxed, energy accelerated. The natural tendency is to resist the transformational sensation. Anytime I feel pain, it reminds me to do a muscle scan. Near the end, I had the feeling my skeletal structure was free from the flesh.

From 10:40 pm to 12:30 am, I sat and worked the meridians. I recall there was strong work in the shoulders and I blanked out with my head tipped back and my mouth open and felt a large circle of energy moving through the TMJ's. I think I was a long time like that.

Dream of losing control then I had a dream while in the blanked out state that I had passed out when the growing phase started. In the dream, I was outside and reactions started which were strong and fast. I went out of control and somebody had to take me inside to my bed. Then I woke up. Perhaps it is a message to go to bed.

Sphenoid Directing Body Movements

July 22

I slept long and have much tension. From 6:30 to 10 am, I did a freestyle session immediately. There was intense work in shoulder and articulations related to it. I am sure the sphenoid bone is moving. I distinctly felt that all the cranial bone movements were radiating from this central bone. It is interesting to know that the pituitary gland is nestled into the top side of the sphenoid at the center and is at base of brain and that the sphenoid looks like a butterfly or a bat, which both are symbols of transformation.

The body stretches are difficult. It is as if I hold my skeleton still while large muscle groups around a stuck bone amass an energy charge with increasing tension and then with a tremendous force, the area is popped, twisted or stretched and something releases. From 10:30 to 12 am, I did a freestyle session with strong bone crunching body stretches; for sure, I am being killed.

The energy does not let up so I did many sessions trying to release the tension. Near the end of the day, I felt something in the neck release and then the body opened with tension releases in the shoulder, trapezious and TMJ. Energy work felt to be at the deepest level of bone so far. I do not remember much, only relief to feel the tension go away.

July 23: Bathed In Golden Sunlight, Shivers, Energy Massage

From 4 to 7:30 am, I did a long intense session but not as bad as yesterday. The pain is from bones moving against bone. I do not have neck tension and no irritating popping of the TMJ, which was getting to me yesterday! Energy worked mostly in the TMJ and behind head by occipital bone in the skull and then in both shoulders. I felt the trapezious muscles release. Near the end, I felt like I was sitting in golden sunlight and was floating while work was occurring in the background of my body. That felt wonderful and I was not outside. There were many shivers, yawns and strong body stretches. There was a long moment of high-pitched sound and then total silence. The root chakra is strongly activated with strong pain near right sphenoid wing. I feel good!

From 4:30 to 6:30 pm, it was a difficult bone crunching session with openings up spine, neck, shoulders, hips, TMJ's & skull. The energetic vibration is fast and works more efficiently. Near the end, energy moved super fast going back and forth and quickly changing directions and worked along paths of different muscle groups. It felt like an energy massage was ironing me out. From 7 to 11 pm, I did a long meditation session with Reiki.

Burning On Cranial Sutures, Skull Getting Narrow And Wide

July 24: Strengthening Full Body Stretches

From 6 to 9 am, I did a sitting meditation and from 10:30 am to 12:30 pm, I did a freestyle session. While sitting, there was much cranium bone work and then stretching with strong body and skull crunches. I worked much on the twist in body. The stretches felt effective to open the tissue. At times, it felt fetal, with one arm squished under body left to front and the other arm right to back, with hips turned, like lying on my side. Releases happened with arms in fetal position with shoulders hunched near neck in back. These were difficult sessions. From 7 to 9 pm, it seems my head is reshaping. There is intense burning between the cranium bones as they separate. I can distinctly feel my head going narrow and wide.

July 25: Sternum Release, Going Deeper Into Squat

From 5:30 to 8:30 am, I did urinary bladder and gallbladder meridian work. The shoulders, hips, spine and rib cage were worked. From 9 to 10:30 am, I did a painful freestyle session. The sternum released near the fourth or fifth rib, the one stuck under the right arm.

From 1 to 2 pm, I did a lying session. From 7:30 to 10:30 pm, I did two freestyle sessions. Mostly I was I lying with the majority of work on spine, rib cage and upper shoulders. I keep sinking lower in the squat. The pelvis bones, ankle and toe open more each time. The spine work felt chiropractic with many twisting, pushing and pulling stretches. At times, I felt searing pain going down a line from TMJ joint, jaw, neck, down back and under arm. Now there is work in sacrum where the hip bone meets it and the sacrum is opening.

I feel disappointed seeing how much work there remains to do, the body is dense and takes a long time to transform. The most effective workout for me now is a Reiki acupressure session followed by a freestyle session. I am tired.

July 26: Mandible Releases With Thud, What Sex You Want To Be?

I slept long, which felt great! From 6:30 to 9 am, I used acupressure on the feet meridians together in a sun session. There were many twisting body stretches with work in hip, shoulder and spine. From 9 to 11:30 am, I did a freestyle session with twisting stretches and crunches; most work was in skull, neck and shoulders with some hip discomfort. The TMJ joint moved to the right with a loud thud. There was much cranium bone movement. I used cranial sacral techniques to try to open the TMJ more and likely I over did it. I get desperate to get this over with and to be rid of the pain that often I do too much. The head, neck and shoulders feel broken now. There was a long hold working on the cord of personality mainly in the head. During the hold, I heard the question, "What sex do you want to be?" Immediately I answered, "Male". I thought about my spontaneous answer and came to the same conclusion that I want to be a male. The main reasons are as a female, I do not feel safe in today's world, and that it would be intriguing to change to the opposite sex. I wonder if I have the power to choose and if it is physically possible to change your sex in a kundalini transformation. I arose after forty-five minutes in the hold, as I could not take more.

Lately, it seems higher-self will completely take over at any moment. I feel it strongest during the holds. Perhaps once the skull is sufficiently changed then a strong reaction might happen in the brain and higher-self will completely take over and finish all the body changes that still need to be done.[59] The energy moves so fast now, it does seem likely.

From 3 to 4:30 pm, I did a sitting session where energy worked mostly in the cranium bones while I was in a blanked out state. From 7 to 9:30 pm, I did a slow and easy shoulder opening where I stayed surrendered with less crunching, so I am not worn out.

---

[59] I was still clinging to the hope that I could change instantly without having to go through the grueling process that is necessary to completely transform.

Sphenoid Bone Moves Body, Energy Balls Work Body, Burning Lines

July 27: Burning In Sternocleidomastoids, Head Whips To Open C7

I slept long and felt the wavy growing reaction during the night. I am stiff with much body tension and I have slight swelling in the shoulder. I have menstruation with strong cramps. From 4:30 to 6 am, I did a stretching session that was difficult because my head, shoulders and back are stiff. I went back to bed.

From 7 to 9:30 am, I did a sun session and stretched afterward. Energy work concentrated in the spine. I still have much body tension. The body is spontaneously moving to align the skeleton. I am physically moving in the sessions like the energetic rotation patterns and energy circuits I have felt for so long inside me. In the freestyle sessions, body parts are stretched in many combinations, such as left skull with right shoulder, shoulders together, or right hip with left shoulder and every permutation the body can move through. Reality sets in; I will have to do all these physical movements, as part of the transformation, there is not going to be any energetic instantaneous healing.

From 10 to 12 am, I did a freestyle session with spontaneous movements with yoga poses for about thirty minutes and then there was intense work on shoulder and TMJ. The yoga poses felt good. The energy in my body powers them and thus the spine stretches are effective. Seeing this motivated me to continue with the hope to release some tension. Once, the facial bones moved more than before, which felt weird and was painful. There were many deep pops and crunches in the TMJ and sphenoid wing area in the skull. I am still twisted, but feel somewhat straighter. It always seems like one more stretch and I will be finished. My naval cavity hurts.

From 7 to 8:30 pm, I did a freestyle session, stretching down to squat, and then down to the floor. It was amazing! I was in a long hold lying on right side with right joints lined up and energy worked the skull and body simultaneously. I felt a deep burning pain in the center of my right hip. Later, the sphenoid bone felt alive, like it was orchestrating the body movements. I continually felt spiraling energy coming from the eye orbit no matter where energy worked in the skull. Energy traversed all parts of the skull with no restrictions. I felt parallel patterns of muscular work in skull and body in different places. I felt figure eights between TMJ's and shoulders, a spiral at top of skull and a spiral elsewhere in body. It felt like a body part was aligning vertically somewhere in the skull with a continuous circle of energy, while energy worked along that circle. The energy was moving very fast at times. Most of the work was on cranium bones, joints and spine and the TMJ's moved radically. Energy worked concentrated on right side, and worked strongly in both sides of the skull. I felt that irritating ligament under my jaw move to another position, which felt great!

From 10 to 11:30 pm, was another amazing session! I was sitting outside with crystals and ring in chair. Energy quickly activated the body, and entered skull and slowly worked on the bones going down. I felt numerous energy balls cushioning my joints and my head was rolling around cushioned by them. I barely felt any pain. There was work on the facial bones and the TMJ's moved. A tremendous force was used on the sternocleidomastoid muscles on both sides of my neck at once with a burning feeling. It was difficult on the shoulder joints and the sternum. Something released in the abdomen with a snap, followed by energy puff outs. One time I felt higher-self take over strongly and my head starting moving around fast and then there were quick whips of my head downward, which snapped the C7 vertebrae. For a long time I had an intense sensation of itching and feeling of insects biting me all over my body. The energy moved even faster then in the previous session. Again, I felt the skull was connected with the body and both moved and changed as one unit. I am tired.

Insight about sphenoid bone It seems the body is as a marionette and can be fully controlled by moving the sphenoid bone. The sphenoid bone is unique in that it articulates with every skull bone. When it moves all skull bones move with it and when a skull bones moves, body parts connected to those bones move via nerves, muscles and other tissues. The nerve center that regulates movement of the sphenoid I suspect is above the sphenoid in the brain, but the higher-self decides which movements to make. The brain now can spontaneously move all parts of my body, maybe more when this is done!

July 28: Energy Balls, Arrows Pierce Chest Muscles, Tooth Powder

I awoke at 5:30 and slept long and deep. The TMJ joint, mandible and along the scapula line by the spine feels tender and sore. The left shoulder has a tender spot, which I have been noticing for weeks. Menstruation continues strong. From 5:30 to 7:30 am, I did a freestyle session, mostly lying. There was similar work as yesterday with lining up joints, working spine, rib cage, neck and mandibles.

From 7:30 to 9:30 am, I did a sun session. The head was bobbing around with quick head movements and work in TMJ's with many energy balls working down my body again. There was much sweating and opening of cranial sutures. I felt something deep in the skull open near the TMJ after much crunching and pops in this area. There was crunching work down the cord of personality. The hip continues to open. From 11:30 am to 1:30 pm, I went to lie down but there were strong stretches working to open the TMJ & shoulder joint.

Vision of yellow house: I had a visual image in the sun of snow-capped mountains. In the foothills, I saw a yellow house with green trim made out of wood. This keeps returning for some reason. The house was two stories and is large. It looked like a farmhouse with no other houses around and was on flat ground.

From 7 to 8 pm, I did a sitting stretch with crystal and ring outside. It was a strong session with difficult work in skull, back of neck and at base of shoulders. I was relaxed and it was still painful. Once, I felt energy going back and forth through my shoulders and upper chest from left to right. It was like many arrows of energy cutting through the dense tissue of my body. I felt like I was being remade. Lately, I smell tooth powder, like when the dentist drills on a tooth. From 8 to 9:30 pm, I did a lying session with much head crunching.

Insight of ratcheting skull plate movement: I observed how the skull plate movement happens. Energy moves along the suture lines of the plate with small up and down muscular actions, charging those muscles. This is done to move the plates in the direction the energy is going. Energy then traces around the edge of each skull plate that needs to be moved as a group in sequence. It is like preparing an area of bones for moving. When all areas have built energetic charge then there are strong muscle contractions, which then carry out the actual bone movements. Because the movement is by microns and each movement needs this long procedure to charge the muscles, I call it ratcheting.

Tailbone Release With Vertebrae Adjustments, Shoulders Release

July 29: Healing Reactions, Trapezoid & Sternocleidomastoid Releases

I fell asleep doing the session last night and woke at 3 am. It is 5:30 am, and I am sore all over as tissues heal. My head is congested, I blow my nose often, cough and grains of sand come from my eyes. My menstruation continues strong. There is a strong urge to stretch now. From 6 to 10 am, I did a freestyle session and later gave acupressure to toe meridians in a sun session. It was not difficult. The acupressure energizes muscles along a pathway of stretch, and later when I stretch that path, it is more effective to open the blocks.

From 10 am to 12:30 pm, I did a long freestyle session, it was difficult and I feel dead now. Starting, there were stretching crunches along the path of the cord of personality. Once, there was strong pain in sacrum, by tailbone, neck and skull and I cried uncontrollably, feeling like a baby while much crunching occurred. It felt like being in labor and I cried out to The Creator to help me. Then I felt a release along the spine near the tailbone and then a correction was made to all the vertebrae moving up slowly and ending at the wormian bones by whorl on skull. That was difficult; I hope I do not have to do it again.

From 12:40 to 2:40 pm, I did another session to relieve tension. There was a long hold with my head tipped back and extreme pressure was exerted on both shoulders at once, which I held until the tension released. After the release, energy flooded into backside with a massage feeling starting at base of spine and working up. There were some nice releases in the trapezious muscle. I cannot take more now!

From 9 to 11 pm, I did a sitting session. It seems the neck work is almost done. There is nerve pain on each side of neck near the sternocleidomastoid muscles. I do not remember much as mostly I was blanked out. From 11 to 12 pm, it was a nice and easy freefall session. There were crackly, snappy, small energy balls all over the upper body. It felt like adhesions were opening all over and I was melting.

Hip, Scapula, Sternum, C7 And Rib Cage Release

July 30: Energy Tracing Of Each Rib In Rib Cage (Like Skull Plates)

I woke at 7 am, with much soreness but good spirit. From 7:30 to 9:30 am, I did a sun session. Energy worked in the right hip and I noticed I do not let energy enter the right side of pubic area because I fear the stinging prickles. I allowed the energy to enter there and shortly after this the right hip released with a small pop and settling of the hip. Then I felt an energy circuit go up in a straight line from the pelvic area to the stomach muscles, through ribs and on up to the TMJ. From 10:30 to 11 am, I did a freestyle session stretching through all the positions.

From 11 am to 1 pm, I did a freestyle session and went quickly down to squat and to lying on stomach and stretching lower back. It was physically difficult. Eventually something released between the spine and the right scapula, and this set off a healing reaction. After this, I was in an hour-long hold lying with strong pressure exactly on the C7 joint in back and in the front on the sternum exactly in the center. It was difficult to get out of the hold. I did so by rolling over very slowly onto my side using my hands to lift my head. Many high-pitched sounds occurred during the hold, I have never heard that before. While sitting I feel a sharp pain in the lower ribs on the back. It seems I have no choice but to keep going.

From 1 to 5 pm, I continued with sessions with work mostly in spine, rib cage, right hip and shoulder with much neck crunching. The torque in my rib cage is ready to release. From 8 to 10 pm, I did a two-hour meditation session outside on crystals with mosquitoes. Energy work in spine and right hip continued. Then I felt a strong pop in C7 and later felt my right shoulder pop. Then the entire rib cage released and shifted toward the left shoulder. The energy zoomed after that and I heard high-pitched tones several times. The spine was starting to feel raw from so much energy moving up and down it. Now, I feel many sore spots.

From 10:30 to 11:45 pm, energy is working deep in the right shoulder crunching away, which feels good to get down in there. I did a freestyle session stretching down and lying on back with neck and skull crunching. I think what is occurring is that after a bone is released in the body then a bone adjustment in done in the skull. I felt the energy work in the skull going around all the bones in a certain order. It seems the rib cage needs to adjust in the manner of the cranium bones, because it does not have much range of motion. Energy is going systematically down the rib cage, moving each rib a little bit and then starting over at the top, this repeated several times.

12 midnight: energy was quickly working between the shoulders tops and the TMJ. After this, there were a few neck adjustments and then energy moved fast and strong and I fell asleep.

July 31: Time Flying By, Forgetting, Burning Lines, Heart Jumps

I slept soundly and rose at 5:30 am. From 6 to 10 am, I did a freestyle session to release the body tension. Soon I was lying on my stomach in the cobra position and energy worked lower back, sacrum, spine, neck, rib cage, and TMJ's. It was difficult but not too bad. The time flew by fast and I could not believe I went that long. After this, I did a sun session. Energy work was mostly in skull and TMJ. There were some gentle stretches afterward. I feel it is near to finishing so I want to keep going. From 12 to 1 pm, I did a stretching session and recall little of what transpired. I think the right shoulder released and I felt bone moving against bone and afterward it seemed in lower position.

From 5:30 to 10 pm, I tried to lie down and rest and it ended up with neck crunching. I kept doing different sessions all this time. There was much work on the C7 joint. In the lying session, there was work on right side of skull that hurt the most so far with burning and nerve pain. In the stretching sessions, I felt streaks of painful burning lines in my legs and other body parts as I stretched through those areas. When I was blanked out, my body jumped twice centered in the chest area. This woke me up! Perhaps it was my heart. There were many shivers in the sitting meditation and intense heat about thirty minutes later. Energy worked in the TMJ or C7 area. It is difficult to remember what happens. The root chakra activates strong each day with more burning. It seems the energy is calm and wavy so perhaps I can sleep.

Chapter 16: Skull Lift Off Atlas & Brain Stem Change

Abdominal Muscle Pulsing & Contracting

August 1: Rib Cage & Shoulder Release, Energy Moves Up & Down Spine

I did seven hours of sessions this morning. It is like being in labor. I cannot stop this, it hurts to do it and it hurts not to do it. There were good releases in middle back, much work on right hip and a few interesting twists of torso and stretching over top of head. It was difficult to surrender fully all this time; I did the best I could. I am stiff, sore, and have much tension. Each twist hurts more. My right ear hurts and keeps popping.

In the afternoon, I did several freestyle sessions and worked with the urinary bladder and hand meridians. The urinary bladder meridian is open compared to the last time I worked it. While working the thumb meridians I felt energetic work in rib cage under the arm. Later there was a release, in the rib cage and C7 on the left side, which felt great. Then I felt the entire shoulder girdle release with many openings all over with energy zooming around. Afterward, the rib cage felt suspended and free of the shoulder girdle. There was a long period of heat. There was much work in a straight circuit up and down the spine. Energy would work in the skull and then move down to body and back up fast. Later both directions occurred at once.

August 2: Abdominal Muscle Contracting, Reliving Birth Process

I slept long. For two hours, I worked with the urinary bladder meridian. My body continues to crack open. It is great, not much pain at all. For the first time, I felt tension release from the sternocleidomastoid muscle. I did a two-hour sun session. There was work behind skull and some strong passes through the shoulders and rib cage. Near the end, it seemed at the point to make a strong spinal adjustment.

My bowel is active; the digestive system does another clean out. For a half hour, I stretched the spine and felt energy going along the path through the digestive organs. There were nice stretches and crunches along the right lumbar spine. In addition, energy worked all the way up the spine, with several good pops near T1 and C7. There was work in shoulder, up neck, with many cranium bone movements and energetic rotation in TMJ joints.

I did a long freestyle session, mostly lying. Spine work was done while in cobra position on stomach. Lying in this position there was a strong pulsing and muscular action that felt to be just below the xiphoid process and above the navel near the diaphragm. I never felt that before. It felt like a strong muscle was used as the power horse to do the work above in the chest, sternum and spine. There was more work in spine and hips and a long stretch, which seemed to be a reliving of the birth process. There were strange contortions in a spontaneous stretch along the cord of personality line through all the joints. Then I sat for thirty minutes and skull work occurred. All the cranium bones moved with my mouth stretched open very wide, and then there was a physical rotation of head up and over and back, moving the bones in the upper mouth.

In the afternoon, I did a two-hour freestyle session with another round through the spine in cobra position. Something in the lower back near the hip was loosened with a strong force, perhaps the sacrum. Energy then rippled up and I felt a loose cord running along the spine up into the head. It shifted in position feeling like it went over my shoulder. Then there was neck work with my head stretching to turn further and further to the right, it seemed that cord was caught and moved around the mandible. Then my head was frozen into that position and I felt a strong pressure build in skull on right side. For sure, I did not dare move. I blanked out while some work occurred. I did not detect cranium bone movement in skull. I presume something was worked deep in skull. After this, the normal shifting patterns and crunching in the skull lasted about forty minutes.

For one hour, I was lying with work on the ligament in the right neck. It popped around more and I felt pain deep in skull. Then I worked the gallbladder meridian for fifteen minutes with work on neck ligament. Something behind the neck, in the shoulder crook snapped loud and the area appears to open. It seems many structures support this ligament. My chest opens more and there is much crunching in the ribs. Next, I did a long freestyle session ending in cobra position. There was crunching of bones and work on same ligament, it keeps springing back. For thirty minutes, I gave acupressure to the urinary bladder, gallbladder and middle toe meridians. My head hurts now.

August 3: Hips And Shoulders Move As Unit With Cranium Bones

I slept long. I feel slight swelling on the side of my neck and upper shoulder. I stretched it easy and there were two cracks, which felt good. My head and the areas in backs of shoulders by trapezious still hurt a little. I feel like going back to bed. I am a little depressed, seeing the density of the body and the reality there is much more to do. I want to finish and it is difficult now.

From 8 to 9:30 am, I did a freestyle session, going quickly down to lying on back and doing skull work. The position was back of head angled with wormian bones on floor and sacrum pressed flat to floor. When the head was turning, it was usually pivoting on the wormian bones. The head and sacrum were glued to the floor and I could not move either part. While lying this way, the chin is pointing toward the sky as far as possible, and then the head turns to the right as far as possible, then tipping head up to center and back toward neck. The muscles of the skull seem to wrap around my head. When the head comes toward the neck, often the mouth opens and the TMJ's align on both sides of head and the facial bones shift. I see that this movement engages all the bones and muscles with strong force to move them. I felt much loosening of muscles between the shoulder and TMJ's. This work is difficult to do. With these lying sessions my hair ends looking like a bird's nest, and I want to cut if off.

The working pattern along sutures in skull is: 1) opening coronal suture at top of skull. 2) Energy goes across coronal suture, and then loosens frontal bone at top and parietals. 3) Energy goes down sides of skull, opening edges of frontal bone, temporals, zygmatic and mandible. 4) Energy goes across back of skull along occipital bone. 5) Energy goes up through center of skull to maxillae, palatine and nasal bones.

I felt distinct energy circuits between the cranium bone movements and movements of hips and shoulders, they move together as one unit. I think that eventually the body will move as one fluid unit, which seems the overall goal.

From 9:30 to 11:30 am, I tried to sit and relax, but my head was tipping back with work going on in neck and skull and it was painful. I will never allow that position again! Instead, I went to the floor and sat on my knees, body to front with arms on floor, this was much nicer, with legs slightly spread apart **(see figure).** In this position, there is leverage of hips and sacrum to help do the work. I did this until my legs were too numb. My head was moving around most of the time. After this, I sat in upright position with legs to front. There were a few shifts in the vertebrae with my chest slowing lowering to the knees. Then I was in a hold position, sitting almost upright for about forty-five minutes, where I almost fell asleep. The power is much stronger everywhere. All the cranium bones move with powerful forces moving down the back muscles. A clear tone sounded when something on the right opened.

Insight about Inner sound: I think these sounds are due to neurons making new connections in the brain. These sounds happen as a brief reaction after an energy circuit in the spine opens and energy rushes to the brain. The more neuron connections that form, the more melodic it sounds.

From 12:30 to 2:30 pm, I was lying, with cranium bone movements and much TMJ work. There were several large releases in the TMJ. I felt work on muscles deep in the joint, working on the face down the frontal, temporal, zygmatic and maxillae line. There were several big releases of related muscles and the skull movements felt stronger. Much tension released from the hip, shoulder and neck. It has been difficult; I am worn out from this.

From 7 to 8 pm, I did toe meridian work. Things continue to open well. There was a big pain in the back of skull. At 8:45, I was sitting, reading, and stretching the trapezious muscles, which were pulling hard on both sides. After a few of these I sat up, spontaneously opened my mouth widely and felt a strong crack in the right TMJ that sounded like a bone broke. I do not feel pain anywhere. From 8:45 to 10:45 pm, I did acupressure on the hand and gallbladder meridians. I was falling asleep doing them. My head is sore.

Ligament Snapping In Skull

August 4: Painful Skull Work, Mandible Release, Spine Snap, Sutures Open

I slept long and deep until 6:30! I am a little stiff, but the head pain has lessoned, the shoulder area still feels a little puffy. From 7:30 to 8 am, I worked the urinary bladder and gallbladder meridians and I did shoulder stretches. There were several cracks along the spine, nothing painful. From 8 to 9:30 am, I did a sun session and worked leg meridians from the knee acupoints, this worked well! It easier to reach the knees than to bend at waist to reach the toes and it allows energy to move easier in the hips. The feet activate well from the knees.

From 9:30 to 11:30, I worked the stomach meridian and did back, neck and head crunches. Something still feels stuck in the right TMJ. There is an area of the skull that is tender and hurts, which seems to be the top of the spine. I am reluctant to allow any energy to enter that area because I fear the pain. I cried, prayed, and allowed energy to work there. It is difficult to do as it does hurt, not only there but in other places in skull too. It felt like something released. I do not want any more head crunches.

Insight for book title: "How to Get Your New Light Body"

From 12:30 to 3:30 pm, I tried to lie down to escape, but had to do skull crunches. When I could not take more, I stood and it started again. Now I am sweating and do not want my walk. There was much work in the sore spot in the skull and the scapula. I am tired but the energy does not let up.

From 4 to 6 pm, I worked the urinary bladder and gallbladder meridians, and laid down for head crunching. At the end, the mandible felt looser from all sides and from front to back through all the bones. I felt a burning pain in the left TMJ and then I felt a release in the right TMJ. Immediately after that, I felt a new power and force in the joint that I never felt before. After this, there was a snap, different from a crack or pop at the base of my skull at top of spine. Now my head feels broken. It is difficult to stop the energy

From 6 to 7 pm, I did a little stretch through the shoulders. It hurts to stop now, so I will keep going but I do not want to. I hope for some relief soon. From 7 to 8:45 pm, I was focusing on feeling the vibration in the skull to allow energy to move freely there. While doing this several times there were loud snaps, which felt like a ligament pulling and letting go. I think it was loud enough someone could hear it in the room. Then there was an immediate relief of tension in that area.

I continued with it and watched energy move along the sutures in various pathways. I could distinctly feel a spiral of energy behind my eye. Most work was in the right skull. Then

I heard a crackly squishy sound at back top of head. Energy rose from there cracking on the way up, which did not hurt. Next, I noticed a strong path of energy movement down a suture line and soon another snap. This repeated about ten times. Then I felt energy gathering in the right skull and then the left skull started activating. The snaps were at back of head, in right sphenoid wing, around the ear, in jaw and down in tops of shoulders. As energy moved down the skull into body, there was fluid movement between the skull and body. Some process continues while I sit here, because I can hear the sphenoid (?) bone making periodic crackling sounds. Now, the inner sound is like a motor revving, not like the marcher rhythm.

From 9:20 pm to 12:30 am, the work continued like before, with many more snaps in the skull, then the work moved into trapezious area along side of neck. This was like the previous work with muscle pummeling, yet stronger. I blanked out once and later toppled over for sleep. Awakening, I felt much energy working in the body. There have been several snaps in various areas of head and body. I am tired but I want to release tension in the trapezious muscles so I can sleep better. I did some stretches from 1 to 1:30 am, and a strange sensation happened. Suddenly, my entire left leg including the hip joint filled with energy and felt liquid, like it melted. It startled me when this happened. It is the first time I ever felt it like this. After that, I fell asleep.

Ligament Snapping Goes Down Body, Energy Circuit In Spine

August 5

I slept well and deep, it felt great. There is much tension in the trapezious area so I stretched it. From 8 to 10:30 am, I did a sun session. The ligament snapping continues working slowly down the body going snap, snap, snap. It feels great with little pain. The energy is powerful. I think this process has been going on constantly. The energy now moves down in a path from TMJ into shoulder releasing the tense or short ligaments. I think that is what it is; they are shorter on one side of the body. So the tight ones are released with the SNAP, and eventually all will be the same on both sides.

Insight about acupressure: When you use your energy to press on an acupoint, it causes the bone near that point to vibrate. When the bone vibrates, it activates nerve impulses in surrounding muscles. As the muscles receive the stimulus, they build energetic charge and expand. After the muscles are charged, they contract which does work to stretch and open the tissue. Then tension energy is released and overall nervous system energy rises. The sensory and motor nervous systems are moving energy back and forth between the brain and body. The energy boost is used to change the programming in the brain, and the new program is sent down to body to carry out the new instructions, which might be done by making new neural connections or strengthening them.

When I stopped the last session, I noticed a shift in the energy. I think it was after a big snap on C7 or T1. Energy was rising from the tailbone and joining force with energy coming down from skull. I guess an energy circuit was made. When an energy vortex forms

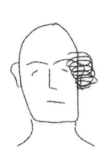

by frontal and temporal bones on side of head, deafness happens in the ear **(see figure).** I think this is an effect I noticed many times when all would go silent. It is like the ear is momentarily cut off from sensory input.

From 11:30 am to 3 pm, there was mostly skull work, crunching around the TMJ joint and shoulder crook, and opening the hip joint. For a time, I was on my back with my legs apart and felt strong pressure on right hip and TMJ joints. The hip was held stationary and was quite painful. I held it as long as possible. Now my entire right leg hurts and I can barely walk. After I rose, there were little snaps all over my body. This was the hardest session to date.

From 5:30 to 7:15 pm, I did another session with work on shoulder and right TMJ. Two times, I experienced high sweats and blanking out while work was done in the skull. From 8 to 9 pm, I did a sitting meditation with meridian work. The front of the face opened and the TMJ's were worked as a pair. My hearing seemed better than usual. I did a freestyle session and worked the gallbladder meridian before bed. Most was head crunching with work in TMJ's. It seems the TMJ's are held in position with the shoulder and hip positions. I guess to realign them; all joints have to be done together somehow.

Parietals Open, Burning Streaks Through Shoulders

August 6: Huge Force On Spine, Blanking Out & Brain Flashes

I slept long. The shoulder relaxes and I feel an opening in the TMJ and hip. I did a two-hour sun session, with work in shoulder and skull. The shoulders, TMJ's, cranium bones, rib cage, clavicle and scapula all loosen more. Near the end, it seemed the work with TMJ's was to align them through the back of the head through the shoulder joints, mandible and occipital bone.

Now, the two halves of the parietals rotate up and down with a marching rhythm **(see figure).** The center point of movement is the wormian bones. The shoulders are moving with this too. The lamboid suture line across the back of the head is loosening, which helps to loosen the occipital bone.

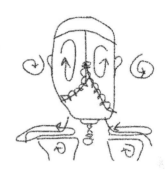

In the last weeks, it feels like sprinkles fall on my skin from the sky.[60] I always look up to see if there are clouds, but there are none in the desert. It localized on the left side of my face and shoulder.

I did a two-hour acupressure session, working the urinary bladder & gallbladder meridians. The shoulder opens with burning streaks all over it, especially in front by clavicle and at top of shoulder-arm joint. I have been doing some amazing twists through the spine. When the sessions get too difficult physically, I stop and work meridians. The meridian work builds an energetic charge in muscles along a path in the body, which later will be physically stretched. This makes it easier to open the areas with the boost in energy. The general order of my sessions is meridian work (build energy), stretch (do the work) and then freefall (relaxation/growing phase). When tension builds, I start over.

In the afternoon, I did a freestyle session with much crunching in spine and skull and at end sexual energy rose to the skull. The stretch was fast; it seems the entire spine is opening. During the session, I heard loud melodic inner sound and something loosened in the right TMJ area. The energy in the spine is powerful like a big snake working its way down, smoothing all the twists. My legs and arms activate and grow tingly.

Later for two hours, I did acupressure on all toe acupoints at once and the energy was so strong I could not believe it. It felt like I was being ironed out. Next, I was lying on back

---

[60] I call this external rain.

with head, neck, spine and shoulder crunches. My right shoulder was on fire with streaks of pain going through it many times; I felt this a little on the left shoulder too.

I did three more sessions before retiring. There was work deep in neck on right side, this was one of the most painful areas so far, but it did not last long. I am sore in many places. I did an acupressure session and fell asleep while doing it. I woke because the energy is too high, making sleep difficult and did another session. I felt pressure building all over the skeleton. I relaxed and felt a huge force and my mind blanked out, like seeing stars while I was pressed on. Something moved, but I am not sure what. A little later, it happened again, with deep pain in my right thighbone, then pain in the hips and the blank out sensation. After this, I had to stretch the upper shoulder, now my head hurts again.

Insight about external rain symptom: I think this is due to intense heat generating internally. Then pressurized water squirts out of the skin pours, with the sprinkling effect. Right after the external rain, I sweat profusely all over the head combined with active skull bone movements. It is strange how it seems to fall from the sky.

Elastic Sheets In Skull

August 7: Sacrum Release, Puff Outs, Tooth Powder, Numb Legs

I finally fell asleep, slept well and woke with a stupid dream. There was much tension in the neck and skull so I immediately did a freestyle session. Energy focused on opening the hips. I lowered into each hip, feeling the sacrum opening and the hip joint loosening. Then I lay down on my back. Immediately there was a crunch and the sacrum dropped closer to the floor. From 8 to 10 am, I did a sun session with much sweating. At first, there was much work in the spinal column and hips. Next, strong energy radiated upward from the tailbone rippling into the large muscles on back and chest in front. Next there was work in shoulder, neck and head, with a neck release from the right shoulder. There were alarming spontaneous stretches through the head and upper shoulders; it felt like bone sliding against bone, moving rapidly around with not too much resistance.

There were stretchy pulls across the bottom row of teeth and the entire face, doing both sides at once. I felt this work had to be done from the back through the spine, and it was all centering on the wormian bones. A change would be made in the right TMJ, then energy moved up to the wormian bones, then a shift, then down to the left TMJ and lower bones, then back up to the wormian bones, etc. I felt pulling of muscles along either side of neck. Near the end, the TMJ's felt more aligned.

My mind goes quiet quickly into the session. I think the second brain flash last night may have changed the brain. Although the work is difficult, I feel good because I see progress.

From 1 to 2:30 pm, I did a freestyle session. The hip opened more and there was twisting and stretching spinal work, until the energy moved up to some muscle or ligament in the right side of my neck at the base of the occipital bone. Then tension was applied to this area and when it let loose, it felt to be a significant release, because after this there were releases in the hip, shoulder, neck and skull.

At 5:30 pm, I went for a walk and before I got back, I had a bad gallbladder attack. I was belching strong and my ribs hurt. I think it is because my rib cage and spine are near to release. When I got back, I did an acupressure session right away working all toe meridians on both feet.

From 6 to 7 pm, the session was amazing, the energy is fast and strong, it seems like one loop inside and I did not feel pain. The energy worked the skull as a unit. It felt like the skull was in motion owing to muscular action and strong elastic sheets. I had the sensation this was reshaping my head. There were many adjustments in the skull and up and down through my body. Many times, I smelled the scent of tooth powder. There were many adjustments in the maxillae and mandible. Then the shoulders were worked similar to the skull with many movements and more work in left shoulder this time. There was high body heat with sweat and external rain during the skull and neck work and my legs kept going numb. I felt that all muscle tension in the body was released when these actions finished. As I sit here, I feel sporadic energy puffs and I hear the marching music strong.

From 7:15 to 8 pm, I did a freestyle session. Energy moved down and there was much pain in the front of the rib cage near the liver. It was difficult to stretch into this area. Soon the rib cage released, then tension released from the trapezious muscle in the shoulder, which felt great. Then harder work started with crunching in shoulders, hips, rib cage and TMJ's simultaneously.

From 9 to 10:45 pm, I did a strong freestyle stretch, but soon it was back to bone crunching in skull. There was work on ligament behind neck near occipital on right. It seems this ligament works to slip up and over another bone. From 11 pm to 12:30 am, I was in the most excruciating tension hold on that ligament for over an hour. That hurt and it still does not budge. Later, there was work on the hip while lying with it open, which takes me back to the early days. Finally, the hip relaxed but then I could barely rise. I am sore all over. I fell asleep quickly.

Maxillae Bone Moves In Ratchet Fashion

August 8: Work In Mandible, Hard Palate & Top Of Neck Near Atlas

I slept well. I had much tension and did a session immediately. From 6 to 6:30 am, I worked all the toe meridians. I went until the hips activated and my legs started to straighten. Lately, I cannot reach my toes, so I activate my legs physically by grabbing the floor with my toes and lifting the heels off the ground and putting pressure on the balls of the feet. I went until the freefall was over and head crunching started. It feels too early for that and I wonder if it is necessary to keep going like this. When I stopped, I felt the freefall sensation. This feels like I am supported by a huge energy and 'behind' the path my body falls through I feel gentle snaps repeatedly. That lasted about two minutes, then back to crunching. It appears there is no way to avoid the harder physical work. I just felt a crunchy snap and release in the left TMJ.

From 6:30 to 9:30 am, I did a sun session and something opened in the neck. I had to stretch each side of my head, then letting it flop down in all positions. I guess this is about loosening the atlas or occipital bone. It was difficult at first and I heard the one word, "Relax". Then I went into a breathing pattern for the entire session. Inhale, rise and move with the energy and exhale, fall, relax and sink down. At times, there was intense pain in the skull, and I shifted my focus to feeling energy in the root chakra to help me get through it. I was dizzy when I rose from the strong rotation inside my body.

From 10 to 11:30, I did a sitting session with "head surgery", where you stay very, very, still, and have the sensation that you are healing your own mind. With eyes closed and head straight, I look with both eyes turned as far to the right as possible, which helps to stop my thinking quickly. Then I feel and observe where the energy is working in my head. I think the mind must be completely still to allow energy to change certain brain areas. These holds with work in the head, seem to be the first stage of removing a body blockage, and later the area related to it is stretched in the body physically. Usually three passes or more are made through an area like this, and then you move on to the next.

There was work on the sternocleidomastoid muscle and the mandible. It seems the ends of ligaments are rolling over the joints. Later I was lying and there was work on the mandible with many passes over the maxillae from right to left, moving it every time a micron. This happened with my head tipped back, rocking on the wormian bones while lying on my back. It felt like the roof of the mouth and the wormian bones in the back of skull are directly connected to each other. There were wide-open mouth moves and cracks in the mandible joints and I felt a tendon or ligament move under the jaw.

At 11:45, I felt cold so I went into the sun for fifteen minutes. It was relaxing, I felt like I was melting. After ten minutes, the right shoulder started popping and like a coiled snake shot out to the right. After this, there were more releases in the body.

From 12:30 to 3 pm, I did stretching sessions. First, the shoulder and spine stretched and I was sobbing like a baby, then there was back work and head surgery. There was work on ligament under lower right molar that took quite some gymnastics to move it. At the end I could barely get off the floor, I feel stiff and sore all over.

From 4 to 6:30 pm, I tried to lie down and rest but it was impossible, there was more work on that muscle under the jaw. It felt like the hard palate was remade, there were many stretches through it. This transformation seems endless and it does not get easier. I do not know what to do to accelerate this or to live with it. I took a walk and there is much tension again. I feel like crying and I feel alone with this. I want to know how much longer and no answer comes. I would quit if I could. From 7:30 to 9:30 pm, the session was difficult and now I am exhausted. There was work at base of neck near atlas, with several pops deep in the skull. From 9:30 to 11 pm, I did acupressure on the toe meridians.

Skull Plates Move Together, Both Sides Of Spine Open, I Will Take Over

August 9: Energy Balls At Skull Base, New Opening On Both Sides Of Spine

The energy never settled and I rose three times in the night to stretch. From 7:30 to 9:30 am, I did a sun session with much skull work. I watched closer to try to ascertain what is occurring. I observed small movements along the sutures, gentle stretches in neck and through all the bones of the skull and the hyoid bone. Then the skull plates started to move as a group together, and then there was a searing pain in the right side of the skull, which lasted about a minute. After this, energy increased substantially and all skull plates started moving together again. I imagined the skull plates are like a shell, which floats on the surface of the brain. All this movement was centered on the mandible and working to align the TMJ joints. I do not believe this is the end goal, only the hardest part to do because all plates have to be free to reposition the jaws.

I was sitting there thinking sometimes I feel good and sometimes not, and it was as if another voice chimed in and said, "I will take over soon." That startled me, but I knew it was truth speaking. The transformation is easier when higher-self takes over, so I hope it is true.

From 9:30 to 12 am, I gave acupressure to toe meridians for about thirty minutes, then sitting. There was much difficult skull work. I observed the same movements with the skull plates, first a few loosen, then groups of plates move together and it is as if the entire skull adjusts. Looking near, the large strong movement is hundreds of finer muscle movements combined into one. This grouping of energy gives the strength to manifest the change in the body. If I look at any larger movement this way, I can detect the millions of tiny muscle movements that make it up.

The session then changed to fast spontaneous head movements. After the head moved around much, then I felt the energy in the head connect to the left spine and move down. Once arriving at the tailbone, my hips released on both sides and melted as they flooded with energy. Then energy moved back up left side and I felt energy balls all over the bottom edge of the skull in back. This served to move the cranium bones even more. Once I felt all the body tension had left, and thought that is it, here I am. Hahaha. There was a strong snap behind lower right molar and several loud pops along side of spine by right scapula, as well one under the scapula in the lower back.

From 12:30 to 2 pm, when I started, sexual energy was strong and eventually was released and rose up the spine. After this, there were many spontaneous head movements with skull crunching and spontaneous stretches up spine through skull joints. After this, something opened in the right mandible and energy went down the right spine. When it reached the tailbone there was work in right hip, and then energy went up on right side of spine with energy balls at base of skull, like it had before with left spine. Then the energy went down the spine and when at the tailbone, the energy started working in sacrum, right hip and mid back. Then the skull work was calm. After that, there were spontaneous stretches in spine up through skull. My spine grows powerful, it is much like a coiled serpent, and I can see how it gets that name. It is not like the pictures with a snake around the spine, instead the spine and skull as a unit is the snake, it is more like the shape of a tadpole or a sperm cell.

From 2 to 9:30 pm, there was intense crunching in spine, head, neck, shoulders and body in freestyle and sitting sessions. There were spinal twists and work on C7. The work in the shoulder was difficult. Later, it felt like super strong energy was remaking my skull, while I sat in the center, barely feeling anything. This lasted hours. Later, I was back on floor and physically crunching again, with focus on right shoulder. The big energy was gone and I was on my own. I think this sudden burst of strong energy is owing to new neuron growth in a localized area of the body and after that work is done, it is like new channels open, and energy rushes in and joins other channels creating the big surge in energy. After an event like this, the energy moves down to the tailbone and another round starts. My head hurts now.

From 10:30 to 11:30 pm, there were rapid spontaneous movements again; I was in outer space, until it got to the shoulder. I felt the right hip fill with energy as the left leg did last week. My right shoulder is a mess, I am very sore.

Change In Brain Stem, Body Can Move Spontaneously

August 10: Energy Circuits In Spine, Hard Palate Stretched Apart

6am: I slept long. One side of my head hurts a little. I had much body tension so I did a session immediately. From 6:30 to 9:30 am, I did a sun session. The main work was in the shoulder, neck and the TMJ. The upper neck through the skull felt alive and the right hip strongly energetically rotates. The healing is moving down and I have to continue to go through the solid material. I 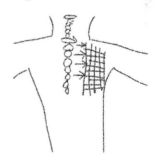 guess what I am observing is increasing levels of energetic vibration, owing to dendrite growth of the neurons. Always the area above where work is currently done in the body has higher energy overall. Each pass through the spine, makes stronger neuron connections all over the body. I felt neuron growth in waves in sections across right side of upper spine and back **(see figure).**

Insight about expanding nervous system changes: I think the energy whorls I felt when this started were due to nerve cell changes. I think this neural growth has been going on since this started. Now transformation accelerates because of the neuron connections that have been made, it is like the snowball effect. I think the energy circuits that are forming are stronger neural connections. It is all moving toward the goal to make the body and mind as one 'light filled' unit.

Vision of brain stem: When I was in the sun session, an image came to me, sort of like a mushroom growing out of the ground. Looking up the image on the Internet, I felt this image most closely resembled the picture of the brain stem. I thought this is what was worked on. If so, I know things will pick up, because this structure controls the motor and sensory pathways between the brain and the body. I think about how the vision, color and light of the eyes are related to the cones of the eyes. Greater neuron connections between them and brain would then make vision more intensely colored and one could probably see at night. This explains the momentary reaction of intense colors and vision. I guess it is like the other symptoms, a new neuron connection is made, you feel a momentary effect and it fades. I think many of all these healing reactions are likely owing to changes in the neural structure. I wonder why this image was relayed to me. At the time, I took it as a message to stay still and unidentified to allow some critical change to be made in the mind. Perhaps it might be an answer to explain a difference in how my body will soon react.

From 10:30 to 12 am, I did a freestyle session, folding quickly down to floor, then on back, mostly with work on the TMJ's in skull, neck and shoulders, with head tipped back on point of wormian bones. There were many side-to-side movements of the head. I think the brain stem image is telling me I can now let go of body control and it will move spontaneously. Indeed, when I let go of body control, my head started moving spontaneously with jerks in a ratchet fashion, back and forth and left to right many times. My part in this was sitting in center. I cannot believe its noon already. My body is more energetic and stronger each time. The head, neck, and shoulder movements feel like a continuous stretching elastic sheet, it is fluid and smooth. I felt a drop in the left shoulder when something released between it and the left TMJ. I feel cold after these sessions.

From 12 to 1 pm, I did a sun session to warm up. There were ligament snaps along the entire cord of personality line. The sun was giving me energy. I was sweating heavy the entire time. From 1:10 to 2:30 pm, I did a session that did not meet my expectations and feel disappointed. Right away, I was on my back with work behind neck, shoulders and TMJ's (arch work) most of the time. There was a period of about thirty minutes of intense head pain. I think this occurs when there is a big shift in all the cranium bones. This has happened a few times. Then there was a hold with head in arched position, with wormian bones on ground, for about thirty minutes, with about three small adjustments in position. Doing this there was no pain and no thoughts, I was blanked out. I could sense energy coursing very fast up and down my body in all parts, seemingly making new energy circuits in the spinal column. After this, I was back doing arch work again. I quit! I am eating. I am finished with this!

From 2:30 to 4:30 pm, there was so much tension that I could not relax, so I did a freestyle session. It was very physical and I went until I was exhausted. From 4:30 to 5:40 pm, I tried to sleep and blanked out for about thirty minutes. Then my body activated strongly, melting the right side of my face and energy rose with a huge force releasing tension from neck and then moved down. It is work now so I stop!

From 8 to 10:15 pm, I feel miserable, I will try a session next of not moving. None of that worked, even the meridian work failed, I had to do 'arch work'. Finally, the muscle stuck in the clavicle, neck and TMJ released, and then the head repositioned with the TMJ joint. There was a big crack near the top of my head and my hard palate was stretched to the max and pulled apart. It took over an hour. The muscles in the right TMJ joint somehow twisted. The left joint seemingly had to be aligned with the right, and the attaching shoulder muscles had to be pulled together. It was a complicated movement. I was grateful I did not have to know how to do it. Much tissue had to be opened in my body, to get to this area. I do pray this is behind me and I can now be rid of that irritating tugging on my jaw, neck and shoulder. It is strange this has been with me so long; I cannot tell if it is healed. The left TMJ still pops out and that irritating tugger is still there, so I presume I will have to endure more.

Cranial Bones Shift As Group In Different Directions In Skull

August 11: Head Snaps, Huge Energy Goes Down Spine, Nose Moves

I slept well and woke with much tension in upper back, trapezious muscles, and with soreness in TMJ area. Last night there was a strong growing reaction all over my body. I saw sparkles of light in the air, which look like dust particles or insects, backlit from the sun. I never noticed that so pronounced before. I pray for relief of this neck and skull tension.

From 6:30 to 10:30 am, I did meridian work for about an hour and then a sun session. After substantial work in shoulder and neck, I felt energy whorls all over after the meridian work. Then the work started in the head. It is strange how the skull changes. The jaw muscles loosen which is not difficult. A few times, there was intense burning pain between the nose and cheekbone and above my crooked teeth in right maxillae. I observed many amazing things. The coronal suture was fully open, and all the bones were shifting to the left, ratchet style, around a circle in my head, which connected somehow with the mandible (**see B in figure**).

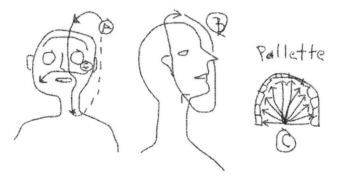

There was another circle (**see A in figure**) which moved all bones down in the same way, going through the palatine bones from back to front. The maxilla was moved under the cheekbones (**see figure**), below the nose with a ratchet action in the palatine bones. When I felt energy moving in rays on the hard palate, I felt the teeth shifting (**see C in figure**).[61] The left incisor had a sharp pain in it. Then there was movement with the temporals going in circles, which affected the occipital and mandible, moving that part to the left. There were many ways that the bones moved in groups to shift the cranium bones. I watched as (A) would be done, then (B) and then (C). However, I do not recall the actual order. Occasionally the energy went down the neck, worked there, and came back up.

---

[61] In figure C, pallette is misspelled, and should be hard palate, or the palatine portion, which forms the anterior half of the hard palate, or the roof of the mouth.

There was much work on the cervical spine with snapping of the head to the chest. I presume this was done to loosen the neck vertebrae, especially at the junction of the neck and the occipital bone. After this, strong energy descended, stronger than I have ever felt. It felt like stronger neural connections were made at a higher level in the spine. This work went down to the tailbone, activated the pelvic bowl, and then went up the left side.

From 11:20 am to 1 pm, I did a powerful freestyle session that moved many vertebrae. Then I did a sitting session where I felt tension release with much work in shoulder and skull. There were many cracks in the scapula, near C7 and T1. There were many loud cracks near the top of the head and much stretching of spine, opening of hip, and stretches and releases in the rib cage. It is fantastic how powerful this is. From 3:30 to 5 pm, I did a powerful freestyle session! I floated through most of it. At the end, there was skull work. This is amazing; I have no words to describe it.

From 8:20 to 9:40 pm, there was work on skull and tension released from spine. I worked toe meridians first and then there was hard head, neck, and shoulder crunching. The mouth and hard palate were worked much stretching them the most so far. Once, my nose moved to my right and down all in one movement. My right arm released with much tingling after. There was burning in shoulders and back. From 9:55 to 11 pm, I did meridian work and then a long hold established. From 11 pm to 1 am, I did more crunching. I am exhausted, but regenerate quickly. There was an amazing stretch through my spine and full circle around the shoulders. Skull work continues. Before sleep, I felt neuron growth behind skull along both sides of cervical spine, for about thirty minutes.

Insight about energy fills: I think the bursts of energy that suddenly fill an area with elongation, filling and melting sensations, may be due to an explosion of neural connections. An explosion happens, like a nuclear reaction when an energy block is opened and nerves meet nerves. These happen sporadically and quickly recede.

Insight about oscillation loop with self-Reiki: Often I get exhausted with the sessions. I start with much power and it fades as I go. When I put my fingers on my toes, the vibration rises. Touching my body with my hands creates a loop in my body and acts like a ring oscillator. Knowing key acupoints is helpful when stretching is difficult because I can boost energy to those areas by using acupoint treatments.

Skull Lifted Up Off Atlas

August 12: Hard Palate Energy Circuits To Back Of Skull & Upper Back

I slept long and got up once to stretch. From 8:30 to 10:30 am, I did a sun session. The skull work seems to have the purpose of fluid articulation of cranium bones. I observed the energetic path of work. It goes over coronal suture in right skull, then down squamosal suture and travels laterally to back of skull, then up lamboid suture to wormian bones, then reversing and going to right down lamboid suture, then tracing lower edge of temporal bone around ear, then traveling back up via the squamosal suture to the coronal suture again. This circular path was moving all those bones in a ratcheting fashion, and I presume the ones that articulate with them. This work occurred most of the time. The mandibles loosened with the other bones as a side-to-side joint movement, like an infinity sign pattern from ear to ear. I felt external rain and then there was a strong stretch of the right mandible and shoulder, which released something. Then energy worked behind skull on both sides of spine all the way down. After this, the skull lifted upward, like it separated from the atlas, and it felt like the skull moved to the left two notches. That was incredible!

From 11:20 am to 1:45 pm, there was much skull work and tension released from the TMJ's. There were many passes through maxillae and mandible. My face feels broken. I did a long freestyle session, following the point of light in my 3rd eye, trusting my body would follow my head movement. I did the entire session this way. I feel this is the key and what I need to do. At 5 pm, I went out and much tension rose and I had to return because my head felt ready to explode. From 5:10 to 7 pm, my hearing and sense of smell are amplified. Last night I smelled the backyard; it was rich, fragrant and interesting. A haiku comes

The sound of leaves
dancing on dry pavement
signs of things to come.

I worked meridians and sat still while tension released from the neck. When stretches started, I did a freestyle session. It ended with skull work on the TMJ. The work was in the painful cord that runs inside the eye orbital, under the cheekbone, then across to the TMJ, down in neck toward back, ending by scapula near spine on right **(see figure).** The muscles and ligaments through the TMJ's and shoulders on both sides, feel like they are on the wrong side of the bones. In the last move, the chest puffed out while lying with back and neck arched and somehow the shoulders were pulled upward. There were many passes through maxillae and mandible. It was difficult and now my head hurts.

From 8:20 to 9:40 pm, there was a spontaneous stretch of my right arm and scapula, while lying on my left side. It felt like the shoulder was pulled apart. There was much cracking and snapping sounds on the muscles attached to the scapula when they loosened. After this a vertebrae in the spine released with a rubbery feeling and pop. After this, more things released. I felt a big shift in the skull and both jaw joints followed. It seemed something key went into position, like the sphenoid bone was centered. This was a difficult session. I am tired of this skull work, awkward positions and headaches.

From 10 to 11:20 pm, it was mostly jaw crunching. The right shoulder top opened and energy worked in the trapezious muscle for a long time. The rib cage released. There was a movement in the hard palate with pain in area of crooked teeth. It felt like a vertical slit opened and that is where it hurt **(see figure, looking up at hard palate** 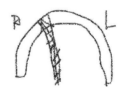 **in mouth).** It seemed an energy circuit was made from the hard palate directly to the back of the head. With each shift of the hard palate, this connection grew stronger. Near the end, there were energy movements down the back of the skull into the spine and shoulders that seemed to match each ray of the hard palate (one for each tooth).

From 11:30 to 12 pm, there was release of tension energy again. I did meridian work until I blanked out. There were several strong snaky spine movements, working on twists in upper spine and neck. A huge energy came down the right side at the end.

Chapter 17: Spine And Sphenoid Circuits, Body Pulls

Frontal Bone Opens, Energy Circuit Down Spine, Rib Cage Release

August 13: Energy Circuit Down Spine

I slept well. More energy works in my body than usual. From 7:30 to 9:30 am, I did a sun session with some spine stretches and mostly skull work. Energy went around edge of frontal bone, stretching it with many crackly crunchy sounds. Then work shifted to right TMJ area. I think the entire right side of my skull is compressed like the shoulder. All skull work relates to making an adjustment near the wormian bones. I see the same patterns and new circle patterns around the sutures. Ratcheting movement still happens with bob of head, turning it a little each time with wide-open mouth and hard palate stretching. Several times, strong waves of energy went to root chakra after energy circuits formed in skull. It appears neuron growth expansion continues and more connections are made between root and crown chakra. It seems the end of the spine is located at whorl at back skull where the wormian bones are. This main energy center seems to connect directly to the circular round pattern of the hard palate.

From 9:50 to 11 am, the TMJ released and the skull stretches apart and loosens, but the crunching is difficult. Most skull work has been in right side. Energy worked long in the shoulder crook and there was a large release of trapezious muscle in both directions. I think after the TMJ's rotate energetically, a connection will form with them and the wormian bones as the anchor point. Then a big circle of energy will form from there going down the body.

From 11:10 am to 1:15 pm, I did a sun session. I feel like I am melting. An energy circuit formed between the skull and tailbone, like a first meeting. After this, there were many skull movements and bone crunching and I cried like a baby. It felt like the TMJ's were loosening. Then energy worked strongly down the spine with pulling and twisting in muscles along neck, back, shoulders, and hips. There were several loud cracks, one at top of skull and one in neck, where afterward the neck released much. The arm still feels to be in the wrong position with a tight band under it going across the chest. Probably I will have to do some crazy maneuvers to open that up. The energy is very high, I am not sure I can calm this down.

From 2 to 3 pm, I did an easy freefall session with much ligament snapping and pops. There was a big skull movement, where it felt it glided over to a new position. A strong growing reaction continued until 8 pm, with activity in TMJ's, hips and skull. It has been a nice break. When I lay down, a huge energy arose and it felt like my entire body enervated and the energy kept increasing. Near the end, it felt like my skull and lower skeleton were aligned as a single unit.

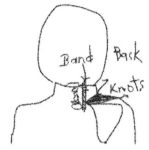

From 9 to 11 pm, I did a freestyle session, talk about power yoga! I folded to the floor with crunching in shoulder. The rib cage released by chest, before it felt like it was compressed under the shoulder. Several ribs, the scapula, and the clavicle held it in place. The tight cord that went under clavicle to upper neck released. The neck and trapezious feels free, it was compacted in there and feels great now. The energy keeps building and I feel waves of energy descend in the body every time something releases.

I did another session before going to bed. There was a tight cord behind the neck, which caused excruciating pain when it was worked. When it released, it was like a rubber band popping. All the muscles in the dark triangle region in my shoulder were twisted in a big knot **(see figure)**. When the large muscles release, the bones release too.

Release Of Muscle Under Jaw, Skull Connects To Tailbone

August 14: Spontaneous Orgasm, Light Explosion, Sphenoid Wing Release

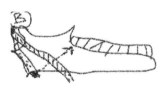

I woke with tension in shoulder crook, but none in skull. From 6:30 to 7 am, I sat and I felt much energy coiling out of the trapezious muscle with many ligament snaps. It felt good.

From 8:30 to 10:30 am, I did a sun session. There was work in shoulder crook, around cranium bones and horizontal stretch from spine through scapula. Eventually there was a release. The energy was high and powerful with little pain. I was amazed to see the new fluidity of the skull bone and plate movements. Energy glides through energetic paths around the hard palate, eye orbits, temporal, mandible and all sutures. The ligament below the inside right mandible (**dashed line in figure**), was the source of the constant tugging under the right molar. Today it slipped from the underside over the top at B in the figure. What a relief! This might be the lateral pterygoid, probably in combination with medial pterygoid, which moves the mandible under molars and attaches to the sphenoid bone. Energy work in skull was down the lamboid suture, going back and forth on each side and repositioning the TMJ's. There was much work by the wormian bones too. I think this will finish soon because there is increased energy and increasing skull articulation.

From 11:15 am to 1:30 pm, I did a freestyle session that was like power yoga! It was a long session, which started easy and got harder at the end. I ended sitting with feet together and my spine was turning a small amount and ratcheting in a circular pattern. After that, the spine was straight and all the twisted energy held in the cord of personality went out the top of my head. I am sore now. Near the end I was blanking out, I could have stayed like that a long time but I wanted to stop.

From 2 to 4:30 pm, the growing reaction started and I rested. From 4:30 to 5:30 pm, I did a stretch with rising sexual energy. I am exhausted now. It does not look like this is going to finish soon. I am starting all over with everything. From 6:15 to 8:15 pm, the energy does not let up. While sitting there are strong neck movements, and I feel I cannot stop them. I did a meditation on the crystals outside, where I focused on the energetic vibration in my body. What you pay attention to grows; it was exactly what I needed. Some head and shoulder work occurred, with energy building in root chakra.

From 8:15 to 8:45 pm, when I came inside there was a strong spontaneous orgasm and after this, waves of energy were sent up the spine to the head. Then there were different reactions. The tailbone activated and energy moved up spine with spontaneous shoulder and head stretches. After this, my head was aligned straight with the tailbone and held in place with it. Then I felt an intense piercing line of energy move down on the right side of tailbone. After this, light exploded all over my body and was darting around. This grew in intensity to where there was excruciating pain everywhere, especially in the head. Then I felt work in spine and right rib cage. Next, there was an energy fill from pelvis down legs. After this, energy moved up and starting working in head and TMJ's. I need a break.

From 9 to 11 pm, sitting I hear cracking noises. I feel like I am melting, gravity is pulling me down and I am sleepy. The main work was in the skull and it was amazing. First, a ligament snapped near the temple. Perhaps it separated the zygmatic from the frontal bone. Energy worked a long time in this area near the sphenoid wing. After this, there were stretches through the face. It felt different because a large band under my jaw moved out and over. I cannot remember everything. After this were shoulder moves. Near the end, there was a loud thud as my entire jaw moved back toward my head. I kept blanking out, like sleeping while something was worked. Then I would suddenly awaken, do a stretch and blank out again. This happened about ten times. At 11:20, I went to bed and the gravity feeling returns. I hope I can sleep and awake transformed.

Skull Flexion & Extension, Many Spine Circuits, Skull & Pelvic Vortices

August 15: Barrage Of Tones, Neurons Firing, Powerful Freestyle

I fell asleep quickly and slept well, the growing reaction is strong. From 6 to 6:30 am, I did a freestyle session with many releases. From 7 to 9 am, I did a sun session with mostly spine and skull work. The sexual energy is strong. From 9 to 11 am, I did a lying session with work on neck and head crunches. There were strong spinal stretches with pulling apart of shoulder, hips and neck on right. After this, the spine opened and felt powerful like a strong snake. It seems my body is compressed on one side with a large curve **(see figure).**

From 11 am to 1 pm, for a half hour I sat and energy worked in spine from tailbone on up which felt great. Then I did a spinal stretch. At 1:30 pm, while sitting I felt a sharp pain in the right side of my head and it felt strange like higher-self is taking over. I can barely lift the pen to write, my hand feels glued to the table. Energy prickles are starting here and there, my head hurts and I hear crackles in it. In the last week, I can keenly feel the extension and flexion head movements and the pulsing of the dura mater. My face is squished then expands out to the ears.

From 1:40 to 3:40 pm, spinal energy circuits formed between skull and tailbone that get stronger each time. This time there was much firing of neurons with high-pitched tones sounding one after the other. I felt strong tingling and vortex of energy in the pelvic bowl and at top of head. I felt strong muscular actions going down along the sides of the spine. When the inner sounds were intense, there was the deepest blue and galaxy view in the 3rd eye. I thought, this is it, it has finished. I could barely feel any pain anywhere in my body. I want that. Some pain returned with neck alignment and lower back and hip work. My neck is sore.

The entire session felt like tension was flowing out of my body through my skull from the articulation path that was worked. Lot's of tension released from the right TMJ. In the session, my body moved but I kept my head relaxed with mouth open and relaxed jaws and not thinking. It seems I am coming alive. The skull and pelvic bowl vortices get stronger each day. Most work was deep in skull, now energy works by the right temple.

From 6:25 to 8:15 pm, I did a freestyle session noticing a huge increase in body power. I stayed standing most of the time. I wanted to stand, because I am tired of rolling around on the ground. The force in the spine was so strong that it was difficult to go against it to stay standing. I kept at it, took the copper ring and raised it over my head to the ceiling. I felt the spine responding. I kept stretching and then felt strong power in my body. For about forty minutes I stretched though all the twisted areas and felt tension releasing through cranium bones. Some of this work was done on the floor to release tension from the hip. When on ground there was shoulder and TMJ work and head crunching. Once, it seemed the upper part of the skull moved. After this energy moved down and worked in maxillae and mandible for a long time. Next was a long time of ratcheting the jaws to the left, and moving my head along the line of sutures around the temporal bone on right.

From 9 to 10 pm, crackles in head start with rising sweat. I worked the toe meridians with acupressure for about twenty minutes, and then stretched in TMJ's and shoulders with much ligament snapping. Finally, I did a freestyle session and now I am exhausted.

Pelvic Pushes, New Circuits, Bones Release, Hormone Release

August 16: Spine, Hard Palate, And Clavicle To Sternum Circuits

I went to bed early and slept well. From 4:30 to 6:30 am, I did a freestyle session. There was constant ligament snapping concentrated in cervical spine and mandible. An energy spiral formed across the mandible, down the sides of neck and around shoulder girdle. Most physical movements were counterclockwise (looking down), around my body. My mind is quieter than usual and my energy is high. Energy builds in the root chakra and a strong energy cord comes up the spine, like a long snake with a big ball on the end. I feel warm and tingly all over.

From 6:30 to 8 am, I did a freestyle stretch down to floor, with work in spine and hip. After this there were intense pelvic pushes, it was difficult like when you strain for a bowel movement, the entire body was involved. This repeated about twenty-five times, and seemed to have the effect to open the hips and lower back. Next, I felt ratcheting movements in right pubic area. After this, I was sitting still and felt energy in the root chakra grow. Then I felt strong pressure on the spine and the body was held in various positions with small adjustments between positions. Much energy released from the spine in various places.

At the end, a strong energy circuit formed from tailbone to skull and I was freezing cold. It is difficult to remember all the details. Thirty minutes later, I am still cold, with goose bumps all over my body. From 8:20 to 9:30 am, I did a sun session to warm up. Starting out, the shivers continued and my head began to hurt with the crackly sounds and the groin was tingling. Mostly I was in a hold with my head cocked slightly to the right, while skull work occurred in right sphenoid wing and on back of the head (in same line as in front), where I felt intense pain. This was not comfortable but the sun helped. After the hold, skull bone movements increased and I felt the cord under my jaw release.

Then I started crying uncontrollably while there were strong twisting movements of facial bones. I felt the sobs going down to the root chakra, each sob racking my body and fueling the kundalini pump and sending energy up the spine to do this 'feat of engineering' in the skull. After this, I felt a huge energy ball form above the hard palate and this strong force started pummeling the left side of the head. It was like rays of energy going out from a center doing the entire half of my left skull. This did not hurt at all.

Next energy went into right skull and TMJ, and then went down neck to shoulder tops and sternum. Then energy went through the cord of personality path, filled with fine energy threads that felt to be burning the flesh. Each muscle stretch had these threads of energy burning through them. Energy was moving down the sternum toward the root chakra. That was the hardest skull session so far.

From 10 to 12 am, energy was in the neck and I started sweating. Energy worked there for a long time with many snaps in the cervical spine that felt good, but lasted forever. Then larger body movements happened which included the shoulders, neck and head together. When the first bone released it felt strange. The bone released with a thud sound and when it released I had the sensation I had no flesh. This started in the cranium bones, moved down neck and then into the shoulder girdles. Each bone released with a thud all the way down. I feel strange, like a skeleton coming alive. Then energy went back to work on the twist in the shoulder. My bones hurt and I am tired. Much energy released from the right shoulder crook.

From 12:10 to 1:30 pm, the energy does not let up. There was difficult work especially in the neck and shoulders. Now strong energy works in the spine. I am sore. 1:40 pm, now there is a freefall and my right arm released! There were many shoulder stretches with the tissue stretching up the back of the head with all the ligaments connected to the TMJ's. There were several strong pulling stretches in sacrum and between the shoulder blades by spine and right scapula. Several times, my spine elongated, so much that I felt the couch was shrinking. Then there was a big pop at C7, and energy connected across shoulder girdles to TMJ's and started moving through its patterns. Then energy went up to skull and now comes down with several snaps.

From 1:45 to 3:30 pm, head crackles start again. I tried to lie down and rest. A strong reaction occurs with much neuron growth, even in my hands. Then there was head surgery for about thirty minutes where I was blanked out. Then head crunching and a big shift to move all the bones of skull to the other side, up or down or something. Once, it felt like my shoulder joints were inside my mouth. It was painful and hard to endure because I am tired. The work was concentrated on TMJ's, shoulders and shoulder crook.

From 5:10 to 7:10 pm, there was more shoulder, skull and right TMJ work and back of neck crunching. The left side of my body filled with energy and it felt like I was melting. It seems huge energy is waiting on both sides of a blockage to make a connection. I am tired.

From 7:20 to 8:30 pm, I was outside sitting with feet on crystals with skull crunching the entire time. Energy worked on pathways with both sides of head together, leaving no path untouched. Near the end, something popped over the mandible knob of TMJ toward the cheekbone. This was 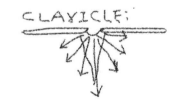 physically tiring work, with many crunchy noises. Then energy moved down to sternum and radiated from the U shape made between the clavicles, in a half circle making new energy circuits **(see figure)**. Then there was crunching in neck, rib cage and shoulder.

When I was lying, I heard a pop like a bag of liquid under pressure was spilling fluid into the right side of the skull. I thought a hormone was released in a large quantity, maybe it was oxytocin. There were several sounds later in that area, like aspiration of air, with periodic small puff outs. Lately, in the wavy growing phase my legs jump, like the reflex response when the nerve by the kneecap is hit with a hammer.

Body Pulls, Tailbone To Hard Palate Vortex, Two Alien Beings

August 17: Many Joint & Vertebrae Circuits Form

From 1:30 to 3:40 am, I woke with intense pressure in shoulder crook and hip so I had to stretch. Tension released and work shifted to cranium bones and shoulder. Energy circuits formed between shoulder girdles, skull and TMJ's. When I was sitting, the upper body was making large circular stretches. This action continued until the head felt like it was smooth and elastic with the shoulders. Next, I had the urge to stretch the side. Shortly after this energy rose from the tailbone with pressure that filled the body and rose up into the skull. The pressure felt similar to the sensation you have when you strain to make a bowl movement. I went with the sensation and allowed my body to relax and it felt like my spine was straightening as the energetic stretch rose in one strong movement. I was making loud groaning sounds and my tongue was hanging out, while movement after movement happened in rapid succession.[62] I felt ligament releases in the neck and the TMJ. After this there were a few lighter stretches working in sides of the body. **It felt like being born and dying at the same time.**

From 4:45 to 5:45 am, there were spontaneous head and shoulder throws involving the upper body, with loud sounds in skull bones and I was making gagging sounds in the throat, interspaced with freefall periods between. During the throws, I was blanked out with the galaxy view. Perhaps this happened ten times. Then energy moved to skull and back down to sacrum. I have uterus cramps and my head hurts. I am tired, that was difficult.

From 6 to 8:25 am, I went to bed when the growing phase started. Neurons are firing all over the body and concentrated energy works in the groin. The energy slowly made a circle in my spine and ended at the crown of the head. There was one short powerful stretch of the hard palate. Then I felt the energy of the spine connect in the middle of the hard palate. I must have blanked out, later I awoke feeling an energy vortex sucking out like a vacuum. I was dreaming much. There was a twist in the cervical spine with crackles. I did not open my mouth and barely moved; only I was tilting to the side. After that, I felt shivers as energy

---

[62] I call this stretch through upper spine a Neck Stretch.

went down the entire spine and it felt as if I was sewn with needle and thread on both sides around each vertebrae in a crisscross pattern.

Dream of helping hands: In one dream, I was lying meditating and two pairs of hands without bodies came to place them on me. At first, I jumped and was frightened. Then I felt they were trying to help so I lay back down and said, "Okay, thanks". Getting up, I hope the dream is real, I would love some help at this point.

From 8:30 to 10:15 am, I did a sun session and worked hard to relax and allow head work. While doing this, I felt an outside pressure was assisting, as if I was receiving help. As the skull moved to the right, there was a crack in the upper back. After this energy was released across shoulder tops, and then there were powerful cervical spine movements and muscular shoulder moves, in an eggbeater fashion. This opened the shoulder crook and TMJ's, and was followed by a round of head crunches. Then energy went down the spine and into the hips, with energetic rotation in hips and TMJ's simultaneously. It surprised me to see this energetic rotation connection between the TMJ's and hips. Then there was more skull work and I got out of the sun!

From 10:20 am to Noon, there were more openings with neck stretches. Then I did a long session with head, TMJ and shoulder work. I intuited that the work going on now is making a change of structure in how the shoulder girdle, TMJ's and skull work together, to allow a more freely moving skull. From this insight, my resolve increased and I allowed the weird rearrangement of the facial bones. My mandible was pulled up and over the top of the maxillae on both sides. The hard palate was worked much as well the other cranium bones. There were energetic rotations around the head and energy circuits formed between the TMJ's through the mouth. Then energy circuits formed from the TMJ's to the shoulders. I feel free from the waist on up, but my head hurts.

From 12 to 2 pm, while lying on my stomach, there were many simultaneous strong pelvic pushes and neck stretches, where I though my head would explode.[63] It reminded me of labor when giving birth. Slowly the bones opened. I am tired, that was difficult!

---

[63] I call this phenomena body pulls.

From 2:15 to 4:15 pm, a hundred energy balls came went down from the top of spine to the tailbone, doing work on the way with snapping sounds. This happened about three times and was intense and not comfortable. Then I blanked out while skull work was done. Coming to, there were bone movements in the TMJ's. Work then was in shoulder, neck & TMJ's, and I felt a cord slip over the mandible again. After this, there were several spine adjustments with energy zooming up and down. Next, all the energy coalesced as a big vortex in the center of the brain. Looking up in top of head with eyes closed, I saw intense blue with galaxy view and saw tiny pinpoints of lights firing.

From 5 to 7 pm, there was a long growing phase where my body feels more electrified every time, and then head and TMJ work. There was opening of frontal, sphenoid and zygmatic bones down the line of the face. Then the lamboid suture opened and it felt like the cord moved in that path, under the occipital and up and under the jaw. It wears me out doing these movements on my back. Most work is focused on center of hard palate and sphenoid. From 7 to 8 pm, I did rolling around stretches and some body pulls.

From 9 to 10:40 pm, I decided to sit still and surrender, and allow tension to release. A change occurred in the growing phase, but I cannot recall what it was. My body got very hot two times. The energy went up and down the spine a few times, and then I felt increased swirling action in hips. Then there were spinal stretches upward with cracking sounds and the sensation I was getting bigger each time. Meanwhile the energy in root chakra was building, and then there were pelvic pushes. My body and arms have the heavy gravity feeling making it difficult to write.

From 10:50 pm to midnight, I did a freestyle session. Soon after I started, my body lined up on the right side. It felt like there was a straight cord of energy going though all the joints on right side. I never felt this so strong and straight before. Next energy was released all along this line and as it did so, there was pain. I saw that this released energy was moving down to the root chakra and was building there, as if a conversion process occurred. I decided to lie there and allow it to pass. It felt like my body shrunk as the cord of personality grew shorter. For a long time, there was intense pain at the back of the head. Near the end I blanked out, then woke and did a few more head, shoulder and neck movements. I fell asleep to the strong wavy growing reaction in the root chakra. Whew, what a day!

Neck Stretches, Spine To TMJ Energy Circuit, Sternum Release

August 18: Head Pops Through Shoulders, Entire Body Numbness

I slept well; rising there is strong wavy growing reaction. Later I did a freestyle session with crackly popping and stretching in the shoulder crook. Then energy was moving around and working on each vertebra in spine. It seems the spinal cord is enlivening from head to tail. The stretch feels powerful with increased ability to open the adhesions in the body.

From 7 to 9 am, I did a freestyle session, powerfully stretching down though hips and lower back, and then slowly stretching with pelvic pushes and some stretches rippling up spine. After the hips were energized, energy started working up the spine and twisting it powerfully, it was difficult. Then there was difficult work in the shoulders and neck. These stretches on the spine that are pulling my body apart, have the same intensity as being in labor. Next, I felt energy center on spine from hard palate to tailbone. Then suddenly I felt this energy circuit connect sideways, over to the TMJ and I immediately felt a fast physical rotation in the joint. Then I observed energy releasing from the TMJ and going down to the tailbone.

From 9:05 to 10:10 am, it was a strenuous session working the upper spine. There was an opening around C7 and after I felt a flood of tingles around it spreading in all directions with neuron growth, what a good feeling! After this, there was so much neck stretching that I thought I would die; it felt like my head was exploding. The neck stretches are difficult; it requires much force to do it. There were many big cracks in the thoracic spine. It seemed energy worked on a cord on the neck from the back of head down to C7. Energy released from the cord of personality and went down to the tailbone, where sexual energy was building.

Insight about the cord of personality is all over the body: I think my cord of personality is not due to a single injury; rather it's a physical collection of energy collected over my entire lifetime. This stored energy is scattered all over my body and when it releases it goes to the spine and back to the central nervous system.

From 11:50 am to 2:15 pm, I did a strong freestyle session where I was successful with letting go of body control. Most of it was difficult with neck pulls. The spine feels notably stronger. A cascade of energy balls went down the body. A bit later, I did another session and skull bones were moving. Then there was a neck stretch through shoulders where it felt like my head popped through the shoulders. The image of a skull getting through a barrier and being happy to be through came and I laughed hysterically. Then I was back to crunching and again multiple energy balls cascaded down. When energy reached the buttocks, I felt them flood with energy and expand, for a moment they felt huge. I am tired.

From 2:40 to 4:10 pm, I feel strong muscular pulls down all sides of my body, rhythmically alternating, like a strong freefall. Then the body energized while head and shoulder work occurred and body heat rose. Then my entire body turned to the left, pulling my bones in the stretch. It felt like energy worked to open the sternum with strong body stretches though the shoulder and hip girdles. My body is being remade into a single unit. That was difficult! It looks like there is much more work left; I do not want to know that.

From 5 to 8 pm, I lay down with a strong growing reaction. There were several jerks in my right foot and leg. A bit later, I did a meditation outside with the crystals. I barely felt any pain. I wonder what goes on in these phases where my body barely moves. Does my body only move when necessary? Is this the easier softer way? It would be great if I could fully transform by sitting in a chair, the body stretching is much more difficult. At the end, the energy in root chakra was high and felt it was near to making an energy circuit in the top of the head. There was rising heat and burning over much of my body.

From 8:40 to 10:30 pm, a growing phase happens. Once I felt a strong heat arise and energy filled my body and went up to the head and it started cracking. There were a few strong movements in cranium bones, and then I felt an energy circuit forming at tailbone and going up spine. Next, I felt energy descend with the expansion feeling in the buttocks. Then energy worked slowly up the spine with skull work going on simultaneously. It seems I have changed as it easy to sit in center. For an hour, I watched the energy course around in the body. My entire body went numb and there were stinging prickles all over with intense heat and sweating. Small adjustments were occurring in the skull. Finally, I rolled over onto my side and fell asleep.

Vortex Between Mandibles & Maxillae, Double Spine Circuit

August 19: Crisscross Pattern Between Shoulders And TMJ's

I slept well, waking there is tension at the back right of neck under skull. I feel stiffness in upper shoulders and right part of the skull. I guess as the muscles heal springiness and flexibility in the body increases. I am shifting my identification away from personality and toward higher-self. "I" do not want to stretch out, yet it is me either way.

From 6:30 to 7 am, I did a sitting session, allowing the energy to flow which felt great. My tailbone and hips opened right away and there were several gentle stretches with pops in cervical spine that felt good. Energy is building in the root chakra. Hearing and sense of smell are enhanced.

From 7 to 9 am, I did a freestyle session. There are strong rocking motions in upper body, which seem to shake the bones loose from the muscles. There's no way I can use a technique for the transformation, the most I can do is quiet my mind and allow my body to move. The bones in right body are moving closer to alignment. The body vibration gets stronger with increased spontaneous movements. I am slowly changing and more aware each day. I accept there will be no instantaneous transformation; it is a long slow growing process.

From 9 to 10 am, I did a sun session with many rapid movements, where I had to work hard to relax and allow them. The energy worked to establish a horizontal energy circuit through my skull, primarily through mandible and maxillae. This was done with muscular bone movements. This area is the top of the spine. As this occurred, it felt like infinity signs coming through the mouth and nose area and pulling on opposite sides, bringing all to the center at top of spine *(see figure)*. With each movement, the

mandibles loosened and energy darted around to loosen plates. It was more like a spiral forming, pulling the tissue in the area to the center. It took full surrender to allow this because my face was squished, but it did not hurt. After this, neck vertebrae released starting at C7 and went up a few more vertebrae. My head and neck were stretching in a full circle around the vertebras. Far out, I have a free neck! With the neck loosening, the spine feels more powerful.[64]

From 10:10 pm to 12 am, spiraling energy moves in spine. It is working in the shoulders and mandibles and is creating a working pattern between them. A crisscross energy circuit is forming from left shoulder to right TMJ and from right shoulder to left TMJ. After this, root chakra energy rose up spine and there were spontaneous jerks of the body that shook the bones in right shoulder, mandible and neck on right. The jerks were combined with gliding and ratcheting movements of skull bones. After this, some work was done in spinal column. Then heat and energy rose to the head with tremendous energy zooming fast all over the body. I laid there about forty-five minutes, while the skull and body were shifted in various ways. It is difficult to stay in an immoveable position for so long. Later, there were many skull crunches, which seem to have larger range of movement. Then the energy went over to mandible, then above the zygmatic and under the eye orbit, and from there across sutures to sphenoid wing. The painful spot is on the hollow of the frontal bone, above the sphenoid and zygmatic bone (the temple). I did not want the energy to go to that spot. I braced myself, got quiet and allowed the energy to work there, and shed more tears. I observed energy moving through circuits between all the main joints.

From noon to 2:30 pm, the sitting session started with the growing reaction and freefall. The energy is strong. It pulls my entire body strongly to center and a spiral vortex of energy forms in the head and goes down the spine into the tailbone. I did two hours of head crunching. It seems the right side of my lower skull is glued to the top of the shoulder, when I compare it to the other side. There was difficult stretching in this area. Another energy circuit was made from tailbone to skull. I blanked out for about twenty minutes. My right leg jumped several times, my left hand and my heart jumped. I know I have a heart murmur, so I guess that heals.

From 6:20 to 8:20 pm, I took a break, it was nice to get out but constantly my neck was twisting and there were snaps and head cracklings. The energy is building and I am sweating. I did a freestyle session. I am better at staying focused and can glide through many difficult body stretches without identifying with the transformational pain symptom. It was mostly skull work which got harder with back and neck crunches. I think I did about four rounds of head crunching and body stretches. There were releases in zygmatic bone and

---

[64] The energy pattern that forms seems to prepare for the stretch of the head around the top of the spine on atlas. Perhaps this charges certain muscles to move the bones. This is the first time I noticed this pattern. The neck cannot change this fast!

mandible and much work on hard palate. I felt a small puff out under the crooked teeth on the right, and heard teeth roots crunching. The energy spirals get stronger in the skull. It feels like energy goes through all the solid material. The right collarbone hurts.

From 8:30 to 10:30 pm, I did head and neck crunches. A strong energy circuit formed between the tailbone and head, then immediately energy went up, then down and then up the spine again and came together at the top of the head. Then energy came down both sides of the body in halves and made changes to the body as it descended. I did more crunching and fell over in exhaustion.

Lying was difficult due to the force of energy going up and down my spine. A strong gravitational force is holding me down. I feel the same when I do freestyle sessions it is difficult to stay standing and go against that force, yet it is a good force for counter stretch. Maybe the force of gravity has something to do with the creative force. I think this sensation is what happened to me in January 2006, when I felt pinned to my bed and could not rise. Energy worked while I slept making passes up and down the spine.

Body Pulls, Pulsing Abdomen, Top Of Skull Opens, Spine Circuit

August 20: Springy Alive Sensation In Body, Intense Work In Groin

I awoke at 3 am with a springy feeling in the body. Feeling stiff and tired I went back to sleep. At 6 am, strong energy worked in sacrum and hips and it was uncomfortable lying, so I rose. From 6:35 to 8 am, I did a freestyle session with powerful stretches in the spine. I felt pressure in the skull bones and they moved when the spine stretched. There was work by C7 and scapula by spine and at same time intense work in lower back and hips. It hurt like being in labor. I felt exhausted and noticed my resistance, so I did a big let go. Then there were stretchy body pulls I never could have done by myself nor would have chosen to do!

It felt like I was dying as the tailbone rotated and a vortex of twisting energy was rippling up the spine, stretching the entire body. My head felt like it was exploding, there were no thoughts and many skull plate movements. My tongue was hanging out and my eyes were bulging. I made gagging sounds as energy moved through the neck because it squeezed my esophagus. I was gasping for breath between the body pulls, not thinking about it, merely letting it happen. I felt no fear, knowing this death was necessary and part of being reborn. The pulsation in the abdominal muscles under the diaphragm grows like there is a new life there. While lying on my stomach, I rest on this area as a pivot point with my hip girdle resting on the floor, and body pulls ripple up the spine. With each push-pull, I felt rising sexual energy and the strengthening pulse in the abdomen was attractive, like a growing heartbeat, as if I was coming alive. There are no adequate words to describe what it is like to go through this. You have not felt fully alive until you feel this.

From 10:30 am to 12:30 pm, I have been stretching continuously since 6:30 am. It has been difficult and has brought me to tears. There were many twisting stretches in the cervical spine. In the last stretch, I was folded into a fetal position, then there was one strong body pull going through right shoulder, and it felt like my neck released all the way to top of the skull. Right after this, the head felt weak as if I could not hold it up, it was a strange feeling like being a baby. I ate and now I feel sick.

From 1 to 2 pm, sitting, the head is crackling and energy swirls in the root chakra and body heat builds. I hope this is near the end. I am VERY TIRED. It would be nice to have a contact with someone who understands this so I can talk to them and share my excitement and the difficulty.

From 2 to 4 pm, there was a big crack in the frontal bone fontanel area at top of head and then, I felt like I was a marionette suspended between strings of energy from the skull to the tailbone, being turned between those points. Then there were strong crunches in C7, shoulders and head. The work went laterally across tops of shoulder, with anchor points at tops of shoulder joints and at C7. This area is opened by tipping my head to the right and back and hunching the shoulders. Apparently this movement brings the mandible, C7 and shoulders closer together, which I feel is done to loosen tight ligaments. There is another area like this in the front of the body, under the right molar and down the side of the neck to the clavicle.

Insight of mandible & sphenoid for skull movements: I think the reason the mandible repositioning happens while lying on my back and rocking on the wormian bones is that the mandible is used as a lever to turn the sphenoid bone and to determine the head position. Now I see why there is much head crunching. The crunching is opening and moving the sphenoid, above the hard palate. The basic ratcheting action for a skull movement emanates from the mandible with repeated skull turns in the desired direction. This accumulates energetic charge in the muscles needed to move the sphenoid that way. When all is ready, the sphenoid moves and all the rest of the cranium bones articulate with it in that movement. The sphenoid articulates with all skull bones.

From 4:10 to 10 pm, I did several sessions. In the last one, I was sitting with legs to front. It was nice to sit still and allow the energy to move me. I guess it is the central nervous system and higher consciousness together which moves me. I was in hold for a long time as energy worked through the legs, hips, lower back, and last the energy went slowly up the spine. I was lowered a notch at a time as vertebrae were worked. There was strong swirling in the root chakra. As the hold progressed, I was sweating profusely and the lower body parts were going numb. I am sitting, head crackles begin and I am tired. From 10:10 to 12, intense energy works in the groin that is a killer. I worry I will have to experience this intensity all over my body. My spine is stiff.

Body Pulls, Blacking Out, Energy Circuits Front & Back Of Spine

August 21: Wide Vortex Coil In Pelvis, Higher-Self Taking Over

I woke at 1 am, and did a long sitting session until 4 am. I was bent over most of the time, while energy built in the root chakra and energy slowly moved up the spine. At the end, energy rose up right side of spine to head, like a fist of spiraling energy and I went back to bed.

From 7:30 to 7:55 am, I woke with a nice feeling of finger-like stretches going down my spine. I did a sun session. The hips and tailbone feel powerful and integrated as part of myself. Energy worked in upper spine and then the upper neck and shoulder muscles melted.

From 8 to 10:30 am, I did a freestyle session. Energy worked in higher vertebrae, and it became a body snapping, stretching and jerking affair. Notable, was my head turned while work occurred in the TMJ. Then it felt like the head moved from its current position, it was difficult. The pelvic bowl kept opening wider to where I felt it would break. The pelvis was a large circle that expanded and contracted while energy formed a coil along the entire spine.

There were intense neck stretches with total cutoff of air supply, I blacked out a few times yet was watching. I made spontaneous groaning sounds at maximum stretch, which sounded like a cow. I think the sounds are due to movement of energy from one form to another. I laughed at the weird sound. It is quite the experience to witness this body death and be around to talk about it later. I clearly see it is a transition. Knowing I am always here, I have no fear to transform into something else. Overall, it is not pleasurable, but the feelings of bliss and being intensely alive are enough reward to keep me going.

I am amazed that not one drop of blood has been spilled with all these violent moves. I think the dura mater is like a cushion and protects from injury. Because I feel it is safe, I can allow the bones to pull apart. I still hope this finishes soon as it is difficult.

Insight about taking over: There is typically a transition near the end of a session. I start by sitting in center and allowing body movements to happen. Near the end, there are strong spontaneous movements and I am drawn to merge with that rising energy. At this point, being on the sidelines as the observer no longer works. I then accept the strong stretching force and unite with it, using all my strength to stretch toward new life. At these moments, I feel as one with my body and realize I am doing the transformation and have been since the beginning. Many people say they have been reborn but they have no idea what that is truly like.

From 11:10 am to 1:10 pm, I did a freestyle session, down to tiptoe squat with body moving slowly into each position of the pelvic bowl in a full circle, stretching it slowly open in each direction. After this, I lowered from toes to sitting and there was a ratcheting rolling action, from thigh to buttocks to thigh, having the same purpose. Then I saw a connection. The pelvic bowl and tailbone area with its strong muscles are like an engine to provide the power to straighten the spine. In addition, the sphenoid is directing the movements of the body.

As the pelvic bowl stretched in a direction, a corresponding movement in associated body parts occurred. Seeing this renewed my determination. I found I could allow what was occurring by keeping my focus on the big energy ball spinning in the root chakra.

The head straightened more and there was deep crunching of the shoulder and right side of the neck. Afterward the neck felt straight, and energy moved into the skull and the mandible opened widely on both sides. There was an hour-long strong body pull session at the end, going up through neck and skull. I was exhausted. Then higher-self took over and I went beyond myself for several super human body pulls, stretching up into the shoulder, neck and head. Then strong energy flooded my body and I thought it was over. My head crackles and I am tired.

From 1:30 to 2:30 pm, I did another round of labor-like intense body pulls. From 2:30 to 4 pm, there was strong energetic rotation in my hard palate and jaws. Then my mouth stayed opened wide and I felt an energy circuit form between tailbone and center of the hard palate up back of spine while the sphenoid turned. After this circuit formed, there were many strong body pulls through the skull. Now energy moves down in freefall and builds in root chakra. As the freefall sensation gets stronger, I feel like pure energy.

From 4:05 to 7:30 pm, I did a sitting session with legs to front. An energy circuit formed vertically between the pubic symphysis and the top of the head up front of body. A strong growing reaction starts. It has been thirteen-and-a-half hours without rest. I have not eaten yet. I had to do another skull crunching session, it was not what I wanted and I cried. I cannot give up the notion this will finish soon. The last round of skull work opened the jaws. The right mandible can activate the left shoulder girdle and vice versa. With this connection, there is a muscular cross pull, creating a stronger ability to do work in the body.

From 9 to 9:45 pm, I did a freestyle session and folded quick to a position on my back with a strong growing reaction. Eating was not a good idea. The muscle in lower abdomen becomes like a flattened taut balloon, I feel it is used to propel the twisting stretches upward in the body. It feels foreign to me. It is not the uterus; it is the entire abdomen from the inguinal canals over to pubic symphysis and up to under the diaphragm.[65] It gets stronger with each body pull. At 11 pm, the growing phase started.

Handy items: This is partly a joke and partly serious. 1. Vaseline for chapped lips and from stretching the mouth wide. 2. A big yoga pad or futon for rolling around on preferably covered in silk. 3. A squatting stool with a pot underneath and bars on the wall to hold onto.

Tornado Vortex On Spine, Spontaneous Orgasms, Hollow Tube Circuit

August 22: Sacrum Opening, Squeezing Of Each Vertebra

From 1:10 to 3 am, I did a sitting session with energy releasing from the cord of personality and collecting in the root chakra. From 3 to 4:30 am, there was work on jaw and

---

65 This may be due to enervation of the fascia sheet that covers the abdomen.

lower back with pelvic pushes. From 4:30 to 9:30 am, it has been continuous non-stop torture. The main work was opening hip and sacrum and stretching through a twist in the spine. The root chakra swirling is getting strong.

From 10:30 am to 12:30 pm, when I started, I felt a twisting tornado in the hollow of the neck and it was moving slowly down. It is amazing to see tissues change as it moves down. It is spinning fast and pulling on all the tissue with it. I think the vortex started in the sphenoid and is working down to the tailbone in freefall.

From 12:30 to 2 pm, I have uterine cramps and energy is repeatedly stimulating the genitals, causing spontaneous back arches and intense brief orgasms. I did some pelvic pushes, which feel more natural. A push happens downward through pelvis combined with the spinal stretch upward, and I allow my neck to angle in the direction the energy is moving up the spine. Then the bones in the skull ratchet with mandible action as the energy moves up. It seems the roof of the hard palate and the mandible work similar. Understanding these relationships, while sitting with legs to front, I allowed my body to move around in a circle with the pelvic pushes and relaxed my jaws to allow energy to move easier into skull. There was much energy moving up the spine for a long time with continuous body pulls.

There was a new energy circuit made in the front from the hard palate down to the pubic symphysis. A different opposing stretch happens in the front as compared to the back of body in the spinal stretch. When the stretch is in front of body, you bend forward bringing ends of spine closer together. It seems the developed abdominal muscle facilitates making this connection up the front of the body. In the frontal stretch, you feel the muscular pull coming up through the throat strong. From 2 to 4:30 pm, the growing phase started and I fell asleep. From 4:30 to 6 pm, I woke with much tension. A vortex of energy goes around spine and works down. The sexual intensity heightens; I had a spontaneous orgasm during the nap, and felt an energy circuit formed. I made a comment during sleep, "you found that connection". I am sweating.

From 6:20 to 7:15 pm, the energy keeps rising strongly to my head, which makes it uncomfortable if I do not stretch. There are continued stretches up spine from tailbone. The front energy circuit from hard palate to pubic symphysis just opened the breastbone and ribs. The three circuits on the spine, the double one along the sides and the one in the front, work together. The large bones of the skeleton feel like they move. When I stretch down on the spine in freefall, the jaws rotate energetically three times to accumulate released energy, and then this accumulated energy is sent down the spine. The energy goes down to the next vertebrae, circling it, like a boa constrictor and squeezing it, and then it snaps.

From 7:15 to 8:30 pm, I am sweating all over. I did a sitting session sitting with legs to front. There were body pulls then freefall sensation and energy building in root chakra. After a while, a new energy circuit was made which felt like a hollow tube coming up the center of my body, from my vagina up to inside my mouth, air rushed into this tube, and I gasped, breathing! Then I felt a huge energy ball form in the root chakra, sexual intensity skyrocketed and this had the side effect to shake the upper body and release much muscle tension. There were many brief spontaneous orgasms.

From 8:40 pm to 12:45 am, the heat builds and freefall starts, I am sweating and there is work on hip. I am tired and can barely move. There was work on the ligament under right mandible and a release, which caused a shift in all the cranium bones. My neck stretched up and energy filled the skull. My head felt like the Earth's crust, with fluidly moving plates on the outside and filling with heat energy (light) on the inside. My head felt like it was alive.

Marionette On A String, Floating Head Sensation

August 23

From 12:45 to 2:40 am, there were continued body pulls and work in skull. The growing phase started, and when I laid down strong energy zoomed around and was difficult to follow. I felt my legs elongate with much energy in root chakra and skull. I felt like a marionette on a string. It felt like energy from top of head directed moves in the lower body, and an energy cord ran from there to lower body. There were several body moves like this before I fell asleep.

I awoke at 8 am; I feel stiff but not sore. I do not see any visible outward changes. I recalled a message from a dream, "It's started now." From 8:30 to 10:40 am, it started with neck stretches, and then neck tension released and the area melted. I have strong sexual energy and the abdomen muscle moves much. In this session, there was a workout like yesterday and ending in freefall. From 10:45 am to 1:36 pm, there was a loud snap in C7 and continuous difficult stretching work this entire time. At the end, it seemed I reached a plateau.

From 1:48 to 3:35 pm, there was continued skull work and a release under right mandible. My head feels lighter and freer. This is taking forever; I am disappointed. 8:35 pm:

The head feels strange, like it is supported by energy versus the muscles in my neck. From 8:40 to 11:30 pm, I did more body pulls. Exhausted, I went to sleep when the growing phase started.

Spontaneous Orgasms In Sleep, Pain In Inguinal Canals

August 24: Body Pulls, Quick Cycles Of Stretching Followed By Freefall

12 to 1 am, a few spontaneous orgasms woke me up and I felt an energy circuit form from the head to the tailbone. I did a few more body pulls then finally went to sleep.

From 7:30 to 8:30 am, I did body pulls. The pelvic push has the purpose to open all the bones that comprise the pelvic bowl, which includes the sacrum sutures and tailbone. The pelvic bowl seems open in most directions. The spine feels more energetic. My head still feels weird. I feel a restriction in the right shoulder.

From 8:30 to 9 am, I was sitting and stretching the spine; it is difficult but feels good. I feel like I have strong power now. This work is like physical therapy, as I am not used to moving my bones like this. I feel like my body is being revitalized. The muscles around the spine charge and build tension as the spinal stretch moves up the body. Then this accumulated energy in the muscles works to loosen other restrictions in the body. It is like pulling myself apart and removing all the restrictions in my body. As the spine gains strength, it becomes an effective tool to open the body. The spine gains more strength when tissues directly connected to it open. From 11:30 am to 12:50 pm, there was a growing phase.

At 4:47 pm, the skull, TMJ's and shoulder feel looser, sexual energy is still strong. From 5:25 to 6:50 pm, I did another round of pelvic pushes. I felt a nice energetic rotation in the hip. I am tired; I can barely raise my arms. My cheek has an abrasive rash on it from rolling around on the floor with the skull work. From 6:55 to 7:40 pm, I did a strong session of bone crunching. I felt a release of the ligament behind neck. I do not want to move another inch. From 8 to 9 pm, there was freefall and some light stretching. Freefall comes again; this time I will lie down, as I need it.

From 9 to 10:20 pm, there are quick cycles of stretching and freefalls. I am too tired to surrender or even to fall asleep. From 10: 30 pm to 2:30 am, there was a growing phase with much work in pelvis along inguinal lines and along line where inner thigh meets pelvis. This was painful and difficult to endure and lasted hours. Eventually I fell asleep.

Non-Stop Body Pulls, Energy Puff Outs, Large Tension Release

August 25: Huge Vibration Increase, Body Elongation, Body Flopping

When I awoke, all was quiet with strong sexual energy. From 9:50 am to 2:45 pm, I did sessions all day. It went well and my spine straightens. Energy moves fast.

From 2:55 to 6:40 pm, every round goes faster. I feel my entire body elongating. I have stretched the spine much. I feel work is at the energetic level. Once, I blanked out for a while and woke with a sudden snap in the middle of my neck with no pain. It felt like something came through the neck from the back to the front.

From 7:10 to 9:50 pm, all goes faster and faster, it was more than an hour with intense uterine pain. It is like the pain of having a baby, but there is no pushing. I wonder why there is no outward physical change in my appearance after all this work. I feel energy puffing out here and there with light energy prickles all over the body. In the last session, there were many releases in the shoulders, hip and neck. After each release, there was a huge firing of energy with a clear tone in my skull. Each of these events seems to double the already high energy. This is awesome. I was happy and laughed when this happened. My head and body felt free. My skull feels like it is suspended above my shoulders.

From 10 pm to 12:30 am, the work is starting to hurt. It is intense and non-stop, like giving birth to a baby. I will go down to a squat and see if that helps. Tension is building in the neck muscles, so I think it means the pelvis needs to be opened more. Today was one of the hardest so far. It was continuous the entire day and I stayed up most of the night. They were all sessions of deep surrender and letting go of body control. While like that, there were wild energetic jerks of the body and I was flopping everywhere, like having epileptic fits. It was the only thing to do. Many times my head rotated around and energy went down the spine to the root chakra. There were strong body movements that released huge tension from postural problems. There were many skull bone movements and large openings in the sutures. The jaw moved everywhere. There was strong growing reaction in the root chakra that was sensitive and hard to endure. I am at a new stage, with strong body movements and large amounts of energy are releasing from the cord of personality.

Sphenoid Moves, Circle Around Atlas, Skull Ligament Snaps

August 26: Coronal & Temporal Sutures Open, Breastbone Released

From 1 to 4:30 am, I did a long difficult session. I fell asleep at 5 am, and it seems I slept a long time but it is only 9 am. At 9:30 am, I sat outside and observed energy going down spine from head to tailbone. A large energy ball collects behind my right jaw.

From 10:30 am to 2:30 pm, I did a freestyle session that was not too difficult. Waves of energy continue to go down the spine and energy builds in root chakra. I did stretches in pelvic bowl, legs, knees and the ankles. There were more jerks of the skull on the neck. I think this has the purpose to loosen the skull from the atlas or axis vertebrae. It is difficult to relax while my skull is stretched and my body is arching and twisted into weird configurations. I do the best I can.

There is strong sexual energy. There was a long growing phase of about three hours, lying in surrender with activity in the groin and imagining testes were growing there. Whatever happens in the groin, it hurts much. I was blanking out whenever it got painful. After energetic work in root chakra, it seems there is more energy for skull work. The skull bones stretched open the widest so far, apparently to open the coronal suture. After this, my face felt like it was reorganizing. I imagined this might be the making of a new face.

Insight about levels of consciousness: Lately, I have noticed these different levels of consciousness: 1. I think and experience pain and am identified with it (conscious). 2. I see myself breathing heavy and sleeping (semi-conscious). 3. I sense pain but it is in the background (centered). 4. I have the galaxy view and can barely feel my body; I am distanced from most sensation (outer space). 5. I feel I am out of my body and I do not feel or sense anything (OBE).

At 5:40 pm, I went outside and took a break. The energy was pushing against the base of the skull the entire time. It was hard to endure. Now something snapped at the base of the skull and my head feels loose and free. Then a suture opened on the right immediately after this. Sexual energy is still high.

From 5:50 to 7:15 pm, the main work was loosening the mandible from the TMJ. It was difficult done while I was lying on my stomach with my head pressed to the surface with the head turned to one side. My spine was tautly stretched, and energy worked to loosen whatever holds it there so tight. At first, there was much jaw stretching, and then my head was adjusted in small angular turns about three times. Then the suture down the side of the face opened and after this, my jaw released. A bit later, the skull was adjusted to a certain angle and held in that position. During this hold, I felt energy pouring down the spine to the tailbone.

After the jaw released there were many skull bone movements. The sphenoid jumped with a big ripple around all the edges. Then ligament snaps with releases were occurring in facial bones and all over the skull. This was still going on when I took a break. It was difficult to lay in this awkward position and stay very still, allowing my facial bones to move like that and hear all the crunching and ligament snapping. Something hurt behind my right eye and in my left ear. There is a strange thumping action of the abdominal muscle while I lie on my stomach during this work and an intense feeling in the root chakra.

Insight of cranium bones hold energy of personality: I think much energy of the personality is locked into the cranium bones because I observe a huge increase in awareness as the energy releases from them. On the top of the spine, I feel like I am dying as the skull crunches and facial bones rearrange. On the bottom of the spine, I feel like I am coming alive, as energy in root chakra increases and the spine enlivens.

From 7:40 to 7:55 pm, releases continue to happen all over the body and energy builds steadily. The TMJ's feel looser. Something released off the back part of the shoulder girdle above the right scapula. There were many tinkling noises, like jewels. I think this is from the teeth moving in the sockets. At 8:15 pm, there were two more snaps and releases, one at the back of the neck and I think the other at the occipital bone. Now energy circles around the atlas (C1 vertebrae) and feels weird. I had a spontaneous liver cleanse.

9:55 pm, the ligament snapping continues in skull, TMJ's, neck, shoulders and down the back. I felt a big energy ball form behind the right TMJ, and then it went down the cord of personality path and opened it. Then I felt movements in the skull with TMJ's, sphenoid and hard palate, move the cord of personality toward the center, my body moving as necessary to allow it. All the while, the growing reaction in the groin grew.

When this cord hit center, I was pulled from a bent over sitting position. An energy circuit formed above, pulling energy up from the tailbone. After this, I heard many inner sounds and saw the galaxy view. Next, there were a few strong head and neck twists. Then my entire body pulled toward center bringing the energy together toward the spine. Simultaneously, there was strong energy in all parts of my body, working to form a new energy circuit on the spine. I feel large energy balls on both sides of the perineum and multiple energy balls collect at the base of the skull.

From 10:10 to 12 pm, I feel like I am pulled to the ground by strong gravity. A suture in the right skull opened. I did a long freestyle session, which felt different because the energy goes into the hips. I stretched upward looking at the sky by raising my head upward, and then I went down to squat. The squat really opened the hips, where both have strong energetic rotation. Finally, there was a long hold with energy building in root chakra.

I did another freestyle session from standing, to squat, and then sitting with soles of feet together, then sitting with legs to front and ending with gradual lowering to ground on back. All this time energy zoomed around. In the stretch, I could see energy was slowly collecting to center. Each body part was activated in the sequence below, and after activation, energy zoomed around in it. One time, I rose from the sitting position and suddenly the breastbone pushed out. After the breastbone released, the head and shoulders activated, and the growing phase started.

Insight about body activation: The energy activation pattern of the body starts from the toes. It moves in this order: Left leg, left arm, left body, right leg, and then energetic rotation in pelvis, which activates pelvic girdle. Then energy moves up spine and activates right arm and then right body activates. Next, the shoulder girdle activates and then the rib cage and sternum activate. Now the entire lower body is activated. Energy then goes down spine again and pelvis rotation is stronger. Then the tailbone (base of spine) activates with common side effect of increased sexual sensation. I think the highest energy that can be generated in the body happens with orgasm. With or without orgasm, the energy built in pelvic bowl will eventually travel up the spine into the brain where actual healing takes place.

Parietals Open, Stinging Prickles, Energy Tube In Chest

August 27: Electric Shocks, Leg Jumps, Whiteouts, Mad Jaw Snapping

From 12:10 am, when I lay down the energetic reaction was strong and I was blanking out. Then, there were stinging prickles like dots that started at top of head, moved down my face and then traveled down my body to the toes. After this, I felt electric shocks in both legs, causing them to jump together at once. Watching the energy, there were waves of total darkness between, which at first was scary, there was absolutely nothing, I could not feel myself at all. I was in this black void feeling dead with nothing to grasp or sense. This alternated every minute or so. I was more comfortable with the reaction the next few times, but did not like that feeling.

At 5:30 am, I woke with the sutures opening at the back of my head and with movement of the cranium bones. The back of my skull was like two halves, lifting and shifting and coming down together like a joint would. It paralleled the lamboid suture lines with movement of parietals.

From 6 to 6:30 am, there is strong growing reaction all over with light energy prickles around the legs, a wavy rocking motion, and the root chakra swirls. I feel I am being slowly energized. The heavy gravity feeling increases. An energy ball is forming behind the right side of neck. Now I feel energy fills in my back and chest. From 6:30 to 9 am, I did a freestyle session with spinal stretches, then I did a squat with pelvis and sacrum work, at the end, I was lying stretching.

From 9:20 to 11:35 am, I did a sitting session, then another session lying on my stomach working on the sacrum and facial bones. My face is quite sore from this. The skull released and then the facial bones shuffled for quite some time. After this, I lay on my back and there were more skull adjustments and popping in jaws.

Next, I felt energy circuits form as I angled my head to several points in the lower body. Then I felt a funnel sucking in my chest below the rib cage. I felt an energy circuit going through the windpipe to the head and going back down to the root chakra. This area kept sucking in; to the point, I could barely breathe. It felt like my chest touched my spine in the back. Then for ten minutes, the jaws snapped continuously. There were repeating snaps in a circle around the skull. Eventually, my head stopped in the center. Then I felt puff outs and energy prickles here and there in the body with heat building.

11:45 am: I feel head crackles and strong energy in root chakra. From 11:55 am to 12:30 pm, I have to stretch, the energy does not let up. I go insane. First, a crazy dance, getting that energy out, and then back down on floor with the chest funnel and jaw snapping again, as I described above. Then I made a joke, "I refuse to lie down". Then I laughed hysterically and could not stop.

12:45 pm, my throat hurts and I have to stretch it anyway, there is no let up. From 12:45 to 3:45 pm, there was a growing phase. I want to quit. From 3:45 to 8:45 pm, it is non-stop; I take small breaks. Mostly I am sitting or lying watching the energy as it zooms around and makes changes. I am blanking out often. I guess the energy continues to go like this for a while. I heard a whoosh sound like energy coming up a tube from the root chakra. I also felt stinging prickles in a vertical line on the abdomen.

From 8:45 pm to 4 am, the energy is high and it is working all over the body. It is difficult because it feels painful. I have to sit in the center to get through it. I think this was one of my first long surrenders, which lasted seven hours. I was suspended in the middle, finding a place of comfort to ride out the transformative energies. I was disappointed when I realized this was not enough energy to complete the process. I confront the realty that I have to go through all this. It is an in-situ metamorphosis, like a caterpillar turning into a butterfly in the pupae. All the energy of the old has to be released and burned to make the new. I felt stinging prickles moving up from legs into hips, sacrum, rib cage, sternum and spinal column. During the night, I felt strong activity in the groin and perineum.

Insight of spinal transformation from old to new: I was watching the working path of the energy. It comes down the right side of the spine to the pelvic bowl which collects energy there as a swirling gyroscope. As the rotation gets stronger, the tailbone activates and sexual intensity rises. I see sexual energy as the growth factor or as new life-force energy. With or without orgasm this vortex of energy is sent up the left side of the spine to the brain. Then this energy is used to pattern a new organization in the brain. It is like a big machine once it is going, breaking down the old body for fuel to build the new body. It was strange to see how the two ends of the spine are like old and new in the growth process. So here I am, a new life of swirling energy forming at the tail with an old face at the top.

OBE, Sphenoid Cracks, Energy Circuits Hard Palate To Body

August 28: Skull Lift, Hyper-Speed Changes, Maxillae Moves With Mandible

From 4 to 5 am, when I lay down there was work, which felt like pulling the skull upward and off the neck. I endured much and then fell asleep being massaged with strong waves of vibrating energy.

At 7:30 am, I awoke feeling energy circling the spine. Now there is a huge vortex building in the neck. A few of my teeth hurt and are sensitive to hot liquids. My neck feels free at the shoulders, but there is much tension in the shoulder girdle, cervical spine and skull. I do not feel like doing anything. Yet, I am still curious, what will the new me look like? What will be the rewards? That drives me on.

From 8:45 to 10:30 am, I did a freestyle session, down to squat. While doing pelvic bowl stretches, I relaxed my upper body and allowed the spine to move. Then I did lying work. Near the end, my left side of body was deeply relaxed. I felt a different energy sensation flood my body; it was like cosmic energy, cool, dark, refreshing and relaxing. These waves were occurring periodically, with strong energy swirling in the root chakra. The inner sound is the marcher music; the other inner sound is like crickets chirping at night.

At 10:40 am, a big energy ball forms at the right side of skull in back with intense burning there, in groin and other body parts. From 10:45 to 11:45 am, I did a stand down to squat. There seems a transition to a growing phase that does not hurt. When I fully surrender, I feel united with the universe. I felt that often this last hour, yet knowing I had a body on Earth, the body was filling with light, and it felt good.

From 11:50 am to 2 pm, I feel the cosmic rain falling on me from within and it is cold. I felt burning in this session in the shoulder, arm, mid back, head and neck. At end, there was work on right jaw with a release.

From 3 to 5 pm, the root chakra is vibrating strong and energy is going strongly down the spine, my entire body is rocking with the marching rhythm. The spine becomes an energy recycler. I did a freestyle session with unpleasant body pulls. The neck and skull opened more with many twists in facial bones. It was difficult. Again strong energy travels down the spine, with marching music. I know only to sit in surrender and allow it to pass. The energy movement is like a big machine. There were some stretches and arches of neck, then galaxy view. Then I was sitting 'above my body' (out of body), while the fastest healing reaction I have every observed occurred. I could not feel anything in the body at all; I watched the energy course around all over the body. Then there was a transition to lying flat on my back. I had one leg frog style to the side and I clearly heard, "Move that leg!" Then I reached down and straightened it. It was not easy to move, as it was so heavy with energy zooming in it.

Vision: Top part of head with only the eyes: Then an image came into my 3rd eye of the top part of a head with only the eyes. I felt it meant I was to stay still and was showing me what would change.

I continued watching and internally saw a rapidly moving energy with black background and light sprinkles in it. It went through the entire head; it felt like the skull was changed in the lips, cheeks, the jaw, top of head and the overall shape of the head. Then the hard palate would crack with the skull and the sphenoid bone, and I felt nerve impulses sent into the body from the hard palate area. It felt like the skin was changed somehow, the energy curled around each toe, each finger, through the legs, through the entire body. Then when this was over, I felt energy fills in various places. There was one prolonged stretch of the spine.

From 8:15 to 10:10 pm, I did a quick stretch down, and then I was on my back with work in right skull. After that, the rest of the skull was worked and then the blue wavy energy started in the skull and filled the entire body fast. I could not tell what was going on, as there was not much feeling. Then nerve impulses were sent down from hard palate to various parts of the body. Next, I felt the body activating energetically and the growing reaction increased intensity. When all the body parts were activated, then the TMJ ratcheting started. I felt energy circuits made from the TMJ'S to the hips, to the shoulder girdles and to the rib cage. The root chakra energy still is strong and I feel painful uterine contractions.

From 10:30 to 11 pm, it was another session of pelvic pushing and hearing marching music with an energy ball twirling in root chakra. There was skull work, and another release of the skull as a single unit. I fell asleep in the growing phase. During the night, there was work on my face, with a growing reaction feeling all over it. The big event was the teeth, energy worked a long time on them, going over each. Then I felt the mandible widen and the maxillae and mandible moved toward the back of the skull.

Chapter 18: Skull, Pelvic Bowl, & Body Vortices

Sacrum Sutures Open, Vertical Energy Circuits On Sides Of Spine

August 29: Energy Circuit Up Front Of Body With Whoosh Up Windpipe

I woke with a stiff spine that cracked when I stretched. From 9 to 10:30 am, I did a freestyle session down to squat, with stretches opening hips from all sides. I worked most parts of the body and there was a long period of opening the right hip on all sides. At the end, I was lying on stomach with work on facial bones and sacrum. When energy moved to skull, I felt sleepy, and felt energy whorls on the skull plate sutures and at the top of the head that hurt. Then I experienced the galaxy view with cool wavy blue clouds and blanked out while work was done in the skull. Then energy went down the spine and worked tailbone and sacrum. There was a long clear tone during the spine and skull work. I laid there a long time in a hold with pain in the sacrum with uterus contractions. After that, there were strong stretches into the sacrum and hips.

From 10:45 to 12 am, I did a freestyle session down to squat where the stretching feels different. There was work in the TMJ and I felt energy building in the spinal column. Then I felt two swirling energy balls like a vortex; one was in the pelvic bowl and the other in the head. It was a difficult session, my chin is raw and I do not want to see my hair. I feel the right sacrum needs to open more.

From 1 to 4 pm, I did a freestyle session with work concentrated on the joints along the cord of personality. There was a large release of tension from the right hip and energy built in the root chakra. Then I laid down. A strange thing happened. I started crying because I felt my body was centered. There were many hard crunches in the joints, with strong activation of the root chakra and energy repeatedly went up spine to skull. I coughed often in regular intervals, and felt the voice box was worked. I repeatedly blanked out, and would awaken when something startled me. There was neck work with strange crunchy sounds and then energy whooshed up my windpipe and made an energy circuit from the stomach area up to the brain. Does all this have to do with healing or is something very different constructing in my body?

From 6 to 7 pm, I meditated in freefall while sitting. From 7 to 8 pm, there was opening of left hip, plus work on both hips and opening of sacrum. I felt energy turn fully around my left hip, as it did with the right one a week ago. Mostly, my body was in a torque position with work in the chest and jaws. It was difficult. Then I lay on my stomach with the hips relaxed, and then the buttocks spontaneously rose upward. I felt this was due to the hips straightening suddenly on both sides. Next energy went down the lines of the sacrum sutures on both sides. I presume there was a release. All the while, the hip joints were rotating energetically, and I felt this rotation was generating a strong force to do work in the joints. I felt adjustments in the shoulder girdle and skull.

From 9 to 10:30 pm, I was sitting meditatively allowing energy to work. I like these sessions when everything settles and I can relax and watch the energy zooming around and making changes. Next, I did a freestyle session. There was work on left hip, both hips together, neck crunches, shoulder and spinal twists, and the sacrum pushed out strong just before I arose. During this session, the two bones you sit on were vibrating very fast as the left hip straightened and was worked. Next, I felt two parallel bands of energy forming and

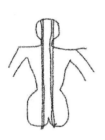

going up the back vertically, a little out from spine on either side **(see figure).** Perhaps these lines are the same as the urinary bladder meridian. Several times energy flooded into my right leg and buttocks. I felt much pain in the pubic bone with the sensation the public symphysis might be separating. There were a few cracks in the skull near the top of the head. Frequently I have amplified hearing during these sessions; it is as if I am outside when I am inside my house. I can hear everything around, loud and clear. I fell asleep quickly.

Balls Of Energy In Pelvic Bowl & Skull With Cord Between

August 30: Bands Contract To Stretch Spine, Chest Compression

From 4:30 to 8:15 am, waking I have the feeling that those parallel bands that formed last night in the spine have just connected to the head. Then I felt those bands contract and my body pulled into a fetal position with my arms crossed under my neck. Then the spine started stretching and I felt higher-self take over, there was nothing to do but allow it. It was not comfortable but not painful either. My body rocked often while lying on my stomach with my arms crossed under me as my legs extended out. This movement seemed to have the purpose to extend the tailbone. Eventually I felt a release in my skull and neck. Next, I was on my back with relaxed arms and doing spontaneous stretches with the sensation of body elongation each time. Next, my legs were slightly raised and then slowly lowered at the hips, until my legs were fully open and flat on the surface **(see figure).** This was the hardest part. I stayed in this hold for about an hour, and then I felt stretching in the sacrum and tailbone areas.

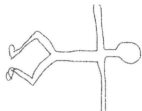

In the third round, energy worked in my chest with compression and stretches into the hips and neck. Then I was lying in the cord of personality position in freefall, while energy worked in the body. It felt good to relax. After this, spontaneous body stretches happened with much force and even this felt good. The energy in the root chakra and all over the body continues to increase.

From 8:45 to 11 am, there was skull crunching. A big energy ball sits in the neck area with my legs in the position like previous figure. Then my legs were drawn to the chest while on my back in a reflexive contraction, and I felt a burning sensation in the entire genital area. Next, my legs slowly lowered while apart, burning the entire time. When they were flat on ground, there were a few pelvic pushes, which I did not like. Then two big energy balls formed, one in pelvic bowl and one in the neck, with a cord between them. Then the neck straightened and I felt this energy ball move from the neck and form a vortex in the skull **(see figure)**. Energy from the tailbone was sent up to top of the spine and an energy circuit was made. From 11:15 am to 12:30 pm, freefall, I feel swirling on my skin and the genitals.

From 12:45 to 2:30 pm: I continued with sessions and now feel dead. From 3:45 to 7:30 pm, finally the hips released, probably much crying helped. It was painful in the shoulder, pelvis, back, head and groin. Energy works in the chest, back and shoulders and there is much skull crunching. I cried because I do not want this anymore, I am exhausted and disappointed this goes on so long. On the positive side, there was another release in the rib cage and right shoulder.

From 8 to 9:45 pm, there was a freefall with shoulder relaxing; the energy is strong now. There was a long session of stretching and skull crunching. Lying on my back after the stretches, I feel more centered and balanced. From 10 to 11 pm, jaw tension releases and I am getting sleepy. My saying for today, "You don't get something for nothing". I did a few more skull stretches before bed. Now, continuous coils of tension energy pour out of my shoulder through the jaw.

Insight about brain controlling body: I observed there are energy circuits going from hard palate to various body parts. When the head and jaws are pointed a certain way and move, then there is also a movement in the hip girdle, sacrum, spine, rib cage or shoulder girdle. I guess this has to do with the energy circuit between the sphenoid bone and motor part of the brain. It is like the analogy that you can control a horse or large animal by controlling the head. The body follows the head.

Insight about freefall and tension cycle: The stretch reflex has capability to do work by moving a muscle to open blocks in the body, which releases the stored body tension. In the freefall phase, the stretched area is relaxed and it is like growing or healing occurs in the area, where the tension was released. After the freefall phase, energy charge gradually builds in body muscles, preparing to do the next opening or stretch to release the stored tension.

Insight about character of faces: The personality shows on the face, with our features getting more chiseled as we get older. Could it be that facial expressions reflect in the rest of the body and by repeating these expressions, we store tension in the face and body over time? I think this can be an important contributing factor to stored tension in the body.

Body Lifted While OBE, Energy Circuit From Throat To Tailbone

August 31: Energy Waves Go Up & Down Body With Quiet Mind

It is 7 am. There is a deep muscle in right shoulder crook that holds much tension. Last night I worked on this area. I now understand my skull will be free when my body is free, as the body is worked as a single unit. From 7:45 to 8:30 am, I did stretching and opening of the tailbone and sacrum, hips, and jaws. I feel like an eel, undulating to enliven myself while lying on my back. Energy in the root chakra is strong.

From 8:45am to 1 pm, this session was mostly sitting in center and allowing the growing phase. This is getting easier to do each day. Each time I feel more centered in all regards: emotionally, mentally, physically and spiritually. There were strong pelvis pushes, opening the pelvis bones wider still. The sacrum and hip on right is stuck and needs to open more.

I had an orgasm and spontaneously the tailbone tucked and the pelvis and legs tightened. Afterward the energy rocketed straight up the spine. Then I felt sprinkles of rain and increased awareness and less body identification. Then cosmic energy waves strongly went up and down my body. Many body parts melted as they filled with energy. This was concentrated in the lower parts of legs and pelvis. Then energy came in waves, as each passed over I would lose identity with the personality. I was thinking and when the wave passed over there was nothingness. This happened repeatedly. I felt no fear seeing what it was. I said aloud, "Hello Creator, nice to meet you" and laughed.

Then the quiet state remained and it felt like my body was down below, I knew it was there and I could observe it while tremendous healing occurred, it was so fast. I felt like I was only a head of yellow light sitting there. Then I felt undulating and swirling energy waves full of tiny colored dots, pick up my body and an adjustment was made to the skull, neck and shoulder area. I was awed at the power to do that. I was not picked up much, only what was needed to adjust the skeleton. I felt no pain. I laughed thinking how hard I have worked, to see something like this done spontaneously. After this, energy worked in the neck while my head was turned repeatedly to the left and right.

It is 1:15 pm; I need a break for my sanity. The marching music is going strong. At 1:30 pm, there was freefall with a shoulder release. My shoulders feel broad. There is much ligament snapping occurring, feels great! From 5:30 to 8 pm, I did a stretch down spine in spiral fashion. The muscles under the tongue activate in chain reaction with other muscles going down the front of my body with stretchy pulls.

An energy circuit forms between the lower mouth and throat area to the tailbone. I hold my mouth open and then my head turns around with it. Above I feel the sphenoid and below the tailbone. It is a sensual feeling with strong root chakra activity. In this session, I easily sat at center and did not feel pain while a strong growing reaction occurred.

Mostly I was lying on my stomach with sacrum work. It is more comfortable to lie on my stomach, since the skull released from the atlas. I do not feel the ratcheting pulls upward of the skull anymore and my chin heals. I guess there were significant energy circuits made along the spine to make a difference in healing power and increased awareness. There was a period of thirty minutes of work along the cord of personality. I blanked out several times. The lying on the stomach position seems the most effective position for working on the spine. The rocking action in the pelvis is what opens the hips and sacrum. It is fascinating to go through this. Each day I feel more aware, bodily and mentally. While laying on my stomach sexual energy was rising, yet I could not feel it at all, I felt nothing in the body. It was as if I was pure awareness, allowing the body to transform itself. Waves of increasing awareness settled on me as this occurred. I am drawn to feeling myself as pure bliss, it is refreshing and pain free. It is like everything.

From 8:25 to 9:30 pm, my body is cracking all over. It is getting intense. Higher-self is taking over strongly. I stretched and ended curled in position of the cord of personality and felt energy work along that path. I did not feel pain this time as the hip, sacrum, back and groin were worked, and usually that kills me. From 10:15 pm to 1:15 am, a growing phase sets in. Perhaps I luck out and can eat and sleep.

Past Life Dreams, Brain Halves Connect With Two Funnels

September 1

It is 6:30 am, and energy zoomed all night. I woke with the strong marching rhythm. My eyes or the eye socket was worked often last night. When I woke, I had to keep them closed because there was much energetic rotation going on behind them and they were dry. In the night, I had strange dreams, feeling they had to do with past lives.

Dream of past life with alligators: I saw myself as a beautiful young woman swimming with an inner tube in the water. There were several other young friends with me in the water. Then I turned my attention to a photo album, which felt to be from a family vacation. In the album, I looked from one photo to the next. The first showed alligators on land, then the next photo showed them creeping toward the water. Next was a photo of the swimmers, who were not aware of the approaching alligators. Then the dream ended. This is interesting because as a child I was fearful there were alligators under my bed in the morning. This fear started unexpectedly for no reason. I was so afraid that I did not want to put my feet on the ground to get out of bed. Perhaps in one life an alligator got me.[66]

Dream of drawing with many faces: I dreamt about a drawing I made and I was showing it to someone. I was pointing out to them how the portrait in the drawing had many other faces in it if you looked from different perspectives. Then the drawing disappeared and I was frantically looking through paper files for it but could not find it. I got angry and wanted to blame this man for taking it.

Dream of being caught in a time loop: I dreamt I was in a store caught in a time loop where people did not know what was occurring. Suddenly, many buyers would appear in the store and a huge line formed at the checkout. I saw this happening and was thinking about how to get through the line. The store workers had to be ready to go in hyper-speed to process them all. The male clerk said, "It starts soon". I asked him if I waited here in line, would I be the first to checkout next time. He said yes. Then he said, "Soon now". The sound stopped, all was quiet for a moment and then boom, here came all the people to get in line. I wondered why they could not get out of this repeating loop. I felt what I purchased cost far too much. I do not remember what it was but was glad to pay to get out of that store.

From 7:30 to 10 am, it was a long session with a strong growing reaction. I was fidgety longing for peace. My body felt heavy, it flopped around as if it weighed one-thousand pounds.

It is 3:10 pm and I have been lying all day in discomfort. Now it is 6:30 pm and I need a break, this is continuous. From 7:30 to 9:40 pm, there was an opening of tailbone and straightening of the spine. Now I need to sit with my head cocked back, sitting with legs to front, while the spine stretches. It is difficult to do and stay surrendered because there is much

---

[66] I believe this was a dream of my most recent past life, and the one that was healing.

pressure on the neck. When I stopped to change locations, I could barely move. I feel I am through that part. At 11 pm, there was work on shoulder, skull, hip, back and pelvis.

At 1:15 am, something happened. Two parallel lines went up the back, came together, and closed in the skull and then I blanked out. I remember having a dream about my head being filled with energy that was zooming around inside. I remember an infinity sign forming horizontally, like two funnels connecting at the apex and cracks going up the back. Probably it was not a dream and really happened. I am sore in the head and shoulders. It has been a difficult day. I hope the worst is behind me. The energy took me over there at the end.

Energy Bands Form Down Spine From Crown To Root Chakra

September 2: Floating Cranium Bones, Large Release In TMJ

It is 5:50 am. There was a strong growing reaction last night and I felt I was filled with light energy. At 11:15 am, I did several stretching sessions working on shoulders and hips.

At 2:15 pm, I did a long sitting session. Next, I did a stretch down through cord line with full-length body stretches and then I lay down. Frequently I feel the reaction of strong vortices of energy on spine working down to the tailbone. Then I sit in center as my head is quickly turned from side-to-side while lying on my back. The pelvic girdle, shoulder girdle and skull, all of which connect to the spine are opening more. Cosmic experiences are frequent with awareness increases. Finally I lay down on the stomach to do sacrum and spine work. There were many TMJ pops alternating with a stretch from right TMJ through left hip and vice a-versa. After this, I raised sexual energy and there was a strong reaction of vortices going down the spine with the cosmic energy feeling. I dreamt I needed to raise sexual energy. It does help. From 3 to 4:30 pm, the energy got so strong I had to lie down. There was work in head, shoulder and arms. I am sweating.

From 6:30 to 7:30 pm, there was skull work while sitting outside. I felt the skull plates loosening more and the mandible felt like it was moving everywhere. A deep blue enters my 3rd eye. Since this morning, it is easy and feels good to sit floating in the cosmos, while the skull work goes on in the background. Once, I felt elements of my face moving up to the top of the sutures and out of my body. Tension energy was releasing upward and out of the face. From 7:30 to 8 pm, there was work on back of neck work while looking upward. It is difficult.

From 9 to 10:30 pm, it was mostly skull work. It felt like a bone broke near the right TMJ area and my cheekbone moved around. There was a release in the cord down my back. The spine was worked down to mid back and while lying on my stomach I could raise myself that high in cobra position. My head felt free. My head, jaws and shoulders are sore now. I think this work is about widely opening all cranial bones. I guess that is necessary to rebuild the body.

From 11 pm to 1:30 am, there was freefall with several long holds with work in the head. Once I blanked out and woke with two powerful bands of energy forming from crown chakra to tailbone. After this, energy went down to the root chakra. I am tired.

September 3: Freefall & Stretch Merge Into One, Facial Bones Open

I vaguely recall energy working all night with a few spontaneous stretches. The tailbone feels strong. I do not feel sore. There is a big energy ball behind neck on right.

Dream of a coming storm: I had a dream of a coming storm. I saw a big vertical white light that was like an explosion barreling down on us. People were running for their cars and trying to avoid it. I was fleeing with my Dad and my sister. I saw my black purse tied to a door. I saw it and took it wondering why it was there.

Dream of teeth breaking off at base: I had a dream about two molars in the back breaking off at the base. I could see the root was still there in the gum. Is it an omen? I think it was Freud who said when you have dreams of teeth falling out it means masturbation. This may be a message to increase the sexual energy. With low spinal energy, the teeth have problems. Sexual orgasm brings energy to the teeth.

From 7:30 to 11:30 am, I did two sessions with work on skull, spine and tailbone. My face was smashed into the pad while lying on my stomach with notable pressure on the bones at midline of face. Much work was done on the coronal suture in an awkward position. I had an orgasm and after this, the maxillae or some bone behind it released. The pelvis opened another notch. While lying on stomach my left kneecap is rolled around and my chin has abrasion, both of these areas are tender. The work in the skull does not hurt.

From 11:50 am to 2 pm, there was a freefall. The cycles of stretching and freefall merge into one. My head is like a loose ball on a stick, I only hear the rattling of teeth. I am exhausted. From 2 to 8 pm, the energy does not let up. I did much skull and shoulder work that bothers me because nothing releases. I did some Reiki on the meridians. I am not comfortable sitting or lying; perhaps I can do it upside down?

September 4

I slept almost nine hours! There was a growing reaction all night, working in shoulder, rib cage, under the arm and both sides of body and skull. I cannot believe this is still going on with this intensity. My skull hurts and I had cleansing dreams. I am not hungry and when I eat, I do not feel good. I am belching, maybe the gallbladder is cleansing due to the shoulder releases.

From 6:30 to 8:30 am, I sat with legs to front in a hold for thirty minutes, followed by a few twists in the skull. Energy worked in the shoulder and neck area and then went down the spine, working each vertebra separately. After this, energy went back up and I stretched the spine. Then energy worked in head. Slowly energy moved back down the spine to other body parts and strong energy built in root chakra. At 9 am, the skull released. At 10 am, there were large body spirals and high-pitched tones with growing reaction.

From 11:45 am to 1 pm, there was a long growing phase, hanging out in the cosmos with strong energy, which I could only take surrendered. My head hurt so I lay down and then the TMJ snapping started. I could not endure it, so I sat up. At least it stopped. I blanked out several times and then came back quick. There were releases in the shoulder, skull and TMJ. I feel like I am coming alive.

From 3 to 5:30 pm, I did a stretch, which opened the vertebrae including the joints, and then I stretched down to lower back, sacrum and hips. It was difficult. From 5:30 to 6:15 pm, there was a growing phase and from 7:45 to 9:30 pm, I did another stretch. I felt I did a good job with surrender while on stomach, working sacrum, pelvis, spine and neck. There was a loud crack in the neck near C7. From 9:45 to 11 pm, there was more work on shoulder while lying on my back with many crunchy openings.

Past Life Healing, Physically Lifted, Whiteouts

September 5: Bag Of Bones, Marionette On A String, Alligator Biting Leg

From 12 to 2 am, I did a sitting session with legs to front and spine was gradually lowered, ending with head on knees. Then I sat upright and blanked out. There is a strong energy ball in the root chakra that is pulsing. After this, a strong energy rose and worked in the pelvis, shoulders and neck. The intensity surprised me. I sat in a hold for about an hour while energy worked. It was difficult. Many clear tones sounded.

At 3 am, I woke with sexual dreams and had the idea to raise sexual energy. I did this and soon fell asleep to a nice wavy growing reaction. 7:30 am, during the night I felt a growing reaction. When I woke, I felt energy descending the spine to the tailbone. The body feels tight all over, ready to burst open.

From 7:55 am to 1 pm, I feel a slow wavy energy, increasing body heat, swirling energy in the root chakra, and I hear the marcher music strong. I stretched, with my head going around in a circle and felt crackles going down the spine. I went through many cycles, with repeating steps that get stronger each time. I give up trying to guess when this finishes.

From 1:45 to 4 pm, the growing reaction starts and I am tired. The bones in the neck and shoulder feel next to each other. I feel like a bag of bones. There is much skeletal separation and it is difficult to stop this momentum. There was a big release in right bottom corner of skull with mandible and occipital bone. There was a big crack somewhere near the TMJ and another big crack on spine.

From 6 to 7 pm, I was lying with body crunching. The nervous system is so strong that spontaneous movements can lift my body up and turn my head and neck. It is like a string of energy attached to top of head that goes down the body at different angles, I move as a marionette on a string. From 8 to 9 pm, I did a freestyle session, mostly lying. There was release of left hip and sacrum, and then the right TMJ released by upper bone. I heard a squishy sound then felt an energetic rotation in the joint. It was difficult. There has been much work on the cranial sutures. I felt pain in the right parietal at the back of the head, and the coronal suture fully opened. Then energy was moving around the edges of the temporal suture.

From 9 to 10:30 pm, I did a lying session with a strong growing reaction, and felt small adjustments periodically made in the skull. At the end, there was a long pause where I was in outer space and then a loud crack in the right TMJ area. Sitting, I am sore. I did a long stretch with tension release and more crunching before I retired. The shoulder was worked strongly. I finally fell asleep exhausted.

During the night, strange things are occurring. Many times, I felt the energy going up and down the spine and moving me around. I experienced a state of total nothingness, but this time visually it was like being in a field of closely packed stars. One time I felt intense prickling start in the toes, but soon it felt like an animal was biting my right calf and taking chunks of flesh from it. At the time, I thought perhaps it is due to the intensity that it feels like this. I have never felt this sensation before. It felt like an animal was eating my legs. It did not last long. I was greatly relieved when that feeling stopped and went back to normal. It was almost unbearable. Later, I thought it might be a past life healing of being eaten by an alligator. Perhaps the body memory released last night.

September 6

From 8 to 10 am, I did a nice and easy sun session. There were many head circles while energy worked down the spine without much jaw movement, a nice break. From 10:30 am to 1 pm, there was freefall and then energy worked in the skull. The energy goes up and down the spine, through hips and head. Now, there is intense skull work with loosening of all sutures. My head turns spontaneously. This effort seems to be about making an energy circuit with the spine and neck. At times, the TMJ's are worked together with the hip joints. The temporal bone and other skull bones are getting quite mobile. There is still work along the coronal suture above TMJ on right side. It is tiring work with some pain in skull at times.

From 1:30 to 4 pm, there was much head crunching, pelvic rocking and a spontaneous orgasm. From 6 to 8:30 pm, it was the same stuff, with difficult work in right hip. The energy rising from tailbone is strong and the body quickly opens. There was much skull suture work. The spot at right bottom back of skull, seemingly glued to the shoulder, released some. Now the shoulder opens, great! There was a reaction with strong waves of energy felt in the tissue behind each opened area. Energy continues to gain momentum each day. From 8:30 to 9:30 pm, I am exhausted.

Electrified With Pinpoints Of Light, Spontaneous Pelvic Pushes

September 7: Blanking Out, Laughing And Crying

I went to sleep early and slept until 4 am. All night I had the repeating sensation of being electrified. It was like many pinpoints of lights going into various parts of my body. This was not a pleasant sensation and thankfully, it did not last long. There is much pressure behind neck. I am in a growing phase still. At 8 am, I went back to bed. A strong growing reaction continues with slow wavy energy. I feel so heavy it is difficult to stay upright. There is no indication to stretch; I cannot tell what is worked as energy is all over. I blank out often and see a geometric pattern in the 3rd eye. Energy frequently increases and gets strong and spontaneously moves and stretches my body. From 8:15 to 9 am, while lying on my back, my body moved spontaneously while head crunching went on. There is high sexual energy.

From 9 to 10 am, I did a freestyle session with body pulls and skull work. During the pelvic pushes, it felt like higher-self took over and they automatically happened. It is amusing to watch the body move spontaneously. There was burning in the genital area. I felt tension energy releasing from cord of personality and accumulating as swirling energy in the root chakra. From 10:20 am to 1 pm, there were more body pulls with many skull bone movements. At times, it was very difficult; I wanted to die and sobbed. The next minute I would be laughing hysterically.

From 1:40 to 4:30 pm, my head and shoulders have much pressure and tension. I want to stop but did a freestyle session, down to squat and then lying on stomach position. This position relieved the neck tension and felt good. It was difficult work! I cried more and I think my skull rotated fully around three times. Several times tension released from twist in spine, as well in the shoulder and neck. Break!

From 7 to 9:30 pm, head destruction. I allowed more than in the past; the face is messed up. I gave acupressure to the toe meridians after and went into freefall, but it was not an easy hold. There was a good release in jaw and shoulder blade. Now strong energy has entered into the skull and the plates seem to move and glide spontaneously.[67]

---

[67] From the notes, I notice intense work in all major parts of body in one day: first in hips & pelvis, then in neck and shoulders and finally in skull, ending with energy release in skull. The time between working on major joints is decreasing.

September 8

From 4 to 6 am, I did a freestyle session with body pulls working from head down through tailbone. I felt more openings in sacrum and mandibles. **I feel like I am sleeping when this work goes on**. From 6 to 8 am, there was more skull work. I have a pain in upper right skull near sphenoid wing where I resist allowing energy to enter. I saw my resistance then thought I heard, "A bone needs to be broken.", so now I worry about that.

From 8 to 9:30 am, I did a sun session, but it was not tranquil! There was strong pelvis work and much jaw snapping. The root chakra energy is strong. From 9:45 to 10:45 am, I did a sitting session with opening of pelvis bones. I am getting tired and the shoulders feel stuck.

From 10:50 am to 2 pm, it has been difficult. I did ten hours of session's non-stop. I need a break. At end, I was on my back and different moves happened. There was a big release in head and hip. At 9 pm, I have been going continuously all day, difficult stuff. I was lying in the cord or personality position and tension energy was releasing from it and gathering into the root chakra. From 10:30 to 11:30 pm, I folded into yogic child pose, and sat like that in a long hold. There were strong movements of the entire body, especially in the spine. In the night, there was pleasant and intense tingling all over the vulva with waves of pleasure.

Snap-Crunch In All Cranial Sutures

September 9: Cranium Bones Move With Facial Bones

I woke at 6 am. I rose several times and did stretches to relieve the neck tension. The growing reaction is strong. From 8 to 10 am, I did a sun session and most was skull work. The cranium bones are loose enough to move with the facial bones. I hope for an easier day, yesterday was one of the hardest.

I often see a deep violet color in my 3rd eye. I sweat more, especially when energy works in the skull. I wonder about the strong vibration energy that goes all over the body, what is it and what is it doing? I do not move physically with it. Is it only nerve expansion? Sections of my body activate with increased vibration then energy moves in this area as if it is mapping a path of stretch. Next, I physically stretch through that area after. By watching where energy works, I know what part will stretch next.

From 10 to 11:30 am, there was skull work. I believe a bone was broke or snapped in the upper right, perhaps by the zygmatic arch. After this, there was more skull work and I sat in center easily distanced from feeling pain. I am very still not moving at all. Once in center, my head moved everywhere, ratcheting around and doing stretches in a full circle in combination with the shoulders and TMJ's. After this, the skull stretched with the spine in back and chest in front along vertical circuits. Next, the right hip released and I was in the growing phase. Lastly, I did a sitting session with spontaneous pelvic pushes.

From 11:35 am to 1 pm, my neck is cracking open. Wow! Hard to believe one-and-a-half hours elapsed! I did a sitting session with legs to front in freefall, but it was not easy. I had pain in the left shoulder, cranial sutures, back, neck, and I had uterine cramps. Next, there was a stretch into the head, which sounded like seashells clanking together. This sound appeared to be in every suture. I have never felt this snap-crunch along all the sutures before. Lastly, I was on the floor doing body pulls, which feel more powerful.

From 3 to 5 pm, most of the time was skull work with precise movements and some work on right hip and sacrum. Then there was a long hold in prone position while energy coursed around. From 6 to 9:30 pm, I did a freestyle session and skull crunching. The skull bones move more fluidly with the spinal column. It seems the body is progressing toward one unit. I was better at surrender, when I get tired then this ability falls apart.

From 9:30 pm to 12:30 am, I was sitting with legs to front in a strong hold. I felt like I was falling asleep. I sensed the work as painful and intense, but sitting in center, I did not experience pain. I sat like that for a long time, and stopped when the pressure on the right hip and neck was too much. I fell over to lie down and noticed a strong growing reaction in the skull, which hurt. I heard a strong musical sound like the cosmos the entire time. It took awhile to fall asleep, as the energy was strong.

Body Pulls With Gagging, Vortex Balls In Pelvic Bowl & Skull

September 10: Electric Pinpoints Of Light Filling Body

In the night, electric pinpoints of light energy were filling my body. I had many cleansing dreams and rose a few times to allow spine and hip movements. I feel full of energy ready to burst open. There is an energy ball high in the neck close to the skull. The C7 joint and shoulders feel fluid, a new sensation.

From 7:30 to 10 am, I did a sun session, with work on cord in right skull and right sacrum. There was a long hold at end. I was trying to 'fall sleep' to allow the skull work. I was sweating much, yet feeling a cool breeze. From 10 to 12 am, I did a freestyle session; it was difficult work from head to tail. Many times, I was gasping for breath with the twisting body pulls and choking and gagging sounds coming from my throat. This sensation feels like my head will explode and much like dying. I am sure nobody wants to know about this!

From 12 to 1 pm, there was more skull work and the right hip and sacrum feel like they have more range of movement. I felt pain in the left TMJ like a sharp bone, and later the same on the right while the jaws opened wide. There was a little blood from the nose; otherwise, I am still intact.

From 3 to 6:30 pm, I did a freestyle session with body pulls. It was difficult and I cried. The right and left shoulders released. There is still something stuck going down line from back of head, to neck, to shoulder crook and on down to sacrum. I have stretched until I am almost dead. I think in the last session I got too desperate and went too far. This happens when I get too tired or feel I want to get it behind me. I pray to The Creator this is over soon and ask The Creator for help! From 6:30 to 8:45 pm, I did a sun session with energetic rotation of pelvis and head crunching. The pelvic bowl feels open, the right hip and lower back released. After these releases, vortex balls formed, one in the pelvic bowl and the other in the skull.

From 8:45 to 10 pm, I sat and the growing reaction started. When movement started, I rose to take a break. Energy worked along the spine and seemed to be aligning the skull with the tailbone. I think there will be a big push at both ends of the spine and then I will feel like I have died. Okay, I have some fear. From 10:15 to 11:30 pm, I was sitting with legs to front, with strong energetic work on both shoulders. It is the first time I felt much work in left shoulder.

September 11: Mandible & Maxillae Pulling Apart

I slept long. I felt energy work going on in the body all night. I had many dreams and I have much tension. From 6:30 to 8 am, I did a freestyle session, with mostly sacrum work. I have to go out for an appointment.

From 11:30 am to 1:30 pm, it was too long to be out; there is much tension in my body. I wanted to sleep but did a freestyle session ending with lying on back and skull work.

First, the right mandible and cheekbone released and then energy was systematically going around the facial bones and around the sutures in various patterns. This energetic work was often combined with a body pull.

Interspersed with this were spine movements caused by jiggling of the body from side-to-side and up and down, like a physical vortex was moving up and down the spine. I felt tension energy releasing from the cord of personality and collecting in center of spine. Now energy is working strong in a diagonal line on the face between the bridge of nose and the eye that goes down to the outside corner of the mouth. I think I surrendered well this session.

From 1:30 to 3 pm, I was sitting outside, with more skull work and crying, wondering if this will ever end. I thought I heard a message, "You are almost there". From 3 to 6 pm, I did a lying on stomach session with work on facial bones. Work was on temporal bone and maxillae with more lateral side-to-side movements. There were about fifty turns of the head fast on one side, and then a hold and a stretch. There was much crunching in area of the teeth. My mandible and maxillae was pressed into the surface and leverage was used to pull the jaws apart. The hips and pelvis were rocking side-to-side, with twisting body pulls upward while the mandibles were pulled apart. I felt a huge wave of energy arise on the right up through the buttocks but not higher. From 6:45 to 10:30 pm, I did a lying on back session with skull work concentrated on frontal bones that move strongly.

Teeth Snaps

September 12: Large Energy Puff Outs

I went out for another appointment. It was too long. From 12 to 1 pm, I did a freestyle stretch with skull work and my mind went a mile a minute yet it still worked, almost spontaneously. From 3 to 6 pm, I did a freestyle session, which started easy, with adjustments made to the skull and body. Now it is difficult with strong body movements but not with pain. The facial bones continue to separate. The same work happens but the time between working separate parts in the body is decreasing. From 6:15 to 7:20 pm, I did a lying on stomach session. It was difficult with much crunching and breaking sounds. All bones feel like they shift and move. From 7:30 to 8 pm, there was sacrum and pelvis work.

From 8 to 9 pm, I did a lying on stomach session with head, spine work and sweating. There is a strange effect in the mouth, which I have been noticing for a few weeks. When the maxillae and mandible are stretched widely apart, it seems like the teeth are attached to elastic cords and they snap out and back with a popping sound. Several times, I thought a tooth flew out of my mouth and I looked for it on the ground. I never found anything and no teeth felt loose. I call this symptom 'teeth snaps'. As the energy gets stronger, larger areas of my body puff out, such as the buttocks, the back and the chest. From 9:15 to 11:30 pm, I did a freestyle session ending in a hold.

Pelvic Bowl Vortex, All Cranium Bones Move At Once

September 13: Uterine Cramps, Leg Elongation

I slept long, with much energetic work going on and some spontaneous stretches in sleep. I rose often. There is tension in upper back and shoulders. The root chakra activity is strong and I hear the sound of marcher music. From 8 to 8:30 am, I did a sitting session and until 10 am, I did a sun session. There was much pelvic rocking and I felt I surrendered well. After this, the hips and skull feel more open.

From 10 to 12 am, I did lying on the stomach and freestyle sessions. The lying on stomach sessions, take a toll on my face from the skull turnings. The nose itches from the drooling, the left chin is chapped and the right side of my neck has many pimples on it from the twisting. The left eye has a scratch on it and the left kneecap is sore from the side-to-side body movements. I do not want to talk about my hair.[68]

From 12 to 1 pm, I did another lying session, my nose is red and my face is sore. From 2 to 3:15 pm, I did an on the back session, something finally releases in back and shoulders! An energy vortex forms as a big circle in the pelvis. Now the head opens, the sutures separate and I am flooding with energy. From 3:20 to 5:30 pm, I did a freestyle session stretching down to squat, which opened the pelvis. Then I lay down on my back and there were skull crunches with different moves. After this, I blanked out in a hold for about an hour. I woke to energy moving down from my head. There is a strong growing reaction now. From 5:40 to 6:30 pm, there was skull work and another cycle in the sacrum starts, with lying on stomach. I need a break.

---

[68] When I had extreme pressure on sacrum and base of skull, the lying on stomach position was the only one that would relieve this tension.

At 6:50 pm, I took a walk but had too much tension so I returned home. I cannot eat and am tired. From 7 to 8:30 pm, I was sitting outside in the chair. When I sat, strong energy rose and opened the tight jaw, neck, shoulder and ribs. The there was freefall for the last thirty minutes. I need to lie down again. From 8:30 to 10:15 pm, I was lying on the stomach with skull turns, which were difficult because my face is sore. My nose is swollen. Near the end, there were long holds of about fifteen minutes where it felt like all the bones were moving at once in the skull. It is somewhat painful when this occurs. Simultaneously, I felt three or four strong uterine cramps. Then I felt my legs elongating.

Physical Spinal Vortex

September 14: Acute Senses, Swarm Of Bees Sound, White Energy Prickles

I slept long with strong growing reaction and dreams. I am stiff on right side of skull and shoulder quadrant. From 7:30 to 8:30 am, I did a sun session. My legs fill with warm tingly energy that feels different, which happened last night too. Right after this, I felt energy puff outs in the groin. Then strong energy moved up the spine. The torso and head rotated as it rose. It was easy to sit in center and allow this. There does not seem to be any division between the old and the new, the ONE is growing, gradually making the new from the old.

From 8:30 to 9 am, I did a sitting session. Strong energy goes up the spine from the tailbone, and I hear cracking noise as it rises. This does not hurt. From 9 to 10 am, there was work in spine and on back of head. Each time, energy works on same areas, but it is stronger and I have more range of movement in each area.

From 10 to 11:15 am, I did a lying on stomach session with skull work. It was not difficult. There were about three passes through maxillae and mandible with much popping of TMJ's. Between each pass, a vortex physically shook the spine from head to toe. Then energy would rise up spine as strong waves enveloping my body. In each round, the energy increased. Once, there was an upward stretch, which loosened cranium bones vertically. From 11:30 am to 1 pm, I did a sitting session with skull crunching and a lying on stomach session with work on facial bones.

I took a walk, my right ankle is looser, and I feel different like I am more alive. The wind on the walk felt invigorating and the trees and the world leaped out at me.

From 2:45 to 4:45 pm, it was a nice and easy sitting session. I barely felt anything even with my head tipped back and sitting for more than thirty minutes. The work was along cord of personality line. I felt like I was suspended by a huge force of energy that was gently removing the body tension. From 4:45 to 5:45 pm, I did a difficult pelvic rocking session. From 5:50 to 8 pm, I did another long sitting session, which was nice. The amount of tension releasing keeps increasing, its unbelievable how much there is. Energy worked on the twist at the back of the neck. I am belching often and food does not digest well. From 8:20 to 10:30 pm, I blanked out during a growing phase while energy worked the spine from head to tail. The work in the shoulders was difficult.

At 10:40 pm, huge energy builds and I hear a different sound in my head, like a swarm of bees. I feel energy prickles all over and something like 'white energy'. I am going to bed. When I put the sheet over me in bed, I was acutely aware of the feeling as it gradually settled on me. I felt every contact of my skin with the sheet; it seemed to settle on me in slow motion. The feeling sensations were vivid and alive in the body.

Chapter 19: Ligament Snaps, Elastic Body

Energy Circuit: Chin-Sternum, Skull Lifts, Neck & Rib Cage Release

September 15: Loud Breaking Noises With Cranial Bone Separations

I slept long with kriyas and dreams and rose once to stretch. Energy works deeply in skull and neck on the twisted ligament that affects the shoulders. The head feels free, like one thread holds it on the neck. From 7:30 to 8:45 am, energy worked at neck skull line and right TMJ and then there was a big release. I felt the strongest shiver ever a few minutes ago. From 8:15 to 10:15 am, energy wound down neck and spine and there was sacrum and hip work and finally a long hold through back, hip and neck. It was difficult.

From 10:15 am to 12:30 pm, I did a sun session. There was much jaw popping. At end, the shoulder and upper rib cage spread apart with much ligament snapping. This was hard. Then energy moved down spine to mid back and worked on vertebrae there. While I sat in center, energy worked on the neck ligament.

From 2:30 to 4 pm, energy worked in breastbone, TMJ's and shoulders with much loosening of cranial bones. From 4:10 to 5:40 pm, I did lying on back session with skull work. It never ceases to amaze me what still needs to be done. The cranial bones continue to separate with loud breaking and crunching noises. I think they need to fully open like a newborn baby. Most work has been in right side of face with some work on the left TMJ. There was loud popping and it felt like the TMJ joint was breaking apart. Now I know what a loose maxillae and nose feel like. The maxillae, nose and cheekbones now move with other bones by lifting up, out and down in a big arc. I felt the flattening and widening of the skull more pronounced. An energy circuit formed down the front of the neck with the chin right after the maxillae released. Energy works strong now in shoulders and neck.

From 6:45 to 9 pm, there was more skull work. It was painful in area of the right sphenoid wing and on the cord line in the neck. I felt much work on the sutures especially down the lamboid. Several times the skull lifted and adjustments were done 'in the air' to the neck and shoulders. I marvel at the strength now present. From 9 to 10:45 pm, I did a sitting session with acupressure on meridians, with work in right skull. After the acupressure, stretches are much easier. I did some more and fell asleep.

Elastic Skull, Sacrum Suture Opening With Clarinet Tones

September 16: Cracks In Left Skull, Energy Puffs All Over

There were kriyas and strong growing reaction in the night. I woke with much tension in the right hip; it seems the entire body will open. From 7 to 11:30 am, I did a freestyle session to relieve the tension. The stretches pull up from the hip and twist up through the head. I did more sacrum work and twisting upward through spine. There were many skull movements and release of neck ligament after many turns of head from left to right. The skull is like an elastic machine.

From 11:30 am to 1:20 pm, I did a sun session with head, spine and sacrum work with much jaw popping. The sacrum released several times and tones like a clarinet sounded. These tones last a few seconds and are clear and beautiful. Energy also worked through the shoulders.

From 2:30 to 7:30 pm, I did three sessions with sacrum and spine work with pelvis and upper body openings. It was difficult with many bone releases. A huge energy descends now feeling like its making large changes to the body. Then there was much ligament snapping in different patterns in the shoulders. With almost every stretch through the tailbone, my legs feel longer. When I sit, it feels like energy rises from the tailbone although it is moving down.

From 7:30 to 9:45 pm, after the ligament snapping there was a long hold with much pain all over. This never let up and was intense for a long time in the shoulders. Now there are movements in head and neck, which seem shorter and snakier with stretches spaced farther apart. Many times, I heard multiple cracks in the left side of skull. Maybe a suture opened. Then there were energy puffs outs all over my body. There were several sweats and going through different states of consciousness. There is strong swirling energy in root chakra and premenstrual cramps. From 10 pm to 12:30 am, it started with pain in shoulders and a long hold while energy worked in upper back and neck area.

September 17: Cranium Bones Move With Body Stretch

Arising I feel free of tension in hips and spine. I feel a little pain at top of left shoulder and tension in upper right quadrant from scapula and up side of neck to base of skull. From 5:30 to 6:30 am, I did a stretch through that area. I did a spontaneous stretch through skull and it felt like all cranium bones moved with the direction I was stretching. This is amazing!

From 6:30 to 8 am, I did a sitting session with pelvic opening. During the pelvic work, there was a vertical hold then shiver after shiver. I am still shivering. From 8 to 9:10 am, I was lying on stomach with facial bone work and saw my split clearly. I saw the one with the attitude resisting this work and the one performing the work. It is me doing everything. When I sit in center it is easier, if not it is harder. I can either be myself or resist being myself that is the only choice. I laughed hysterically when I saw that. From 9 am to 5 pm, I did four sessions, with much skull work in facial bones and shoulder work. I heard a tone and blanked out one time.

At 6 pm, I did an hour-long freestyle session with body stretches. From 7 to 8 pm, I did a sitting session with pelvic rocking. There is a strong tailbone to skull energy circuit now. Energy worked in area of skull and neck down to shoulders. The bone snapping hurt.

From 8 to 12 pm, there were many big movements at first and a long sitting session with a hold. I am sore now. There was much pain in the left shoulder. I am made of flesh and bone and it takes time to heal. Just before sleep, a huge energy rose from tailbone and traveled up spine to right side of skull and then my head moved spontaneously for about ten minutes. I could not tell what was worked because the energy was so strong.

Moving Of Frontal Bone, Ligament Snapping In All Joints At Once

September 18

I fell asleep to strong energy working in my body, each time it is stronger. I think the spine was worked all night. Several times, I knew I was turning to different positions to release tension. I had many dreams. I am stiff but not sore anywhere. Growing phase still occurs. It is 5 am and crackle sounds are starting all over the skull.

From 6 to 7 am, I started sitting with work in spine with head in held position looking up for a long time. I felt the cranial bones moving and energy moving along the cord of personality. It is difficult to sit with the head like that. At 7 am, the energy moved down with the head relaxed. Just before 8 am, I was on the stomach with around five stretchy pulls through the maxillae. From 8 to 10 am, I did a sun session where energy worked the spine from head to tail.

From 10:45 am to 12 pm, I am so tired that surrender seems my only option. All this time I was on the stomach with movement of facial bones, mandible, maxillae and the frontal bone! This is the first time the frontal bone moved. This was hard, my face is all sore again.

From 12 to 2:30 pm, energy worked while lying, I fell asleep and had dreams. From 2:30 to 3 pm, I feel strong energy moving down and gently snapping ligaments and stretching muscles. From 5 to 6:30 pm, I did a freestyle session the entire time with many movements. Wow, my body feels so strong! The right shoulder, chest and back opened considerably. From 6:30 to 8:30 pm, I did a freestyle session with ligament snapping in the joints all over the body in full surrender. I feel dead. It stopped and a high-pitched tone sounded in my left ear, which lasted a few minutes. From 11:30 pm to 2:15 am, I did a sitting freefall session where I blanked out at end.

September 19: Spontaneous Stretchy Pull Down Both Sides Of Spine

Awakening at 7 am, I feel good with little body tension. It was a restless sleep with many crazy dreams and kriyas while the energy worked in the spine. I feel healing in my right ankle. I did a small stretch and the spine feels strong like it can remove any adhesion. The root chakra energy is strong. I did a lying on the stomach session with skull work, a sun session with tension releases and a freestyle session with many movements in joints and adjustments in skull.

From 12:20 to 2 pm, I did more of the same work on back. The sessions are strong and need much muscle power to do them and I get exhausted. Yet the desire from within to transform is strong so I surrender to the forces. It is hard to do normal activities in comfort. From 4 to 6 pm, I did a difficult sitting session, with long holds with head looking up and work in shoulders.

From 6:30 to 8:30 pm, there was a long growing phase. Near the end energy pulled on both sides of spine from tailbone to skull, it was intense. It was not comfortable to sit while this occurred so I lay down. This lasted about thirty minutes. Then skull work started which seems stronger with larger movements.

From 8:30 to 8:50 pm, the cranium bones separate more and I feel the tugging muscle under the jaw is ready to release. I went a little crazy trying to release the right shoulder because I am desperate to get relief. The ligaments keep loosening and the right chest, right shoulder, hip and sacrum feel like they are opening much. There are many puff outs in the right body now. It seems the sutures are opening wider on both sides of head. From 8:50 to 9:45 pm, the skull continues to open and spine work happens after. At times, I feel pain at once all over and have to change positions. I am sweating most of the night. From 9:45 to 12 pm, there was more skull work while sitting and something released horizontally across the right clavicle toward the shoulder joint. I did more work before I went to sleep.

Elastic Body Pulls, Horizontal Vortex Squeezes Skull

September 20: Energy Vortices In Both Ends Of Spine

It is 5:30 am. I had many dreams and kriyas. From 6 to 8:30 am, I stretched down and it was easy. I feel healing in shoulders on both sides along side of spine. The tailbone movement gets strong. At one moment, there was energy vortices on both ends of spine and it felt like my neck was centered. A new stretchy pull action starts in the body. I feel spinal compression down to tailbone and then a spinal stretch up into head (body pulls). All the joints engage with this action; I especially feel the TMJ's engaging with the hip joints.

From 8:30 to 10:30 am, I did a sun session with mostly skull work. Near the end, I felt a physical vortex encircled my skull horizontally. In front, it went under the cheekbones and above maxillae at intersection of TMJ's. In back, it was between the occipital and parietal bones. It felt like a physical indentation had formed all the way around. Then the ring squeezed in and the right TMJ released. There were more releases in right chest, shoulder, hip and sacrum. There are many energy puff outs now in right side of body. From 11 am to 1 pm, I was lying on back with spine work. It now feels good to surrender body control.

From 1 to 10:30 pm, I did four sessions. Energy worked facial bones, and intensely worked cranial sutures, back of skull and shoulders. Energy worked on the stuck ligament behind neck under the parietals and occipital bone. It hurt while that was done. There were several releases in skull and shoulders and crying.

Sacrum Suture Opening Followed By Cracking Of Vertebrae

September 21

It was the typical sleep with kriyas and dreams. From 9 to 12 am, I did a sun session, which I enjoyed, as it was easy to surrender. All the time energy rose from the tailbone. The spine feels strong. Energy moved groups of muscles on side of neck up to jaw area, and my head turned with strong force. The shoulder released. Energy worked in muscles behind throat and there were strong movements of cranial bones. After tension releases in skull, my head feels hollow.

From 5 to 6 pm, I did a freestyle session. The hips and pelvis are like a powerful machine in the squat. From 6 to 7 pm, I did a meditation outside in chair. From 7 to 9 pm, the sacrum released after constant pressure up spine and on right sacrum. Then energy ripped up the spine with body pressure that opened tissue up to the skull. Then energy went down the spine going around each vertebra and cracking them, which felt good. From 10 pm to 12:30 am, there was skull work and now I am tired.

September 22 - Autumnal Equinox

From 7:30 am to 2 pm, I did continuous sessions with similar work as before while energy worked up and down the spine. It was easy to surrender with little pain and feeling I was strong. From 5 to 5:30 pm, I did a sitting session with pelvic pushing. From 6 to 11:30 pm, I did two sitting sessions with skull work.

September 23: Sitting In Center, Riding On Edge Of Tension, Skull Lifts

From 9 to 11 am, I did a sun session. At first, a strong spiral stretch went ripping up the body moving much tissue for about thirty minutes. It felt like I was being pulled apart. Next, there was skull work. Then energy moved down with simultaneous work in shoulders, right hip and skull, with pressure on twisted cord in right shoulder. The shoulder snapped and released a few times.

From 11 am to 12:30 pm, I did a sitting session. There was strong pelvic rocking with torso rotation and root chakra activation. When I fully let go of body control, it moved madly everywhere. That is how much energy there is now. There is no controlling my body or trying to follow what is going on. It is so fast it drives me to sit in center to ride out the storm.

From 12:30 to 3 pm, I did a torturous laying session. Now I am beat. From 6:30 to 9 pm, I did a sitting session. I quickly went to center and it was easy while stretches happened in the skull and shoulders and skull lifts were going on. There were body pulls too.

From 9 to 10:30 pm, I sit in center while large body movements occur. While surrendered its like I am following a path through the maze of my body's twists and turns. I think what is going on is a transformation of the energy of personality into a body that can be fully aware. A deep spot in skull was worked and the shoulder opens more. My right shoulder is a convoluted mess. There is no way I could figure out how to unravel it, surrender is the only way. Several times tones sounded at once in both ears and after I felt a profound quiet. It is easy to sit in center and endure these changes. I scan for the strongest tension in the body, and relax that area to allow energy to move through it and release tension. I willing do this, because I am greedy for the pleasure I gain as my awareness rises.

From 10:45 pm to 1:30 am, there was a growing phase. Energy works on the stuck ligament behind neck and shoulder. The work is different in that it is very slow.

Insight about riding on edge of tension: when I sit in center, it is like riding along following the edge of tension. The edge of tension is where there is the sensation of pain or pressure in the body. At this edge, I feel the sensation of tension energy releasing and converting to pleasure as rising awareness. I can easily follow it.

Insight about 'I am healing myself': most of the time I've been in the transformation I've felt like a victim, like I'm forced to do this and hoping for a magical instant healing. I have the persistent idea I only need to open one more thing and then the energy of The Creator will heal the rest for me. My split identity dissolves and I feel more unified. I see I am the one doing this healing since the beginning. I did not know who I was, as I was mostly identified with my formed self. The more I transform energy from the personality, the stronger I get. It is beautiful how it works and it makes much sense.

Pelvic Pushes, Body Pulls And Blacking Out

September 24

From 1:30 to 2 am, I did a session before sleep. From 9 to 11 am, I did a sun session, then a strong freestyle session with spontaneous stretches.

From 1:30 to 3:30 pm, I did a sun session and lying on stomach session with spontaneous stretches for about forty minutes. It is difficult to let go of body control when lying on my stomach with facial bone movement. When I am tired, I note I am not surrendered. When I return to surrender state, facial bone adjustments are made that, "I" never would have allowed. The personality quickly learns a new technique, even to the point of pretending to surrender. Hahaha! On the stomach is one of the best positions because it forces you to surrender to distance from the pain. I hate this position, mostly because I do not want to give up control.

From 3:30 to 6:30 pm, there was a long growing phase, then blanking out and coming back to extreme pain in shoulders and upper neck. I took it as long as I could and then lay down for thirty minutes.

From 7 to 9:30 pm, I did a sitting session with opening of sacrum. A big energy ball formed behind neck and skull, that hurt and I could not get relief from it. After this, pelvic pushing started. There were many body pulls with strong pressure filling the entire dura mater. The spinal column feels like one elastic sheet and stretches to the max. I hold my breath and black out while the body pulls happen. I pushed much and worry I will hurt myself. It does something, as the right hip and sacrum released. From 9:30 to 11 pm, there were more pelvic pushes.

September 25

From 7:30 am to 2:30 pm, I did a long sun session and a laying session. My ability to surrender control of body is better. Many times, I was united with the fast movements, feeling I was doing it, liking it, being it and filling with energy. The hip and sacrum opened much on right to where physical rotation of the hips feels good. The time goes by so fast; it is difficult to believe I did this for seven hours. From 6:30 to 9 pm, there was a release in cord behind neck. From 9 to 12 pm, it was a difficult growing phase. There was work in various positions ending with skull work. Much tension released from facial bones with energy filling the skull after.

September 26: Symphonic Inner Sound, Snake Shaped Spiral In Spine

I rose twice and the energy was so strong it felt like gravity was pulling me down. The sleep was uncomfortable with strong growing reaction, especially in the hip. While this went on, I heard beautiful internal sound, like a soft symphony. Waking there is still a strong growing reaction and I am not comfortable. From 8:30 am to 6:30 pm, I did several sessions with skull crunching.

From 7 to 7:30 pm, I did a sitting session with release in right hip. I get tired of writing the same thing. The energy goes up and down and there is work in various areas and positions. Today was difficult, hurting more than usual, the energy is strong and non-relenting. I am constipated, so now I drink more water because of the intense sweating. It is difficult to digest food and I feel nauseous when I eat, which is partly due to the strong pushes and stretches. Higher-self takes over more and I am more willing to do this work and not complain. Now, a strong physical spiral forms in the spine from head to tail. It feels like a big snake when it moves and undulates. I float on that huge energy that rocks my body. From 7:30 pm to midnight, I did three freestyle sessions with spontaneous body movements and crunches.

Fast Spontaneous Body Stretches

September 27: Increasing Awareness

It was difficult to sleep and I rose twice. Awakening, I feel good with not much tension. Sitting, there is a gentle opening of the back of the neck with pops and snaps. I have estimated the number of skull turns so far during the transformation at about two million. From 7:30 am to 1:30 pm, I did three sessions.

From 4 to 5:30 pm, the energy is incredibly strong. I feel like I am being ironed out. When I let go of body control, the speed of spontaneous body movements is incredibly fast. I can tell when I am resisting or pretending to surrender body control, because it is too slow. The personality is an adapter. The head must have been worked a hundred times. A loud tone sounded about thirty minutes ago.

From 6:30 to 8 pm, I did a freestyle session, which I have not done for a while. I let go of body control well while standing but after the squat "ego" took over and I was using the new strong force of the spine to stretch through the bones and muscles. I was wearing myself out in the process. Then I was lying on my back for an hour and my body was being controlled and moved from skull bone movements. From 8 to 11 pm, I did lying and sitting sessions. There were releases in shoulders and cord behind neck. I feel the cord moving around and twisting under the scapula on right.

Insight of ability to surrender gradually increases: The ability to let go of body control increases gradually. While on my back, stretches occurred in directions that I never would have chosen. I have better ability to stay in center, which helps immensely. I see the process of enlightenment right before my eyes.

September 28: Spine Straightening, Fast Spontaneous Spine Stretches

It was difficult to sleep with strong growing reaction. From 8 to 11 am, I did a sun session. It was difficult to get started because my shoulder, head and rib cage ached at the beginning. I kept at it and eventually I enjoyed it. Energy worked on both sides of the spine to straighten it. Then there was a sudden strong movement up the back of the neck through shoulders and over top of head. Afterwards, my skull felt better aligned with the spine.

From 11 to 12 am, I did a sun session with energy working down to hips. From 12 to 2 pm, difficult work continues while lying on stomach and skull work. There was a big crack near top of skull and the right TMJ hurts much.

From 4 to 6:30 pm, there was much pelvic pushing. When I sat there was a strong reaction of spontaneous stretches and crunches going in all directions. I was not sure who was doing it. I did not feel surrendered yet it kept going on for all this time, I guess the split is blurring. When it stopped, tension was gone from the spine. From 6:45 to 8 pm, I did a freestyle session down to squat with opening of hip and sacrum and down to lying on stomach with big releases in skull. The sound from the bones moving and popping is loud. From 8 to 11 pm, I did two rounds on the back. The little tugger muscle released off the outside top of the right shoulder. The last round was painful in the skull.

Insight about the more 'you' give, the more 'YOU' grow: For years, I have wondered how self-realization manifests. Now I understand higher-self IS but self-realization has to be grown, which happens through reorganization of the mind. Each time I quiet the mind-voice, higher-self is there and changes the mind. The change to the mind is later reflected in the body as cells are replaced. Changes are made to the mind to create a body of light. I am creating my new body from my old body.

Energy Circuits Between Joints, Entire Spine Feels Elastic

September 29: Frontal Bone And Maxillae Pull

Sleep was uncomfortable and I rose twice. From 9 to 11:30 am, I did a long sustained surrender in a sun session. Daily I feel stronger and can take more. There were releases in shoulders and skull and a tone sounded. I watched energy circuits form between joints: TMJ to shoulder, shoulder to hip, hip to TMJ, on both sides and opposite sides of body. Now, a spiral of energy goes down from the top of the head to the tail, with the growing reaction like it is removing energy blocks all over. There were perhaps one-thousand head turns, where I can sit quietly and allow it, but lose focus after two hours.

From 11:30 am to 1 pm, I did various lying positions with spontaneous stretches, and then was on the stomach for about an hour. This felt good because it is the only position that can release tension from base of skull and sacrum. With each release, my body flattens and has more contact with the surface I lie on. I also feel increased body relaxation. From 1:30 to 2:30 pm, I was lying on my back with body pulls that felt good and powerful. It seems I am stretching toward perfect spinal alignment. From 4 to 6:30 pm, I did a sitting session with freefall.

From 7:30 to 9 pm, I did a lying session. It seems the entire central nervous system encompassing the spine is forming into a single elastic sheet. The stretches through body at different angles continue. I become more elastic and can move larger bones and tissues. I stopped when energy moved to skull. Then the frontal bone and maxillae were pulled down together in one strong movement, which frightened me when it happened. From 10 to 12 pm, I did a sitting session with body stretches from head to tail. I keep doing too much because of my belief that if I do only one more stretch then I will be done. It is difficult to drop this belief. I need to face the reality that there is much more to go.

Vertebrae Crunches, Ligament Snapping In Face & TMJ's

September 30: Horizontal Bands In Chest, Spine Circuit, Neck Releases

7:30 am: it was a restless sleep. Waking, sheets of energy work upward in my body and there are horizontal bands across my upper chest and shoulders. From 8 to 11:30 am, I did a strong sitting session, with releases in shoulders, skull and neck.

From 12:30 to 3 pm, I did a sitting session with many body pulls. Then I blanked out for a long time. I think an energy circuit formed from tailbone up the spine. From 3 to 5:30

pm, I laid down with skull crunching the entire time. Near the end there was strong crunching of vertebrae down the spine, I thought it would never end. It was a difficult session, I could not drop my attitude of feeling it hurt too much and not wanting more. Once, I made a joke, "Drop the pity-party Betsy, feel joy, oh yeah, feel joy!" Then I did laugh. Something released off the right shoulder and the spine lined up through all the joints.

From 5:30 to 7 pm, I did a freestyle session. While lying, in desperation I took over and wore myself out. I cannot clearly tell the difference between my control and higher-self control of my body. From 7 to 8:20 pm, I was laying on my back with head and shoulder releases. The node behind skull released and there was a release in the adhesion between spine and scapula. After this, energy expanded and I felt a fluffy warm tingling in my legs and lower torso.

From 8:30 to 9:30 pm, the energy is still strong. I did a sitting session with more head and shoulder releases and the tingling feeling persists. From 9:30 to 11:15 pm, I lay down and there was ligament snapping in the TMJ's, and later all the facial bones were popping with them. I wondered if the cord of personality would release from the bottom of spine. **It felt like energy was coming up the spine continuously and the popping in the TMJ's was releasing this energy.** Wow, was that boring and hard to endure and my face is so sore! Eventually it stopped or I quit moving not wanting more. I blanked out and woke later at 12:15 am. It is strange how that ended suddenly. I guess I am in growing phase. My head hurts.

Insight about elastic sheets: My guess is these elastic sheets are the result of increasing enervation of muscles of the body, primarily those directly connected to the central nervous system. I think it is the phenomena of energized fascia, which cover the entire muscular system. With this new capability, different parts of the body can be spontaneously moved. I guess this elastic feeling is what it may feel like physically to be an enlightened being. The energy circuit patterns have formed before but now they manifest physically more near the surface. Perhaps I can review the notes and know what is next on the physical level.

Paired Joint Energy Work, Non-Stop Ligament Snapping In Skull

October 1

I woke at 8 am. It was a restless sleep with many kriyas. There is strong tension in the upper right shoulder quadrant in back. The growing reaction is still strong; I feel no urge to stretch. From 9:30 to 10 am, I did a sun session. There were easy head, shoulder and TMJ stretches. I feel a stretchy pull of muscles along the path from left scapula to right TMJ.

From 10 to 12 am, I did a freestyle session. I think the session last night, which popped apart the facial bones and TMJ's must be a new phase. Energy descends both sides of the body working on the spine. The joints on both sides of the body are worked in various combinations, the right hip with the left shoulder, the right hip with the right shoulder, the right hip with the left TMJ, the left shoulder with the right TMJ, and all other combinations thereof. Now I understand that all joints on both sides of the body will work together. The spine feels like a strong and efficient machine. The movements in the body are fast and there are many releases.

From 12 to 1:30 pm, I did another freestyle session. Wow, the time flew by! From 2 to 3 pm, I did a lying on the back session. The spine feels straight on the right side. While sitting my chest and ribs feel free and loose. From 5 to 8 pm, I did a lying session with body pulls. When I stopped, a rib hurts under my arm. From 9:30 to 11:30 pm, I have been resting since the last session, I am sore. There was an intense period with spontaneous ligament snapping and cracking in skull bones with constant jaw snapping; even more than last night, maybe there were five-thousand of these. From 11:30 pm to 1 am, I continued to stretch and at the end there was a release in sacrum and hip. I just felt a strong shiver with leg elongation.

Squeezing Of Skull

October 2

From 1 to 2:30 am, I stretched until exhaustion then went to sleep. From 10 am to 2 pm, I did a sun session. There was work in tailbone, skull and spine. There was much pelvic pushing with the feeling my skull was squeezed. It felt like the entire body was squeezed. At first, it was difficult to allow this sensation but I kept at it. Soon I could sit in center; it was like holding my breath at first until I relaxed my body and disengaged as the witness. In this state, the body pulls happen spontaneously. I like the body pull because it is effective to open the body. The left side of the occipital bone and left shoulder were worked; I think this is the first time on this side. There was more work in cheekbone and TMJ areas.

From 5:30 to 6 pm, there was a slow tension release and freefall session, it was a nice break. I am still sore from this morning. From 6 to 7:30 pm, I was lying on stomach with facial bone work. It was not hard. I stayed in the sweet spot of the warm and fuzzy feeling even with painful jaw and shoulder work. Repeatedly I went back to that spot if things started to feel like work or painful. I have been zooming in on this spot the last few days wondering why it feels good. Is it that any pain can be taken while there, or is it that because I am one with myself it feels good because I have no resistance? From 11 pm to 1 am, I felt a huge energizing of my body and then skull work started. I think I need a broader perspective of what is going on with this work, when I look too near then I keep getting fooled it's going to end soon. The entire central nervous system is increasingly like a single elastic sheet.

Insight about sexual energy: A vortex of energy builds in the pelvic bowl, which as it speeds up, concentrates around the spine and then moves down to the tailbone. As energy moves to tip of tailbone it energetically twirls and this stimulates the genitals to raise sexual energy. As far as I know, sexual climax from orgasm is the strongest energy the human body can generate. Expressed sexual energy is the spark needed to bring new life into being. Sexual orgasms are inherently part of kundalini transformation because they are the source of new life and are the growth factor.

Flexing Of Tailbone (Tucks), Suffocating Body Sweats

October 3: Energy Works In Stretched Tissue, Both Sides Of Body Worked

From 1 to 4 am, I did a sitting session with tension release and freefall. From 8 to 12 am, I did a sun session with body pulls. It was easy as I have much energy. I feel energy working immediately behind the path of stretched tissue. There were intricate paths worked on both sides of body in shoulders, rib cage, and skull. This seems to be a new stage, with both sides of body now worked in parallel.

From 12:30 to 2:30 pm, I did a freestyle session with lying and rolling around with work on right shoulder, rib cage, hips, and sacrum. Both sides of spine are worked together. From 5:30 to 8:30 pm, I took a break and a loud tone sounded. I do not feel much tension in my neck and skull, which is rare. I did a sitting session with the same work from before from head to tail. From 9:30 to 11:30 pm, the same work continues and I am exhausted and feel desperate. It seems the shoulder and TMJ is so convoluted it will never open. There were many stretches through paths of rib cage, shoulders, hip and skull. The right side of my neck is sore with pimples and rash all over it from the stretches. Tones keep sounding, energy continues to increase and the tailbone and sacrum puff out energetically. The tailbone is drawn toward the anus (tailbone tuck) to straighten it or open vertebrae. The root chakra activity has been light. In the growing phase, I often have suffocating heat and full-body sweat with energetic movement all over the legs and wonder if it is owing to nerve growth. This gets stronger each time. The heat periods are stronger than a menopause hot flash. In the night, I constantly alternate between covering up with blankets and then tearing them off.

Shoulder Energy Circuits, Cervical Spine Work, Sacrum Flex

October 4: Atlas & Occipital Bone Work, Energy Circles Cervical Spine

I slept in until 9:30 am! It was a restless sleep. I go up twice and had high energy in night. From 9:30 to 12 am, I did a sun session. Sitting in center makes it easy. From now on, I will stop if I cannot do that. I think to do fewer concentrated sessions, as this may be more effective.

From 2 to 3 pm, I did an effective lying session. Even though it is work, it feels good to release this tension. From 6:30 to 8 pm, I did a sitting session with stretchy pulls. I feel there is good progress. Energy worked deeply into all parts of the left shoulder and left TMJ, and opened much. After this, there was crisscross energetic activity between and across the two shoulders. Then energy moved toward the center by C7 joint and area of the spine between the scapulae. Next, there were many passes up and down the spine popping the vertebrae and T1 released during this. Then there was a strong stretch down to the end of the tailbone, which now feels close to full extension.

There was much work on upper cervical spine. It was like a slow surgery, rotating the head around in a full circle, while energy worked on the occipital bone and back of the skull near the atlas. I felt the energy rise substantially during this. Then energy went up and down twisting around the neck. I feel the head is clear and I am at the beginning of the big spiral of energy that will form along the spine. The base of the skull at the atlas now feels open. I felt neural growth near the end and the stretch reflex stopped so I wait.

From 8:30 to 10:30 pm, I did a lying on the stomach session with skull and sacrum work. My lower back arched with sacrum and hip articulation (sacrum flex), a first for this. It feels close to the skull aligning straight with the spine. I am going to bed early.

Insight about new body: I think when our vibration and awareness level is high enough then kundalini transformation triggers from activation of switches in our DNA. I think all human bodies will react more of less the same way. The DNA program exists and the instructions to grow the new body will activate once the conditions are right.

Manifesting as higher-self in the physical body is a learning process. We can move our body but higher-self is not moving, rather it is a programmed physical reaction coming from our central nervous system. My body is reacting and moving and I thought by being harmonious with that movement, then I was moving as higher-self. However, that was not quite right. When my body is reacting and I accept the reaction, then I am one with the reaction with no resistance and I have done an act of being aware. The kundalini transformation is the field where I learn how to surrender control to my higher-self and the more I do that the more I grow. The reaction will eventually stop and having gone through the process, I will then have the result of full awareness in the body.

Vision of being a man: During a short hold in a session, I had an image of myself as a tall thin man with wild light colored hair. In this vision, I saw myself as this person and was acting as them. Coming back to stretching it dawned on me that I was seeing myself as another person and it was male. The hair was like mine, gnarled like a bird's nest. Was it a dream, a past life, or an omen?

October 5: Shoulders Worked With TMJ's, T1 Pop, Shoulder Release

From 2 to 4 am, I did a sitting stretch down through spine. It was difficult because I had to keep pointing my body at different angles, not what a sleepy person wants to do. Energy popped all vertebrae in each direction from top to bottom. The T1 and C7 vertebrae were worked intensely. After this, I lay down and was turning to find comfortable positions where tension and leverage was used to open adhesions. Lastly, I did a lying on the stomach session for about an hour. From 9 am to 1 pm, I did a sitting session outside with good surrender. There were a few large movements of the skull and tailbone. The skull movements are intense.

From 2 to 3 pm, I did a lying session. There were big cracks in skull on right and the right jaw and neck is sore. From 6 to 8:30 pm, I did a freestyle session that was not going well, so I switched to a sitting session. From 8:30 to 10 pm, there was a strong growing reaction. Energy was slowly going back and forth through the TMJ and shoulder on right in many directions and opening adhesions. There was work of left shoulder with right shoulder and both shoulders with the TMJ's. There was a loud pop on the T1 vertebrae. After this, there was a release in the shoulder crook and on lower edge of right occipital bone. Energy was moving down the spine when I arose. It feels open in the TMJ, neck and shoulder. From 10 pm to 1 am, I sat while energy worked and blanked out when energy worked in spine.

Vertebrae & Rib Cage Ligament Snapping

October 6: Release In Left Side Of Neck With TMJ, Tones

From 8 to 9 am, I did a freestyle session, with work on right shoulder and C7. From 9 am to 1:30 pm, I did a sun session where work was mainly on spine. It was easy to stay surrendered. From 1:30 to 7 pm, I took a long break! It is the longest I have taken in a long time. It felt good without much tension building.

From 7 to 9 pm, the session was different. Energy started at top and worked down, with popping in vertebrae, snapping each with a twist. Simultaneously, the corresponding ribs in front were worked along the sternum. Perhaps it was loosening all the ribs and other attachments of muscles to the spine. It was popping and snapping all over which did not hurt at all. Next, I felt intense expansion of energy in sacrum and tailbone area and an elastic sheet moved up the spine over the skull.

After this, body pulls started in succession. There were many strong pelvic pushes, which were intense but did not hurt. There were many releases in rib cage, spine, sacrum and neck and much stretching of cranium bones, more than I thought I still needed.[69] I sense the tailbone is not fully open. The energy is high. I am not tired but would welcome a freefall session. From 9:20 pm to 12:15 am, it was more of the same work, this time in slow motion. It was not pleasant. At the end, the shoulder was near to release.

Neuron Growth Immediately In Stretched Tissue

October 7

I awoke at 8 am after a long sleep. I have much neck tension. From 8:30 to 10 am, I did a slow and easy sun session. I feel energy work along main cord path. From 11:30 am to 2 pm, I did a freestyle session. I grow stronger and can barely feel the larger movements. The reaction of new neuron growth occurs immediately in the stretched tissue. That is distinct. The squat was strange, I could barely feel my body at all and a deep blue light filled my 3rd eye. Energy worked on the main cord path down the back.

From 2 to 3 pm, I did a lying on the stomach session. From 5 to 6:45 pm, I did a lying on the back session. It is amazing how much the energy has grown from this morning. Energy moves vertebrae and works in the shoulders. Everything in the body is worked as one unit now, with energy moving up and down the spine. The ability to clear energy blocks is greater, and the transformation goes faster. From 7 to 8 pm, I did a lying on the stomach session, I am not superwoman after all and I need a break! From 8 to 10 pm, I did a sitting session until I could not move my jaws anymore. There were many passes through the body zigzagging everywhere. The C7 area feels loose.

October 8: Intensity Of Skull Work Goes Up A Notch

I slept almost ten hours! From 9:30 am to 2:30 pm, I did a sun session with many bone movements, which were difficult at first until I remembered to relax. Even after I relaxed, it was difficult until there were some releases. After the releases, it was easier to surrender and allow work to go on in ribs, spine, skull and sacrum. The sacrum opens more.

---

[69] It is easy to see here how the body prepares for the stretch, as vertebrae and ribs are loosened before hand, then the fascia sheets energize, then the spontaneous pulling stretch happens with many releases.

From 5 to 7:30 pm, I was sitting outside after having done a few strong pelvic pushes. The pushes felt different and stronger but did not hurt. Then I heard a loud tone and felt energy rising. I came in, did some freestyle movements and ended with lying on my stomach. From 9 to 11 pm, it is difficult to get started as my shoulder and jaws are sore. There were different energetic paths of work, mostly on the right side. The stuck muscles across the shoulder and down the back of the neck have been snapping all day. All day, there is much activity in the tailbone with many openings there. I just finished an intense round in the head different from all other sessions. The skull bones were separating and moving and then my skull moved over a notch with a strong move at the end. It was difficult. It has been difficult all day. I have been crying, sweating much, and am sore in many places. I am tired and wonder how much is left.

October 9: Increased Vibration, Galaxy View, Bliss Feeling

I arose at 8 am and slept long with many dreams. There is tension in neck. Another month has flown by. From 8:30 to 9:30 am, I did a sun session. It is unbelievable how strong I am, sitting and barely feeling anything as if I have an epidural all over. During the sitting session, strong adjustments were done to the skull, shoulder, back and hip, all along the main cord path. My mind is active yakking away, but still the healing goes on.

From 9:30 to 11:30 am, it was fantastic! The growing reaction continues winding its way down the spine, working much in the shoulders and T1 vertebrae area. Energy works in one place then goes to another and makes a connection. For example, I feel adjustment in a vertebra, then in shoulders, TMJ and skull. The sacrum opens easily. I can sit in center and allow strong bone movements that would hurt without this strong energy. It was pleasant.

From 11:30 am to 1:30 pm, it was the same stuff. Energy moved up the spine to the skull for another round working at deepest level of the bones. There were many big cracks in lower part of skull on right and then moving down to shoulders. It was painful so I stopped. From 5 to 8 pm, strong work continued and was easy until it worked in shoulders.

I am amazed by what is occurring. How is it possible that my skeletal frame can correct so quickly? The body twist I had a week ago is gone since bones released in rib cage and spine. After a few hours, all pain is gone and it is healed. Can nerves do this? At this accelerated rate, I think it can finish soon. I long to see the result. Will something even more amazing happen, when this huge energy is no longer occupied with moving my muscles and bones around?

From 10 pm to 12:30 am, I sank into a growing phase with pressure on shoulder crook. I laid down because it was hard to endure while sitting. Just before this, I was sinking into a pleasant warm tingly sensation, while difficult work occurred. The energy continues to rise.

Energy Circuit Connects Left & Right Spine Over Coronal Suture

October 10: Energy Work Between Right Skull & Sacrum, Dolphin Music

I rose at 9:30 am and slept in late again! It is difficult to start because there is much tension. From 9:30 am to 3:30 pm, it went so well that I kept it up for six hours. At the end, a spinal alignment occurred in the skull. Favorite sayings lately: resistance is futile, you want this, you are doing this, surrender, you do not have to do anything, shut up Betsy and finally relax. If I can relax, it is like floating in the Milky Way with a warm and fuzzy feeling. I guess this is what they call bliss.

From 4:30 to 6 pm, I did a lying session and the head opens more. It seems the sacrum needs to open more on right side. From 6:15 to 7:45 pm, I did a sitting session with skull and shoulder work. I made much progress, but there is much more to do. There were several strong crunches in right lower skull in back, by TMJ, jaw, neck and shoulder. I wonder if these snapping and crunching sounds are popping of ligaments.

From 7:50 to 9:45 pm, it was a difficult lying on the stomach session. There was work lining up the energy points of the sacrum on right with head on right. There was a strong twisting energy going up the spine to the left. There was much ligament snapping in skull, with jaws popping and pelvic rocking. I was sweating strongly. I tried hard to sit in center, but it was difficult with the pain and pressure.

From 9:50 to 11:30 pm, I did a sitting session with much crunching in right skull. Near the end, a circle formed across coronal suture, down sides of head and under jaw.[70] I fell asleep to awesome music of dolphins singing. My entire body was warm and tingly.

---

[70] From the notes, it appears this circuit connected the right and left energy circuits of the spine, in a loop over the top of skull. A long growing phase follows, with energy working down both sides of spine at once.

Excruciating Pain In Sacrum And Hip

October 11

I awoke at 7 am and had a restless sleep. There is strong tension in right sacrum and skull. An energy circuit forms between the two ends of spine and pulls on both sides. Yesterday there were stretchy pulls up right side of spine where it felt to be in a straight line.

From 9:30 am to 2:30 pm, I did several sessions that were difficult near the end. The entire time the hip and sacrum area hurt. I think a twist in the spine is near to release, so there is strong tension on these areas. I can barely walk. The head and shoulders released. I did strong painful spinal stretches with sweating. The hip pain is excruciating right now.

At 7 pm, I went out and walked and did some work, with constant excruciating pain in sacrum and hip. I had no idea how to deal with it. When I returned I was all prepared for a killer freestyle session but was tipped over and a growing phase started. I felt energy zooming around the hip, lower back, abdomen and rib cage in front. It was not comfortable but there was nothing to do but allow it. That surprised me. I hope I can rest.

From 7 to 8:30 pm, I am in a difficult stage. The energy continues to work on the hip and now it works in the skull. It is strange to feel the bones move around without me stretching. There is some pain but it is not too bad. There is much body heat and sweating. The energy in the legs feels different like its cool and ironing everything out. From 8:30 to 10:45 pm, intense pain continues in the hip. In the last hour, the focus shifted to hard work in shoulders and spine with many crunches and large releases. I feel some relief in the hip. From 11 pm to 1 am, it was mostly shoulder and spine crunching. The hip still hurts.

October 12: Tender Ovaries, Root Chakra Swirling, Release In Hip

I awoke at 6 am. It was a long night. Energy still works in the hip and it holds much tension. Last night a loud tone sounded with a short flash in my brain as it passed through. There was much work in the shoulder and TMJ. From 9:30 am to 12:30 pm, I did a sitting session outside in the sun with much shoulder and spine work. I have appointments outside.

At 7 pm, growing phase continues. I feel work on my sacrum, left hip, right ankle, right skull and left and right shoulders. I have uterine cramps and the ovaries are tender. There are many energy whorls in the vulva. The hip finally feels better. From 7 to 9:30 pm, I did two sessions with work concentrated in head and shoulders. From 9:30 to 11 pm, I did a freestyle session with powerful hip work and it straightened much. I feel totaled. I just felt a big shiver. I feel much more power moving the body versus sitting. I am good at letting go of body control and allowing spontaneous movements in various positions. At the end I was in a hold lying on my stomach while energy worked strongly on right hip and sacrum

Extreme Skull Pressure, Energy Working Both Sides Of Spine

October 13: Spiral Of Energy Presses On Base Of Skull, Elastic Skull

I woke at 5:30 am. I feel rested and slept well. A strong energy spiral rises up spine and presses on the skull. From 6 to 6:30 am, I did a freestyle session and there was a release in skull and sacrum. The hip and back feel much better and I feel energetic. From 6:30 to 9 am, I did a freestyle session ending with lying on stomach. From 11:30 am to 2 pm, I did a sitting session outside with head, shoulder and lower spine work.

From 6 to 10 pm, I did two sessions. The second was difficult. The work in the skull felt different as if it was widening or opening the skull. Many times, it felt like my head was squeezed or held in a vice. It was not painful only there was strong pressure. From 10 to 10:30 pm, the adjustments feel different in that I feel strong work occurring in the body as energy descends. Energy just worked strongly on the twisted muscles in the shoulder crook. Energy works down both sides of the spine at once and then comes up to do parallel TMJ adjustments from back of neck to front. It is like lifting the joints together and rotating them from back to front. My head feels elastic and the cranium bones moving fluidly. From 10:30 to 11:30 pm, I did more of the same. I am tired.

Constant TMJ Pops, Sacrum & Skull Pressure, OBE With Alien Being

October 14: Strong Body Stretches & Skull Work

I woke with tension in the entire skeletal frame. I feel bent. From 8:30 to 11:30 am, I did a sun session with work on spine.

From 3:30 to 5 pm, I did a lying session and from 6 to 7 pm, I did a sitting session. In the latter session, it felt like I was sitting on an energy ball with strong energy streaming up the spine from the tailbone while I was stretched with it. There were big releases in lower skull and right of neck with loud crunches. It surprised me there is this much left to open.

From 7 to 8:30 pm, I did a laying on stomach session with many more skull bone movements and much sweating the entire time. The skull work was on the frontal bone, the TMJ's and temporal bones. The entire spine was worked with many tailbone tucks and spontaneous undulating stretches along the spine. It was difficult, now my head hurts.

From 11 pm to 2:15 am, it was a long session with many skull crunches and the jaw popped much, it was maddening. After this settled there was a long period of strong energy swirling with extreme pressure on right sacrum and skull at TMJ. The pain was so intense that I must have gone out of body.

Then I felt an outside help. Something was pulling at my shoulders, neck and head, all over me. A little bit later, I sensed it was a person. I felt they were trying to kill me and I tried to strangle it and had a hold of the neck. I know I was not moving yet I had my hands around the neck of this person. I distinctly know I felt it. When I felt the skinny elastic neck then I remembered the encounter of the alien being from last year when I went out of body. When I recognized what was going on I stopped struggling and I silently voiced, "Help me and thank you". After this, there was more help. Then I lay there for a while and could not move. There was a huge loud clear tone, which sounded near the end.

My thoughts near the end were strange because it was impossible while in the midst of this pain I had drifted off into a dream. I think I had an experience in a non-physical dimension and met another kind of being. I cannot remember it well. Perhaps when there is intense physical pain you leave your body. That is what I did before when I encountered the same elastic-like being. Perhaps the being arrived again for the same purpose, to help me stay near my body so I could return to it when the extreme pain had passed. This experience is amazing; it tells me there is much I do not know.

The common factor of these two experiences is I was intensely focused on complete surrender. The other time I was lying in meditation trying to go as deep as possible, wanting badly to surrender so I could awaken. Last night the pain in the sacrum was excruciating, so I intensely wanted to distance from the pain. I guess it is a capability to go out of body. It is interesting to know I can have experiences like seeing, feeling and hearing while out of body. I always believed I needed a body to do that. I wonder who this person is, that is ready to help me exactly when I need them. I think it has to be an advanced being perhaps having evolved to a consciousness that does not need a physical body.[71]

Sacrum Release, All Skull Bones Move At Once, Twenty-Minute Tone

October 15: Sacrum Pain, Ligament Snaps In Sternum & Spine

I awoke at 7 am. I am stiff. The energy still works along the spine near the scapulas and neck. From 8 am to 1:30 pm, I did a sitting stretch and felt a growing reaction in the spine. The entire day I want to go out of body to escape the intense pain in the sacrum and skull pain.

From 1:30 to 2 pm, I did a freestyle session. It seems I have to work on the sacrum, it hurts when I do it, but it hurts more if I do not. From 5 to 6 pm, the pain makes me desperate. I tried many ways to stretch my body to get leverage and open the sacrum. Finally, there was a release in the sacrum and it feels good for the moment.

From 9 to 10:30 pm, I had a long break with a growing phase. Then I did a freestyle session where there was much snapping of ligaments in ribs at sternum and spine.[72] Then the energy worked in right TMJ and the top of shoulder twist. There is a strange movement when my jaw is stretched toward the tip of my shoulder and it seems they are tied together in the stretch. Energy works to release some muscle connection between the two.

There were some strong elastic stretches along the sides of the head through the shoulders and TMJ's. I do not recall this occurring before. A couple of times I felt all the skull bones adjusting to new positions spontaneously. I have been noticing this over the last days and feel a strong headache when this happens. From 10:30 to 11:30 pm, I did a sitting session with more head and shoulder work. A loud high-pitched tone sounded for about twenty minutes. This has been the longest tone so far.

October 16: Letting Go Of Fear Of Hurting Myself, Tones Sounding

I arose at 7 am, it was a restless sleep and I rose twice. Like yesterday, my entire frame feels bent along the spine and is uncomfortable. I had to stretch immediately. From 7 to 8 am, I did a freestyle session ripping through the muscles. I am not comfortable with the idea I can stretch and pull my body apart like this. I have the fear I will hurt myself. Noticing my fear, I let it go and went with the powerful pulls and stretches. I heard many snaps as

---

[71] I think I am becoming elasticized in this transformation, so perhaps this being is the next life form.

[72] The sequence starting here is nearly identical to that starting on October 6th that ends when the sacrum releases. It is interesting to see the repetition and quicker pass through the second time.

ligaments and bones popped and I did not hurt myself. It seems the big tension in the spine released. From 8 to 12 am, I did sitting and lying sessions, wow, everything opens.

From 12 to 1 pm, I did a sitting session and my right shoulder is quite sore now. From 5:45 to 7:30 pm, it is going good lying and allowing this pulling, twisting, stretching and crunching. The shoulder releases more as well everything else. Tones are sounding again. My hair is a disaster; it is funny to see it sticking out at every angle. From 7:30 to 11:30 pm, I did two lying on stomach sessions mostly with skull work. The area worked in neck at shoulders goes deep to the bone. It is strange to have no tension in areas where the old knots dissolve.

October 17: Pain In Background, Brain Flashes, Burning Muscle

I awoke at 7 am, and my head is tilted to the left. I did a few stretches and the tension released. From 8 to 9 am, I did a freestyle session down to squat and sitting. Wow, my body is powerful! There was no strong crunching, loud noises or pain. I barely felt my body. While standing with eyes closed, immediately brain flashes blanked out my mind with the galaxy view. This happened many times during the hour. I felt energy work in neck, shoulders and spine and heard little snaps and pops. My body felt like it was smoothing out and I was moving slowly with ease. Once, I felt intense burning in my left shoulder yet it was not painful. I experienced NO PAIN, even though this session was the most intense so far! I guess the nervous system vastly changed after the neck opened.

From 1 to 2:30 pm, I did a freestyle session. It started easy like floating on an energy wave, but was difficult near the end. I am tired. These body movements are foreign, it is hard to get used to them. From 6 to 7 pm, I did a lying session with head and shoulder crunching. From 8 to 10 pm, there was much work in neck, TMJ and shoulder. The work gets harder as the day progresses.

October 18: Sprinkles On Face

I awoke at 8:30 am. I slept long and have little tension. From 8:30 to 10:30 am, I did gentle stretches in a sun session. From 1:30 to 2:30 pm, I did a freestyle session with strong work on spine. From 6 to 7:30 pm, I did a freestyle session, stretching compressed area on right. I surrendered well. I keep feeling sprinkles on my face in the last weeks even when I am not working out. From 9 to 11 pm, I did a lying session on stomach. I fell asleep in that position during a hold. I awoke at 3 am, and went to bed.

Sacrum Suture Fully Opens

October 19: Opening In Skull With Squishy Sound, Tailbone Tucks

In the night, I had pain in my right hip joint. I woke at 8:30 am, and had to stretch immediately. I did a freestyle stretch for thirty minutes. A tone sounded about halfway through and the sacrum opened more. I am aware of my thinking and can watch it with crystal clarity. From 9 am to 3 pm, I did continuous sessions wanting to move this along faster. Near the end of the last session, there was a big opening in the back of the head with a squishy sound.

From 6 to 8 pm, there was strong pulling, stretching and popping in the body and the sacrum opened on right. The suture feels open down to the tailbone. The sacrum almost pulls together at the center tucking in the tailbone. From 8 to 10 pm, I was in a freefall with tailbone energy rising up the spine. There were strong holds in the freefall with tension pain in head and shoulders. I feel it was good work.

Chapter 20: Burning Lines, Skull Sides Open

October 20: Crack In Sphenoid Wing, Pulling Apart Right Shoulder

I awoke with much tension and did a freestyle session from 1 to 2 am. The stretches were strong and elastic covering the entire spine and going up and over my skull and were moving my skull over a notch. After this, I went to sleep and woke at 7:30 am. I feel stiff in the spine and bent to one side. From 8:30 am to 2 pm, I did various sessions and there was much work in lower right skull, mandible and back of skull. There was one big crack, opening right side of skull by sphenoid wing, work in upper rib cage, clavicles and much work down spine by right scapula. I feel almost dead.

From 7 to 8 pm, it was an intense session pulling apart right shoulder with lower skull and mandible. Loud tones sounded twice, I think good progress was made to open that area. At the end, I was lying on stomach. From 10 to 11 pm, I did another strong session. It is amazing I did not feel sore from the last one. I fell asleep in a hold until 12:30 am. The energy was strong during the hold going all over the body at fast speed.

October 21

I did a session from 8 to 9 am. The energy is strong. I feel strong elastic stretches down the spine on right side connecting head to hip and stretching the area on right of torso between TMJ, shoulder and hip. Starting was easy and pleasurable, like being supported by a huge wave of energy and effortlessly moving with no crunching. Strong energy filled my body and I felt buoyant with waves of pleasurable feelings. The freefall energy goes through same path as what was stretched prior. From 9:30 to 11:30 am, I did a sun session, mostly with spine work.

From 12 to 1 pm, I did a freestyle session down to lying with long stretches through spine and I felt large movement of bones. It seems energy works deeper, directly on structural problems in the bones. From 6 to 8 pm, I did a session with strong energy working in shoulder, and up and down the spine. From 8 to 12 pm, I did continuous sessions until I was exhausted.

Ten-Thousand Skull Turns, Elastic Sheet Over Skull

October 22

From 8 to 9 am, I did a freestyle session, down to squat and from 9 to 10 am I did a sitting session outside. The cycle between work on skull and tailbone is about five minutes. From 12:30 am to 3 pm, I did a sitting session. From 5:30 to 7:30 pm, I did a sitting session with many crunches in the shoulder and up right side of skull. The work went deep into the shoulder and was somewhat painful when muscles released. I am sore. At 9:30 pm, the growing phase starts. When I rose from lying, I was bent and it was difficult to rise. The last workout was difficult. From 10 to 11 pm, I did a difficult lying on the stomach session. There were about ten-thousand continuous skull turns, which seemed to move the cranium bones over. Tension increases on sacrum, I do not want more.

October 23

From 5:30 am to 11 pm, I did six different sessions. The long muscles are connecting and the energy keeps rising. There was difficult work in skull and spine with fast movements of body. I went to bed at 11 pm.

October 24: Twisting Spine Stretches, Elastic Skull, Many Skull Turns

I woke twice in the night. Rising at 8:30 am, there is strong tension. From 9 to 10 am, I did a sun session. It was difficult. Energy worked in the shoulder girdle and right rib cage area from sacrum to right shoulder. There were long stretches along the cord of personality. There are twisting stretches pulling up spine, neck and head. From 10 am to 2 pm, I did continuous sessions, which were easier than this morning. I worked harder to focus on the body vibration, which makes it easier. I was surprised with strong crunches in vertebrae starting at the shoulder crook and going up the neck. I had no idea there was that much adhesion left in there. Much energy released and afterward, strong energy worked across the shoulders.

I took too long a break and now body tension is unbearable. From 7 to 8:30 pm, I did a lying on the stomach session. There were many skull turns to the left like an elastic sheet stretching across my skull repeatedly, moving the bones very slowly. Eventually something lined up behind neck and then energy strongly opened tissues on the right. Then my body flooded with warm and fuzzy energy. Once, the cranium bones in right skull were moving with a big energy ball while I turned my head. It felt weird. I had to go to deep surrender to endure it. At the end, I relaxed in a growing phase for about ten minutes.

October 25: Squishy Cracks Behind Skull By Atlas & Jaw

I slept long and had many dreams and kriyas. I awoke at 9 am, and did five minutes of stretches to relieve neck tension. From 10 to 11:30 am, I did an easy sun session with strong stretches opening the skull, shoulders and back. There were several squishy cracks behind skull by spine on right and in mandible area. Afterward, it felt like the back released and energy works there. So far, there is no pain. I did another sitting session outside from 12 am to 3 pm, with more work in skull and shoulders.

I did a lying session from 6 to 8 pm, on side and on stomach. There was skull turning like last night but today it is a continuous elastic sheet around the skull. When I was on the stomach, there was a long hold and I kept at it and then high heat developed and I felt I would pass out. I think energy worked in the skull because after the hold there were cracks in the mandible. From 8 to 10 pm, I did another lying on the stomach session then went into a hold and fell asleep. Two tones sounded during this session.

I feel sad because I know everyone in my family thinks I am crazy and I am without support. I have no idea what is occurring or how long this will continue. I am getting tired of this routine. I want to do something else but the strong tension leads me to keep doing these sessions to get relief and feel better. It has been nearly a year since this started. I wonder if I can take another year of this.

Ligament Popping In Spine, Rib Cage, Shoulders And Jaws

October 26: Getting Up In Night, Many Skull Turns, Strong Leg Activation

It is difficult to tell when morning starts as I rise every few hours to stretch. There is much energy moving in the body and I am thirsty I guess from sweating. From 3 to 4:30 am, I did various sessions, there was pulling on both sides of the spine up through the skull, many crunches in shoulder, skull work and work by T1 vertebrae. A muscle across the top back of the shoulder girdle moved around painfully. There is much burning and sweat in the skin in the side of the shoulder crook. My hair is totaled on all sides. I slept and then awoke and had to stretch immediately. I did a session from 9 to 10:30 am. I felt some pain in the upper right front skull when I started.

The freestyle session felt different in that stretches went up the spine on both sides extending up through the skull, I felt it in the long muscles running vertically on the back. Then I did a lying session with snapping of ligaments in vertebra, ribs, shoulder and TMJ's, stronger than I have felt this before. It felt good but was tiring. Short holds occurred between the fast movements. From 10:30 to 11:30 am, I did more of the same sitting outside in the sun.

From 12 to 1 pm, I did a freestyle session. There were powerful stretches up back and into shoulder, which felt good to do them. From 6:30 to 9:30 pm, I did various sessions. My entire body is stretched with energy going through all the flesh and bones. The majority of the movements are long vertical elastic stretches through the body often with a spinal twist that creates a force on areas of the back or ribs to open them. I understand this is another phase, there are probably many more to pass through. Lying on the stomach, there were five-thousand more skull turns where the elastic sheet feels more continuous. It stretches the skin and moves the cranium bones slowly. I have a rash on the right side of my neck again. I felt pain in the upper right front of the skull. During holds, my legs activate strongly especially the right one.

Insight about fading mind-chatter I often stop the mind-chatter. I will see I am chattering and recognize the activity as desperate, futile and senseless. Then I quickly stop it and go back to quiet mind. Mind-chatter is no longer the main show.

Both Sides Of Neck Release

October 27: Energy Ball Moves Down Neck With Burning Trail

It was a restless sleep. I awoke at 6 am, with some tension along the spine mostly in the shoulder crook. Growing phase still occurs. From 7 to 9 am, I did a short sitting session then lying on my left side. Notable was a twisting and pulling stretch encircling the cervical spine down to tops of shoulders with work in muscles across shoulder tops over to the spine. There was slow movement of all cranium bones to the left, with gliding elastic stretches. I felt the cervical spine moving closer to line up vertically with the rest of the spine. There was a simultaneous stretch horizontally across lower back and head, both to the left. As the neck moved closer to vertical alignment, there was pain in the sacrum. There were a few crunchy sounds behind neck and a hold of about ten minutes.

After this, there were a few head stretches and TMJ adjustments then another hold of ten minutes. During the holds, energy zoomed around the body forming neural connections. I can detect this with my inner eye as flashes of energy similar to a supernova. Usually when energy moves in the body it is a predictable pattern. When neurons fire rapidly, I detect energetic flashes in bursts occurring all over my body. I have been observing this a long time but forgot to write it down.[73] Different was a burning sensation in skull areas and left maxillae. Cranium bones repositioned without skull movement, only the TMJ moved.

From 9 to 10 am, I did another session and the right neck released. Then I felt an energy ball moving through the flesh with a burning trail behind it. Energy worked deeply in right shoulder crook more toward the back. The right sacrum is painful and I have uterine cramps. From 10 to 11 am, I did a sun session. From 11:30 am to 12:30 pm, I did a lying session, with mostly holds.

From 2 to 3 pm, I did a strong sun session. The neck released on the left with a brain flash and a loud long tone. From 4:45 to 6 pm, tension energy releases from my entire body with gentle stretches. The TMJ's adjust with big lifts of the jaws. There are strong crunches in right skull and shoulder crook and the T1 vertebrae opened. From 6:45 to 8 pm, I did a lying on the stomach session with much skull turning and after that, I rested. When I tried to rise at 9:30 pm, it was difficult because I was stiff with the growing reaction. I have sacrum pain and uterine cramps and the head, neck and shoulders hurt. I went to bed early.

Burning Lines In Neck, Skull Feels Like Bag Of Bones

October 28

It was a restless sleep with kriyas and getting up a few times to stretch into painful area by sphenoid wing in right skull. Arising at 5 am, there is much neck tension. My nose runs, I am cold and feel strong swirling energy in the root chakra. From 10 to 11:30 am, I did a sun session.

---

[73] This may have started on September 1st, from the notes I cannot tell for sure.

From 11:30 am to 12:30 pm, I did a lying session. First energy worked deeply in the upper front of skull and right cheekbone with intense pain. Then I recalled what I wrote about pain a few days ago, that it is a sign of healing so I allowed it. There were strong crunches and stretches in the skull with all skull plates moving together in a ratcheting and popping action. I felt much tension energy release from the skull. Then there was strong stretching of back muscles in various directions with spinal twists across backs of shoulders, neck and the back. I felt the lower body connect with the skull, and both stretched as one elastic sheet covering the entire central nervous system.

From 1:30 to 3 pm, I did a sitting session. From 5:30 to 6 pm, I sent long-distance Reiki to a sick cat. Long breaks are difficult, because when I return I have too much tension. The upper right front skull and TMJ still hurts. It is difficult to stop the energy. From 6:30 pm to 12:30 am, I did two sitting sessions and one lying session. In a sitting session, energy worked on the sternocleidomastoid muscle, on side of neck and across back of shoulder girdle. The flesh repeatedly burned as twists of energy pulled through the muscle. Before I only felt burning in my neck. It feels like being burned with a hot coal, but on a very thin line that runs through the muscle. Later in the lying session, my head opened. After this, my head hurt and felt strange like it was lying on a pile of rocks even though I had a pillow. The skull bone movements were so strong that my head no longer felt cushioned by flesh anywhere. After that, there are stretches up the trapezious and back of head.

October 29: Lower Back Flexible, Increased Vibration, Tailbone Tucks

When I rose, I felt increased flexibility horizontally across my lower back. It bends more now. I did lying and sitting sessions from 6:30 to 8:30 am, which were difficult. There were many releases in shoulder and skull and the spine twist is less. There were long powerful body stretches in various directions opening the spine, rib cage, hips and sacrum. My energy keeps increasing. Just when I think, I have run out of energy and cannot do more, energy increases greatly after a release. There was burning on neck muscles and pain in cheekbone and sphenoid wing, but not as bad as yesterday. The sacrum hurt much but deeply surrendered I endured it. The tailbone tuck feels close to center, which feels good. Lately, the hips and sacrum engage more in the stretches. From 8:30 to 11:30 am, I did a sun session.

I took a nap from 12:30 to 1:30 pm, and from 5 to 6:30 pm, I did sitting and lying sessions. There were more burning lines in neck muscles and across shoulder. The work goes deeper. The shoulder crook is deeply stuck by spine, rib, and under scapula at back. From 6:30 to 8 pm, I did two sessions, sitting and lying on stomach. I rose when a hold established.

Crisscross Energy Pattern On Shoulder & Neck Vertebrae

October 30: Extreme Tension In Sacrum & Skull, Elastic Vortex Stretch

It was the usual restless sleep. From 5 to 7 am, I did sitting and lying sessions. It was difficult to start because I had extreme tension on both ends of spine in skull and sacrum. First energy worked in muscle at side of neck and across shoulder back. Apparently, it released because the burning pain and twist went away. Then the body feeling changed and energy worked a long time going back and forth over the back and front of shoulder girdle. After this, the upper back felt elastic and continuous with the skull and neck. Then strong elastic stretches ensued stretching the entire spine and skull with no popping. Quite often, I felt intense brief pain near the right cheekbone when the energy stretched into the skull. Later there was tension on the sacrum with painful work in the left hip in the line to the right TMJ. The entire body was involved with stretching and pulling from sacrum to skull. It was difficult.

From 7 to 8 am, I did a sitting session with elastic stretches popping apart bones in ribs, spine and shoulders. I am held in various twisted positions to gain leverage to open certain areas. Then I am stretched in all directions, opening the area with popping sounds as bones or ligaments moves. Primarily this occurred in the right side of torso, right hip, rib cage, spine and shoulder. Energy was rising from the tailbone in a vortex shape mostly confined to right body. The sweating and heat is suffocating. The prickly raindrop feeling on my face happens so often I do not record it anymore. I know when a skull adjustment is coming because the sweat droplets precede that movement. Strong shivers have occurred about five times that cool the body. The last session was physically difficult, but it felt good too.

The energy does not let up. From 8 to 10 am, I did a lying session. I did a total surrender to the strong body pulls, as there was no other way to endure it. Starting out, energy worked in right skull that hurt much while this area was stretched open. Next there was work in my right shoulder and my head moved dramatically. It felt like tight tendons were holding the shoulder and head in a tilted position. When this loosened, it felt like fine cords of bone moving and snapping. After these released, energy went up to the head and I felt a thud as the skull was lifted and turned.

After this, a crisscross energy pattern started in upper back and moved up the neck in the same pattern. The working pattern resembled the shape of a butterfly **(see figure).** Most work was on shoulder backs and neck. There were some stretches into right hip and a squeezing tailbone tuck. Most stretches had the elastic feeling with little popping. The skull hurt when growing phase started. I slept from 10 am to 1:30 pm.

From 5:30 to 6:30 pm, I did a sitting stretch. There was ligament snapping mostly in right shoulder and right rib cage and several times into skull near TMJ and cheekbone. It hurts every time the work goes up there but it is brief. Mostly this session felt good. From 7 to 8:45 pm, I did a lying session with mostly stretching and later I did a sitting session with mostly ligament snapping down the spine. From 11 pm to 1 am, I did a sitting session starting with freefall. This morphed into a big workout with pain in skull on starting in typical places. There were many burning lines in right shoulder, right side of neck, mandibles and other shoulder areas, also around five-thousand skull turns.

Insight about stretching: I still do not know why there is so much stretching. What comes is that stretches open and enervate the tissue. I feel like a baby chicken trying to get out of the egg. Strong energy is needed to break out of the shell to be born. It is like stretching toward the light and it is difficult.

Energy Circuit Thru Atlas & Occipital Bone, Vibration Rocking Bed

October 31: Burning Muscles

From 6 to 8 am I did stretching and from 8 to 9 am, I did a lying session working with surrender. I get sore already. From 9 to 11:30 am, I did a sitting session in the sun. Work was on shoulder top, side of neck and TMJ. There was a big burst of energy then a hold sitting straight where energy concentrated on neck at skull line, with intense burning sensation for about twenty-five minutes. It was hard to endure. I do not recall ever having a hold like that in a sitting position. After this, circular paths of energy worked through shoulder, neck and jaw with many burning lines. It was difficult; I wanted to cry but did not. I have a rash on my neck.

I worked on the computer and at 1:30 pm, the area in shoulder crook had intense burning in all the muscles. I had to sit back and stretch for about fifteen minutes. The tension builds but I do not want to work out. From 4:30 to 5:30 pm, I did a freestyle session down to squat with much work in the torso. It felt great; I have much strength and power to open the body! From 6 to 8 pm, I did a sitting session with shoulder and skull work, and there was one long hold. At 9 pm, I went to bed. The biggest energy show I have experienced so far occurred in my body. My body was vibrating so strong there was obvious movement of the bed. I fell asleep quickly and slept soundly until 4 am.

Burning Line Goes Up Spine, Blizzard White Out, OBE

November 1: Shivers, Heat, Spontaneous Orgasm, Tailbone Tucks

I awoke at 4 am, with tension in spine and some in neck. It is a big relief and I feel straighter. From 5 to 6 am I did a freestyle session, down to squat and sitting. The entire time sitting, I was meditative and barely moved while strong energy rose from the tailbone and worked wonders on the spine. A few times, I felt pain in the skull, by the cheekbone and TMJ region on the right. I periodically felt brief intense burning lines in shoulders.

From 6 to 8:30 am, I did a sitting session. The huge energy continued with burning lines in neck and shoulders. A strong burning line ripped up the right spine, feeling it unzipped it. The feeling was like getting your flesh caught in a metal pants zipper, but went so fast that there was no lasting pain. I heard loud thud sounds in shoulder bones as they released.

After this, energy activated in root chakra with shivers, intense heat and a spontaneous orgasm with many tight squeezes of sacrum bone tucking in the tailbone with releases in hips. Next, there was strong skull crunching. Work was in coracoid process of scapula, muscles attached to ribs near collarbone, and back near C7 and scapula (bones of shoulder girdle). I feel all these muscles are holding my right shoulder in a twist. In the front, the line worked runs up the neck under the right mandible, under the cheekbone toward nose and up by eye orbit. In the back, it runs up the spine on right to occipital, through TMJ, to outside edge of eye orbit and into sphenoid wing.

Near the end, I heard a strong tone and felt like I was in a blizzard; it was a total whiteout, while my body stretched with crunches all over. This lasted a few minutes, much longer than I have observed so far. This was an intense session with much burning in various muscles and strong vertical stretches up through the spine to the head. I am sore now. From 9 am to 12:30 pm, I fell asleep to a strong growing reaction.

From 1 to 2 pm and from 6 to 8 pm, I did sitting sessions with work in skull and shoulders, with many burning lines in neck and shoulders. There were many crunches in cheekbone, TMJ, mandibles and passes up both sides of neck into skull.

November 2: Neck Burning, Heat, Shivers, Numb Arms

I slept long and deep and have tension on rising. From 6 to 7:30 am, I did a lying on stomach session with skull turning and strong tension on the sacrum. The TMJ's and shoulders have much tension. From 11 am to 12:30 pm, I did freestyle session with much bone popping all through the torso. It is amazing that the strong skull and shoulder stretches with bone popping does not hurt. It is another level, it appears there is much more transformation to do.

From 1 to 2:30 pm, I did a difficult sitting session with skull bone crunching and burning lines in neck. From 5 to 7 pm I did a freestyle session down to squat and then on my back. When I started, energy was so strong that I felt no pain and moved as higher-self while energy worked up the spine to the head. The floor work was harder. I think in the previous session something must have opened in the neck.

I had a relaxing walk, where I could turn my head and observe the nature and not be consumed with the body tension. The energy is so strong there is no rest. From 8 to 9:30 pm, I did a sitting session with difficult work in the head and shoulders. I went deep into surrender to endure it. As I sat erect, I felt energy going up and down the spine with strong pressure on the shoulders. After this the entire body activated, the root chakra started swirling and I felt alternating heat and shivers. The right side of body was noticeably more energized and my arms went numb. The growing reaction was intense and I went to deep center to where I felt I was out of and above my body. It is still going on in the body. At 11 pm, I went to sleep.

November 3: Energy Wave Rises, White Flash In Brain

I rose once to do skull stretches. After arising at 8 am, I feel good. There is some tension but also I feel a rising energy that lifts my spirit. From 8 to 8:30 am, I did a few lazy stretches and then felt a big wave of energy rise, which produced a white flash in the brain followed by a warm and tingly feeling. From 9:30 to 11:30 am, I did a freestyle session down to squat and lying. I am so strong that I feel no pain while energy is working. It feels good to do the freestyle session. It is like power yoga. I allow my body to move into various postures and hold still when the movement stops. The end of these sessions get harder as work moves into new territory when the popping and crunching starts. I stayed quiet about half the time. Now I know to rest in the growing phase, until ready to go again. The turn around time is amazingly fast. After I stopped, I had many shivers.

From 5 to 6 pm, I did a freestyle session with the same thing as before. The torso easily opens with the powerful stretches. I need a different word for stretch; it is more like being pulling apart. So far, it feels good. The vibration in my body rises. I did normal things today, which feel great! From 6:45 to 8 pm, I did a sitting session with difficult head and shoulder work. From 9:45 pm to 12:15 am, I did a freestyle session and a sitting session with difficult work in skull and shoulders. I am sore now.

Sides Of Skull Open, Skull Plate Popping, Padded Bone Feeling

November 4: Snapping In Shoulders With TMJ's

From 8 to 9:30 am, I did a freestyle session with spinal work and from 9:30 to 11:30 am, I did a sitting session with difficult head and shoulder work and a growing phase after.

From 12 to 1 pm, I did a sitting session with head and shoulder work. There was a big opening in skull where it cracked on both sides several times. From 1 to 2 pm, I did a lying on back session. There were brief intense burning lines at side of right skull. The entire right side of the head is stretched from back to front.

From 6 to 9 pm, I did a freestyle session and sitting session with head and shoulder work. While doing this, the bone movements near the neck and skull changed from the snappy and crunching sensation to one with padded bones. When a bone released, it felt more like a thud than a crunch. Shortly after this, the skull plates started popping with a loud sound, similar to the wooden sound you hear if you knock on top of your head with your mouth open. It was snappy and strong and lasted about twenty minutes. It happened all over the head and both the left and right TMJ's were snapping too. It did not hurt but I did not like the sound of it so I went to sit in center.

After this, energy moved down to the shoulder tops and then ligament snapping started there together with the TMJ's. Later the energy worked deeply in the right side of the skull combined with shoulder movements. It was difficult. This lasted more than an hour. At 11:30 pm, I wanted to go all night to finish but I cannot. I am still sore and feel bad about it. The days feel long as the months go by, it is the hardest thing I have every done. Tomorrow I hope that I feel better. This work never gets easier; there is always a new challenge.

Somebody asked me why I pop my jaw, which I did not realize I did in public. I tried to explain but their blank gaze told me everything. I do not doubt it looks crazy. I pray this can be over soon. I get no confirmation from the outside and have nobody to talk to about this.

November 5: Strong Skull, Shoulders & Neck Work, Skull Shift

I woke in the night and from 12 to 1 am, I did a surrender session with intense skull work. The energy was so strong my body did its thing. A long loud tone sounded and the right TMJ felt clear of tension. Afterward the body vibration was strong and I fell fast asleep. I awoke at 8:30 am and feel rested. I have tension in front of neck and skull at jaw line. The shoulders and rib cage feel closer to center with less twist in spine to the right. From 8:30 to 10 am, I did a sitting session with work in right shoulder and skull. There were many burning lines across shoulders from front to back. From 10:30 to 12 am, I did a sitting session. Work was deep in shoulder crook, with many burning lines especially along the line up the neck.

From 12:30 to 2:30 pm, I did a freestyle session with strong stretches and large bone adjustments. From 6 to 7:30 pm I did a freestyle session and sitting session with intense work in skull and the normal work in shoulders. It feels near to a release in the shoulder crook. I hear light thuds as the skull is shifted slightly to the left. From 7:30 to 10 pm, I did a sitting session with much neck work with burnings lines and then a loud tone sounded. The neck muscle feels close to releasing. This is difficult.

Rising Into Cobra As Crisscross Pattern Works Down Spine

November 6: Skull Plate Pops, Padded Bones Move Down, Sacrum Release

From 5 to 8 am, I did a freestyle session, down to squat and sitting with shoulder, neck and skull work. The work is going deeper in the path: across the shoulders, up side of neck to TMJ, then down to C7, then across to shoulder in back, then down to T1 vertebrae with a little bit of work in left shoulder. There are many burning lines across shoulder backs and vertically up back of neck. In front, the work goes vertically down to muscles of pectorals, under rib cage and shoulder. I think everything needs to be opened. There are many muscles, bones, ligaments and tissues. The wooden popping sound in the skull plates continues.

Before this session, I was at the computer and experienced an intense burning in the right trapezious muscle that caused me to double over at the neck. I could not endure it long and did a freestyle session from 11 to 12 am. It was a killer session working on torso twist. The padded bone feeling now moves down to the TMJ's, neck and tops of shoulders. I think this padded bone feeling is owing to huge energy balls encompassing the bones. Perhaps this is the first time the bones move because there is enough energy now. There is no feeling of crunch or friction, only soft gliding and sometimes a thud when they reposition.[74]

From 5:30 to 7 pm, I did the strongest freestyle session to date, and remained deeply surrendered for most of it. There were strong twisting body pulls with popping and crunching of bones with tremendous force. Later when I was on my stomach, there was a horizontal torque across the lower back and sacrum area, which loosened the lower spine. There was much crunching as it passed through this region repeatedly. Then energy worked between the shoulders in a crisscross pattern of the infinity sign while my head lowered to the ground. Then this pattern started working down the spine and as it did, I slowly and painfully rose into the cobra position. At the end, my torso was nearly vertical with legs and hips flat on floor (see figure). I could never do this position before. While in the cobra position, there were strong twisting pulls down the spinal column from the skull down to tailbone. During the strong vertical pulls, I felt the cranium bones and plates crackling and moving. Then there were crisscross pulls of shoulders with corresponding movement in the hips with vertical body pulls and tailbone tucks. Eventually I sat and there was twisting of the torso and crunching through the cord of personality all along

---

[74] I think the padded bone feeling is due to enervation of cartilage that surrounds the bone.

the spinal column. Then I was lying on my back for a few more crunches and was in a long hold where I blanked out for about ten minutes. It is quiet for the moment and I am sore in many places.

Squeezing Full Body Elastic Stretches (Body Squeezes)

November 7: Coiling Release Of Neck Muscle, Burning Lines

I slept long. Rising, there is tension in left shoulder and activity in skull. I do not want to do anything. From 10 am to 1 pm, I did a freestyle session with full torso twists and with an awesome force stretching and moving the bones, with crackling, crunching, and popping sounds. I guess this is similar to what a 'folded' animal has to go through to be born. This is difficult work!

I took a long break! From 6 to 7 pm, I did a freestyle session. The first half was easy, moving slowly in short holds while strong energy from the spinal column worked in stuck areas. In the second half, a tight elastic band came up my entire body squeezing everything from root to crown, with pops and crunches. When it reached the head, it felt like it was crushed. There were many of these at the end. It was like straining hard to make a bowel movement, pressure reddened my face, and I did not breathe a few times.

The energy did not let up so I did another freestyle session from 7 to 8:30 pm. It was difficult! I had to surrender deeply to allow this session. It was mostly lying on stomach and side with much skull work, jaw popping and shoulder work. Near the end, energy changed to the padded bone feeling. This feeling goes further down and encompasses most of the shoulder. A long clear tone sounded for about ten minutes. From 8:30 to 11 am, the growing phase started and I rested.

From 11 pm to 12:30 am, I did a lying on stomach and side sessions. It was intense with more popping and burning lines. A muscle at side of neck and behind shoulder released as it twisted around my neck like a snake and unrolled in a spiral fashion. I felt many releases and sweated most of the time. There was work on facial bones with skull turns while lying on the stomach. I have no words to describe this experience and I cannot 'be there' to observe how it is done. Several more tones sounded.

Strong Spontaneous Movement Sessions, Fetal Release

November 8: Popping Of Torso Bones, Head Fills With Warm Fuzzy Ball

From 1 to 2 am, I did a lying on the stomach session. At the end, there was a hold and I fell asleep in this position. I awoke at 5:30 am with the sensation of a spiraling energy working on the middle of my back. I arose and went back to bed. I woke at 8 am, with strong tension in the spine. From 8:45 to 10:30 am, I did a freestyle session down to sitting and lying on my stomach sessions.

From 11:30 am to 7:30 pm, I did three sitting sessions with head and shoulder work deep in shoulder muscles. There were many loud skull plate pops. The energy is still strong. From 8 to 11 pm, I did freestyle, sitting and lying sessions. In the lying session, popping of the torso bones started with strong force. After having worked so hard in the head and shoulders, I thought, "Oh no, now I have to go through the same in the entire body!"

Eventually this stopped and energy switched to work intensely in the head. The head was stretched and popped all over with crunching noises. Then it switched to elastic sheets all over the surface of the skull with much skull bone movement. I cried uncontrollably, my head hurt more than it ever has. The crying was a spontaneous reaction. The crying was not like sobbing. I was shaking all over, my head hurt, tears were rolling down, and I was making strange noises. The crying seemed to last a long time and gave me the feeling it was a fetal emotional release. I surrendered to it.

Then the feeling in the skull changed when my entire skull filled with energy that felt like a warm fuzzy ball. Large movements of the cranium bones were occurring but I could barely feel them, I only felt the thud-like movement. Then there were strong stretches going down the cord line. Later there was a hold and I was grateful for the rest. I stayed without moving for about thirty minutes. It is quiet. I am sore and energy works all over the body.

November 9

I slept well, on rising at 6 am, there is much tension in the spine. From 6:30 to 7 am, I did a freestyle session with strong stretchy spiral-like pulls from hips up spine that opened the hip and sacrum. From 7 to 8:30 am, I did the hardest freestyle session so far yet it felt great because I felt like I accomplished something. The power in the body is so strong that I can now stretch all along the spine and move the big bones. It makes sense that the spontaneous body movements would get stronger over time and have greater ability to open the bones. Before I thought, the bones might pop into place spontaneously. Hahaha, I have to move them, what a revelation! I always have to do the work! For the entire time, I have to go against my tendency to want to remain the same, down to the last fiber of my being.

I stretched into both hips much deeper than ever before and finished this session with horizontal stretches across the lower back which exhaust me. There was one long session stretching through cord of personality where I could sense the pattern clearly on the backside. The hip was stretching and releasing tension.

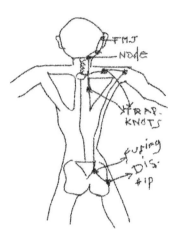

The **figure** illustrates the problematic areas in my body with the dots. The right TMJ joint, shoulder joint and hip have been dislocated since birth. My entire life these joints pop and make a noise. The node at base of skull on right side of spine seems connected to knot inside scapula near spine, which I thought was a cyst when I was ten years. I think it is related to a twisted muscle or ligament between skull and spine in a vertical line, perhaps it is the alar ligament. The spot near the right sacrum suture and hipbone is tight like it is fused. Because of this deformity I could never do a yogic bridge posture even when young doing gymnastics. I have never had flexibility in the sacrum. This deformity caused extreme lower back pain during childbirth. I have never slept on my stomach, because my back would hurt.

From 10:30 am to 2 pm, I did another killer head and body session. I was crying spontaneously like last night while the right skull was stretched with much jaw popping. After this, I did a sitting session with a growing reaction while energy worked in the spine. Lastly, I did another session with more crying and skull work.

From 4:45 to 6 pm, I did two freestyle sessions with strong energy. The spontaneous movements are powerful. From 6:45 to 8:15 pm, I did a sitting session with skull work and popping in jaws. The skull work is different. There were many snapping sounds in the right skull plates and crunching noises with loud cracks from deep in the skull. The path of work was cheekbones, TMJ and down back of skull and over to shoulder. I feel a strong connection between muscles from TMJ to shoulder and a muscle releases under the cheekbone. From 8:15 to 11 pm, there was a growing phase. I rested and went to bed.

Right-Left Pumping Between Shoulders & Hips, Strong Spine Vortex

November 10

I slept soundly, yeah! I woke at 5 am and from 6 to 9:30 am I did a freestyle session, down to squat and lying on stomach session. Later I was sitting in a long hold for an hour while energy worked in the spine. From 9:30 to 12 am, I did more sessions.

From 5 to 6 pm, I did a difficult freestyle session. There were interesting moves at the end while on stomach in cobra position. There was left and right swaying of shoulders, and simultaneous right and left pumping of hips. After this, a large vortex formed and was spiraling fast going up the spine.

From 6:30 to 8 pm, I did a session with much work on area around right TMJ, cheekbone and under jaw and into side of neck behind shoulder. Skull adjustments were made on both sides of neck with much skull pressure. It was an uncomfortable session. From 8 to 11 pm, I did a sitting session with head and shoulder crunching. This seems endless but I detect the stretches go through different paths of muscle and tissues. From 11 to 12 pm, I did a freestyle session and now my skull hurts. I did thirteen hours of sessions today.

Chapter 21: CCW Rotation, Double Helix Vortex

November 11: Tension Release From Spine

From 10 to 11:30 am, I did a freestyle session with incredibly strong energy and no pain. It took little effort. I sat in center and allowed my body to move spontaneously. I feel spiraling energy rising up spine while the spine relaxes and releases tension energy.

From 12:30 to 8 pm, I did four sessions. When doing a lying on back session I tried to rest but the reaction continues. There was strong skull work, working on right shoulder back and neck muscles. My head hurts all over. From 9 to 11 pm, I did a freestyle session and could not take any position for long, as all is sore. The energy is strong and I want to continue but I cannot. Several times, I felt energy puff outs in my legs and buttocks and the feeling that my legs elongated. After I laid down for sleep, my arms went numb.

Popping By Clavicles, Upper Rib Cage & Under Arms

November 12: Skull Pressure, Inner Sound Like A Million Crickets

I awoke at 6:30 am, and feel rested. From 7 to 8:15 am, I did a sitting session with work on back of neck and entire line of cord from skull to hip. I already feel tired. From 8:15 to 10:30 am, I did a freestyle session with about an hour of lying on stomach and doing skull work. I needed that. After a while, the skull needs to be adjusted and this position seems the most effective way to do it. The spine activates in an undulating fashion and the body uses leverage on the skull to move the cranium bones. The same stretching work repeats all over the body, always opening it a bit more. From 11:30 to 12 am, I did a sitting session with head and shoulder work. There is strong skull pressure with pain and I am tired.

From 1:30 to 2 pm, I did lying on stomach session with orgasmic arousal. From 4:30 to 6 pm, I did a sitting session. At first, there was much popping and snapping in the torso with a twisting stretch. It was predominately in the front rib cage, under arm and up to parts of shoulders and some on the back. After this, energy worked on shoulder girdle and especially on both clavicles. There was more work on the front than usual. After this, there was an opening up back of the neck, across along skull line and ending in front by the throat with a stretch and crackle going deep into this area. After this, energy worked slowly down the cord line and I felt tight muscles relax. It was difficult, but I see progress and the hope to finish drives me to continue. I need the carrot very much. From 6 to 7:30 pm, the work was similar with more skull crunches. There are still crunching noises in side of the neck and under jaw.

Lately, when I go to sleep the energy in my body is amazing. I hear the sound of a million crickets chirping. Visually it is as if I am in outer space, as one with the stars in the galaxy. Bodily, I feel like I am humming and the energy feels soft and fuzzy all over and the vibration rocks the bed. It is difficult to tell where the energy is working in my body as it quickly fills the entire body. I did not do more as the growing reaction started.

CCW Torso Rotation Starts, Physical Energy Circuits Between Joints

November 13: Rig Cage Twist, Bone Popping In Head, Neck & Shoulders

I slept well and woke at 7:30 am. The rib cage in front feels twisted, the spine feels bent and I have neck tension. From 8 to 9:30 am I did freestyle session. My ankles are sore so I could not hold the squat position long. Next, I was sitting and then lying on the stomach. While I was sitting with legs to front there was something new. My torso circled counterclockwise with simultaneous stretching. (Further references call this CCW torso rotation.) I felt energy rising from the tailbone, spiraling up the spinal column, and radiating into the problem areas. There were many crackles and pops as the spine, rib cage and shoulders stretched.

The larger muscles along the path of stretch activate as a group. I am stronger because the larger muscles enervate. There was work in left hip up to right shoulder and vice-a-versa. There was work on the cord in front of right body. The right body cord starts near the inguinal canal inside the hip, goes up to rib cage, then under ribs over to arm, then across to clavicle and first ribs, then up to jaw by molar in back, then under cheekbone and up to sphenoid wing region. On the stomach, energy worked in a similar spiral pattern on the shoulders and energy circuits formed from shoulders to TMJ's. Bones release in the skull with a thud. There were horizontal infinity patterns across tops of shoulders and then stretches from left shoulder to right TMJ and vice-a-versa. This session was not difficult.

From 10 to 10:30 am, I did a sitting session with strong body pulls. I think the sacrum released and then huge energy popped all bones frantically in upper shoulders, neck and head.

It was crazy and fast, but felt good. I am sore now. From 11:30 am to 1:15 pm, I did a sitting session with snapping and popping of neck and head. After this, I did a lying session with stretchy pulls along cord paths through entire body.

From 1:15 to 2:15 pm and 4:30 to 5:30 pm, I did sitting sessions like previous one with more popping and crunching into different areas of the torso. From 6 to 7 pm, I was lying on side with head and shoulder work. At end, I felt my upper body as one unit with no pain; I only felt the thuds as bones shifted. It is a strange feeling. From 9 to 11:30 pm, I did a sitting session, alternating between crunches and smooth elastic stretches going over different paths in the body. A big muscle released across shoulder back that felt great. I fell asleep to awesome energy coursing through my body.

Insight about gradual transformation: I am reminded this is not about freeing a muscle or fixing one thing. A growing process remakes the entire body. Trying to speed it up does not help. When I do that, I get tired and frustrated. The most important thing I need to do is surrender control of my body and mind. The body is complex and these elements of my personality have been with me a long time. I cannot expect my entire body to be remade instantly. When I stretch into a tight area that action alone is the beginning of new growth there. The stretch energizes the tissue and starts the growing reaction. There will not be any sudden healing. To transform, energy has to move through physical flesh and that only happens if I allow it to happen.

Knife Feeling In Flesh As Bones Move

November 14: Skull Feels As One With Lower Body In Spinal Stretch

Waking at 7:30 am, I am sore in the body. The right side of the neck, skull, right hip and ankle feel looser. Yesterday, it struck me I have physically changed much, due to the work I have done. It feels foreign and weird. It is not visible outwardly, but it is there.

From 10 to 11 am, I did a freestyle session with was physically difficult yet I had no problem to bodily surrender. There were long stretchy pulls through the body and more work on shoulder crook, mandible and side of neck. When the shoulder and TMJ's released, there was a strange sensation of bones sticking out at weird angles. I guess this is due to shoulder girdle movement as a single unit. From 11:30 am to 1 pm, I did a sitting session. There was much popping of jaws, on side of neck, and in left shoulder. I am sore and feel like sleeping.

From 4:30 to 5:45 pm, I did a sitting session with more work on shoulder, shoulder crook and TMJ. At 5:40 pm, I felt shivers for about five minutes coming up spine. From 6 to 7 pm, I did a freestyle session with long twisting torso stretches up entire spine. While sitting, there was CCW torso rotation. There were many crunches all over central nervous system area. When I quit, it felt like the skull loosened and united with the lower body in the upward stretching body pulls. These are powerful stretches. From 9 to 11 pm, I did a sitting session with head and shoulder work. Energy worked deeply in front of skull and under mandible, in neck and shoulder tops with many burning lines in all these areas. I felt cranium bones expanding and shifting around. There were strong crunches up the right side of face and work on left shoulder. My skull, shoulders, back and hips hurt.

Loosening Of Shoulder Girdle Bones

November 15: Moving Up And Down In Squat, Cranial Suture Crunches

I slept well and rose once for a few skull stretches. After rising at 8 am, I feel I could stretch a few times and the spine would be nice and straight. While sitting, there is looseness in the upper shoulder, neck and skull on the right, that I have never felt before. The neck tension is much less. It felt natural to sit and do CCW torso rotations so I went with that for thirty minutes. From 8:30 to 9 am, I did a sitting session with work in skull, neck and shoulders along lines of tension without crunches. The stretches glided over these areas repeatedly and later moved down to lower back. I feel much stronger in the spine than ever before.

From 9:30 to 11 am, I did a freestyle session with long pulls through entire spinal column. Then I was stretching into hips with horizontal pulls across lower back. Then I was lying on stomach and side, moving everywhere even going back to standing. At the end, I did a CCW torso rotation session. At one moment, I felt energy tracing and crunching around in a circle, on all the edges of the right scapula bone. I felt work on clavicle and left shoulder top. Then there were about four intense pulls through the shoulder joint. From 11 to 12 am, I did a sitting session with work in the muscles in right skull, TMJ and shoulder.

I took too long a break and now I have too much tension. From 5 to 6 pm, I did a powerful freestyle session. I was moving up and down to squat, standing, sitting and lying positions and experiencing strong twisting stretches up the spine in all of them. While in the squat position, the legs came together squeezing above the hips. While in cobra position there were strong stretches alternating between shoulders and hips.

From 7 to 8:30 pm, I did a sitting session with skull and shoulder work. I felt bones jutting at strange angles and felt muscles shifting to new positions in the shoulders. There were many crunches at line of occipital bone to TMJ and to shoulder joint by coracoid process of scapula. The muscles between the TMJ's, work to connect to the shoulder muscles,

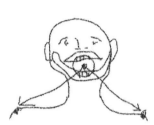

in an upside down 'V pattern' through the mouth **(see figure).** I feel the muscles move between the TMJ's when the mouth is wide open. It is as if the muscles pass inside and through the joints and then down the neck to the shoulders. There is less tension in left shoulder after the right shoulder and TMJ released.

From 9 to 12:30 pm, I did several sitting and freestyle sessions. The last one-and-a-half hour was difficult work in the skull. After some painful crunches through the jaw, I was in a phase of short holds with work going on in the skull. I felt tiny crunches around the cranial sutures, which sounded liquid with squishy sounds. It is difficult to describe. It was like little bubbles of movement in the skull accompanied with intense head pressure and a migraine headache. Then a slow turn of the head would happen and it would repeat. After this, energy moved down the body. Several times, there were big energy puffs out in the pelvic area. Near the end of the skull session, there was intense pain in the pubic symphysis. This seemed strange because there were no frontal stretches down the body. During this session, my left arm went numb for about ten minutes and my lips were numb.

Shoulder Crook Opens, Skull Vortex, Night Vision

November 16: Skull Pop At Top Of Neck, Skull Shift

I slept well and rose at 7am. It felt like my body was straight except for the shoulder and head, which felt cocked to the right. I feel tension in the shoulder crook. From 7:30 to 9 am, I did a CCW torso rotation session, round and round the shoulder and shoulder crook, sometimes working the entire shoulder girdle **(see figure).** Then I lay on my side and stretches were going through entire cord of personality. Then I was lying on stomach doing skull turns. The energy in the skull steadily built as the bones shifted in the skull and there was increasing pressure on right side of sacrum. From 8:30 to 12 am, I did three sitting sessions. There were strong 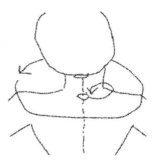 twisting movements around the skull and several times, I felt releases. It was difficult with intense skull pressure and tension in shoulders.

From 12 to 1:30 pm I did a freestyle session. The first notable thing is there was a strange pop in the skull near the top and back of neck. It felt like the skull moved over one notch and was now balancing on a point. After this, there was a HUGE release in the right side of the neck in shoulder crook. It felt like the surface area was a circle of five inches in diameter. Suddenly, it went squishy with crunching and my head felt erect and straight.

After this, I did an intense lying on the stomach session. There was a release in the right TMJ and afterward I felt a large vortex form in the skull. This was one of the best releases ever, releasing much tension that I have felt for about one year in the right TMJ. About ten minutes later, another release felt great. There was much work in facial bones. There is still tension between the skull and sacrum.

From 5 to 6 pm, I did a strong freestyle session. The shoulder and skull continue to open more. There were many spontaneous spinal stretches. From 6:30 to 8 pm, I did a sitting session with more skull and shoulder crunching which went deep into skull and shoulder. I feel movements of bones deep in center of skull. I am sore now. From 8 to 11 pm, the growing phase started and I rested. From 11 pm to 12:30 am, the energy increases and I did one more session.

The energy inside my body zooms. The last two nights I saw light in my room and thought I needed to turn the lights off. They were not on. When reading my close vision is less blurry. My face is getting sore and chapped from this skull turning.

Skull Pressure With Slow Motion Moves & Holds (Head Surgery)

November 17

I rose twice with much sweating, kriyas and dreams. From 7 am to 12:30 pm, I did four sessions with many body stretches, some spontaneous. I am tired.

From 12:30 to 2 pm, I took a nap. From 4:15 to 5:30 pm, I did a freestyle session ending with lying on stomach and doing skull turning. From 5:45 to 7 pm, I did a sitting session outside with crystals. There was much skull work and crunching. From 7:30 to 12 pm, I did three more sessions and feel sore now. Often I feel pressure in the skull and the skull plate's shift without stretching. There were slow arcs of torso with short holds between the movements. It was difficult because of the skull pressure. Several times sweats arose. It was like a slow head surgery, opening right side of skull muscles with many crunches and hard pops of TMJ and loud snaps and thudding noises. I do not recall a session quite like this before and lasting for so long. When I stopped, energy was moving down both sides of neck and back of skull. It felt like the muscle under the cheekbone is now in the correct position and the TMJ and mandible feels more open. I like to release tension from skull before bed because then lower bodywork starts and I sleep better.

November 18: Gliding Energy On Cord Path, Parietals Open

From 7 to 8:30 am, I did a freestyle session ending with lying on stomach. My ear is sore and chapped. From 8:30 to 11:30 am, I did another freestyle session.

From 12 to 1 pm, I was lying with head crunching. Notable was a different pattern of stretch. It was side-to-side horizontally through skull and I felt the cheekbone rolling to a new position. From 4 to 5 pm, I did a freestyle session. At first, energy worked on right hip and sacrum in squat and sitting position, done with twisting spinal stretches. Next, I was on stomach in cobra position with alternating shoulder stretches. Then I was lying and there was ligament snapping in rib cage, shoulder girdle, cranium bones and spine. There were many shoulder and hip releases. It was a difficult session, but not painful which is amazing.

From 5:30 to 7:15 pm, the fast ligament snapping in torso continued and when I sat it was even stronger. After this, a strong gliding energy formed along the cord of personality on front and back of body. There was much work on shoulder and TMJ's. It feels close to releasing a muscle between the right shoulder and TMJ again. Later there was a release in the skull by the cheekbone and jaw with both shoulders. The parietals opened up to the wormian bones in the skull. Several times strong energy shifted cranium bones without me moving.

At 7:30 pm, there is a strong tugging feeling inside my left thigh. I have not felt anything like this before. From 7:30 to 8:30 pm, I did a sitting session with head crunching. Each time the head turned, the jaws constantly popped with fast rhythmic opening. I am sore.

Tailbone Vortex Rips Up Spine, Body Squeezes With Black Outs

November 19: Rib Cage Release, Energy Bands Around Sutures

In the night, I sweated and had many kriyas and cleansing dreams. There was much skull pressure with skull bone shifts and the right hip was worked. I rose twice to stretch. I got up at 6:30 am. There is much tension and pressure at base of neck and skull. It feels like a bone rather than a muscle holds tension.

From 7 to 9:30 am, I did a sitting session with TMJ popping and ratcheting of the neck to the left with skull plate movement in right skull for about forty minutes. Then I did a freestyle session ending with sitting. The freestyle session helped release the tension, and the cord of personality relaxes. Energy traverses the twisted path as one continuous loop in the body. There was intense work on the muscle under cheekbone, in TMJ and near the coracoid process on the scapula. There was much skull pain with strong pressure and spontaneous bone movements. I am sore.

From 9:45 to 10:30 am, I did a sitting session with ligament snapping all over the torso concentrated around shoulder and full circle around neck at shoulder level. While laying it felt like my body was one unit, with continuous energy snapping ligaments all along the cord.

From 10:30 to 12 am, I did a lying session. Immediately a vortex formed in the pelvic bowl and moved up the spine. As the vortex moved up the spine, I was stretched to the maximum, which pushed out the rib cage, the spine and moved the entire skeleton. As it rose higher, it got stronger. At first, I was afraid I might get hurt, then trusted and let go of body control. Energy rose all the way to the skull with blacking out intervals where I felt swallowed by the muscular waves coming over the skull. At times, I could not breathe between the stretches. How can I describe this? It is like breaking out of a shell. After this, there was head surgery, with short holds, crunches and pops. There were many skulls turns. My ear is sore.

From 2:15 to 3:30 pm, I did a freestyle session with much ligament snapping. There was a long time stretching the right side and sitting with strong spinal twists pulling the bones to new positions. The shoulder girdle on right moved with the cranium bones. Lastly, I was lying on stomach. Near the end, there were horizontal pulling stretches across base of occipital bone and across lower back. By the occipital bone, it was squishy and crunchy with a bone against bone sound. It is hard to believe what my body is capable of doing. I am tired.

From 3:30 to 6 pm, I did a sitting session with much head and shoulder work. I feel movement in the cranium bones during the holds. There were more openings in the facial bones followed by stretches over opened areas. Sometimes muscles are released on both sides of the skull. This is the most skull-bone separation I have experienced to date. The movements under the mandible are difficult. I feel bone under it and wonder if that is the roots of the teeth. There was hard pressure on this area and the maxillae. I felt an intense pain and something firmly stuck under the back molar under the jaw. Then energy zoomed in here and kept popping something. One of my wisdom teeth never erupted; maybe it is related to that.

I feel tight energy bands on the sutures as the skull plate's shift. I felt energy under the eye orbits. There is much activity and I have little idea how this is done or what the work is trying to accomplish. Near the end, I was feeling parallel pulls of muscles up both sides of front of face with the hard palate feeling to be in the middle. Then there was work in the shoulder crook and intense burning lines down the back of the neck below skull from TMJ. I felt another burning line in the shape of a curve. It went along the lower edge of occipital bone to mandible and then arched up under cheekbone and went up to frontal bone along side of nose. I long to have my skull and shoulders free of all this tension and pulling.

From 6 to 10:30 pm, it was a different casual sitting session. The cranium bones were moving spontaneously for more than two hours, but I could not detect what was occurring. There was intense pain at times with strong pressure. I presume energy worked on deep bones in skull. There was a squishy sound, which I think may be cerebral spinal fluid sounds owing to the strong pressure. After this, there were stretches into the shoulder combined with movements of the cranium bones. Then there were hard stretches deep in vertebrae, moving down the spinal column. I felt the skull was aligning to the corresponding body part, which was previously adjusted. I am super sore.

From 10:30 pm to 12:15 am, I did a freestyle session with similar things. There is skull surgery and ligament snapping. There was deep work in the shoulder crook which felt it went down to bones of cervical spine. It was a difficult session.

Not many tones sound lately. When a new body area opens, energy floods into it with a deafening quiet. It is like being in a blizzard with a total whiteout. The nature of the body stretch changes, from the harder pops and crunches to a softer bone gliding feeling. This softer feeling lasts for a while and then gets harder. The inner sound is like a million crickets chirping and the 3rd eye view is like what you might see if you were floating in the Milky Way Galaxy surrounded by stars and I feel like I am one of them. I hear and see this constantly.

November 20: Large Release In Right Side Of Neck And TMJ

From 7 to 9:15 am, I did a CCW torso rotation session. The rotation worked around the neck with stretches into shoulders, neck, and skull. After this, energy got strong and I had to lie down. Then there were strong expanding torso stretches concentrated on the upper right rib cage and shoulder and going down spinal cord on back. It felt good to stretch the body and feel the energy course through it. Lying on the stomach there was simultaneous skull turning and pelvic rocking. Once, the sacrum pain was intense. My left ear is chapped and sore which makes this difficult. I get many episodes of shivers after these sessions and get very cold.

From 9:30 to 10:45 am, I did a freestyle session. Notable was how long I stood and went up and down from squat position to standing and back. In squat, it gets closer to feeling open on both sides in the hips. Later there was much more stretching and popping in the shoulders. After this, I lay down and a growing reaction lasted for twenty minutes. A tone sounded.

I took a long break and the tension did not build much, it was a nice break. From 1:30 to 2:20 pm, the session was amazing. The right side of the neck and jaw just released and the side of my neck feels great! From 5 to 6:30 pm, I feel good. I feel much relief in the neck and right TMJ. I felt a notable rise in energy this session. The neck, shoulder and TMJ work continues but it is not difficult. From 11 to 12 pm, I did a lying session with head crunching. It was difficult to fall asleep after this.

November 21: Painful Stretching, Facial Bone Work, Crying, Teeth Snaps

It was a restless night with kriyas. From 8 to 10 am, I did a freestyle session with strong pulls along the spine with crunching in skull and other places as the spinal energy twisted upward. It was painful. From 10:30 to 12:15 am, I did a sitting session with stretching of right skull and shoulder. I felt two teeth snaps and a few days ago, I felt this many times.

From 12:30 to 7:45 pm, I did four sessions. There was much crunching in shoulder, jaw and skull. In one session, the shoulder work was very difficult and I cried. Lastly, I did a sitting session similar to freefall but more intense with skull pressure. It seems the sphenoid is moving and articulating with the other loosened cranium bones. There were many stretches through the right trapezious muscle. Work continues on the upper right temple, TMJ, mandible, shoulder crook and shoulder. The jaws, area in back by spine and scapula are sore.

From 9:30 pm to 12:30 am, I did a sitting session with more facial bone crunching than ever before. Several times, I felt energy puff out in the left side of the body. I was sweating most of the time. I did thirteen hours of difficult sessions today.

November 22: Horizontal Stretches On Both Ends, Head Whips

I awoke at 8 am and slept well. There were a few skull stretches with pressure on the sphenoid wing with fleeting pain. From 8:30 to 9 am, I did a CCW torso rotation session and spinal stretches. The shoulder still holds much tension. After these stretches, there is some relief and I feel stronger like I can open the shoulder. From 9 to 10:30 am, I did a sitting session with spontaneous stretches with strong swirling in root chakra. From 10:35 to 12 am, I did a freestyle session ending with lying on stomach with skull turns and a horizontal pulling across the lower back. There were many head whips in a full circle that felt good. The tension builds fast so I cannot enjoy the freefall.

From 12:30 to 1:45 pm, I did a lying session with crunching in skull and shoulders. It feels like I am killing myself. From 5 to 6:30 pm, I did a freestyle session that felt different, like something is near to opening in the central nervous system. From 7 to 9 pm, I did a sitting session with head and shoulder crunching. Growing phase started.

Ligament Snapping In Large Bones Of Torso

November 23: Teeth Snaps

I slept soundly until 6 am. It was a nice break. From 6:30 to 8:30 am, I mostly did a lying on the stomach session. There were horizontal stretches across lower back and skull turns with work on mandibles. My face is chapped and sore now. It was difficult to rise from the lying position and stop the reaction, I could barely move against it. The work was in the section of platysma fascia between the scapula and the mandible on right. It feels if something would release here the entire skeleton would release.

From 8:30 to 10:30 am, I did one of the hardest sessions to date. I started with standing and stretched down to squat. Then the stretchy feeling changed to ligament snapping. This time with much larger movements and strong thuds as bones released. This was occurring all over the upper right torso and lasted a long time. There was strong pain in the back and neck with pressure in skull for about ten minutes. Then there was strong snapping of ligaments in the skull. There were two of these episodes and the skeleton felt straighter afterward.

Then I was slowly lowered to back on floor doing strong skull and shoulder work for about an hour where I went to deep center to endure it. I noticed I was preventing stretches from entering into the upper right quadrant of my body. I let the energy go through there, dropping my fear of pain. I said, "Pain is good. It will heal you if you allow it." And, it was painful all over the collarbone, shoulder joint, jaw and TMJ. There were two strong teeth snaps where I have the crooked teeth on top front right.

From 11:30 am to 1:10 pm, I did lying on back session with head crunching. The main work went around the temporal bone in a circle then down to jaw and opened the lower molar area. In addition, the cheekbone was worked much. Then there was work to loosen muscles between right mandible and shoulder in front and back. I felt two muscles release.

From 4:45 to 8:30 pm, I did two sitting sessions with skull crunching. The energy changed in the second session with rising skull pressure and pain and I could sense skull plate movements, which lasted about an hour. At the end, the TMJ and shoulder muscles were ready to release. I cried because I am tired of this. From 8:30 to 9:30 pm, I did a lying session. The work was easy with less crunching and more elastic stretches. At 11 pm, growing phase started.

Large Bone Releases Including Shoulder Girdle

November 24: Puffs In Abdomen, Freezing Shivers

In the night, there were many kriyas and dreams and I rose twice to stretch. It is 6 am, and the left spine feels straight and the right spine is bent from the shoulder on up. From 8 to 8:30 am, in a sitting session there was a large bone movement in shoulder girdle and cervical spine. There was a counterclockwise turn with thud sounds as bones shifted but it did not hurt. My right hand hurts, including the entire thumb from the wrist on down. My hand is weak and it is difficult to hold heavy things. Yesterday I felt a freezing cold line going along my arm while working out.

From 9 to 9:40 am, I did a sitting session. There were large bone movements through entire spinal column, which were not painful only alarming how strong they were. A strong energy rose up and pulled apart tight bones. I am elated with this new power. With a few strong stretches, the shoulder, neck, back of spine, sacrum, hips and TMJ release in many places. I have to trust, that I will not get hurt to allow these moves.

From 10 to 11 am, I did a freestyle session. It was the strongest freestyle session to date. I went up and down from stand to squat through hips, then finally lying on side. I am tired but my energy is strong. Near the end, energy was moving up with crunching in head and shoulders then with a few strong twists there was a big release in both shoulders. The energy increased so from 11:10 am to 12:45 pm, I did a sitting session and my right arm did a spasm or automatic reflex during the workout and jumped off my lap. When I stopped, there were sparkling lights in the air with my eyes open. There were several energy puff outs in the stomach area.

At 1 pm, I had strong shivers with freezing cold feeling for over ten minutes. I had uterine cramps too. When I stopped, work was in the muscles along the ridge of the shoulder going up and working horizontally with some skull muscles in the platysma or trapezoid muscles. Several times, I felt burning lines in this area and the sphenoid wing. Much of what was done was amazing in that it was larger movements of skull, muscles, and bones with no pain. There was twenty minutes of popping in both jaws while skull adjustments were made with connecting lower body muscles and at same time, I did twisting body stretches. This did not hurt but was irritating.

From 1:30 to 3 pm, I took a nap and felt energetic work in the spine the entire time. I felt energy zooming around fast and working all over. From 5 to 5:30 pm, I did a sitting session, similar to this morning with strong ligament snapping and powerful movements of bones. I felt releases in jaw and shoulder. From 5:30 to 8:30 pm, I did two sitting sessions. Notable were intense burning lines in shoulder crook on up to mandible. The shoulder girdle loosens more. This is intense, thirty minutes is enough time. From 10 to 11 pm, I did a lying on stomach session with skull turning. It is amazing how the cranium bones move with little pain. My hand hurts so bad I can barely write.

November 25: Deafness, Release Of Mandible & Maxillae, Teeth Snaps

From 7 to 8:30 am, I did a freestyle session with ligament snaps, bone releases and strong twisting stretches. My right hand is swollen and unusable, I feel down. From 9:30 to 11 am, I did a freestyle session and from 11 am to 12:30 pm, I did a sitting session.

From 12:30 to 1 pm, I did a sitting session and there was ligament snapping in right rib cage. Around 4:30 pm, my hand feels better but it is still swollen and now something hurts in the right ankle. I have episodes of temporary deafness in the workouts.

From 5 to 6 pm, the trapezious section of muscle that is in back between the edges of the scapula and on up to the skull released. When it released I felt a ripple move across the back edge toward the shoulder crook then up from there to the skull and mandible. Then I felt large energy puff outs in the lower body. It feels hollow in the shoulder crook with a big calm empty space. All is quiet for the moment.

From 8 to 9 pm, I did lying session with skull turning with work in cheekbone and shoulder. From 9 to 10:30 pm, I did a sitting session with ligament snapping, gliding stretches and another round of crunching in shoulders and skull. There were intense burning lines up side of neck for about five minutes.

From 10:30 pm to 1:15 am, I did continued sessions in various positions. There was a strong opening in the mandible with several teeth snaps. Then there were teeth snaps in the maxillae but not as dramatic as in the mandible. In general, there has been much opening of the cranium bones all over the face and along the suture lines of skull plates. I am tired and sore.

Body Worked In Halves, Tornado Vortex Rises Up Spine To Skull

November 26: Ligament Snapping All Over Skull With Clavicle Release

From 8 to 8:30 am, I did a sitting session with long stretchy pulls from sacrum on up. I felt releases in the hips, shoulder girdles and TMJ joints. I felt no pain. From 8:30 to 10 am, I did a sitting session, then lying on stomach with skull turns and mandible pulls, then lying on side with work on shoulder and neck. The energy is so strong the only thing I can do is lie down and surrender to it. This has been occurring frequently the last week. From 10 am to 12:15 pm, I did a sitting session with painful work in skull and shoulders.

From 12:30 to 2 pm, I did a lying session with strong energy. I feel a warm tingly energy filling one side of the body while there is difficult work going on in skull and shoulder on the other side. From 5:30 to 7:30 pm, I did two lying sessions, with loosening of bones on right side of face. There was much crunching in mandible, occipital and temporal bones. I am tired and have strong uterine cramps and tingling in groin.

From 8 to 9 pm, a powerful energy arose filling my entire body with a vibrating energy centered on the spinal column. It felt like taking a ride and floating on a huge wave of energy as the body swayed around. There was much skull work with so much movement it surprised me. Interspersed with this were episodes of loud popping of skull plates that did not hurt.

From 9 to 11 pm, I feel I reach a new stage where the skeleton and skull can be moved with stronger force. There was a full round of ligament snapping in all cranium bones and the torso. After this, there were teeth snaps in mandible and maxillae done tooth by tooth. I felt muscles in the neck were connected with the teeth snaps. Then there was snapping around the cheekbone and under the eye orbit, which seemed to be preparing for a facial bone movement. After this, there were holds with slow movement of bones in the skull alternating with popping of skull plates. I cannot take one more pop. Once the clavicle jumped as something released during a strong stretch. A big wave of tissue moved horizontally and changed position.

Energy puffs out happen more in right side of body. The left side of body activates afterward, preceding larger body movements. At times, the energy was so strong and the skull movements hurt to where I could not find a zone of comfort in any body position even while surrendered. It got much harder as is typical. These body changes are very complex.

From 11:30 pm to 12:30 am, the energy rose up the spine like a tornado and I felt it spiraling inside my head. I then did a sitting session until the jaw and shoulder is so sore I refuse to move them. My hand is still swollen mostly by the thumb area. I still feel a pain in the right hip and the left shoulder top has much tension. It is difficult to do this. I do not have the words to describe what this feels like. I sacrifice my entire life for this because I will get no relief until it is done.

Spine Coming Physically Alive

November 27: Teeth Snaps, Burning Lines, Right Shoulder Release

The day's roll by, growing takes its time and cannot be forced. I feel as a new being entering into the world but there is nobody that knows about it. I feel so alone with this. Will there be a welcome from the cosmos when this is complete, a nice warm loving embrace as I come anew into the world? From 8:30 to 10:30 am, it has been difficult with continued work on shoulder, neck, skull and right hip. I wrote a tanka poem today:

> Sea polyps on stone
> frantic jettisons upward
> working to break cord.
> Growing force crescendo
> jellyfish enters ocean.

From 11:30 am to 12:30 pm, I did a sitting session. The spine feels alive with spiraling energy breaking free from restricting tissues. From 1:30 to 2:30 pm, I did a sitting session like the previous one. It is difficult to stop the energy. From 5 to 6:15 pm, I did a sitting session. Work was in areas of TMJ, cheekbone, shoulder and neck with ligament snapping all along cord of personality path. There were many teeth snaps in the right mandible. For a short time, there was intense burning in upper lip in line vertical with crooked canine teeth. Lately, burning lines have been occurring often. I felt brief intense burns in various areas in shoulder, neck and skull. My right ear hurts much during all these sessions and I often feel strong pain in the sphenoid wing when it crunches in there. The left shoulder top is still painful; I sense it will release tension when the right shoulder releases.

From 6:15 to 8 pm, I did a lying session with growing reaction with strong energy zooming around. The right ankle, legs, pelvis and stomach were worked. From 8 to 9 pm, I did a lying session with skull work. There was a time when my head turned fully to the right tucked near the right shoulder joint. Then there was a crunching along the bones down through the TMJ line vertically. The bones were grinding together. I feel a muscle from the mandible will release that is connected to the scapula area below.

From 9 to 12 pm, I did two sitting sessions. The right shoulder, neck and skull released. It feels strange like there is a big empty hole with bones popping around inside. I cannot pop my jaws any more. From 12:15 to 1 am, I sat and CCW torso rotation started. It felt good with no crunching so I surrendered to that. Later, I felt a release in right hip and entire torso. Then a spontaneous head crunching started in the right skull that was fast and painful. I could only take it for ten minutes.

Release Of Neck Leads To Formation Of Double Vortex On Spine

November 28: Floating Shoulder Girdle, Energy Prickles

It was a restless sleep with strong energy and stretching most of the night. From 8 to 10 am, I had to start stretching right away. First, there was CCW torso rotation and popping going round and round the cervical spine. Then work moved into shoulder, TMJ, and cheekbone and I felt pain all over the skull and shoulders. There was a long hold with strong tension in the trapezious muscle where I wanted to go out of body to escape that pain. At the end, it felt good.

From 10:30 to 11:45 am, I did a freestyle session with popping of bones and opening of pelvis. Then I was sitting doing yoga-like twisting spinal postures. Lastly, I was lying on stomach raised in cobra position with alternate left, right, left work in shoulders. Then I did a sitting session with more bone popping and opening in the pelvis.

From 12 to 12:45 pm, I did a CCW torso rotation session. Work was on the mandible by lower molar and top of shoulder joint. I often felt the bone grinding feeling in both places. The shoulder girdle feels like its floating and I sit nearly straight. I wrote another tanka poem:

Promise of pleasure
keeps me coming back for more
I'll face any pain.
Merging with your warm embrace,
I AM alive on Earth.

From 1 to 1:40 pm, I did a difficult freestyle session. I feel dead. From 2:30 to 3:30 pm, I did another strong freestyle session. I think to escape but the energy does not calm. From 3:30 to 5 pm, my body opens with much ligament snapping all over. The snapping goes up and down, then there is freefall and it repeats. I did three or four freestyle sessions. I want to stop because it is torture.

From 5 to 6:30 pm, there were slow movements in the skull while sitting. From 6:30 to 9 pm, there was easy and difficult skull work. One time there was strong crunching in the TMJ and neck, it was so intense I thought I might pass out. The neck feels free from the skull. I cannot believe how strong this was and dread thinking about how much is left to do.

At 10:45 pm, the growing phase started with a strong body vibration. **I feel like I am a point of light in the middle and my body spirals around me.** I feel light stinging prickles all over the areas where energy is working. The entire body is numb with high body heat and sweating.

Double Helix Vortex, Shoulders Worked As Pair, Ethmoid Moves

November 29: Entire Shoulder Girdle Release

I slept long but it was restless. When I rose, my shoulder blades felt closer together with more freedom of movement between them. There was tension on the left side of the cervical spine. The tension no longer keeps the neck bent to the right.

Dream of teeth coming out: I had a dream where I was selecting teeth in my mouth to take out, the bad ones and ones with fillings. I grabbed a hold of them and gave them a little twist and they came out with no pain, no blood and no roots on the teeth. Then I felt gaps all over my mouth from the missing teeth. This is the second time I have had a dream like this with teeth coming off at the base.

From 8:45 to 10:45 am, I did a sitting session. First, there was snapping and loud pops in left TMJ, then CCW torso rotation, and then popping in right TMJ. Later there was intricate work on the TMJ, cheekbone, mandible and neck and shoulder line. Several times, there was a muscular pull down through the maxillae. It was like when you curl your upper lip down and over your upper teeth. I felt work on the maxillae bone horizontally too.

From 11 to 11:30 am, I did a sitting session with popping of bones all along the cord of personality path on back. Then I felt energy twirling up the spine in the body in a clockwise direction and the body was stretching against this vortex with counterclockwise rotation on the outside. There was a stretch going up the spine. From 11:30 am to 12:45 pm, I did a freestyle session with ligament snapping.

From 4:15 to 4:30 pm, I was outside my house and did a session in a restroom. The energy in the skull is strong and there is pain in the cheekbone area. I was glad I could relieve the skull pressure. From 5:15 to 5:45 pm, I did a sitting session. The energy rose as a spiral up the spine branching with long stretches horizontally through my torso. Then I felt the entire shoulder girdle shift and release. Then energy went up into skull, twisting and pulling on tissues, which felt great. There was much popping of TMJ's. There was a big energy ball at the base of the skull, which seemed to make this easier.

From 6:30 to 7:30 pm, I did a freestyle session with the same kinds of stretches without pain, only tiring after a while. The body feels smoother in the stretch and energy is working both shoulders together horizontally! I need a new word to describe the upward, spiraling body stretches that pull apart my skeleton. From 7:30 to 9:30, growing phase started and I rested. From 9:30 to 11 pm, the session started with standing and going down to squat and then I could not feel anything. There was no resistance and I easily moved with the body reaction. I never felt it like this. There were amazing moves in the shoulders and head.

I felt the ethmoid bone moving with air turbulence inside and had a tingly nose. The energy was moving all over and I could not follow it. I only felt pain in the upper right sphenoid wing when the energy would pass through there. Later I did a sitting session with skull work until I was exhausted. There was a high-pitched tone on right side that sounded while sitting. The work is on both shoulders together with the TMJ's. It seems these areas of body are connected and need to release together. Finally, energy goes intensely into the tight muscles of the left shoulder. There were twists going around the neck. The energy is moving up the body with the spinal twisting and pulling apart phenomena.

Chapter 22: Sphenoid Release & Skull Articulation

Neck And Right TMJ Release, Intense Ligament Snapping In Skull

November 30: Difficult Skull Work, Jaw Wraps Around Neck

It was a restless night with many kriyas. I have much neck tension. From 6 to 7:30 am, I did a freestyle session. It was difficult because of neck tension. I stood, than sat and did spinal stretches, then lying on stomach with skull turns that gave some relief in neck. I had to go deep to center to allow the skull work. From 7:30 to 8:30 am, growing phase started and I rested. From 8:30 to 11:30 am, I did a lying session with work on skull and shoulders. It was difficult, like my head is twisting off with many facial bone movements. I wrote another tanka poem:

> Tornado vortex
> twisting apart foundations
> new life comes from old.
> Frozen personalities
> break apart under pressure.

From 1 to 1:45 pm, I did a freestyle session standing the entire time! With swaying stretches, the vortex worked up the spine into the skull. From 5 to 6 pm, I did a freestyle session standing the entire time! There was crunching and popping all over. It did not hurt, but was tiring. From 6:30 to 8 pm, I did a sitting session with skull work, long holds and much crunching in right skull. There were moments when it felt like my jaw was wrapped around my neck and pushing up, but it did not release. It was difficult.

At 8:15 pm, while sitting, energy circled around my neck and the right TMJ crunched and shifted like nothing I have felt before. From 8:20 to 10 pm, I did a freestyle session ending with lying on back doing skull work. There was a long period of strong ligament snaps along all the sutures and skull bones with jaw popping. I thought I was going to die. It was hard to endure so I went to deep center. After this, I felt loose ligaments in the right cheekbone area and the entire right face has loosened bones. The TMJ areas are sore.

Elastic Skull Turns With Pressure On Sacrum, Hyoid Release

December 1: Constant Pops Of Left TMJ, Sharp Object In Throat

I feel tension on left TMJ and at base of skull in back on right side. From 5:45 to 8 am, I did a CCW torso rotation session with constant popping of left TMJ for about forty minutes. I did a lying on stomach position with much skull turning. Then I felt much pressure on the sacrum. I felt the entire skull as one elastic sheet turning to the left. My nose was running and itching I guess because the ethmoid moved. It was difficult to rise with pressure at opposite ends of spine. I feel like a nap, that last session was difficult.

Dream of hyoid bone breaking: I had a dream in the session. I reached to the area on the throat where the hyoid bone is and it came out of my neck in two halves broken it the middle. It seemed another bone came out of the neck, but I do not recall what it was. Is it an omen of a move that will happen or has it happened?

From 10 to 12 am, I did a freestyle session standing most of the time, then squat, then sitting and twisting torso stretches, then lying on side, and last lying on stomach. The majority was skull work with crunching in lower right occipital bone and mandible with much skull bone movement. Then energy went across shoulder backs and I felt a big snap horizontally and then felt a sharp object in the throat. Did the hyoid bone release? I feel energy circling around the atlas bone and the skull feels free from the spine. I feel like sleeping, my hair is totaled and my face and ear are chapped and sore. I am getting many shiver episodes lately.

From 12 to 12:30 pm, my rest turned into another session. From 3 to 5 pm, I did a sitting session. Skull work was deep in sphenoid wing near the zygmatic arch and down. There was much crunching and opening of area under jaw, occipital bone and shoulder. Near the end, a profound whiteout happened with a clear high-pitched tone. My lower back still hurts. From 5 to 8 pm, I took a nap with a strong growing reaction. From 8:30 to 10 pm, I did a sitting session. Starting out there was high energy with soft bone movement without crunches. The last thirty minutes were difficult. Many bones released including the TMJ, cheekbone, palatine, maxillae, clavicle and scapula. From 10:30 to 11 pm, I did a sitting session with twisting stretches up spine with hip and sacrum openings. From 11 pm to 1 am, I did a sitting session with much skull work. I am sore all over.

Maxillae & Mandible Open, Bliss Sensation In Body

December 2: Sustained Spontaneous Moves, Loud Skull Pops, Whiteout

I awoke at 5:30 am, but the growing reaction was so strong I could barely sit so I went back to bed. From 8:30 to 9 am, there were strong spontaneous spine stretches before rising, where higher-self took over. I could only allow them by centering deeply and trusting I would not get hurt. From 9 to 11:30 am, I did a freestyle session where spontaneous movement lasted for more than an hour! Spontaneous movements stretched the entire spine with dance-like movements and swaying. Interspersed with this was work in hip and ligament snapping in skull. The hip popped several times and there were several loud cracks in skull back in upper right. There was a long whiteout with the right ear feeling deafened and a clear high-pitched tone. Something tight at neck back released. Then I was in squat, and after that sitting with twisting of torso to left. It was a difficult session but easy to sit in center.

From 11:30 am to 12:40 pm, I did a lying on the stomach session. At first, it was nice, sinking into a blissful energetic sensation as tension rolled out of the body with skull turning. I have felt this blissful sensation for a week. Then there were the loudest pops all over the skull I have ever heard: Bang, bang, bang, with about five minutes of rapid popping. There were many releases in the shoulder and the right skull. After this, the front of the face opened with the sensation that the maxillae and mandible were floating. There was extreme pressure on the sacrum and sexual arousal most of the session. It was difficult.

From 12:50 to 2:15 pm, I did a lying on the stomach session, which produces the most relief of tension with the least effort. Work was on right temporal bone and down to mandible. From 5 to 5:30 pm, I did a difficult sitting session. Something released under the scapula near right shoulder. From 5:30 to 6:30 pm, I did a freestyle session that lasted for forty-five minutes and a sitting session. There was much snapping and popping in the maxillae and mandible. I do not want to open my mouth anymore. From 6:30 to 8 pm, I did a lying session. From 9:30 to 12, I have been lying with a strong growing reaction and much sweating. There were some cracks on the left shoulder and mandible. As I fell asleep, the energy in my body grew to a strong vibration. Then I felt stinging prickles and energy puffs all over the flesh. I was sweating strongly. It took me a long time to fall asleep because it was not comfortable. The suffocating heat was the worst.

Sphenoid, Cheekbone, Eye Orbits & Nose Releases

December 3: Suffocating Sweats, Skull Vortex, Childhood Memory

I awoke at 7 am, with dry mouth and still feel sore and stiff. From 7:30 to 8:30 am, I did a CCW torso rotation session for about thirty minutes. There was skull, TMJ and shoulder work with significant releases in right skull near temple, in TMJ and cheekbone. Energy spirals up and forms a skull vortex.

From 8:30 to 9:30 am, I did a freestyle session standing the entire time with much skull popping. Fluid movement in body increases, the freestyle sessions are like a swaying dance. I felt a release of muscles between the right scapula and spine. There was a snap and it felt like two muscles separated and went opposite ways. It was like previously it was an X and when apart as parallel lines. Several times, I felt something release on the outside right lower side of skull and slide across like an elastic band. Many times work went into the tender area of the cheekbone and sphenoid wing. I had to go to deep center to allow most of the work.

Insight about spine shortening: An increasing sensation in the last months is that my spinal column gets shorter. Before it was like the hips and tailbone were way down there while energy worked in the skull. As the transformation continues, energetically the body grows toward being one unit and all parts are worked together. It is like there is no longer distance between the body parts. I know there is much more to do. I keep reminding myself growing takes its time. I wrote a tanka poem about it:

One step at a time
I walk on the path of life
finding no shortcut.
Accepting the laws of nature
a fruit will fall when its ripe.

From 10:30 to 11 am, I did a sitting session with work in sphenoid wing and cheekbone, which still hurts. I felt muscles releasing under cheekbone and down to shoulder crook. After this, I rested but tension builds fast. From 11:45 am to 12:45 pm, I did a freestyle session while standing with swaying and body crunching with much work in right skull and shoulder. Starting was difficult as I am stiff and sore but once energy increased, it was not bad. The rhythmic swaying action is effective to loosen skeletal bones. I stand with quiet mind allowing my body to be loose like a rag doll to allow the spontaneous body movements. When I stand long, the toes and fingers get puffy and fill with fluid.

There were several cracks with ligament releases. Both shoulders and TMJ's were worked together. There were many releases in skull, shoulder and neck at a deep level, which took strong energy to pull apart adhesions in there. Increasingly, a smooth elastic sheet covers the entire upper body, the body rotates counterclockwise and muscles relax. It feels open in right shoulder crook.

The main line of work is from sphenoid wing, down at angle under cheekbone, down to mandible in molar region, then down to clavicle near sternum, across to shoulder joint, then down back to scapulae, across to T1 vertebrae, then in a diagonal down to right hip. There is another line going down from TMJ, circling around occipital bone to base of skull, then down right side of spine between scapula bone and down to sacrum.

From 1:30 to 2:30 pm, I did lying on stomach session. From 5 to 5:30 pm, I did a sitting session. From 5:40 to 6:25 pm, I did a freestyle session with standing, squat, sitting twist and lying on side. It was difficult work. Several times, it felt like bones were sticking into my flesh at backs of shoulder tops and I felt muscles burning. From 7 to 8:45 pm, I did a sitting session with head crunching and much popping. At the end, spontaneous skull crunches occurred in broad bands in various directions. I endured way beyond comfort feeling it is near to finishing. I felt pain, as if the bones were sticking into my neck at the back.

The facial bones loosened horizontally across the nose and eye orbit edges. The facial bones, right jaw and clavicle feel loose. It is strange to have that feeling. I felt much pain in the right ear where a dog bit me when I was a child. I recalled that memory and pain, and cried praying for this to be over soon. This was the most intense skull session so far. I am sore. The left side of skull and body are involved in these sessions, but I do not notice the left bodywork so much because there are fewer adhesions. I fell asleep to high energy and sweating.

Hard Work Releasing Mandible & Sacrum, Sphenoid Crunches

December 4: Energy Balls Around Spine, Energy Circuit Up Right Spine

Awakening at 5:30 am, there is not much tension in the neck and skull, only a little in the sacrum. The growing phase continues. The shoulder girdle feels looser. From 6:15 to 8 am, I did a CCW torso rotation session but it was mostly lying on stomach doing skull turning. This was the hardest session like this so far. I felt intense pressure on head and tail ends of spine with the opposing horizontal stretch. There was intense pain in sacrum like giving childbirth and I had pain in the jaws and neck. It felt like energy was pulling the jaws loose. There were many rounds of ligament popping in the skull. Several times a huge energy came into the right skull and I had the padded bone feeling. At one moment, my hip released. I was groaning in pain near the end. I do not recall much because I was deeply surrendered. It was difficult to rise with the extreme pressure in the sacrum; it took me several attempts to rise. After this, the growing phase started with energy working all along spine. I slept until 11 am.

From 11 to 12 am, I did a freestyle session for thirty minutes with ligament snapping in body and skull, and a CCW torso rotation session. Energy balls wrapped around vertebrae while my upper body rotated CCW and the vertebrae snapped gently. The entire time the TMJ's were popping. The ligament snapping moved down the spine to about mid back. Now ligament snapping starts in the shoulder girdle, neck and skull. I have no idea what this was. Later, it felt like bones were sticking me in the chest by the clavicle and upper rib cage. There was a release of the pectoral muscle between the clavicle and a rib. It was intense. I felt squishy crunches deep in the skull. The body vibration keeps rising. I had several whiteouts.

From 12:10 to 12:45 pm, I did a sitting session with spinal stretches and ligament snapping along cord of personality line in torso and skull. There were more squishy crunches in skull and crunches in shoulder. From 12:45 to 1:45 pm, I did a freestyle session with ligament snapping. I feel energy rising on right side of spine and pulling apart the body. I feel popped out. From 5:30 to 7 pm, I did a sitting session that started fantastic with opening in shoulder and padded bone feeling in the skull. From 8 to 8:45 pm, I did a sitting session, mainly with skull work.

From 10 to 11:30 pm, I did a freestyle session, then a sitting session with work in torso and skull. There was much pain in the right jaw molar area and TMJ joint on the stretch, like bone grinding against bone. I stretched that area many times. This time instead of the typical TMJ popping and stretch through neck muscles, the crunches went deeper into the tissues. Several times, I felt bone crunching and internal popping in skull, which I think was in sphenoid bone and up the back of the neck.

From 11:30 pm to 1 am, I did a sitting session and energy increased fast. There were skull movements but more like freefall ending with intense holds down sides of neck and back. I was surprised to stretch into new paths in the skull connected to the body.

Spine Vortex Shaking Body

December 5: Huge Release Of Skull Bones, Fast Spontaneous Moves

From 7:30 to 8 am, I did a lying session where energy worked in right side of skull. There is strong pressure in right sphenoid and I heard several cracks in skull. From 8 to 10 am, I did a freestyle and sittings session, the skull hurts. From 10 to 11 am, I did a sitting session with twisting spinal stretches, work in torso, and ligament snaps along cord of personality. At one time, I had my head against the wall and it was similar to skull turning done on my stomach, so I have another option to do this and not get a sore face. I am exhausted.

From 11 to 12 am, I did a freestyle session. I have increased awareness and it is easier to sit in center and allow the spontaneous movements. While sitting there was a rocking twisting movement in the body corresponding to internal vortex of energy rising up spine. My body feels imprisoned with a strong cord holding me compressed and in constant tension on both ends of the spine. Working out I feel the stretching on both ends of spine. I imagine it is how a chick would feel when hatching. This tension and the desire to be free of it, keeps me going. The growing force continues all our life, and helps to free us from our prison. We want to be aware and free of pain, we want to be free. I wrote a tanka poem about it:

Shell of protection
restricted growth causing pain
desire for relief.
Baby chick's exhausting pecks
spurred by hope of space to fly.

From 12:30 to 2 pm, I took a nap. From 5 to 5:30 pm, I did a sitting session with releases in right hip, neck, shoulder and TMJ; the tailbone comes close to center in the tuck. The stretch is going up and over the top of the head feeling as if I am doing a full circle with my body. The right side of my body opens and forms as one energy. I felt a release horizontally across shoulder back near top that felt like a slowly moving line of energy with a cutting edge, which lasted for a few seconds. From 6 to 6:30 pm I did a freestyle session.

From 7 to 8:30 pm, I did a sitting session with the most skull openings so far. There was much popping, cracking, and stretching all over the skull for about a half hour and I wanted to stop. I changed my attitude and decided it was not painful. I then became one with it seeing myself popping along the lines of the sutures like viewing myself in the past. I had the perception of my head being over there or as having been there. This is real pain not imaginary as I am sore all over. Nevertheless, I can go through it and not have the experience of pain if I do not identify with it. The bones of the face are looser.

From 8:30 to 10 pm, I did an on the stomach session with skull turning. From 11 to 12 pm, I did a freestyle session. Wow! I was sore when I started but got past that feeling quickly when energy rose. The spontaneous movements were increasingly fast and I was moving with it. It went all over the skull, down the spine, into neck and shoulders with quick moves. A big muscle knot, below C7 on right of spine between scapulas, released. My shoulder dropped considerably after this. From 12 to 1 am, I did a lying on back session with more skull work.

Burning Lines Down Sutures At Sides Of Skull

December 6: Head Surgery

From 7:30 to 9:15 am, I did a CCW torso rotation session. Energy worked mainly on shoulder crook in front, and back and neck and skull on right. There were many rotations and it was not easy. I think the body is growing by slowly stretching out and making a new form. At the end, all was calm. From 9:30 to 12 am, I did three more sessions.

From 12 to 1 pm, I did a sun session. There was an intense period of burning lines down side of skull between sutures, which occurred about five times. The vibration is considerably higher. From 1 to 6:30 pm, I did a lying session, a sitting session, and had a nap.

From 6:30 to 7:30 pm, I did a freestyle session and near the end while sitting, I did not want any more crunches in the skull so I stayed still. Then strong energy rose and worked in the skull. It felt different because my head and neck were rigid yet filled with much energy. It was a new level of head surgery. A tiny skull move would happen and then a hold which repeated for about fifteen minutes. At one time, energy in the pelvis was strong and felt like sitting on a cushion. Then there were intense crunches near forehead, by ear, in jaws and by sphenoid wing. I would have liked to pass out. I went to bed early.

Learning To Move As Higher-Self, Sphenoid Crunching

December 7: Elastic Sheets On Skull Sides, Eczema, Baby Powder Smell

There was much sweating and kriyas in the night. I woke at 6 am, with tension in the left TMJ and my head is still tilted to the right. From 6:30 to 8 am, I did a CCW torso rotation session with much popping in the left TMJ. Near the end, there were stretches between the shoulder and TMJ that hurt.

From 8 to 9:45 am, I did a freestyle session. I started standing relaxed as if I was asleep. Then the head was swinging and I felt a smooth elastic sheet forming on the left part of skull and working to include the right side. Soon after that, it felt like my entire body was one energetic unit and I was dancing. This movement occurred when I felt tired and wanted to stop and sit. Instead, I decided to work harder at letting go of body control. This is what was needed and I had plenty of energy in my physical body to move me. The work was more effective when I was 'sleepy'. It was still difficult on right side because it hurt. After this, I went down to squat and lying on back where the cheekbone and side of the face was worked.

Insight about tiredness: Often the tiredness that overcomes me is not physical. Rather it is a sign of mental tiredness and therefore a signal for me to turn off the mind-chatter. When I am quiet, higher-self arises and I am no longer tired.

I have two patches that look like eczema[75]on my body. One is on the left thigh and the other is on the back of my upper right arm. They are a circle about three-fourths inch in diameter with a scaly edge, and clear in the middle **(see figure).**

From 10 am to 12:30 pm, I did a lying on the stomach session, which started with skull turning and then spontaneous stretching along the cord line. It felt like the sacrum lined up with the skull on the right and the spine felt straight. The jaws were moving in tandem with connecting muscles in the mouth and cheekbones. All this movement worked to release a muscle or tendon behind the right cheekbone, which goes down through the mouth. Twice I smelled baby power, like the fragrance used in Johnson & Johnson products. This session was difficult. At the end, the growing reaction was strong and I fell asleep on my stomach not moving for over an hour.

From 4:45 to 5:45 pm, I did a sitting session. The elastic sheet forms more in right skull and feels good. There were releases in jaws and shoulders and a clear tone sounded while walking earlier. From 6 to 7:30 pm, I did a freestyle session. From 9 to 10:30 pm, I did a sitting session with much skull crunching. The elastic sheet formed more over the skull and then a different kind of crunching started. I guess it is the sphenoid loosening because it felt deeper. I felt a release in the cord between the TMJ and right molar area of mandible and shoulder.

From 10:30 to 11 pm, I did a sitting session. The skull work was dramatic. The cheekbone and mandible loosened, with the feeling of knife blades inside as they shifted. Several times both legs elongated. From 11 to 12 pm, I did a freestyle session, which was intense with ligament snapping all over body. Then energy worked in cheekbone and shoulder. It is painful I do not want more. I am surprised I look the same after all this work.

Sphere Forms In Skull, Much Work In Facial Bones

December 8: Teeth Snaps, Maxillae & Mandible Crunches, Jewels In Mouth

I slept in until 10 am! From 10 to 10:45 am, I did a CCW torso rotation session with work in right front shoulder and some popping of TMJ's. From 11 am to 12:30 pm, I did a

---

[75] I had eczema when I was an infant; I presume this symptom is a sign the eczema was healing in the body. It is interesting that the baby powder smell and healing in the skull occurs in same period.

freestyle session standing the entire time. Several ligaments snapped, one horizontally across the shoulder top in back, one vertically up spine on right to skull, and one around the cheekbone. Once the skull jumped and shifted to the left when something released. The energy is strong and my toes are numb from standing. Each day the work is difficult. I do not think it is correct to say this session was the hardest ever or the most intense. Rather I am continually challenged based on my previous work. I feel there is nothing I cannot handle.

From 12:30 to 2 pm, I did a session where the left side of face opened much. From 5:45 to 6:15 pm, I did a sitting session. The entire time energy worked in skull with padded bone feeling and large bone adjustments. From 6:30 to 7:45 pm, I did a sitting session. Energy worked in right skull and shoulder. There was high energy for thirty minutes and then crunching. Energy worked entire skull and then a sphere formed in skull. Then energy worked on cheekbone, along eye orbits, TMJ's, mandible and maxillae. I felt several teeth snaps and the left and right shoulders were worked together.

From 9 to 11:30 pm, I did a freestyle session. Energy was strong. It started with the padded bone feeling in the skull and quickly I went down to squat. I easily sat in squat, slowly swaying, and could not feel much, only an increasing discomfort in the lower legs and ankles. Then I sat a long time while skull work occurred. The last forty-five minutes were maddening, with crunching in maxillae, mandible and bones vertically along side of face. Energy often went through the shoulder and jaw joints. I think the maxillae and mandible need to move[76], and many muscles and ligaments connect to them. There was much crunching with tinkling jewels feeling in the mouth. The left shoulder top is painful. I refuse to open my mouth.

Many Skull Releases From Top Of Spine, Skull Articulation

December 9: Popping All Over, Symphonic Sound, Amplified Senses

I slept long and well. After rising at 7 am, there is tension in the neck, near C7 and the shoulder crook. From 7:30 to 9:30 am, I did a CCW torso rotation session with repeating ligaments snaps in the cervical spine and shoulder crook going deeper each time. Then there was extraordinary popping of shoulder, rib cage and spinal column. I could not believe my body was doing this. There would be a pop, and then a stretch combined with skull and TMJ

---

[76] From the notes, it appears the sphenoid is opening by loosening bones around it.

popping. It felt like the skull was repositioning on the spine. In addition, I felt much movement in cranium bones and joints. The head feels like a precise and powerful articulating machine. The popping lasted an hour. Then I lay down with work in the right lower skull and shoulder and I felt the clavicle release. Several times, I felt energy fills in my legs and strong swirling energy in root chakra. I mostly felt pleasure despite the strong work happening.

From 9:30 to 10:30 am, I did a sitting session with ligament snapping in ribs, shoulders, TMJ, right shoulder and cord down to hip. It hurts now. From 10:30 to 11:30 am, I did a freestyle session. I felt sleepy when starting and allowed myself to be in 'sleep mode'. It was powerful. First there was ligament snapping and then down to squat, where I could not feel much in my legs. I let go of body control and allowed strong stretches, with many jaw and shoulder releases.

From 11:30 to 12 am, I was resting during growing phase. There is a beautiful symphonic sound in my head. My body vibrates strongly and I feel fleeting pains here and there. I have had many shivers. My hearing and sense of smell is amplified lately.

From 12 to 3 pm, I took a nap and from 5:30 to 6:30 pm, I did a sitting session with releases in skull, shoulder and back. From 7 to 8 pm, I did a freestyle session. A muscle released from the shoulder and TMJ. Now energy works in center of the skull. I felt energy move up both sides of maxillae feeling the hard palate in the middle with energy crunching up the sides. In the last half, I had to go beyond myself to allow the repeating crunches in the shoulder and TMJ's. The skull jumped and shifted to the left about five times. My right ear popped several times and I felt pain in the sphenoid wing.

From 8:15 to 10:45 pm, I did a sitting session. Starting, energy was high with work in TMJ, skull plates and occipital bone. Energy then switched to popping and crunching with some work in left shoulder. Crunching happens now in a circle around the mandible projection in the right jaw. Bone is grinding on bone with a squishy crunching sound. There was a long round of ligament snapping in maxillae and mandible seemingly along lines of the teeth. After this, energy shifted to intense holds with strong tension on various parts of the skull. I felt energy worked to move the maxillae. Then there were about ten cracks behind neck and releases of skull to left. **Each day it feels more like a knob is in the center of the skull and energy lines up to it from the back of the neck.**

Skull Feels Alive, Vertical Rod In Spine, Intense Facial Bone Work

December 10: Floating Facial Bones, Skull & Sacrum Release

From 12 to 1:30 am, I did a lying session with much skull turning. Something weird happened that is difficult to describe. The skull coming alive might be the closest. It felt like the cranium bones were moving and floating with energetic rotation of jaws. Often I felt my legs elongate. At the end, it felt like a vertical rod was out of place along the right spine. At this point, I collapsed not wanting more and the growing phase started.

It was a restless sleep with kriyas and cleansing dreams. I awoke at 9 am. From 9 to 10:30 am, I did several sessions. First, I did a CCW torso rotation session and there was loud snapping in the skull, which snapped as one unit for about twenty minutes, but I got little relief from the tension. Then I did a lying on stomach session with skull turning. When I lied down the snapping stopped. There was much work in maxillae and mandible with strong pressure on sacrum. When I stopped, it was difficult to rise but I feel the tension has released. My hair is totaled and my eye, nose and left ear are chapped.

From 12:30 to 2 pm, I did a freestyle session. The entire skull feels fluid. There were several releases in the shoulder with the feeling it dropped. I heard a loud clear tone in right skull. From 5 to 6 pm, I did a sitting session with strong stretches.

From 6 to 7 pm, I did freestyle and lying on stomach sessions with skull turning. Facial bones loosened and I felt my mandible, maxillae and cheekbones as if they had widely floated out. The ligament at back of the neck released, after energy worked this path: up back of skull in center, over top of skull and down front of face, under cheekbone and over to TMJ joint. After work in the TMJ, the ligament released. Then energy worked on facial bones in a parallel fashion. At end, there was difficult work on frontal bone. I went until I collapsed. I cannot believe this is occurring in my body, it is amazing.

From 7:30 to 8:45 pm, I did a sitting session with work in back and shoulders. From 8:45 to 9 pm, I did a freestyle session with crunching and popping of jaw and shoulder and deep in skull. From 10 to 11:30 pm, I did a freestyle session and it was easy to move as higher-self the entire time with no pain. At end, I was lying on stomach. The maxillae, cheekbones and mandible were pulled and stretched with plate movements and opening of the jaws. The working path, dropped down from eye orbit along side of nose, then at an angle from TMJ through cheekbone and into hard palate, then into the mandible, hyoid and working other plates. I could not follow it.

It was STRANGE that I did not mind having my face stretched and pulled apart like this. Near the end, I felt a muscle roll over half of my head on left and working to do the same on right. The maxilla was stretching with the upper teeth slowly with a complicated series of movements. Then there were teeth snaps and pulling, in the chin and teeth area. The mandible projection near top is stuck under cheekbone on right skull. That is where I hear the grating and grinding sound, and is the source of the pain when the cheekbone moves.

Energy Ball In Area Of Sphenoid Bone

December 11: Large Opening Of Skull Bones, Energy Circle Around Skull

I slept long and well. Waking at 7 am, there is strong tension in neck and skull. It is not like tugging muscles; rather it is like bones ready to release. From 7:30 to 8:30 am, I did a freestyle session, mostly lying with skull turns while the skull popped on the neck. Then there was ligament snapping all over various suture lines and then work on jaw. I felt shifts of skull on spine, which were gradually opening the right side of skull. I felt the nose, cheekbones, maxillae, and mandible moving at various times.

From 8:30 to 9:45 am, I did a sitting session with more skull work like previous session. I am getting many shivers after I stop lately even when I sleep. I am sweating occasionally. Now I feel the sphenoid move above the hard palate with softer movements. The articulation is smoother and energy works to increase skull articulation in all directions. When it moves I feel an energy ball above the hard palate with a sort of multi-dimensional projection in the way it is pointed. When I stopped a new section in the upper right of skull was popping.

From 9:45 to 11:30 am, I did some sitting but mostly lying on stomach with skull turning. Lately, this position puts extreme pressure on upper part of skull. It is like a brief headache with head pressure then a loud pop happens in a skull plate. I felt the parietals open on back of skull along the lamboid suture and then felt jaw adjustments made along these lines. The frontal bone released and I felt strong pressure above the nose at the tops of eyebrows and the eye areas. Then I felt the coronal suture over the top open. Lastly, I felt pressure directly on the left temporal bone with pops around it. Interspersed with all this were facial bone movements and shifts. It feels weird, but I like it. I can imagine never having a headache after this is done. I have not felt extreme pain, only a little on right sphenoid wing.

I took too long a break and there is much tension now. From 6 to 7 pm, I did freestyle session standing the entire time with head and shoulder work. There was much crunching in the mandible, maxillae and up side of skull along suture lines and much movement of the maxillae. There were some full rotations of the head, while it was tipped back. There is a circle forming at line of mandible horizontally around the skull. Several times the skull released with big thuds and shifts to the left. The shoulder dropped more. It felt like the stuck area between cheekbone and down to scapula released.

From 7:30 to 7:45 pm, I did a lying on the stomach session. I felt the strongest pressure so far on the left temporal bone. It felt like my left ear was rising and then when this area released it felt like the ear was rotating around the TMJ joint. First, the left temporal was done and then energy traveled diagonal across front to other temporal and then this rotated. There were about twenty of these energetic moves alternating sides. The pressure does not hurt but physically takes a toll.

At 7:50 pm, I was in a hold for about an hour observing the energetic work and sleeping a little. The energy was strong in the legs, hips and pelvic bowl. There were energy puff outs all over the body with a warm and tingly feeling and later it felt like pain all over. Several times, I felt fine tingly prickles on the buttocks with high sexual energy.

After the hold, there was more hard pressure on the skull with strong pops of the skull plates, interspersed with facial bone movements. There were several energetic rotations of the temporal bones. There were many movements of mandible and maxillae with teeth snaps in all teeth. The entire face rearranges with the twisting and stretching vortex forming in the skull. However when there is a gliding spiral muscular twist it feels good. As tension energy releases from facial bones, the body vibration increases rapidly. I think the skeleton alignment holds most energy of the personality. Much energy is held in facial bones, as they are rigid.

From 10 to 11 pm, I did a lying on back session with high sexual energy and crunching and popping all over the right side of skull. From 11:30 pm to 1:30 am, I did a freestyle session standing for an hour, and sitting for the rest. It was difficult to fall asleep because the body vibration was strong and I had pain in the leg bones.

Dream of being a man: In the hold, I had a dream of myself as a man with long blonde straight hair and glasses. Waking I thought that cannot be me because I do not have glasses. He was a small man and not tall.

Energy Explodes In Skull, Sphenoid Releases

December 12: Sphenoid Wing Crack, Freezing, Shivers, Neck Pummeled

I had many dreams and woke at 8 am. From 8:30 to 9:30 am, I did a CCW torso rotation session. The skull pops as one unit adjusting the skull on the spine. The muscle between the TMJ and shoulder joint has loosened and the shoulder drops more. There were several cracks in skull near sphenoid wing. My legs were warm and tingly the entire time.

From 9:30 to 10:30 am, I did a sitting session watching the internal energy. I feel both jaws moving more and muscles on underside of maxillae are shifting. The entire skull is shifting along the main suture lines. From 10:30 to 11 am, I did a sitting session with stretchy pulls through shoulder and TMJ alternating between front and back of body. There was a deep opening of skull up back of head on right and over to sphenoid wing in front.

From 11:30 am to 12:45 pm, I did a freestyle session. In the squat, I had my body balanced over the right thigh. It felt like energy was rising up the spine from there on both sides. It was difficult to sit in center, because there was more pain than usual and the movements were fast. Pain kept drawing me out of center with the voice that wants to quit.

I had a long break and feel great! From 5:30 to 6:45 pm, I did a freestyle session. It was as if I could not feel my body and was floating on energy. In the squat, there were complicated maneuvers in the spinal column and neck with tucking the chin to neck and feeling muscles open through the hyoid bone and over the mandible. Then I did sitting and lying on the stomach sessions. When I first lay down there was hard pressure in the skull on the sutures. Soon a huge energy exploded in the skull and I felt all the bones inside like loose Lincoln Logs jumbling around.[77] Then I felt a huge wave of pleasure as my body elongated several times. I felt a strong rush of freezing cold with shivers after the body elongations. Then there was more pressure on skull with pops and suture openings and I went to exhaustion.

---

[77] Perhaps a release of the sphenoid bone would cause this reaction.

From 7:30 to 10 pm, I rested for an hour with the growing phase and was freezing with strong shivers. After this, I was laying and a huge energy rose and engulfed the entire body. Then neck stretching started, so I sat up. The energy then rose up in a spiral from the tailbone and 'attacked' the jaw, neck and shoulders, concentrated on the neck. It was as if an area of one square inch was worked with hundreds of energy points working on it from all angles. There were slight body movements with much skull pressure and at times intense pain. There were many satisfying cracks at the back of neck, which released the skull to the left. This lasted about an hour and changed to crunching in the skull and popping along line of mandible with intense pain in the TMJ and lower molar. Several ligaments released. A ligament inside my mouth moved from mandible to area under tongue and centered in the middle. After this energy surged and several times, I felt cords moving inside my mouth and felt teeth snaps. This was so strong I thought something was in my mouth. This session was difficult yet satisfying because of the huge energy gain in the body. I went to bed early.

December 13: Complex Skull Work, Energy Rush, Skull Tones

From 4:30 to 6:30 am, I did freestyle and sitting sessions with skull popping. Notable was my head was tipped to right with head lying on right shoulder with all the body weight centered above it. Then there was crunching deep in the cheekbone, TMJ and on up. I noticed I kept protecting this region and not allowing energy to work in there. I have to face whatever old injury is buried in there. I know releasing the pain will feel good so I keep that thought in mind to psych myself up. I allowed more energy to work in cheekbone area this session. From 6:30 to 11:30 am, I did four sessions. Work was on shoulder joint and TMJ, with popping in shoulder and rib cage on right. It was difficult.

From 12:30 to 2 pm, the growing phase started and I took a nap. From 2 to 3 pm, I did a sitting session that had gentle popping in right skull and shoulder that felt good. From 5:30 to 7 pm, I did a sitting session with high energy to start and much crunching and popping in right skull. Loud tones sounded twice in left skull for a long time. There were complicated patterns of stretches. An example, which is not exact: muscles pull down over upper teeth, maxilla slides to left, muscles in jaw need to move, then mandible and TMJ pop, then forehead moves, then TMJ and right shoulder is stretched vertically on same side, then cheekbone shifts, etc. It is a complicated maze.

From 7:30 to 9 pm, I did freestyle and sitting sessions with skull and shoulder work and a strong hold in skull near end. Tones sounded in right skull and after that I felt a huge energy rush. It was the hardest work so far in the skull with extreme pain in right sphenoid wing. From 11 to 12 pm, I did a freestyle session. There was intense crunching in right shoulder and jaw. Several tones sounded. There was extreme pain with burning lines in the back of right shoulder for about fifteen minutes, the longest I have felt that. I felt the cutting feeling in the flesh as the right mandible, cheekbone, clavicle and scapula slid to new positions.

Sphenoid Articulation, Elastic Skull & Gliding Skull Bones

December 14: Shivers, Body Elongations, Burning Ring Around Skull

From 12 to 12:30 am, I did a lying session before bed. I slept well and did a stretch before rising at 8 am. My neck looks elongated. The maxillae and mandible feel they are in new positions.

From 8:30 to 9:30 am, I did a lying session. There was strong skull pressure with opening of cranial sutures. The temporal bones were worked and the jaws glide. I felt muscles between the jaws and shoulder points on both sides slowly move, as the jaws adjusted. Skull pain was like a migraine when pressure was briefly applied, then quick relief after the pop.

From 9:30 to 11 am, I did a sitting session with TMJ and shoulder work. Several times in the last sessions, I felt a pinpoint bubble-like pop at top of coronal suture while bones and muscles moved in skull. There were squishy crunches in TMJ, mandible and occipital bone ridge. Several ligaments snapped by facial bones. There were many gliding facial bone movements, several sneezes and energy elongations in lower body.

From 11 am to 12:30 pm, I did a sitting session. I feel powerful spine stretches with swaying body movements, where the skull and shoulders feel as one unit. I had many shivers. The line from mandible down to shoulder crook opened.

From 12:45 to 4 pm, I did three sessions: freestyle, sitting with spontaneous spinal stretches, and skull popping. I am dead. From 5:30 to 6:45 pm, I did a sitting session with skull and shoulder work, which started with strong energy while complex work was done in skull. This was easy and pain free for about forty minutes. There were strong holds with body tipped to left, followed by strong neck cracks. There was a brief strong pain in the left sphenoid wing and afterward it felt like that area of the skull glided. Energy now works on both shoulders and both TMJ's together. The left shoulder hurts. There were many openings of mandible, back of neck between base of skull and shoulder.

From 7 to 8:30 pm, the growing phase started and I slept. From 8:30 to 9:30 pm, I did a sitting session with skull work where I did not have to move much. My head bobs and sways and is held in positions with strong energy. At times, I feel tingles on the scalp sensing movements. I feel energy radiates out from above the hard palate by the sphenoid.

From 9:45 to 11 pm, I did a lying on stomach session. The strong energy continues with little pain. After some time, the area from the TMJ's to the top of the skull was one continuous elastic sheet. It was pulling down toward the neck in back, which happened several times. I recall a burning ring forming around the skull at the TMJ level or slightly above. There was an elastic sheet stretchy feeling around the skull in a ball like fashion. There was a loud crack in the right sphenoid wing area and another big crack near the mandible and I felt the jaw release. A hold immediately followed this.

From 11:15 to 12 pm, I did a lying on back session. First, I observed work on the parietals and felt pain near the wormian bones. It felt like I was lying on a bone under my head. Then the right sphenoid wing was worked and next the side of right face. Several times, I felt long glides down the lateral side where it felt like the cheekbone was sliding under the mandible. Then the work moved down to the side of the neck and along the shoulder and clavicle line. It felt like this area was inverting.

Chapter 23: Physical Release Of Spine

All Spine Vertebrae Popped, Ligament Snaps In Circle Around Skull

December 15

From 12 to 2:30 am, I did two lying sessions. The first was on stomach ending in a long hold. This process seems about cracking my head open like an egg. In the second session, I was lying on side with skull popping. There was work in chin and down the sides of the head. Near the end, energy changed and I felt muscles pulling up the throat and neck in front. There were many ratchets of temporal bone with movement of TMJ's down on one side and up on the other, interspersed with the vice-like skull pressure. There was work on back of skull, cheekbone and mandible.

From 9:30 to 10:30 am, I did a lying on back session with much skull pressure and suture pops. I could visually detect the twisted path of the cord of personality going down from skull to the sacrum. As this area of skull was worked, I felt releases in sacrum that felt wonderful as tension released. Sometimes my head would turn to the right, then my chin would tuck into the front of my neck, and it felt like one part of the face vertically tries to roll out and over the other. My neck feels free. There is tension in side of skull. My lips look like they have more color. From 11 am to 1 pm, I did a sitting and lying on stomach sessions.

From 1:45 to 2:30 pm, I did a sitting session. The right side of skull finally releases. Yeah! From 5 to 6:45 pm, I did a sitting and freestyle sessions. I feel much better. From 7 to 8:30 pm, I did a sitting session and lying on side with suture pops and work in jaws. This work was difficult. From 8:30 to 10 pm, there was a growing phase and a nap. When I lie down to rest, the energy fills my body and it goes numb and eventually I fall asleep. I always awaken when energy rises up from the tailbone like a tornado usually into neck or skull. It is so strong that when I rise I have to do a session.

From 10 to 11:30 pm I did a sitting session with work on muscle groups between TMJ's and shoulders. Starting out, all vertebrae popped from bottom to top with many pops in the neck. Then there was ligament snapping in a circle around the skull on sides, over top and under jaw. Then I was tipped to left, with work in right TMJ and crunching in the neck. There were many cracks in neck vertebrae with releases of skull to left. As it occurred, the left shoulder, sacrum and lower back accumulated tension. Something released a few times across the left shoulder top, it seems only to release as a pair with the right shoulder and TMJ. This was difficult. From 11:30 pm to 1 am, I did a freestyle session. I think a new spiral forms in skull. I hurt all over.

December 16: Knife-Edge Feeling Along Cord Path, Neck Pops

From 8:30 to 9:30 am, I did a sitting session with cervical spine popping, going round and round with releases of skull to left. Then there was work in TMJ's and cheekbones. Then tremendous tension built in trapezious muscles, which seemed it was done to release the skull. Then I did a lying session.

From 10:40 am to 12:30 pm, I did a sitting session and freestyle session and long hold of thirty minutes. I had the padded bone feeling to start. Then I felt a continuous circle all along the cord of personality and felt knife-cuts all along it. I especially noticed this through hip, up back to right shoulder and right skull. There is strong work now in left shoulder that is painful. It is also painful when both shoulders move together. If I am not surrendered it hurts like hell, otherwise I can endure it. I found a thick soft scarf to tie around my head to protect my face during the lying sessions. When there is a will, there is a way.

From 12:30 to 2:45 pm, I did a lying on stomach session with the scarf, which worked nicely. It is about eight inches wide and four feet long made of a stretchy fleece that allows for a tight fit, yet ability for skull to expand with it on. I wrap it around skull covering eyes, ears and nose. There were many releases in skull, TMJ's, shoulders and neck. From 5:30 to 7:30 pm, I did a standing session with popping occurring in many of the tight areas. I felt like a mad woman because my body was moving fast in many ways. The body bursts apart.

From 7:30 to 9:30 pm, I did a lying on stomach session with two holds between crunching sessions. The middle of the neck released, and immediately after I was in a strong held position. I think the holds have the purpose to make energy circuits between lower body and skull after something opens. The sexual energy grows in the holds. I feel healings in various places: right ankle, left shoulder, skull, left sacrum has burning on it. The body turns were strong; I surrendered body control to allow the reaction. The growing phase started after this.

December 17

From 8:30 to 9 am, I did a CCW torso rotation session with popping going around and around the neck. My neck feels longer and almost free from the shoulder. From 9:15 am to 10:45 pm, I did eight sessions and am tired.

Insight about stretching short cord of personality: It is clear, energy rises up spine from the tailbone, twisting in a spiral fashion to work the upper body. The cord of personality is like a short stiff cord in the body creating a huge tension, like a spring that is wound too tight. This creates continuous pressure to lengthen and open it by stretching it out, which is done to release this energy. Of course, everything is connected in the body all along this cord. With each opening of a joint and each stretch of the spine and skull, the cord gets a little longer and more elastic. In the next stretch, there is greater range of movement, which gives more force to free the next restriction. I predict that at the end, a huge vortex composed of entire energy of personality will form as vortex in pelvic bowl. This will then rise up from tailbone after orgasm to the brain. Then the brain will change greatly and I will be enlightened!

Rod From Neck Into Skull, Gliding Spheres At Ends Of Spine

December 18: Numb Body, Blissful Tingling, High Sexual Energy

From 7 to 8 am, I did a lying on stomach session with skull turning and work to loosen right mandible. The facial bone movements are more dramatic. I feel the parietals moving behind skull with pulls along the lamboid suture. In general, the sutures are looser and the skull feels alive and like an elastic ball. It is amazing the cranium bones can move like this. The mandible will drop down and open, then the cheekbones move, then the cranium bones stretch along the suture lines, repositioning all cranium bones so slowly. My skull seems like a spinning ball on a stick. I feel a strong rod coming up the back of the neck into the skull; I guess it is the spinal column activating more. From 8 to 8:30 am, I did a sitting session.

From 12 to 8 pm, I did four sessions. There were stretchy loops going through skull and over my shoulder as if it is opening this area. I felt several cords release in TMJ's, shoulder, mandible and neck. I have the sensation of gliding spheres on both ends of the spine with only a little twist between them.

From 8:30 to 10 pm, I did a lying on stomach session and fell asleep at end in a hold. I was stretched while I slept. I woke at 3:30 am. The holds are getting interesting; the entire body fills with vibrating energy and everything goes numb. I feel tingling all over; it feels good and lulls me to sleep. The pelvic bowl is getting warm as if it has a heater inside and I feel tingly prickles on the buttocks and genitals. I feel small pains here and there in the body.

All Skull Bones Crunch At Once, Skull Moves Spontaneously

December 19: Right Skull Energy Circuit, Muted Hearing, Whiteouts

From 3:30 to 4 am, tension is building in neck and skull. I did sitting CCW torso rotations. From 4 to 6:15 am, I did a lying on stomach session. It was intense with alarming moves in mandible and skull. It is like every bone in skull crunches at once with much tension on the sacrum. It is difficult to sit in center and not feel pain. I could barely rise because of the pulling energy on both ends of spine. There were strong skull turns with pulls of the muscles from the outside of mandible and down toward neck. It felt like the jaw was turned inside out. There were strong moves of the TMJ's combined with cocked head movements.

From 6:30 to 7:30 pm, I did a sitting session. I had a burst of willpower to get through this by surrendering and allowing the spontaneous stretches. I am sore and tired but there is too much tension. From 7:30 to 9 am, I did a freestyle session. From 9 am to 1 pm, the growing phase started and I slept. From 1:15 to 1:45 pm, I did a CCW torso rotation session. Something feels different in the neck and shoulders; the tension is more toward the spine and up the back of neck.

From 5 to 6 pm, I did a sitting session. It feels close to an energy circuit forming between the sacrum and skull. From 6:30 to 7:30 pm, I did a freestyle session. Starting out I felt tingling on back of the skull. I felt an intense pain up side of skull on right between cheekbone and TMJ joint. I kept having whiteouts with muted hearing and padded feeling in cranium bones. The energy boost did not last long and then it would hurt. These energy surges kept repeating. The last work was on collarbone at sternum, up to molar, over to TMJ and up. There was left shoulder and TMJ work. I am exhausted. From 7:30 to 9:30 pm, I did a lying on stomach session. At the end, ligaments were releasing on right side of face and skull. There was a thirty-minute hold in the middle.

From 11:30 to 12 pm, I did a lying on stomach session. In this session, my head felt different. It was like the skull bones expanded and were moving outside the normal confines of my face shape. The skull felt hard and heavy as if it had life of its own and large movements and turns of the head were occurring spontaneously. It was strong; I could only go to center.

December 20: Left Ear Moves, Nose Squishes, Shivers, Elastic Skull

5 am: Every night the energy in the body is stronger. It is difficult to fall asleep with the sweats, vibration, body kriyas and pain felt deep in the bones. There is frequent stretching of spine during sleep, I get the urge to stretch or turn and do it automatically. This stretch reflex eventually gets too strong and I rise. From 5:30 to 8:30 am, I did a lying on the stomach session, which ended in a hold and sleep. From 8:30 to 10 am, I did a freestyle session. A muscle on TMJ released and there were more squishy crunches on lower back and right of skull perhaps under occipital bone. I was tired the entire time and it was painful. I think the skull work is better to do lying because the weight is off the skull. While standing or sitting you feel bone on bone and this does not feel good. From 10 to 11 am, I did a sitting session.

From 11 am to 12:30 pm, I did a difficult lying on stomach session. It is getting boring writing about it. There are endless stretching passes, work keeps getting harder and range of movement always increases. Holds between stretches are common. I felt the strange left ear movement and the nose was squished much and itches internally. Work was on both TMJ's and shoulder joint points simultaneously. There were many shivers and sweats. It is torture.

From 5 to 10 pm, I did four sessions. There was much crunching in lower right skull. A muscle released in back. When lying after difficult skull crunches, there was a rhythmic turning of skull to left. It felt like my entire skull was one elastic sheet. At the end, there was a hold with strong growing reaction and pain all over. I hope I can sleep.

December 21 (Winter Solstice): Jelly Nose, Intense Skull & Body Crunches

I slept well and rose when the kriyas were strong. I am not so bent. From 6:30 to 7:30 am, I did a sitting session. From 7:30 to 8 am, I did a freestyle session. In the molar area on right mandible, I felt a crunch and then a muscle wrapped around the bone released. From 8 am to 12:45 pm, I did two sessions and had a nap. There is less neck tension and release of muscles on right mandible continues.

From 12:50 to 7:45 pm, I did four sessions. There was a difficult period of mad crunching through entire body. There has been much skull crunching. From 10 to 11 pm, I did a lying on stomach session, like last night with endless turns to left with the smooth gliding feeling without crunches. These turns are rapid, perhaps one every second. Once, my head felt solid or stiff, which is a new sensation. Perhaps it is due to numbness. It is difficult to observe what happens because I go to deep surrender and cannot remember. I was sweating profusely. Each time I feel the heat rising into the body from the pelvic area. Tonight my face is soaking the sheet I was laying on which then sticks to my face because it is damp. When the facial bones smash, they feel like jelly. One time the mandible opened wide and it felt like it went out to the sides beyond the normal face contours. I was in hold at the end and at 11:15 pm, I fell asleep.

Full Take Over Of Higher-Self For Ten Minutes

December 22

From 4 am to 1:30 pm, I did four sessions. There was work in skull and shoulders and at end everything felt like it was burning. I am sore and it is difficult to do the sessions.

From 5 to 9 pm, I did four sessions. The left mandible dropped several times. Energy now works muscles going up both sides of neck in back. There are new paths of stretching through skull, the energy is high and the work is not too difficult. There was another round of crunching down the right side of skull and neck. I am tired.

From 10 to 11 pm I did a freestyle session mostly surrendered. Starting out the energy was so strong that higher-self took over and my body was moved as needed, it did not matter if my mind was quiet. It surprised me when this happened. It lasted about ten minutes. Then I centered well and continued. I am better at surrendering and allowing spontaneous body movements.

Insight of sensation of bliss: sleeping is a relaxed state. Everyone knows what sleep feels like, and craves it because it is blissful. Everyone has experienced bliss. It is that warm tingly vibration feeling where you feel no pain anywhere in the body or mind and you sink into this sensation and could stay there forever. When I am doing these sessions and I am surrendered then I feel blissful. I can tell it is the same sensation as the feeling of deep sleep. I think I will have the blissful feeling all day long when I am enlightened. Cool!

Full Vortex Forms On Spine

December 23: Vortex Balls On Ends Of Spine, Vortex Rotates Upper Body

I arose at 4 am, and feel rested. There is much tension in the skull. I did a CCW torso rotation session and from 5 to 6 am, I did a sitting session. The energy is very high. Soon after I started, I felt vortex balls on both ends of the spine. It felt like the entire spine was rotating from head to tail and the upper body and head were swinging around with a centrifugal force removing the kinks. There were small whorls of energy rapidly forming in the pelvic bowl and rippling up. I got into it. It felt like I was sleeping, while my body moved round and round while energy moved up toward the head. Just before I stopped, the entire body shivered, and it was like being in a deep freeze that lasted about five minutes. I am tired.

From 6:30 to 10:30 am, the growing phase started and I took a nap. From 10:30 am to 12:30 pm, there is intense tension on the line up the back of skull. It seems all tissue is loose around it and only a thread holds it in place. Lying on stomach feels easier to do, I do not feel pain. I feel elastic sheets stretching over my head in various directions. The pelvis is active with rhythmic motions and alternating hip joint action and sacrum flexes. Once, something released in the skull and my head swung to the left. Then it felt like the skull was supported by a cushion of air. That feeling lasted about five minutes. There was more work deep in shoulder crook and the left shoulder released much. My mind races with intelligent thought and insights come, a symptom I recall from my crown opening seven years ago.

Insight of I will always be in control. Ever since the Kundalini triggered, I have wondered if some strong reaction might happen when I am in public and I would lose control. I asked about that and heard the answer: "You will always be in control, you can quell any reaction. There is no need to worry." Finally, I have my answer!

From 12:30 to 9 pm, I did four sessions with strong energy. There were tension releases in TMJ, neck and shoulders that felt great. There was mandible and maxillae repositioning with much facial sweating. From 10 to 11 pm, I did a sitting session. There were big loosening crunches in neck, shoulders and back that felt like marbles rolling around. Several times tones sounded in right skull. There were several brief searing pains in skull near TMJ and on up the suture line. It felt like a muscle uncurled under the cheekbone and eye orbit.

From 11 to 12 pm, I did a difficult lying on stomach session. There were five-thousand more rhythmic skull turns to left and brief searing pain in right TMJ. There was a period where the left skull, felt hard like a rock and little stiff adjustments were done here and there with much force behind them. These moves are the hardest for me.

The rhythmic skull turns seem at the rate of the frequency of respiration. I think this action is moving the skull plates. I try to describe it. There is pressure on left upper front of skull. Then as my head turns to the left, there is a pulling down on left side, which I feel down to my toes. Then there is a pulling up through the body, where the head returns to the start position in center.

Along the edge of right mandible, there is a bone or muscle in parallel with it that seems too low. I had the feeling this muscle was pulled out, up, and over. I had a sweaty head most of the time, felt like I was suffocating, and the nose ran much. I think the latter is a reaction from movement of the sinus cavities, which serves to protect the bones. I do appreciate the sweat because I know the high heat makes these moves easier.

Pelvic Opening With Huge Release Of Both TMJ's

December 24: Ligament Snapping In Cranium Bones And Teeth

From 12 to 1:30 am, I did a sitting session with many teeth snaps in maxillae and mandibles. There was snapping and popping in new areas of skull too. I am popped out.

The energy is strong, but difficult to get started, I still feel sore from yesterday. From 8 to 9:30 am, I did a sitting session with popping of bones in various paths through central nervous system. I have pain in the lower abdomen as if the intestines have an infection and the area feels tight and stiff with a dull ache. Near the end, rotational energy built in pelvis and suddenly the stomach muscles in the lower abdomen engaged and there were spontaneous pelvic pushes for about fifteen minutes followed by a spontaneous orgasm. I felt this action was loosening the bones in the pelvic bowl. Later there were some stretches up through right hip and shoulder with horizontal pulls across the lower back. Today was the first time I felt a stretching movement and a clear release of tension. The entire central nervous system area comes together.

From 10 am to 11 pm, I did five sessions. The last session was lying on stomach session with skull turning. Then there was a long hold and I fell asleep. All the time in the hold, I felt strong work going on with fleeting pains here and there. After the hold, the TMJ's released and internally it felt like big wheels spinning around on both sides of the head with no resistance. It felt great.

December 25: Spontaneous Orgasm, Skull Surgery

From 6 to 8:15 am, I did a lying on stomach session. I observe that the undulating spine action in this position is what is effective to open the spine from tailbone to skull. There was work on back of neck, shoulders and sacrum. I could barely feel anything during the session. It is as if my entire body is filled with energy. Sexual energy is high and I felt several pains near pubic symphysis. I feel like I have a sore throat with a rough sounding voice after this session. Does the voice box change too? From 8:15 am to 12:45 pm, I did four sessions.

From 1:45 to 7 pm, I did three sessions with one spontaneous orgasm. From 7 to 9 pm, I did a lying on stomach session where I blanked out and was not even aware I went to sleep. I have no memory of it at all. At 10:30 pm, the growing phase continues. My left shoulder hurts, as if it is swollen. The sessions were difficult.

From 11 to 12 pm, I did a lying on stomach session. There were more holds than movement. This sequence repeated: a few slow and precise strong moves in skull, then in an instant freeze and hold for abut fifteen minutes. I fell asleep. The growing in the body is strong. I feel pain in various areas and have to change body positions frequently to get comfortable. There are many kriyas. I could sense the spiraling energy moving up, stretching, and working on blockages in the holds.

December 26: Pelvic Rocking, Spontaneous Orgasms, Centrifuge In Skull

I arose at 4 pm because of pain but sitting did not help so I went back to bed. I awoke at 6 am, and feel stiff. From 6:30 to 9 am, I did two sitting sessions with strong body pulls through TMJ's, neck and shoulders while popping the bones in these areas round and round. It felt good. There was sacrum work. It felt like the inner side of right hip opened far down toward the tailbone. Then there was work on right skull and shoulder.

From 10 to 12 am, I did a lying on stomach session. There were the typical body and skull turns to left. Notable is the hips and pelvis engaged more with more range of motion in the sacrum flex. Sexual intensity rose spontaneously when I was surrendered and the more I surrendered my body the higher it grew. I felt an energy ball spinning in the root chakra, used as a force to open the right side of groin. There was alternating pelvic pushing and sacrum flexes. Then there were intense spontaneous orgasms where I screamed about five times. After this, the pelvis settled then the energy rose up the spine with strong pressure on the skull. Then there was strong crunching work on right shoulder, neck and skull.

From 12 to 7 pm, I did four sessions. One was lying on stomach, nearly identical to the previous session. From 5 to 7 pm, I did a sitting session with a release in area of back of neck and shoulder that felt great! When it gave, there was the sensation of a knife-edged bone moving toward the skull fast. Perhaps it was a release of the scapula. There were several burning lines after and more muscle releases under the jaw, in face and neck. There were several burning lines around cheekbone. There were many pelvic pushes with a large energy ball in the root chakra. There were many pops in right ear, shivers near the end, and I felt cold.

From 11 to 12 pm, I did a sitting session with more releases in the shoulder to where it feels clear. A centrifugal force works in the skull. The skull has bands of rotating clear energy going around it in various directions. One is over top of head and one is behind neck with TMJ's. I felt these bands extend way down over the shoulders to mid back. It felt like all this area was clear with no crunch and no resistance. The formation of these bands felt great.

Sensation Of Making Love With An Invisible Partner

December 27: Burning Ring Around Skull, Energy Ball On Perineum

From 12 to 12:45 am, I did a sitting session and heard a clear high-pitched tone sound in right skull for about three minutes. From 1 to 2 am, I did a lying on stomach session and fell asleep in a hold. From 5 to 5:45 am, I did a sitting session. A circle is forming in the skull connecting the TMJ's. From 6:30 to 9:30 am, I did two sessions.

From 1 to 3 pm, I did a lying on stomach session. The jaw gets loose and I feel it moving around. Energy worked around the mandible, it seems its inverting. I feel an energy ball pressing on the perineum and it seems something happens with the genitals. The sexual energy is high. I made spontaneous moaning sounds when there were body pulls with stretching on both ends of spine and crunching in skull. Several times the pelvic area contracted and it felt as if a bone was between the thighs. It felt like making love with an invisible partner.

From 6 to 7 pm, I did a freestyle session moving through the cord area and popping everything at a new level and in new areas. I felt the pelvic energy ball action with some upward stretches. I felt balanced at times in the squat with body resting above right hip. It feels clear as one line up through the body. There is always another level and more to do.

From 7 to 10 pm, I took a nap with a strong growing reaction. I woke drenched in a sweat. From 10 to 11 pm, I did a CCW torso rotation session. At start, I felt a burning ring around skull at TMJ, mandible and occipital bone line and I continued to rotate for about fifteen minutes. Then there was popping and crunching work on all these areas. I am tired.

December 28: Neck Elongation, Spontaneous Orgasm

I woke at 6:45 am. It was a restless sleep, filled with kriyas, sweats and tension behind neck under mandible and occipital bone at base of skull. My neck elongated physically. From 7 to 7:30 am, I did a CCW torso rotation session, which opened the area behind skull by mandible and occipital bone. From 7:30 to 8:30 am, I did a freestyle session with skull and back work. From 9:30 to 12 am, I did three more sessions with skull and back work with releases in right hip.

From 12 to 12:30 pm, I did a freestyle session. From 12:30 to 2 pm, I did a lying on stomach session. There was a strong spontaneous orgasm and after this energy rose up spine and worked in the skull for about fifteen minutes. From 5 to 8 pm, I did a sitting session with release of tension from jaws. From 8 to 10 pm, I slept.

Physical Loosening Of Spine With Labor-Like Pushes

December 29: Circle Forms Between Ends Of Spine, Constant TMJ Snapping

From 1 to 2 am, I did a CCW torso rotation session working both sides of TMJ's and shoulders together the entire time. From 8 am to 2:30 pm, I did three sessions. The last was a difficult lying on stomach session. There was pressure on TMJ's with popping and pressure on neck and sacrum with uterine pain during the pelvic pushes.

From 5:30 to 6:30 pm, I did a sitting session. There was much ligament snapping. I feel like I am a skeleton popping my bones into place. It does not hurt it merely feels weird. This session concentrated around the neck and shoulders with the TMJ's working together much more and with more turning of cranium bones as a single unit.

Lately when there is centrifugal force in the skull from swaying, a rippling happens on the surface where the force is applied. It is like a gentle rippling of bone movement and inside I can hear light pops and cracks. These generally feel good and I guess it indicates all bones of the skull are sufficiently loose and can move now. The pelvis has a huge vortex or energy ball inside. Often there is swirling energy in root chakra and sometimes with stinging prickles. I feel a circle forming now and an energy circuit forming between the two ends of spine.

There was a large release in right mandible, neck and shoulder and afterward it felt hollow there. There have been strong pelvic pushes lately combined with strong skull pressure. The spine seems it is separating from the body. Often I make spontaneous groaning sounds with the strong pushes. The body makes the sounds because of the strong force moving through it. It reminds me being in labor.

From 7:30 to 9:30 pm, I did a lying on stomach session, like the previous session, and it was difficult. From 9:30 to 10:30 pm, I took a nap. From 10:30 to 11:30 pm, when I arose there was pressure on both TMJ's and the urge to snap them together. Then there was strong incessant snapping. I could not stay upright so I lay down. The only comfortable position was on the stomach, which I did not want. The last stomach sessions have been much more pain than pleasure and I dread them. I fell asleep after this.

Sacrum And Skull Release

December 30: Strong Teeth Snaps, Crying, Tones And Whiteouts

From 4 to 4:30 am, all night there was such strong work going on in the body with sweating, kriyas and constantly turning positions. I rose hoping to turn off the reaction. The tension is along the back of neck and mandible. The CCW torso rotation was difficult. The teeth are moving with strong teeth snaps in the skull. I do not think I can take this sitting.

From 4:30 to 5:30 am, I did a lying on stomach session. It was difficult with increasing pain in sacrum, skull and uterus. Typical work was a turn of the head combined with a pelvic push and strong head popping which happened repeatedly. I was lying there as relaxed and centered as I possibly could be, allowing what had to be done.

From 5:30 to 8 am, I slept. There is still pain in sacrum with much tension in neck and at base of skull. My enthusiasm is low. I do not want to go on. I had some strange dreams.

Dream of being in sea with fish and dolphins: I was being pulled through a large expanse of water hanging onto a towrope and as I passed through the water, I could see many large colorful fish and dolphins near the surface basking in the seawater. I was in awe to see this. I was tired and let go of the towrope, the boat went away from me, and the drivers did not realize I had let go. I had some concern because I knew I could not catch the boat by swimming. Then I relaxed, feeling they would return.

Dream of new penis: I was dreaming I was in bed and saw a large penis freshly born and erect, wondering how it got there between my legs. A man came and was supportive realizing what had happened to me. He looked at it and said it needs some surgery. I said no, my body would take care of it.

From 8 to 10:15 am, I have to go with it there is too much pain. I did a sitting session with much popping of shoulder girdle, mandible and maxillae. From 10:30 am to 1:30 pm, I did a difficult lying on stomach session. A bit of blood came out of my nose. The sacrum still has intense pressure on it.

From 1:30 to 3 pm, I did a sitting session. It hurt as energy pulled apart the shoulder, neck and skull and I sobbed while it happened. After this, it felt like padded bones in the skull and was not bad. Energy seemed to be working at deep level in skull by sphenoid wing. From 3:30 to 4:30 pm, I did a sitting session. The energy does not let up. I am crying much and praying this will end soon. From 4:30 to 7:30 pm, I did a lying on the stomach session.[78]

From 8 to 10 pm, I did a sitting session. After taking a break, the energy was strong, so it did not hurt. I heard a tone in right skull and later, there were two whiteouts in the left skull. After this, my head was supported by a strong energy and I felt new complicated paths of stretch in skull. I have never felt the energy this strong before. I felt some tension down back to right hip. From 11 to 12 pm, I did a difficult sitting session.

Sacrum Separation & Tailbone Release

December 31: Left TMJ Opens And Spreads Far Apart

From 12 to 2:30 am, I did a difficult lying on stomach session. Something opened in the pelvic area near the anus or tailbone that felt like little bones crackling. There was an opening going down the right sacrum hip suture line with a twist of the body.

There was much sacrum flexing and pelvic pushing. It feels like having a child. I recall that experience now, the endless pushes, the sacrum pain, and wanting it to be over soon. While the two ends of spine are worked, the skull pops and adjusts. My face moves more to the center instead of to the right side. I am exhausted. From 8:45 am to 12:30 pm, I did three sessions, which were not painful with work on right mandible. My energy feels strong.

From 12:30 to 1 pm, I did a sitting session and for the first time energy went deep into left shoulder. There was a slow tilt of head to left with strong tension, then a pop of a bone vertically perhaps in left side of neck or near shoulder crook. There were many strong pops like this. I feel ratcheting circles of temporal bones moving with TMJ's on both sides of the skull. I have never felt that so pronounced before. I feel much pain from the left shoulder in a line down to right hip crest. Sometimes I am in a position with left ear next to left shoulder joint tip, presumably to release the molar jaw muscle on left side. I feel increased

---

[78] Most likely, the sacrum released during this session.

ability to move head and neck in leftward turns. It is strange that all my life I never noticed restricted movement of turning my head to the left.

From 1 to 3 pm, I did a lying on stomach session with a strong spontaneous orgasm. From 6:45 to 8 pm, I did a freestyle session, with tension releases in skull. My toes are numb from standing so long. There was a big neck crack and a muscle released afterward. From 8:30 to 9 pm, I did a sitting session. From 9 to 11 pm, I did a lying on stomach session. After about twenty minutes, the left TMJ opened and spread far apart. Right after this there was a long hold. I feel stinging prickles with slight burning feeling but it is not painful. I detect little energy puff outs here and there in the body. There is strong energetic activity in the root chakra and the area feels warm.

To be continued…

Glossary

Acupoint is a small vortex of energy, palpable on the surface of the skin as a faint pulse, an entry point into a meridian pathway. These acupoints were determined long ago, by people that could feel energy on the body. They mapped the meridian pathways and acupoints along them. It is called an acupoint because in traditional Chinese acupuncture, it is a point on the body where the acupuncture needle is inserted for treatment.

Acupressure is an energetic healing technique to apply pressure to acupoints along Chinese meridian pathways. This is the same principle as doing acupuncture, the difference being instead of using an acupuncture needle you use your fingers. The pressure activates the nervous energy moving along the meridian channel producing piezoelectricity. This acceleration is the source for the healing effect.

Aura is a field of subtle, luminous electromagnetic radiation surrounding a person or object like the halo or aureoles of religious art. In people, it extends a few feet out in all directions.

Black Void refers to a reaction that happens in the mind where there are waves of total darkness between being conscious. There is absolutely nothing to hear, see or sense and you cannot feel your body. It is total nothingness and is scary.

Blanked Out is my term for an altered state of consciousness where there is a total absence of thinking and sometimes of feeling. Often there is no memory while in this state, yet you are aware it is occurring. It is like watching yourself sleeping. Time flies by fast where thirty minutes feel like one. It is common that hearing amplifies in this state.

Blockage and Blocks refers to an area in the body where energy cannot flow freely at ideal level to maintain a healthy system. An energy block can be mental, emotional or physical. It is also known as energy being held as form by a person, owing to conditioned response patterns.

Body Pull is a spontaneous stretch along the spine. There is a pushing action downward on the lower spine with sensation of pushing out at pelvis to extend tailbone with simultaneous pulling action along upper spine up through neck and skull to open top of spine in brain stem. It is like being pulled apart at both ends of body, and thus why I call it a body pull.

Body Squeeze is a spontaneous stretch along the spine like a body pull but stronger. As the stretch reaction rises up the spine, it squeezes all the tissue, including rib cage, neck and skull. As the energy passes through chest and neck, the breath is held and vocal sounds are common. When energy passes through the skull, you go out of body or see blackness for a few seconds.

Bliss Feeling is a healing reaction where you feel warm, tingly, calm, vibrantly alive, and free of any pain. It is similar to when you are in a deep sleep state.

Brain Flash is a reaction that happens in the mind, with sudden explosion of light with inner view of a galaxy of stars followed by a completely quiet mind.

Burning Lines is a healing reaction felt as a moving burning line going along a narrow path in the body, most often felt in muscles.

C7 is an acronym for the seventh cervical vertebra, at bottom of base of neck. This is the big bump on spine at level of shoulders behind the neck.

Center is an altered state of consciousness where your mind is quiet and your body is relaxed. Consciousness is withdrawn from the sensation of pain. You are aware and can easily feel and observe your body but do not identify with it, so do not feel transformation energy as painful. Deep center is less identification with the body, like **Outer Space** or **OBE**.

Chakras are wheel-like vortices existing at different points along the spine. There are also chakras on the palms, soles of the feet, below the feet and above the head. There are seven chakras located along the spine and each is associated with a specific tone and color. The root chakra is in the perineum area. The sacral chakra is above the pubic bone by genitals and with sacrum in back. The solar plexus chakra is by the navel. The heart chakra is by the heart and thymus gland. The throat chakra is at the throat and thyroid gland. The brow chakra is on the forehead. The crown chakra is on the top of the skull.

Chi is an energetic vibration found in all living things. Chi is frequently translated as "life-force" or "energy flow". I tend to think of chi as the interface between outer sensation in the body and inner reception of information to higher-self.

ChoKuRei is the Reiki power symbol

Cleansing Dreams are a type of symptomatic dream that results as a beneficial healing reaction after energy has worked in the mind. They manifest from mind reorganization owing to purging of programmed response patterns we no longer need. The dreams have elements of traumas, repeating scenarios and old history. After cleansing dreams have happened, the associated program no longer affects you in life and you do not have that dream anymore.

Central Nervous System (CNS) is the part of the nervous system that integrates the information that it receives from and coordinates the activity of with all parts of the body. It contains the majority of the nervous system and consists of the brain, spinal cord and dura mater. Together with the peripheral nervous system, it has fundamental role of behavior.

Cold Breeze is healing reaction, where you feel a cold windy, rushing feeling, like cool energy rushing up the spine, or cool rushes of breezes anywhere in body.

Counterclockwise (CCW) Torso Rotation Session – A kundalini meditation session done while sitting either in a chair or on floor with legs to front. This reaction happens late in the kundalini transformation. The torso physically circles spontaneously around in a counterclockwise direction while the torso is stretched. This is owing to energy rising from tailbone and spiraling up around the spine as it moves upward. This reaction is effective to open tissues and popping, cracking and crunching sounds are often felt and heard.

Cranial Extension & Flexion refers to the movement of the cranial bones in terms of a flexion and extension cycle owing to motion of the sphenoid bone, which completes one cycle in six seconds and last our entire life. This flexion extension cycle is the breathing of the cranium, and the sutures are there to accommodate the motion. In extension, the cranium narrows and elongates and the body goes into internal rotation, where an exaggerated example in the body would be pigeon-toed. Flexion is when the top of the sphenoid moves anterior, and the bottom moves superior. The movement of the rest of the bones is called flexion, even though their individual motions are unique. During flexion, the cranium becomes wider from side-to-side and foreshortens from front to back. During flexion, not only do the cranial bones widen, but also the body slightly rotates externally and broadens.

Cranial Sutures are a type of fibrous joint, which only occur in the skull and sacrum. They are bound together by Sharpey's fibers. A tiny movement happens at sutures, which contributes to the compliance and elasticity of the skull and sacrum. These joints are synarthroses.

Cranium (Skull) in human beings, the adult skull is normally composed of twenty-two bones. Except for the mandible, all bones of the skull are joined together by cranial sutures. Eight bones form the braincase, a protective vault surrounding the brain. These are one frontal, two parietals, one occipital bone, one sphenoid, two temporals and one ethmoid. Fourteen bones support the face. Encased within the temporal bones are the six ear ossicles of the middle ears, though these are not part of the skull. The hyoid bone, supporting the tongue, is usually not considered as part of the skull as it does not articulate with any other bones.

Cranium (Skull) Plates – the rounded plate-like skull bones that are on top of the skull that form a protective encasing around the brain. These consist of the frontal bone, the parietals, the occipital, and the temporals. There are cranial sutures between all plates.

DaiKoMyo is the Reiki master and empowerment symbol

Distance Symbol refers to the Reiki long-distance symbol of HonShaZeShoNen

Distance or Distanced from Self means not to identify with your thoughts and feelings, thus giving the ability to observe these reactions occurring in the mind and body.

Distance Healing is an energy healing technique to send energy healing at a distance, without touching the person. This is possible, because at the energetic level there is no such thing as distance. All objects are interconnected with a web of energy, like living in an ocean full of fish. When one object moves, all objects feel the displacement or movement. There is no such thing as time on the energetic level; all times exist simultaneously.

Double Helix Vortex is physical vortex that forms later in the kundalini transformation and encompasses the entire spine and shortly after this, it separates into two vortices like a double helix. One vortex encircles the spine internally in a clockwise direction and the other vortex encircles the spine physically on the outside in a counterclockwise direction.

Drops of Liquid is a reaction where a tiny energy ball or drop of fluid is moving through the body, from mind or upper body to lower body. This may be due to a hormone release, drainage of lymph, or be a tiny energy ball.

Dura Mater is the outermost of the three layers of the meninges that surrounds the brain and spinal cord, filled with fluid and is finely enervated. This structure is like a tough outer lining, which controls flexibility of movement and transfer of nervous energy along the entire cranial sacral system. It is likened to a physical structure that moves chi through the nervous system.

Electric buzzing is a reaction with mild electric shocks going over an area repeatedly. It is commonly felt in the teeth.

Elastic Sheets is a healing reaction felt on surface of body where the body area feels energized, tingly and elastic. This is most often felt localized in a small area. I suspect this is due to enervation of the fascia layer. A stretch reflex is often accompanied with the symptom.

Electric Shocks are a healing reaction where it feels exactly like getting a mild electric shock, such as when touching a live electric wire.

Elongation is a momentary sensation that a body part is gets longer, larger, or expands in size and shape. This may be due to sudden inflow of nervous energy after an energy block opens.

Emotion Symbol refers to the Reiki symbol, SeiHeiKi, pronounced Say- Hay- Kee.

Energetic Rotation is swirling energy localized in an area, most often felt in the joints.

Energy Ball is a ball shaped swirl of strong energy felt in localized areas.

Energy Circuit refers to a large nerve path strengthened or formed between two parts of the body or running along a channel in the body such as along the spine. When it forms it is felt as large movement or rush of energy moving along back and forth between the two parts of body.

Energy Dancing is a fun term for allowing the body to be moved by higher-self.

Energy Fill is a sudden inflow of energy into a large portion of the body, such as a limb, with the pleasant sensation the body part has melted, is warm, fuzzy or liquefied.

Energy Massage is as if energy is massaging the muscles and is deeply relaxing.

Energy Prickles are soft non-painful pinprick sensation felt near surface of skin.

Energy Pummeling refers to a small area of the body being pummeled with strong energetic charges, that vibrate the area and can be felt as strong buzzing or vibration in that body part. It can be seen internally as flashes or explosions of light in the area.

Energy Ray is a line of energy, emanating from a single source and projecting in a radial pattern toward other areas, such as the spokes of a bicycle wheel.

Energy Spiral is a spiral of energy moving through body in a corkscrew shape.

Energy Vortex refers to energy swirling around in the shape of a funnel or a spiral, having a point of origin where it has the smallest diameter, typically getting wider in dimension the further from the source of the flow. I call a strong energy vortex a tornado vortex. When there are two energy vortices traveling in opposite directions, re: one up and one down, such as one on each end of the spine, this then creates the shape of a double helix rather than a funnel.

Energy Whorls refers to energy in pattern of a curlicue or swirl of energy localized in a small area of the body.

Entrainment is the process whereby two interacting oscillating systems, which have different period when they function independently, assume the same period. The two oscillators may fall into synchrony, but other phase relationships are possible. The system with the greater frequency slows down, and the other accelerates while they work to assume the same period.

External Rain is a symptom where sprinkles of water land on skin coming from above, as it feels when in the rain. I believe this is due to high body heat and high pressure in dura matter, which results from sweat squirting strongly from the pores and falling back on you. This symptom is most often felt on the face.

External View refers to visual effects seen with the eyes that are not normal. An example is seeing sparkling lights in the air or more vivid coloring of objects.

Facial Bones are the bones of skull that compose the face which include the frontal bone, sphenoid, nasal, lachrymal, volmer, ethmoid, palatine, zygmatic, maxilla and mandible.

Fascia is the soft tissue component of the connective tissue system that permeates the human body. It interpenetrates and surrounds muscles, bones, organs, nerves, blood vessels and other structures. Fascia is an uninterrupted, three-dimensional web of tissue that extends from head to toe, from front to back, from interior to exterior. Fascia can relax and contract much like muscle fibers. The entire web of fascia can activate such as during flight or fight instincts.

Follow the Leader refers to allowing higher-self to take control of mind and body, done by quieting the mind and relaxing the body, and allowing spontaneous movements.

Fontanel refers to the area of the diamond-shaped anterior fontanel where the two frontal and two parietal bones join near top of skull, which is palpable in an infant.

Freefall is a healing reaction, which follows after energy has risen to brain and done work there. After a change is made to the brain, new instructions are sent into the body. This is felt as tingling cascading energy with the sensation you are melting. There is no body tension or stretch reflex. It is a relaxing sensation and very welcome.

Freestyle Session is a kundalini meditation, done by letting go of body control and allowing the body to move spontaneously. In advanced kundalini transformation, a sequence of yoga–like poses with holds and stretches results. Positions normally progress from standing, lowering slowly down to squat, then sitting with spinal twists and finally lying on back, stomach or side.

Galaxy view refers to an internal 3rd eye viewpoint, which looks like the stars of the galaxy. When this visual image appears, you are often in an altered state of consciousness.

Growing Force refers to the energy that causes things to grow, due to increasing vibration of the universe and all objects in the universe over time since the Big Bang. Ever since the Big Bang all objects continue to move faster and increase vibration. The growing force causes this to happen. The sun is the most obvious source of growing force for the Earth.

Growing Phase, Growing Reaction is a state of reorganization in the body, after energy blocks have been removed, and nervous energy is moving around and making changes to the system. It is a resting phase where the stretch reflex subsides, body vibration increases and neuron growth explodes. This can be felt as elevated energetic vibration, tingling, numbness, prickles, muscle twitches, tones. Discomfort may or may not be felt. It feels like growing happens in body.

Head Surgery refers to energy working in skull with high pressure in the skull typically with high body heat and facial sweating with little or no lower body movement. A small move is made to a cranial bone then there is a hold and this repeats slowly. You stay still in the center and have the sensation that you are healing your own mind. The skull work seems related to removing a body block, as later the area in body related to that area of skull is stretched.

Heaven Symbol is another term for the Reiki symbol for emotions, SeiHeiKi

Helix is like a coiled spring shape. A double helix is like DNA, with two coil shapes intertwined.

Hip (Pelvic) Girdle consists of a pair of coxal bones (hipbones), each of which contains three bones: the ilium, ishium, and pubis. Together with the sacrum and coccyx, the pelvic girdle forms a bowl-shaped region, the pelvis or pelvic bowl.

Higher-self refers to the wise, non-thinking aspect of self that exists as sentient soul or spirit energy. This is the source of our energetic vibration, insights, and healing capacity, yet has no form. It is our true self but is invisible.

Hold, Holds refers to the body being held rigid in a fixed position with strong muscle tension felt in a small area, such as a Charlie horse cramp. This most often happens on vertebrae in spine, shoulder bone, pelvic girdle bone, jaws or skull. A hold lasts from fifteen to sixty minutes. A painful sensation is felt with energy pummeling strongly through an area. The hold suddenly stops and simultaneously the area opens. A pleasant sensation is then felt as energy rushes into the previously blocked tissue.

HonShaZeShoNen is the Reiki distance symbol.

Inguinal canal is a passage toward the front of the body in the abdominal wall which in men conveys the spermatic cord and in women the round ligament.

Inner sound refers to a tone heard by the ears, owing to some movement or event in the body, most often in the brain, rather than being externally perceived.

Insect Biting is a healing reaction stronger than energy prickles or stinging prickles. It feels like an insect is biting you and taking a tiny chunk of flesh.

Insect Crawling is a healing reaction exactly like insects crawling on the skin.

Insight refers to an understanding of cause and effect based on identification of relationships and behaviors within a model, context, or scenario. The understanding is received intuitively.

Internal View refers to what you see when your eyes are closed. Images can be seen as well flashing lights and colors.

Internal Rain is a healing reaction with the sensation it is raining inside your body, perhaps owing to sudden and profound drainage of the lymph. The rain moves from top of body down, and you feel a sudden cooling.

Intuition describes "thoughts and preferences" that come to mind without reflection. It is reception of information from the pool of universal wisdom and is received when the mind is quiet. It is often received as response to a question we wanted answered.

Kundalini Transformation is synonymous with spiritual transformation and is a gradual and slow growing process resulting in higher levels of self-realization. As the transformation progresses your higher-self aspect keeps getting stronger and simultaneously, your lower-self or personality aspect gets weaker. The process is a biological metamorphosis.

Ligament is a fibrous tissue that connects bones to other bones. Ligaments connect bones to other bones to form a joint. They do not connect muscles to bones; that is the job of tendons. Some ligaments limit the mobility of articulations, or prevent certain movements altogether.

Ligament Snapping is a healing reaction, which I presume, happens owing to both ends of the ligament building an energetic charge. After charged, the ends contract and an externally audible snapping sound is felt and heard along the line of the ligament. This effect may be occurring owing to tendons snapping. This reaction may have purpose to increase range of mobility of joint or bone articulations. I think it is a permanent enervation of the ligament and is a capability of the new body that becomes elasticized.

Long Distance Symbol refers to the Reiki long-distance symbol: HonShaZeShoNen

Mantra is a sound, word, or phrase continuously repeated as a prayer, used in Hindu and Buddhist religious practices for meditation.

Master Symbol is the Reiki empowerment symbol, DaiKoMyo

Meditation is a time to practice placing attention on an object that is the meditation focal point not requiring thought. During the time, you repeatedly reset focus to the focal point whenever you notice you are thinking. This practice is done to gain skills at attaining quiet mind and higher state of consciousness. The meditative state is synonymous with quiet mind.

Memory Loss refers to a symptom resulting from being in an altered state of consciousness, where you do not observe external events and thus are not recording memories and cannot remember what happened afterward.

Meridian is a chi energy pathway in acupuncture for Chinese medicine. Chi energy concentrates and moves along several well-used paths in body owing to common human movement patterns, which travel through the neuromuscular junctions and mainly follow the lines of the skeletal bones. Each meridian forms a loop or circle in the body. There are fourteen well known meridians: lung (LU), heart (HT), pericardium (PC), triple heater (TH), small intestine (SI), large intestine (LI), spleen(SP), kidney(KD), liver(LV), gallbladder (GB), urinary bladder (UB), stomach (ST), conception vessel (CV) and governing vessel (GV). There are charts available showing the path of each Chinese meridian in the body where there are palpable points along it known as acupoints. In the journal, specific acupoints are referenced by using the meridian abbreviation letters followed by the acupoint number. For example LU14, refers to lung meridian, acupoint 14.

Moving as Being is an advanced kundalini state, where the body has enervated enough so that higher-self can move the body when mind is quiet and body is relaxed. Spontaneous body movements happen to open larger muscles and tight skeletal joints.

Neck Stretch is a spontaneous stretch upward in upper spine with purpose to open upper parts of spine including shoulder girdle, neck and skull bones at top of spine on up into brain stem. Neck stretch can occur simultaneously with pelvic push in which case I call it a 'body pull'.

Neuron Connections are localized area of synapse formation, very fine, and felt as subtle tingling or shimmering. It is like a fractal pattern branching into smaller units.

Neuron Growth refers to an explosion of synapse formation either in tissue of body or in brain. In the body, it is felt as waves of tingling rushes and because it can be felt in body, I presume it is due to synapse growth in the neuromuscular junctions. Neuromuscular junctions do not exist in the brain. Perhaps the symptom of neuron growth in brain is rather that of internally seeing flashes of light and or hearing inner sounds.

Neuromuscular Junction is the synapse or junction of the axon terminal of a motor neuron with the motor end plate, the highly excitable region of muscle fiber plasma membrane responsible for initiation of action potentials across the muscle's surface, ultimately causing the muscle to contract.

OBE (Out of Body Experience) is an altered state of reality that results when consciousness withdraws from the physical body. This state can happen spontaneously, when there is extreme pain in the body, and is done to protect the person while intense healing happens and to make the healing process more efficient. It is a very different world and experience than anything Earthly. After the work finishes, you enter the body. It is common while having an OBE that you see your body lying below from a position above it.

Observer refers to pure observation mode when you are as one with your higher-self. You are aware and observing but not using your mind in any way. It is direct and clear sight.

Oscillator Oscillation is the repetitive variation, typically in time, of some measure about a central value (often a point of equilibrium) or between two or more different states. The oscillating movement creates an energetic vibration. Used in this book, an oscillator it is like the copper coil I use for healing that is the heart of a motor, which generates electricity.

Outer Space refers to an altered state of consciousness with quiet mind. Your consciousness is more withdrawn from body than when you are in **Center**. It refers to a state between **Center** and **OBE**. You feel little body sensation and the inner view is like that of the galaxy, thus its name. Time passes quickly and you feel energy moving rapidly in your body.

Padded Bone Feeling refers to a sensation of a cushion of air or energy enveloping a bone and you feel it move in a gliding, easy, smooth way. This may be due to enervation of cartilage.

Palpate is the act of feeling or examining the body through the touch of the hands or fingers.

Piezoelectricity is electricity produced by pressure and is one of the known bridges between the mechanical and energetic worlds. Pressure on bone or a meridian acupoint initiates an electric current. Bone resonates with the vibration of impact. A meridian activates and starts moving energy along the channel. If a metal beam is hit, it rings. The force of impact translates into vibration. The beam or channel is set in resonance.

Pelvic Push is a spontaneous reaction to push downward through lower spine in the pelvis area, much the same as a woman pushes while in labor or when having a strong bowel movement. This has the purpose to open lower parts of spine including, lumbar spine, sacrum, and pelvic bones, and to extend and straighten the tailbone. The pelvic push can occur simultaneously with the neck stretch, in which case it is called a body pull.

Pelvic Rocking happens while lying on stomach or while sitting and is a kundalini reaction. An energy vortex in pelvic bowl activates the hip girdle, which subsequently causes a movement in each hip socket alternating from left to right, which causes a rocking motion. This motion is similar to sexual intercourse and often results in sexual orgasm. The movement is more pronounced after the double spine vortex forms.

Physical Rotation refers to a rotation of energetic vibration that is so strong it can be felt in the body and can cause spontaneous movements often in a rotating manner.

Puff outs, puffing out refers to energy puffing out, expanding or ballooning in a small area of the body.

Power Symbol refers to the Reiki symbol, ChoKuRei, pronounced as Show-Koo-Ray.

Sacrum Flex is the sensation and reaction of the sacrum bone articulating, flexing upward or downward between the hip sutures.

SeiHeiKi is the Reiki symbol, known as heaven or emotional symbol and is pronounced Say-Hay-Key.

Session refers to a kundalini meditative session that I did to allow higher-self to move my body or I would meditate if there was no body tension. I typically started with a freestyle session then would end in a certain body position where the majority of work was concentrated or maybe I would only sit in a hold. When the stretch response is strong, there is a twisting vortex of energy rising physically up the spine in a counterclockwise direction which when it reaches the base of the skull turns the skull in the same direction. Different body positions facilitate certain bone movements as is amply described in the journal.

Shaktipat (from Hinduism) refers to the conferring of spiritual energy upon one person by another. It is done through lying on of hands or long-distance via entrainment.

Shoulder Crook refers to an area, where side of neck meets shoulder top (L shape), where the crook is the corner of the letter 'L'. Deeper in this corner is what I call the crook, resulting from muscles within this area connecting to shoulder girdle, rib cage, going up side of neck and to various bones in skull. Much work is done in this area of the body and later in the transformation, an energy vortex forms there.

Shoulder (Pectoral) Girdle is the set of bones, which connects the arms to the axial skeleton on each side. It consists of the clavicle and scapula bones. The only joints between the shoulder girdle and axial skeleton are the sternoclavicular joints on each side. It is as if the girdle floats over the chest and back, allowing for greater range of motion of upper body.

Skull Turning is a kundalini reaction, which typically happens while lying on the stomach. A twisting vortex of energy rises physically up the spine in a counterclockwise direction, which when it reaches the base of the skull, then turns the skull in the same direction. The purpose of this movement is to open and elasticize the fascia, ligaments, tendons, muscles and cartilage of the shoulders, neck and skull and to separate all cranium bones.

Stinging prickles refers to a healing reaction of prickles that sting, like that of being stuck with a needle or of being stung by a bee. Normally felt on or near surface of skin and are perceived as painful. Synonyms are pinpricks, pins & needles and bee stings.

Stretch reaction refers to energy charges building in certain muscle groups, then when a physical motion is performed with those muscles, the energy precedes the physical movement and 'opens' the tissue microseconds before the physical move is made. This leading energy movement disperses the tension in the field, releasing held energy and clearing blockages and adhesions in the body.

Sun Session refers to my meditative sitting outside in the sun, where I had my feet on a large flat quartz crystal, often held a 12" copper ring, invoked the Reiki symbols, and sometimes did acupressure. Doing all these things together would strongly raise my energetic vibration. Most of the time I meditated and observed energy flows in my body, and allowed my body to relax and move spontaneously.

Surrender means to cede control of the mind and body by lower-self to higher-self. You cede control by focusing on something, which does not need thought, such as a feeling occurring in the body. When quiet, you are in the meditative state. It is like lower-self is sleeping and higher-self is awake. The surrendered state is when higher-self is controlling body and mind.

T1 is an acronym and refers to the first thoracic vertebra, at bottom of base of neck. It is first thoracic vertebrae under big bump (C7) on spine above the shoulders.

Tailbone Tuck After energy has formed into a vortex in the pelvic bowl, it sometimes happens that this energy is discharged down the spine, and the tailbone reacts by tucking into a curled shape toward the genitals. A strong sexual sensation is typical with this event. In early kundalini transformation, it is less pronounced and can be felt as sudden rise in sexual energy, spontaneous orgasm, or having feeling of fluttering in the tailbone area. Later on in the kundalini transformation, the tailbone physical moves.

Teeth Snaps refer to a healing reaction when it feels like the teeth snap with a long rubber band attached to them. It can happen to each tooth or only to a few. It feels like teeth are flying out of the mouth. I believe this is due to ligaments snapping.

Tension and tension release refers to muscle tension in a localized area, which has varying degrees of discomfort. I believe this reaction is due to electric potential energy charges building in opposing muscles groups related to a bone that needs to be realigned. When tension builds to its maximum, transformational pain can be strong, but soon after, the muscles contract and stretch, the tension is released and the bone moves, giving relief. It is also used to refer to stored tension of the personality being held in fixed form, releasing from the cord of personality.

Third eye is a sensory structure, located behind the middle of the forehead in the brain, capable of receiving visual images, information and communication with higher planes of existence. This structure is receptive when the mind is completely quiet.

TMJ is an abbreviation for the temporomandibular joint, the joint of the jaw. There are two TMJ's, one on either side of the head. The name is derived from the two bones, which form the joint: the upper temporal bone, part of the cranium and the lower jawbone, called the mandible.

Vortex Ball refers to a large energy ball in shape of vortex. It forms in pelvic bowl or skull cavity at either end of spine. It can happen in both ends simultaneously.

Whiteout refers to a healing reaction with a sudden blanket of silence with completely quiet mind and total loss of all sensory feelings, including sight, hearing, and sense of touch. You feel you have no body and are suspended in a white space. It is like being in a blizzard and not able to see anything.

Windy Storm refers to a healing reaction where energy movement in the body can be heard internally and it sounds like a storm with strong winds.

.

Index

C

I

M

N

T

Anatomy Of The Skull

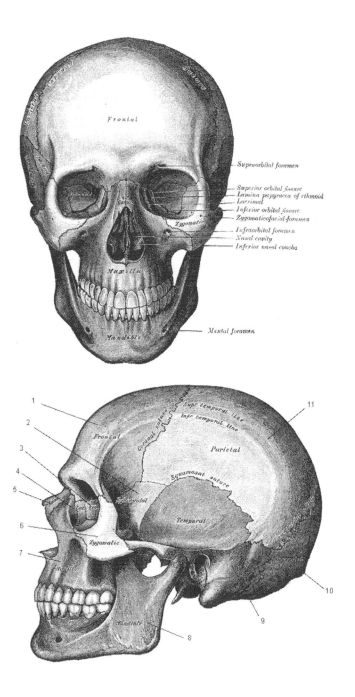

Above are reproductions of lithograph plates from Grey's Anatomy, from the 20th U.S. edition of
Grey's Anatomy of the Human Body, originally published in 1918 and lapsed into the public domain.

About The Author

This photo was taken in Spain in 2006 at age forty-seven, shortly after kundalini awakening triggered.

MARY E. (BETSY) RABYOR was born in Wisconsin and lived in Nevada, Florida and Spain. She went to college and was a computer programmer for 17 years, with family and suburban life. Since 1990, she has meditated and learned self-healing techniques. In August of 1999, she spiritually awakened, quit her job and devoted her life to self-realization and helping others. Shortly after starting Reiki self-healing in 2005, her kundalini unexpectedly awakened. She continues to work with her kundalini transformation today. She lives in Wisconsin and is a skilled distance healer, author, poet, intuitive, and spiritual mentor.

You can contact her at her websites:

http://ourlightbody.com

http://phoenixtools.org

http://distance-healings.com

24434320R00278